Olympiad Champs

MATHEMATICS

CLASS 4

with **Chapter-wise Previous 10 Year** (2013 - 2022) Questions

DISHA™
Publication Inc

DISHA Publication Inc.

45, 2nd Floor, Maharishi Dayanand Marg,
Corner Market, Malviya Nagar, new Delhi –110017
Tel: 49842349/ 49842350

Typeset By

DISHA DTP Team

Buying books from DISHA

Just Got A Lot More Rewarding!!!

We at DISHA Publication, value your feedback immensely and to show our apperciation of our reviewers, we have launched a review contest.

To participate in this reward scheme, just follow these quick and simple steps:
- Write a review of the product you purchase on Amazon/Flipkart.
- Take a screenshot/photo of your review.
- Mail it to *disha-rewards@aiets.co.in*, along with all your details.

Each month, selected reviewers will win exciting gifts from DISHA Publication. Note that the rewards for each month will be declared in the first week of next month on our website.

https://bit.ly/review-reward-disha.

Write To
Us At

feedback_disha@aiets.co.in

Preface

We are pleased to launch the thoroughly revised 4th edition of **Olympiad Champs Mathematics Class 4** which is the first of its kind book on Olympiad in many ways.

The Unique Selling Proposition of this new edition is the inclusion of past year questions till 2022 of different Olympiad exams held at school level.

The book is aimed at achieving not only success but deep rooted learning in children. It is prepared on content based on National Curriculum Framework prescribed by NCERT. All the text books, syllabi and teaching practices within the education programme in India must follow NCF. Hence, Olympiad Champs become an ideal book not only for the Olympiad Exams but also for strengthening the concepts for Class 4.

There is an exhaustive range of thought provoking questions in MCQ format to test the student's knowledge thoroughly. The questions are designed so as to test the knowledge, comprehension, evaluation, analytical and application skills. Solutions and explanations are provided for all questions. The questions are divided into two levels-Level 1 and Level 2. The first level, Level 1, is the beginner's level which comprises of questions like fillers, analogy and odd one out. When the child covers Level 1, it means his basic knowledge about the subject is clear and now he is ready for Level 2. The second level is the advanced level. Level 2 comprises of techniques like matching, chronological sequencing, picture, passage and feature based, statement correct/ incorrect, integer based, puzzle, grid based, crossword, venn diagram, table/ chart based and much more.

The first concern which each parent faces is how to make their children read a book especially when it is based on academics. Keeping this in mind interesting facts, real life examples, historical preview, short cuts to problem solving, charts, diagrams, illustrations and poems are added.

With the vision to remove all the misconception a child may have pertaining to the subject, to relate his knowledge to the real world and to develop a deeper understanding of the subject, this book will cater to all the requirements of the students who are going to appear in Olympiads.

While preparing this book, some errors might have crept in. We request our readers to identify those errors and send it across on **feedback_disha@aiets.co.in.**

We wish you all the best for your Olympiads and happy reading.......

Team Disha

For feedback : feedback_disha@aiets.co.in.

CONTENTS

Unlock your child's
HIDDEN GENIUS!
with Olympiad
Champs

DISHA
Publication Inc

10 Principles to CRACK ANY EXAM

1. Chase consistency, not intensity.

Doing intensive study makes your day. But it also exhausts you in the long run, leading to lesser output and added pressure. Toppers always focus on doing consistent work daily, for consistency is far more valuable than intensity.

Remember consistent study of 4 hours every day is more important and powerful than studying 12 hours a day and then not studying at all for next 2 days.

2. Go beyond the surface.

Most students only see a few reasons (teacher, coaching, books, etc) behind Toppers' success, which is only the tip of the iceberg. What they donot see is Toppers Mindset, self belief, habits and discipline and that is where the real problem is.

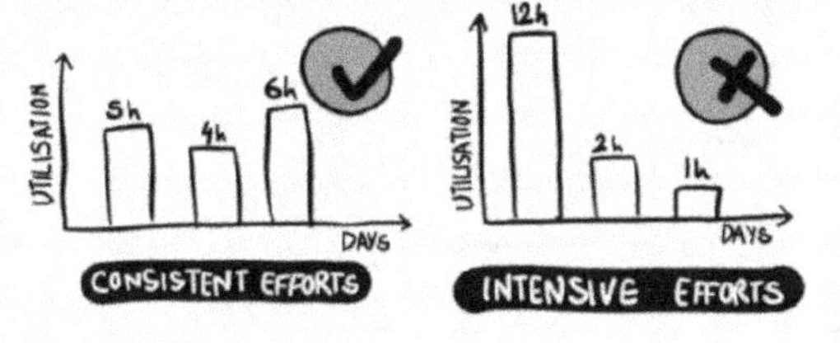

3. Focus on giving your best, not chasing the best.

We want the best coaching, the best teacher, best batch and the best books but we are not ready to give our BEST. Success comes only when we are ready to give our best. We must focus on giving our best than chasing excuses to cover up our failures.

4.

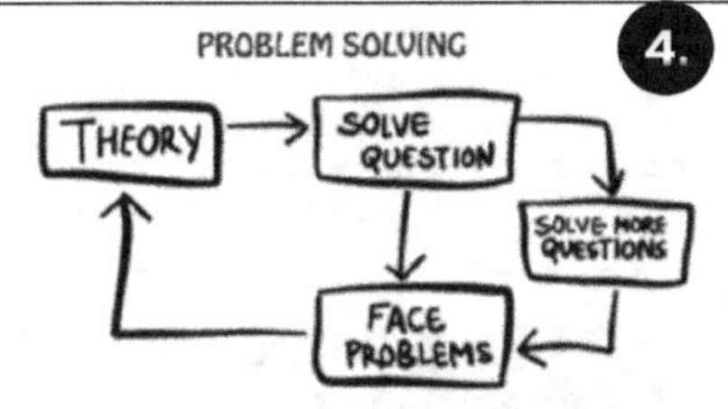

Clarity of concept is the key

Concept clarity is critical. If you cannot solve a question, you must go back to the theory and thoroughly examine the concept instead of referring to the solutions. Remember question is one of the chehra(face) of the concept. When toppers get stuck in a problem, they go back and refer the theory(read the concept again and again on which the question is based)

5. Every failure should be a lesson learned.

Most students do not learn from their failures and repeat their mistakes. Toppers also face failures, but they learn from mistakes and elevate themselves. Making mistakes and learning from them is the key to success.

6. Choosing the quality of resources is more important than quantity.

More than 90% of the questions in most books are the same as their substitutes. Instead of practicing from four books and failing to complete them, it is best to prepare from two books and complete them with thorough revisions.

7. Difficult things become easy by taking it one day at a time.

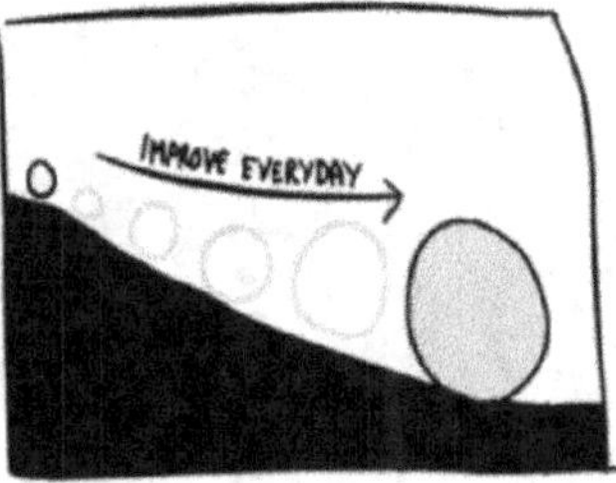

The best way to take any preparation forward is by taking it one day at a time. It makes the impossible possible by taking small steps every day.

Starting a difficult subject. No worries. Keep on working session by session, day by day and week by week and one day you will become unstoppable force.

8. Everything is easy

Before starting everything looks difficult. Once you take a first step, it slowly starts looking easy and over a period of time you become master in the activity. This is toppers secret to become master in any subject.

9. Nobody is gifted

We think toppers are god gifted. We think toppers have high IQ. We think toppers are special/lucky. But the truth is every topper was once an average student (no body is born topper). What makes them different is their consistent and focused efforts

10. Believe in your journey and success will come to you.

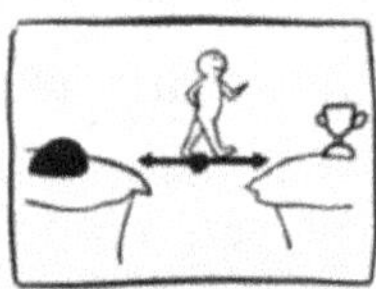

There is never a straight path to success; hard work & patience is required for the results to show up. Keep on working hard without thinking too much about the results and success will come to you eventually.

Counting by 1's in Roman Numerals

1	2	3	4	5	6	7	8	9
I	II	III	IV	V	VI	VII	VIII	IX

Counting by 10's in Roman Numerals

10	20	30	40	50	60	70	80	90
X	XX	XXX	XL	L	LX	LXX	LXXX	XC

Counting by 100's in Roman Numerals

100	200	300	400	500	600	700	800	900
C	CC	CCC	CD	D	DC	DCC	DCCC	CM

Roman numerals can be combined to make larger numbers. For example: 26 is XXVI in Roman numerals. This is how it's made

X	+	X	+	V	+	I	=	XXVI
10	+	10	+	5	+	1	=	26

1 Chapter | *Roman Numerals*

LEARNING OBJECTIVES

This lesson will help you to:—

❖ be able to know the history & use of Roman numerals.

❖ be able to solve real life problems based on Roman numerals.

❖ explore various principles of Roman numerals.

❖ be able to define Roman numerals.

❖ be able to convert Roman numerals into Arabic numerals and vice versa.

QUICK CONCEPT REVIEW

ROMAN NUMERALS

Sam's father brought a new wall clock. Sam was amazed to see some alphabet instead of numbers on the clock. He asked his father about it. Father told him that these are numbers based on the Roman system of numeration. Let us all learn about it.

When Romans learned to write they needed a way to write their numbers. For this they developed a numeric system which uses combinations of letters to signify values. This system is known as Roman system of numeration.

Romans used these numbers for trading & commerce. These numbers are still used today in many different ways.

This system of numeration does not use place value like the Arabic system of numeration.

There are seven symbols used in this system which are as follows:

I, V, X, L, C, D & M.

Each symbol has a corresponding value:

I stands for 1

V stands for 5

X stands for 10

L stands for 50

C stands for 100

D stands for 500

M stands for 1000

PRINCIPLES USED IN ROMAN NUMERATION SYSTEM

1. **Principle of Addition:** Tina wants to meet her brother who studies in class 11, but the number written on the name plate is a Roman numeral, so she is confused whether she is going to the right classroom. Can you help her?

    Class XI ⇒

    X = 10 and I = 1

    Therefore, XI = 10 + 1 = 11

    Hence, Tina is going to the correct classroom.

    This example uses the principle of addition.

    Addition is only applicable when the first symbol is greater than the second, third etc.

    When a symbol appears **after a larger symbol it is added.**

    When the principle of addition is used, a symbol can be used only three times.

    Let us take another example:

    LXX ⇒

    L = 50

    X = 10

    X = 10

    Therefore, LXX = 50 + 10 + 10 = 70

Note:

(i) Repetition of a symbol in a Roman numeral means addition.

(ii) Only I, X, C and M can be repeated.

(iii) V, L and D are never repeated.

(iv) No symbol in a Roman numeral can be repeated more than 3 times.

Historical preview

❖ The history of Roman numerals is not well documented and written accounts are contradictory. It is likely that counting began on the fingers and that is why we count in tens. A single stroke I represents one finger, five or a handful could possibly be represented by V and the X may have been used because if you stretch out two handfuls of fingers and place them close the two little fingers cross in an X. Alternatively, an X is like two Vs, one upside down.

Example : Which of the following is greatest?

(a) XL   (b) XC

(c) CM   (d) XCI

Solution:

XL = 50 – 10 = 40

XC = 100 – 10 = 90

CM = 1000 – 100 = 900

XCI = 90 + 1 = 91

So CM is the greatest among given Roman numerals.

2. **Principle of Subtraction:** Jojo was waiting for his friend on a street. He saw a board on which two numbers were written. One was a Roman numeral another was an Arabic numeral. But he is confused that which number is written on the board.

Roman number written on board = IX

$$
\begin{array}{cc}
I = 1 & \searrow \quad 10 \\
X = 10 & \nearrow \quad -1 \\
\hline
& 9
\end{array}
$$

Therefore, IX = 9

Subtraction is only applicable when the first symbol is less than the second one.

If the symbol appears **before a larger** symbol it is **subtracted.**

Another example,

CD ⇒

$$
\begin{array}{cc}
C = 100 & \searrow \quad 500 \\
D = 500 & \nearrow \quad -100 \\
\hline
& 400
\end{array}
$$

Therefore, CD = 400

Note:

   (i)   V, L and D are never subtracted

   (ii) I can be subtracted from V and X only

   (iii) X can be subtracted from L and C only

   (iv) C can be subtracted from D and M only

3. **Principle of addition & subtraction are used in combination.**

Rohan was reading an article.

Super Bowl XLVIII

The Super Bowl is the annual championship game of the National Football League (NFL), the highest level of professional American football in the United States, culminating a season that begins in the late summer of the previous calendar year. The Super Bowl uses Roman numerals to identify each game, rather than the year in which it is held. For example, Super Bowl I was played on January 15, 1967, following the 1966 regular season, while Super Bowl XLVII was played on February 3, 2013, following the 2012 season.

He saw numbers written in roman numerals. Let us have a look.

Roman number XLVIII ⇒

$$X = 10$$
$$L = 50$$
$$V = 5$$
$$I = 1$$
$$I = 1$$
$$I = 1$$

⇒ (50 – 10) + (5 + 1 + 1) = 40 + 8 = 48

Therefore, XLVIII = 48

This is an example where principle of addition & subtraction are used in combination.

CONVERSION INTO ROMAN NUMERALS

For converting a number to a Roman numeral we break the number into Thousands, Hundreds, Tens and Units and write down each in turn.

Example: Deepika wants to convert her year of birth into Roman numeral. Can you help her to do so?

Break 1987 into 1000, 900, 80 and 7, then do each conversion

❖ 1000 = M

❖ 900 = CM

❖ 80 = LXXX

❖ 7 = VII

So 1987 = MCMLXXXVII

LARGER NUMBERS

Numbers greater than 1,000 are formed by placing a dash over the symbol, meaning "multiplied by 1,000", but these are not commonly used.

5000	10000	50000	100000
$\overline{V}$	$\overline{X}$	$\overline{L}$	$\overline{C}$

SOME BASIC COMBINATIONS

1	2	3	4	5	6	7	8	9
I	II	III	IV	V	VI	VII	VIII	IX

10	20	30	40	50	60	70	80	90
X	XX	XXX	XL	L	LX	LXX	LXXX	XC

100	200	300	400	500	600	700	800	900
C	CC	CCC	CD	D	DC	DCC	DCCC	CM

Shortcuts to Problem Solving

❖ An accurate way to write the Roman numerals is to first take the Thousands, Hundreds, Tens and Units.

Example: 1999, one thousand is M, nine hundred is CM, ninety is XC, nine is IX. Combine all these:

MCMXCIX

❖ Develop a mnemonic device to remember the order of Roman numerals. A common mnemonic like "I Value Xylophones like Cows Dig Milk" puts the Roman numerals I, V, X, L, C, D and M in order from smallest to largest. If you only have trouble with the larger numbers, it may help to remember that "C" is equivalent to "century" and "M" is equivalent to "millennium": 100 and 1000, respectively.

❖ Write the six pairs of "subtractive" Roman numerals on a notecard along with their equivalents in Roman numerals, "IV" is equal to 4, "IX" to 9, "XL" to 40, "XC" to 90, "CD" to 400 and "CM" to 900. These are called "subtractive" because the first letter is "subtracted" from the second. Keep the notecard visible at all times so you know to recognize these pairs when they appear.

Multiple Choice Questions

LEVEL 1

1. Romans used these numbers for trading & __________.
   - (a) commerce
   - (b) finance
   - (c) law
   - (d) exporting

2. Addition is only applicable when the first symbol is __________ than the second, third etc.
   - (a) greater
   - (b) smaller
   - (c) equal
   - (d) greater than equal to

3. **Statement A:** When the principle of addition is used, a symbol can be used only three times.

   Statement B: When the principle of addition is used, a symbol can be used only 1 time.
   - (a) A is correct
   - (b) B is correct
   - (c) Both are correct
   - (d) Both are incorrect

4. Pick the odd one out.

   V, IV, X, XI, VIIII.
   - (a) IV
   - (b) XI
   - (c) V
   - (d) VIIII

5. Pick the odd one out.

   I, V, X, L, C, D, N.
   - (a) X
   - (b) I
   - (c) C
   - (d) N

6. Roman numbers don't have symbol for __________.
   - (a) zero
   - (b) one
   - (c) two
   - (d) three

7. When a symbol appears after larger symbol, it is __________.
   - (a) added
   - (b) subtracted
   - (c) multiplied
   - (d) divided

8. Subtraction is only applicable when the first symbol is __________ than the second one.
   - (a) less
   - (b) more
   - (c) equal to
   - (d) less than equal to

9. Pick the odd one out.

   [Mental Mathematics]
   - (a) X
   - (b) XX
   - (c) XXX
   - (d) XXXX

10. Pick the odd one out.

    [Mental Mathematics]
    - (a) I
    - (b) II
    - (c) III
    - (d) IIII

11. Write 49 in Roman numerals.　**[2013]**
    - (a) XXXXIX
    - (b) LIX
    - (c) XLIX
    - (d) LIX-X

12. Convert : CVI　**[Mental Mathematics]**
    - (a) 100
    - (b) 105
    - (c) 106
    - (d) 110

13. In Roman numerals 'M' stands for __________　**[2016]**
    - (a) 50
    - (b) 500
    - (c) 1000
    - (d) 1500

14. Convert : 1400
    - (a) MCD
    - (b) MC
    - (c) MD
    - (d) M

15. Convert : MXVI **[Mental Mathematics]**
    - (a) 1016
    - (b) 101
    - (c) 1006
    - (d) 1000

16. Write 630 as a Roman numeral. **[2017]**
    - (a) DCXX
    - (b) DXXX
    - (c) VCXXX
    - (d) DCXXX

17. Write 830 as a Roman numeral.
    (a) DCCCXX   (b) DCXXX
    (c) DCCCXXX   (d) DCCXXX

18. Convert : 3010 [Mental Mathematics]
    (a) MMMX   (b) MX
    (c) MMM   (d) MMX

19. Which one of the following is meaningless?   [2016]
    (a) XXIX   (b) IXXX
    (c) L   (d) XC

20. Which of the following is an incorrect match?   [2016]
    (a) XLVIII = 48   (b) LX = 60
    (c) XCIV = 94   (d) CD= 600

21. Pick the odd one out.
    C, XL, LXXXX. [Mental Mathematics]
    (a) C
    (b) XL
    (c) LXXXX
    (d) None of these

22. Write 737 as a Roman numeral.
    (a) DCCXXXVII   (b) DCCXXXVI
    (c) DCXXXVII   (d) DCCXXVII

23. Convert the statement into Roman numbers.
    5 × 4 = 20
    (a) V × IV = XX
    (b) V × IV = VIV
    (c) V × IIII = XX
    (d) V × IV = VVVV

24. Solve: XII – II = ?
    (a) X   (b) XI
    (c) II   (d) XII

25. Roman numeral equivalent to 89 is __________.   [2012]
    (a) LXIL   (b) IXC
    (c) XIC   (d) LXXXIX

26. Ria had LVIII postcards & XI stamps. How many are there in all?
    (a) LXVI   (b) LXIX
    (c) LXII   (d) LXI

27. What number is the minute needle pointing to?   (see fig. A)
    (a) 12   (b) 11
    (c) 10   (d) 9

28. What number is the hour needle pointing to ?   (see fig. A)

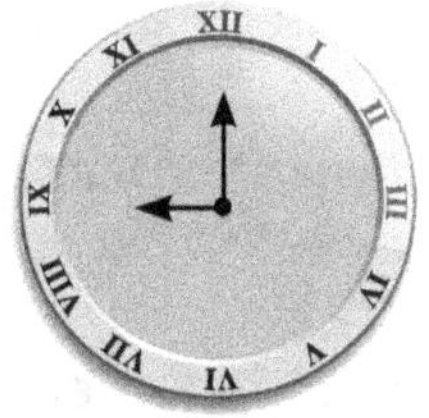

Fig. A

    (a) 9   (b) 10
    (c) 11   (d) 12

29. What time is the clock showing?   (see fig. A)
    (a) 9 'o clock   (b) 12 'o clock
    (c) 11 'o clock   (d) 10 'o clock

30. What time is the clock showing?   (see fig. B)

Fig. B

    (a) 5 'o clock   (b) 12 'o clock
    (c) 7 'o clock   (d) 6 'o clock

31. Solve:
    DVI – XIV = ?
    (a) CDLXXXI   (b) CDXCII
    (c) CDLXXII   (d) CDLXXX

32. DCLV – LV = ?
    (a) LV   (b) C
    (c) D   (d) DC

33. XLIII – ? = XL
    (a) XL   (b) XLIII
    (c) III   (d) II

34. Study the following statements and select the incorrect option. **[2018]**
    (a) Symbols V, L and D can never be subtracted while writing roman numerals.
    (b) The successor of the greatest 4-digit number is the smallest 5-digit number.
    (c) Difference between the successor and the predecessor of a number is always 1.
    (d) The difference between the smallest and the largest 5-digit number formed by 3, 4, 6, 0 and 2 (without any repetition of a digit) is 43974.

35. Find the value of LXXVI + XCVII. **[2019]**
    (a) CLXXIII   (b) LXXII
    (c) CLXXII   (d) CXXIII

36. Roman numeral CM is same as __________. **[2022]**
    (a) 100 – 10
    (b) 1000 – 100
    (c) 1000 – 500
    (d) None of these

LEVEL 2

Direction (Qs. 1 to 6): Solve the addition/subtraction given in the question.

1. MMLXIII – CDLXXXVI =   **[Tricky]**
   (a) MDLXXVII   (b) MDLXXVI
   (c) MDLXV   (d) MDLXVIII

2. DCCCLIX + XXVII + DCCCXLII = **[Tricky]**
   (a) MDCCXXVI
   (b) MDCCXXVIII
   (c) MDCXXVII
   (d) MDCCXXVII

3. MMCMXXXI + MMMCMLXXXII = **[Tricky]**
   (a) $\overline{\text{VI}}$CMXII   (b) $\overline{\text{VI}}$CMXI
   (c) $\overline{\text{VI}}$CMXIII   (d) $\overline{\text{VI}}$CMX

4. MMMLXII + XCII + MMDCXLVIII = **[Tricky]**
   (a) $\overline{\text{V}}$DCCII   (b) $\overline{\text{V}}$DCCI
   (c) $\overline{\text{V}}$DCCCII   (d) $\overline{\text{V}}$CCCII

5. $\overline{\text{IX}}$ CXXX – MMCCCLXI =
   (a) $\overline{\text{VI}}$DCLXIX   (b) $\overline{\text{VI}}$DCCLIX
   (c) $\overline{\text{VI}}$CCLXIX   (d) $\overline{\text{VI}}$DCCLXIX

6. $\overline{\text{VI}}$DCCXII – XIX =
   (a) $\overline{\text{VI}}$DXCIII   (b) $\overline{\text{VI}}$DCXCIII
   (c) $\overline{\text{VI}}$DCXCII   (d) $\overline{\text{VI}}$DCXCI

7. Write 1116 as a Roman numeral.
   (a) MCXVI   (b) MCXV
   (c) MCXI   (d) CXIV

8. Write 2,676 as a Roman numeral.
   (a) MMDCLXVI
   (b) MMDCLXXVI
   (c) MMDCXXVI
   (d) MMDLXXVI

9. Write 2,990 as a Roman numeral. **[2008]**
   (a) MMCXC   (b) MCMXC
   (c) MMCMXC   (d) MMCMC

10. Match the following:

List I		List II	
A	I	1	5
B	V	2	10
C	X	3	1

      A B C   A B C
   (a) 2   3   1   (b) 1   2   3
   (c) 3   1   2   (d) 1   3   2

11. Select the INCORRECT match. **[2013]**
    (a) LVIII = 58
    (b) CII = 102
    (c) XCVIII = 108
    (d) LXII = 62

12. 'Read the statement carefully and choose the correct option.'

    A: Roman numerals use place value.

    B: Roman numerals don't use place value.

    (a) A is correct
    (b) B is correct
    (c) Both are correct
    (d) Both are incorrect

13. 'Read the statement carefully and choose the correct option.'

    [2009, Critical Thinking]

    A. If a symbol appears before a larger symbol, it is subtracted.

    B. If a symbol appears before a larger symbol, it is added.

    (a) A is correct
    (b) B is correct
    (c) Both are correct
    (d) Both are incorrect

14. Match the following:

List I		List II	
A	XVI	1	16
B	VII	2	21
C	XXI	3	7

	A	B	C			A	B	C
(a)	1	3	2		(b)	1	2	3
(c)	3	2	1		(d)	2	3	1

15. Which of the following statements is INCORRECT? [2014, Critical thinking]

    (a) V, L, D can never be subtracted while writing Roman numerals
    (b) Symbol I can be subtracted from V to X only once
    (c) X cannot be subtracted from L
    (d) None of these

16. Match the following: [Critical Thinking]

List I		List II	
A.	5000	1.	$\overline{X}$
B.	10000	2.	$\overline{V}$
C.	50000	3.	$\overline{C}$
D.	100000	4.	$\overline{L}$

	A	B	C	D			A	B	C	D
(a)	2	1	4	3		(b)	1	2	3	4
(c)	4	3	2	1		(d)	3	4	1	2

17. Fill the correct sign. [2014, Tricky]

    LXXVI + XLIII – XV $\boxed{}$ LXXXVII – LIV + X

    (a) >
    (b) <
    (c) =
    (d) Can't be determined

18. 'Tick the correct option.'

    A: 62 = LXXII

    B: 62 = LXII

    (a) A is correct.
    (b) B is correct.
    (c) Both are correct.
    (d) Both are incorrect.

19. Find P, Q, R and S respectively. [2015, Critical Thinking]

	$\boxed{P}$	8	5	$\boxed{Q}$
–	3	$\boxed{R}$	$\boxed{S}$	5
	5	4	3	2

    (a) IX, XI, IV, II
    (b) II, III, VIII, I
    (c) IV, VII, VIII, II
    (d) VIII, VII, IV, II

20. Tick the correct option. [2010]

    A. M – D = D   B. M – D = C

    (a) A is correct.
    (b) B is correct.
    (c) Both are correct.
    (d) Both are incorrect.

21. M × 1000 = ?

    (a) 1000M
    (b) M1000
    (c) M
    (d) $\overline{M}$

22. Tick the correct option.   [Tricky]
    A. V – I = IV   B.   V – II = III
    (a) A is correct.
    (b) B is correct.
    (c) Both are correct.
    (d) Both are incorrect.

23. Tick the correct option.   [2008]
    A. XI + XI = XXII   B.   X + X = X
    (a) A is correct.
    (b) B is correct.
    (c) Both are correct.
    (d) Both are incorrect.

24. There are MMCDXX people in a city. Out of them, DLV are children and rests are adults. How many adults are there in the city?   [Critical Thinking]
    (a) MDCCCLXV   (b) MDCCLXV
    (c) MDCCCXV   (d) MDCCCLV

25. Complete the table: [2009, Tricky]

V × I =	V
V × II =	a
V × III =	b
V × c =	XX
V × d =	XXV

    (a) a = X, b = XV, c = IV, d = V
    (b) a = XI , b =X, c = IV, d = V
    (c) a = X , b =XVI, c = I, d = V
    (d) a = X , b =XV, c = IV, d = VI

26. Tom Sexton was born near Angeles Church on May sixth. Which year was Tom born? (Hint: find all of the Roman numerals you can find in the given sentence and arrange correctly).
    (a) 1950   (b) 1989 [Tricky]
    (c) 1999   (d) 2000

27. The costs of Notebook, Bag, Pencil box and Paper clip are given in the table.

Notebook	₹ LXXXVI
Bag	₹ CLV
Pencil box	₹ LXVII
Paper clip	₹ XXV

    What is the total cost of a Paper clip, a Bag and a Notebook?   [2016]
    (a) CCLXVI   (b) CXV
    (c) CCXLVI   (d) CCXLI

Direction (Qs. 28 to 32): Arrange as per the sequence in ascending order.

28. M,D,X,V
    (a) V,X,D,M   (b) X,V,D,M
    (c) D,V,X,M   (d) M,D,X,V

29. L,C,M,V
    (a) L,C,M,V   (b) V,M,C,L
    (c) M,C,V,L   (d) V,L,C,M

30. X,I,M,C
    (a) I,X,C,M   (b) X,I,M,C
    (c) C,I,M,X   (d) M,X,I,C

31. D,X,V,I
    (a) D,X,V,I   (b) I,D,X,V
    (c) V,X,I,D   (d) I,V,X,D

32. L,D,V,M
    (a) D,L,M,V   (b) V,L,D,M
    (c) V,D,M,L   (d) M,V,L,D

33. While writing Roman numeral for 456, Mary made a mistake as she wrote CDXVI. Which one of the following is the correct notation for the required numeral?   [2011]
    (a) CDLVI   (b) DCLVI
    (c) CDLIV   (d) CDMLVI

34. Match the following :
    A. MLXVIII   (i)   1130
    B. MCXXX   (ii) 1192
    C. MCXCII   (iii) 1068
    D. MCCLIV   (iv) 1254
    (a) A-iii, B-i, C-iv, D-ii
    (b) A-ii, B-iii, C-ii, D-iv
    (c) A-iii, B-ii, C-i, D-iv
    (d) A-iii, B-i, C-ii, D-iv

35. Identify the correct answer for XLIV ÷ XI   [2014]
    (a) 3   (b) 4
    (c) 5   (d) 8

36. Study the following numbers. [2018]

MCCLIII,	MDXCIV,	MCDXC
MDCXIV	MCCCLVII,	MCDV

Find the sum of the digits at hundreds place of the smallest and the greatest number.

(a) 8   (b) 9
(c) 6   (d) 11

37. Match the number obtained after the additions of roman numerals given in column I with their hundreds digit given in column II. [2018]

Column I	Column II
P. MMDCCX + MCDXVII	(i) 9
Q. MCCCXV + MDCIX	(ii) 0
R. MDXCIX + MDCVIII	(iii) 1
S. MCDVII + MDCIX	(iv) 2

(a) P→(iii), Q→(i), R→(iv), S→(ii)
(b) P→(ii), Q→(i), R→(iv), S→(iii)
(c) P→(iii), Q→(iv), R→(i), S→(ii)
(d) P→(ii), Q→(iv), R→(i), S→(iii)

38. Which of the following are arranged in the ascending order? [2020]

(a) CXLVI, CLXXXIX, DLXVIII, CMLXXVII
(b) CXLVI, CMLXXVII, CLXXXIX, DLXVIII
(c) CMLXXVII, DLXVIII, CLXXXIX, CXLVI
(d) CMLXXVII, CLXXXIX, DLXVIII, CXLVI

39. Aman is XXI years old. Raghav is XV years older than Aman. The sum of their ages (in years) is __________. [2020]

(a) 57   (b) 52
(c) 29   (d) 38

40. Arrange the following Roman numerals in the ascending order? [2022]

XXXII, CXXXII, CXXIX, LXXIV

(a) XXXII < CXXXII < CXXIX < LXXIV
(b) XXXII < LXXIV < CXXXII < CXXIX
(c) XXXII < LXXIV < CXXIX < CXXXII
(d) XXXII < CXXIX < CXXXII < LXXIV

RESPONSE GRID

LEVEL 1

1. a b c d   2. a b c d   3. a b c d   4. a b c d   5. a b c d
6. a b c d   7. a b c d   8. a b c d   9. a b c d   10. a b c d
11. a b c d   12. a b c d   13. a b c d   14. a b c d   15. a b c d
16. a b c d   17. a b c d   18. a b c d   19. a b c d   20. a b c d
21. a b c d   22. a b c d   23. a b c d   24. a b c d   25. a b c d
26. a b c d   27. a b c d   28. a b c d   29. a b c d   30. a b c d
31. a b c d   32. a b c d   33. a b c d   34. a b c d   35. a b c d
36. a b c d

LEVEL 2

1. a b c d   2. a b c d   3. a b c d   4. a b c d   5. a b c d
6. a b c d   7. a b c d   8. a b c d   9. a b c d   10. a b c d

11. a b c d   12. a b c d   13. a b c d   14. a b c d   15. a b c d
16. a b c d   17. a b c d   18. a b c d   19. a b c d   20. a b c d
21. a b c d   22. a b c d   23. a b c d   24. a b c d   25. a b c d
26. a b c d   27. a b c d   28. a b c d   29. a b c d   30. a b c d
31. a b c d   32. a b c d   33. a b c d   34. a b c d   35. a b c d
36. a b c d   37. a b c d   38. a b c d   39. a b c d   40. a b c d

Solutions with Explanation

LEVEL- 1

1. (a) commerce
2. (a) greater
3. (a) A is correct.
4. (d) VIIII
5. (d) N
6. (a) zero
7. (a) added
8. (a) less
9. (d) XXXX
10. (d) IIII
11. (c) XLIX
12. (c) 106
13. (c) 1000
14. (a) MCD
15. (a) 1016
16. (d) DCXXX
17. (c) DCCCXXX
18. (a) MMMX
19. (b) IXXX
20. (d) CD = 500 – 100 = 400 and not 600

21. (c) LXXXX, because no symbol can be repeated more than 3 times.
22. (a) DCCXXXVII
23. (a) V × IV = XX
24. (a) X
25. (d) LXXXIX
26. (b) LVIII + XI = LXIX
27. (a) 12
28. (a) 9
29. (a) 9'o clock
30. (a) 5'o clock
31. (b) CDXCII
32. (d) DC
33. (c) III
34. (c)
35. (a) LXXVI + XCVII = 76 + 97 = 173 = CLXXIII
36. (b) CM Roman Numerals = 900
So, 1000 – 100 = 900 is same as CM

LEVEL- 2

1. (a) 26
2. (b)
3. (c)
4. (c)
5. (d)
6. (b)
7. (a)
8. (b)
9. (c)
10. (c)
11. (c) XCVIII = 98 and not 108
12. (b) B is correct.
13. (a) A is correct.
14. (a)
15. (c) As X can be subtracted from L
16. (a)
17. (a) LXXVI + XL III – XV = 76 + 43 – 15 = 104

and L X X X VII – LIV + X = 87 – 54 + 10 = 43
So 104 > 43
18. (b) B is correct.
19. (d) P = VIII, Q = VII, R = IV, S = II
20. (a) A is correct
21. (d) $\overline{M}$
22. (c)
23. (a)
24. (a) MMCDXX – DLV = MDCCCLXV
25. (a) a = X , b =XV, c = IV, d = V

26. **(c)** Tom Sexton was born near Angeles Church on May sixth.

Show all the Roman numerals

ToM SeXton was born near Angeles ChurCh on May sIXth.

Take them out MXCCMIX, and rearrange MCMXCIX which is 1999.

27. **(a)** As 86 + 155 + 25 = 266 or CCLXVI

28. **(a)**

29. **(d)**

30. **(a)**

31. **(d)**

32. **(b)**

33. **(a)** CDLVI represents 456

34. **(d)** a - (iii), b - (i), c - (ii), d - (iv)

35. **(b)** As 44 ÷ 11 = 4

Note : Either give only correct option or correct option with value. Uniformity is necessary. Explanation is required if needed.

36. **(a)** MCCLIII = 1253, MDXCIV = 1594, MCDXC = 1490, MDCXIV = 1614, MCCCLVII = 1357, MCDV = 1405

37. **(a)** P→(iii), Q→(i), R→(iv), S→(ii)

P. (2710 + 1417), Q. (1315 + 1609), R. (1599 + 1608), S. (1407 + 1609)

38. **(a)** CXLVI =146

CLXXXIX =189

DLXVIII = 568

CMLXXVII = 977

39. **(a)** Aman's Age =   XXI = 21 years

Raghav's age = XV + XXI = 15 years + 21 years = 36 years.

The sum of their Ages = 36 + 21 years = 57 years.

40. **(c)**

International System of Numeration

53263217 = 50,000,000 + 3,000,000 + 200,000 + 60,000 + 3,000 + 200 + 10 + 7

Hundred Millions	Ten Millions	Millions	Hundred Thousand	Ten Thousands	Thousands	Hundreds	Tens	ones
	5	0	0	0	0	0	0	0
	3	0	0	0	0	0	0	0
		2	0	0	0	0	0	0
			6	0	0	0	0	0
				3	0	0	0	0
					2	0	0	0
						1	0	0
							7	
5	3	2	6	3	2	1	7	

Billions Family

Hundred Billions	Ten Billions	Billions

, **Millions Family**

Hundred Millions	Ten Millions	Millions

, **Thousands Family**

Hundred Thousands	Ten Thousands	Thousands

, **Ones Family**

Hundreds	Tens	Ones

• **Decimals Family**

Tenths	Hundredths	Thousandths

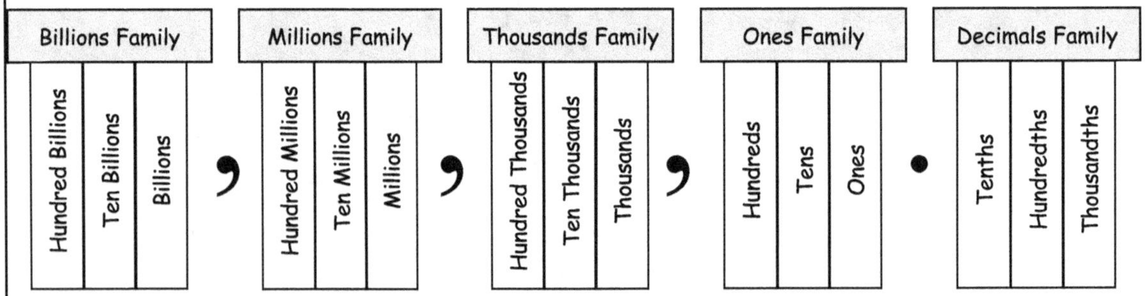

Chapter 2

Large Numbers

LEARNING OBJECTIVES

This lesson will help you to:—

- ❖ be able to recognize & learn numbers larger than lakh.
- ❖ be able to understand the place value chart.
- ❖ be able to identify ten lakh.
- ❖ be able to understand the real life applications of large numbers.

QUICK CONCEPT REVIEW

Large Numbers

A census officer visited Rohan's home. He was confused why she was asking so many questions. He was really curious & asked his father all about census. His father told him that census is the process to count & record all the information of the population of a country.

Rohan says that population of the whole country must be a very big number. His father told him that for this you will have to learn about large numbers.

Let us all learn about large numbers.

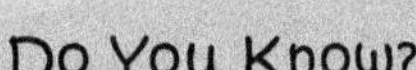

Amazing Facts

❖ Sometimes instead of using commas, we can leave spaces between periods. This helps to read a number easily & quickly.

❖ Abacus is considered the origin of the calculator.

❖ The largest 1 digit number is 9.

❖ The largest 9 digit number is 999999999.

❖ The smallest 1 digit number is 1.

❖ The smallest 9 digit number is 100000000.

Do You Know?

Example : - How many lakhs are there in one million?

Solution : 1 Lakh = 100000

1 Million = 1000000

So there are 1000000 / 100000

= 10 Lakhs in one million.

Let us have a look at the table given below:

Number	Read As
1	One
10	Ten
100	One hundred
1000	One thousand
10000	Ten thousand
100000	One lakh
1000000	Ten lakh
10000000	One crore
100000000	Ten crore

The numbers given in the above table are based on the Indian system of numeration.

As the number increases it becomes larger and larger.

6 DIGIT NUMBERS

We know that 99,999 is the greatest 5 digit number. If we add 1 to it, we will get the smallest 6 digit number.

99,999 + 1 = 1,00,000 (smallest six digit no.)

Place Value

The place value of a 6 digit number is Lakhs in the place value chart.

Have a look at the place value chart given below:

Lakhs Period	Thousands Period		Ones Period		
Lakhs	Ten thousands	Thousands	Hundreds	Tens	Ones
5	4	7	2	8	3

The place value chart has been separated into three groups:

The ones period has three places – Hundreds, tens & ones.

The thousands period has two places – Ten thousands & thousands.

Next period is the lakhs period which includes – Ten lakhs & lakhs.

But we will learn ten lakhs in higher classes.

Use of Comma

If we write the number without using the place value chart, we use comma to separate the periods.

Let us consider an example:

5,47,283

Here, first comma from the right is used when the ones period is complete.

Second comma is used when thousands period is complete.

ACTIVITY TIME

Put commas to separate the periods:

- ❖ 435362
- ❖ 326483
- ❖ 210002

Reading a 6 digit number: 5,47,283

We read a 6 digit number as mentioned below:

Five lakhs forty seven thousands two hundred eighty three.

ACTIVITY TIME

Read the following numbers:

- ❖ 6,47,393
- ❖ 8,72,282

Expanded notation: 5,47,283

Let us learn to write a number in its expanded notation form. Look at the table given below:

5	4	7	2	8	3
1 00 000	10 000	1000	100	10	1
1 00 000	10 000	1000	100	10	1
1 00 000	10 000	1000		10	1
1 00 000	10 000	1000		10	
1 00 000		1000		10	
		1000		10	
		1000		10	
				10	

This table can be summarized as follows:

500000 + 40000 + 7000 + 200 + 80 + 3

Some More Examples

Example : - Write the following number 627891 in Indian system and International system of Numeration

Solution : In Indian System:

L	TTH	TH	H	T	O
6,	2	7,	8	9	1

Six lakhs twenty seven thousand eight hundred ninety one.

In International System:

HTH	TTH	TH	H	T	O
6	2	7,	8	9	1

Six hundred twenty seven thousand and eight hundred ninety one.

Multiple Choice Questions

LEVEL 1

1. 99,999 is the greatest ____ digit number. **[Mental Mathematics]**
   - (a) 5
   - (b) 4
   - (c) 3
   - (d) 2

2. Place value of 5 in 5,43,684 is ________. **[Mental Mathematics]**
   - (a) lakh
   - (b) thousand
   - (c) ones
   - (d) tens

3. Smallest 6 digit number = ________. **[Mental Mathematics]**
   - (a) 0,00,000
   - (b) 1,00,000
   - (c) 9,99,999
   - (d) 99,999

4. 300000 + 20000 +4000 +200 +20 +2 = ________.
   - (a) 3,24,222
   - (b) 3,42,222
   - (c) 2,34,222
   - (d) 3,22,432

5. Ones period includes:
   - (a) Hundreds
   - (b) Thousands
   - (c) Ten thousands
   - (d) Lakhs

6. Lakhs period includes:
   - (a) Thousand
   - (b) Lakh
   - (c) Tens
   - (d) Ones

7. Thousands period includes:
   - (a) Ten thousands
   - (b) Tens
   - (c) Ones
   - (d) Hundreds

8. Pick the odd one out: **[Mental Mathematics]**
   - (a) Hundreds
   - (b) Tens
   - (c) Ones
   - (d) Thousands

9. We use ________ to separate the periods.
   - (a) comma
   - (b) full Stop
   - (c) brackets
   - (d) hyphen

10. 4,37,283 is a ________ number. **[Mental Mathematics]**
    - (a) 4 digit
    - (b) 5 digit
    - (c) 6 digit
    - (d) 7 digit

11. Instead of putting comma, we can ________ to separate the periods.
    - (a) put hyphen
    - (b) leave space
    - (c) put full stop
    - (d) put brackets

12. Ten lakhs comes in ________ period.
    - (a) thousands
    - (b) lakhs
    - (c) ones
    - (d) hundreds

13. Pick odd one out.
    - (a) 6,34,231
    - (b) 1,34,345
    - (c) 1,34,655
    - (d) 12,34,56

14. Pick odd one out.
    - (a) 6,44,245
    - (b) 4,65,345
    - (c) 2,55,666
    - (d) 2,566,55

15. Pick odd one out.
    - (a) 1,00,000
    - (b) 10,000
    - (c) 1,00,001
    - (d) 10,00,00

16. 3,44,567 has ________ lakhs. **[Mental Mathematics]**
    - (a) 3
    - (b) 4
    - (c) 5
    - (d) 6

17. 3,44,567 has ________ thousands. **[Mental Mathematics]**
    - (a) 3
    - (b) 4
    - (c) 5
    - (d) 6

18. 3,44,567 has ________ ones. **[Mental Mathematics]**
    - (a) 3
    - (b) 4
    - (c) 7
    - (d) 5

19. 3,44,567 has ________ tens. **[Mental Mathematics]**
    - (a) 3
    - (b) 4
    - (c) 5
    - (d) 6

20. 3,44,567 has ________ hundreds. **[Mental Mathematics]**
    - (a) 3
    - (b) 4
    - (c) 5
    - (d) 6

21. **6,46,555 = ?**
    (a) 600000+40000+6000+500+50+5
    (b) 600000+40000+6000+500+5+50
    (c) 600000+40000+6000+50+50+5
    (d) 600000+4000+6000+500+50+5

22. **Write One lakh in figures.**
    (a) 1,00,000   (b) 10,00,000
    (c) 10,000   (d) 100,00,000

23. **Write the expanded notation of 5 lakhs.**
    (a) 500000
    (b) 500000+0000+000+00+0
    (c) 50000
    (d) 5000

24. **Put the missing commas in 645333 according to Indian system of Numeration.**
    (a) 6,45,333
    (b) 64,53,33
    (c) 64,533,3
    (d) 645,333

25. **Write the expanded notation for 3,00,123**   [2010]
    (a) 300000+100+20+3
    (b) 300000+00000+0000+20+3
    (c) 300000+000+100+20+3
    (d) 300000+00+100+20+3

26. **The number shown on the abacus is written as ____________.**   [2019]

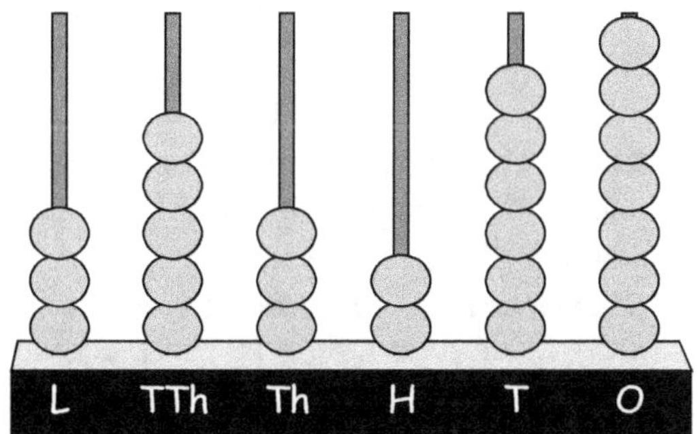

    (a) Three hundred fifty three hundred two hundred and sixty seven
    (b) Three ten thousand fifty three hundred thousand two hundred sixty seven

    (c) Three lakh fifty three thousand two hundred and sixty seven
    (d) Three five thousand three thousand two hundred sixty seven

27. **The XYZ company estimated the cost to build a new baseball stadium which is Rupees ninety four thousand. What is this number in numeral form?** [2020]
    (a) ₹90400
    (b) ₹94000
    (c) ₹90004
    (d) ₹90040

28. **Ramya bought the given microwave. What is the number name for the cost of the given microwave?**   [2021]

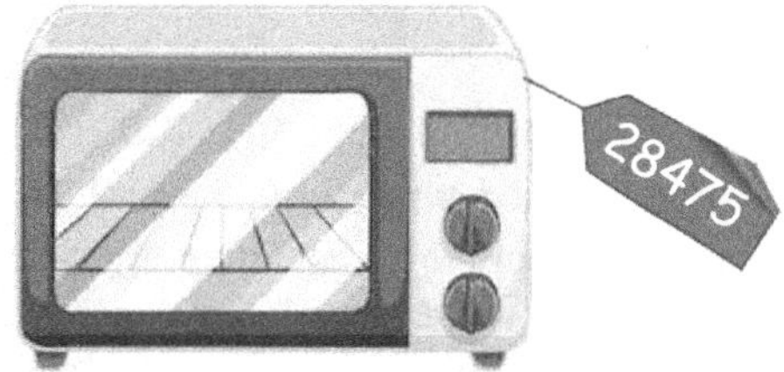

    (a) Twenty thousand eight hundred four seventy five
    (b) Two eighty four thousand seventy five
    (c) Twenty eight thousand four thousand seventy five
    (d) Twenty eight thousand four hundred seventy five

29. **Which of the following has the least value?**   [2022]
    (a) 10 tens more than 20 hundreds
    (b) 10 ones more than 200 tens
    (c) 10 ones more 20 tens
    (d) 10 hundred more than 200 thousands

30. **In the number 275465 what is the difference between the place values of 5?**   [2022]
    (a) 4999   (b) 4998
    (c) 4995   (d) 4875

LEVEL 2

1. Match the following: [Critical Thinking]

	List I		List II
A.	5,45,667	1.	One lakh
B.	1,00,000	2.	Four lakh forty five thousand nine hundred fifty three
C.	4,45,953	3.	Six lakh thirty four thousand six hundred seventy two
D.	6,34,672	4.	Five lakh forty five thousand six hundred sixty seven

```
     A  B  C  D              A  B  C  D
(a)  4  1  2  3         (b)  4  1  3  2
(c)  1  4  2  3         (d)  4  3  2  1
```

2. How many times does the place value of 8 in the numeral 2583219705 is greater than the face value of 8? [2012]
(a) 10000000 (b) 1000000
(b) 100000 (d) 10000

3. Draw a place value chart for 2,00,222.
(a) Lakhs period – 2, Thousands period – 00, Ones period – 222.
(b) Lakhs period – 2, Thousands period – 22, Ones period – 222.
(c) Lakhs period – 2, Thousands period – 02, Ones period – 222.
(d) Lakhs period – 2, Thousands period – 02, Ones period – 22.

4. What is the place value of 5 in the number 45321? [2013]
(a) 50 (b) 5000
(c) 500 (d) 50000

5. Write 4,23,456 in words. [Tricky]
(a) 4 lakh 23 thousand 456.
(b) Four lakh twenty three thousand four hundred.
(c) Four lakh twenty three thousand four hundred fifty six.
(d) Four lakh twenty thousand four hundred.

6. Which one of the following lies at the farthest distance from 0 (zero) on the number line? [2014]
(a) 5694 (b) 49894
(c) 98446 (d) 56942

7.

Lakhs period	Thousands period		Ones period		
Lakhs	Ten thousands	Thousands	Hundreds	Tens	Ones
1	3	0	2	5	9

This is a place value chart for __________.
(a) 1,3,259 (b) 1,30,259
(c) 1,30,25,9 (d) 130258

8. Which one of the following is the face value of 5 in 765001? [2015]
(a) 5 (b) 50
(c) 500 (d) 5000

9. Read the statements carefully and choose the correct option. [Critical Thinking]

Statement A: The place value of a 6 digit number is Lakhs in the place value chart.

Statement B: The place value of a 6 digit number is Thousands in the place value chart.
(a) Statement A is correct.
(b) Statement B is correct.
(c) Both are correct.
(d) Both are incorrect.

10. Find the product of the place values of two 2's in the number │102132│.
    [2016]
    (a) 2 × 2 (b) 20 × 2
    (c) 200 × 2 (d) 2000 × 2

11. Read the statements carefully and choose the correct option.

    Statement A: If we add 1 to the largest 5 digit number, we will get the smallest 6 digit number.

    Statement B: If we add 1 to the largest 4 digit number, we will get the smallest 6 digit number.
    (a) Statement A is correct.
    (b) Statement B is correct.
    (c) Both are correct.
    (d) Both are incorrect.

12. A number has 24 ones, 3 hundreds and 15 tens. What is the number? **[2010]**
    (a) 384 (b) 474
    (c) 24,315 (d) 31,524

13. Fill in the blank spaces:

?	?			?	
Lakhs	Ten thousands	Thousands	Hundreds	Tens	Ones
1	3	0	2	5	9

    (a) Lakh period, thousand period, ones period respectively.
    (b) Lakh, hundred, ones respectively.
    (c) Lakh period ones period respectively.
    (d) Lakh period, thousand period.

14. Place value of 5 in 6,54,321 is ___________.
    [2009]
    (a) lakh (b) thousand
    (c) ten thousand (d) hundreds

15. Tick the correct statement.
    A: 5,34,237 = 5 34 237.
    B: 5, 34, 237 = 5-34-237.

(a) A is correct.
(b) B is correct.
(c) Both are correct.
(d) Both are incorrect.

16. Tick the correct statement.
    [2008, Tricky]
    A: 6,00,000 is the correct way to write 6 Lakh.
    B: 6 00 000 is the correct way to write 6 Lakh.
    (a) A is correct.
    (b) B is correct.
    (c) Both are correct.
    (d) Both are incorrect.

17. Smallest 6 digit number is ___________.
    [2008]
    (a) 1,11,111 (b) 1,00,001
    (c) 1,10,010 (d) 1,00,000

18. Tick the correct statement. **[Tricky]**
    Statement A: Place value of 6 in 1,34,064 is lakh.
    Statement B: Place value of 0 in 1,34,064 is tens.
    (a) A is correct.
    (b) B is correct.
    (c) Both are correct.
    (d) Both are incorrect.

19. Which of the following is equivalent to "five lakhs one hundred and nine"?
    [2017]
    (a) 50109 (b) 501009
    (c) 500109 (d) 510090

20. Match the following: **[Tricky]**

	List I		List II
A.	5,45,667	1.	0 tens.
B.	1,00,000	2.	9 hundreds
C.	4,45,953	3.	2 ones
D.	6,34,672	4.	6 tens

	A	B	C	D			A	B	C	D
(a)	4	1	2	3		(b)	4	1	3	2
(c)	1	4	2	3		(d)	4	3	2	1

21. 12 thousands + 12 hundreds + 12 tens + 12 = ________. **[2014]**
    (a) 12228 (b) 12252
    (c) 13308 (d) 13332

22. Tick the correct statement.   [Tricky]

Statement A: 1,00,000 is largest 6 digit number.

Statement B: 99,999 is smallest 5 digit number.
  (a) A is correct.
  (b) B is correct.
  (c) Both are correct.
  (d) Both are incorrect.

23. Write the number with :   [Critical Thinking]

3 ones, 3 tens, 4 hundreds, 6 thousands, 6 ten thousands & 9 lakhs.
  (a) 9,66,433   (b) 3,34,669
  (c) 3,46,469   (d) 9,33,466

24. Which one of the following is the expanded form of the numeral 7400546?
  (a) 700000 + 40000 + 5000 + 40 + 6
  (b) 700000 + 400000 + 5000 + 40 + 6
  (c) 7000000 + 400000 + 500 + 40 + 6
  (d) 700000 + 40000 + 5000 + 400 + 6

25. What is 1 more than the greatest 5-digit number?   [2012]
  (a) Smallest 6-digit number
  (b) Greatest 7-digit number
  (c) Greatest 6-digit number
  (d) Smallest 7-digit number

26. Find the values of P, Q, R and S respectively.   [2018]

Number	Rounded off to nearest 100	Rounded off to nearest 1000
92684	P	R
43595	43600	Q
S	14600	15000

  (a) 92000, 44000, 92000, 14595
  (b) 92700, 43000, 93000, 14595
  (c) 92000, 43000, 92000, 14680
  (d) 92700, 44000, 93000, 14620

27. Identify it.   [2020]
  • I am a 4-digit number.
  • All my digits are different.
  • They add up to 20.
  • The hundred's digit is double the one's digit.
  (a) 6734   (b) 9236
  (c) 2864   (d) 2963

28. Fill in the blanks and select the CORRECT option.   [2020]
  (i) The number 82564 when rounded off to nearest thousands becomes (P)
  (ii) (Q) will be added to 56492, to make 98492.
  (iii) Difference between largest 5-digit number and smallest 6-digit number is (R).

	(P)	(Q)	(R)
(a)	8000	4000	1
(b)	80000	4200	1
(c)	8000	42000	1
(d)	83000	42000	1

29. The number shown on the abacus is written as _________.   [2021]

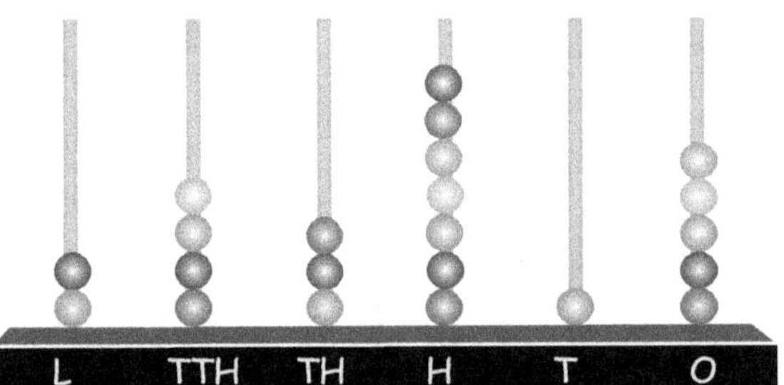

  (a) Two hundred forty three hundred seven hundred fifteen
  (b) Twenty four thousand three thousand seven hundred fifteen
  (c) Two lakh forty three thousand seven hundred fifteen
  (d) Two lakh forty three thousand eight hundred fifteen

30. Difference between the 4-digit smallest number and the 4-digit greatest number formed by using digits 2, 0, 3 where 3 comes twice in both the numbers, is: [2022]
  (a) 1287   (b) 990
  (c) 1269   (d) 972

31. Find the values of P and Q in the pattern given below and then find the value of Q – 2P. **[2022]**

(a) 88   (b) 90   (c) 92   (d) 84

RESPONSE GRID

LEVEL 1

1. a b c d	2. a b c d	3. a b c d	4. a b c d	5. a b c d
6. a b c d	7. a b c d	8. a b c d	9. a b c d	10. a b c d
11. a b c d	12. a b c d	13. a b c d	14. a b c d	15. a b c d
16. a b c d	17. a b c d	18. a b c d	19. a b c d	20. a b c d
21. a b c d	22. a b c d	23. a b c d	24. a b c d	25. a b c d
26. a b c d	27. a b c d	28. a b c d	29. a b c d	30. a b c d

LEVEL 2

1. a b c d	2. a b c d	3. a b c d	4. a b c d	5. a b c d
6. a b c d	7. a b c d	8. a b c d	9. a b c d	10. a b c d
11. a b c d	12. a b c d	13. a b c d	14. a b c d	15. a b c d
16. a b c d	17. a b c d	18. a b c d	19. a b c d	20. a b c d
21. a b c d	22. a b c d	23. a b c d	24. a b c d	25. a b c d
26. a b c d	27. a b c d	28. a b c d	29. a b c d	30. a b c d
31. a b c d				

Solutions with Explanation

LEVEL 1

1. (a)	2. (a)	3. (b)	4. (a)	27. (b)	28. (d)	
5. (a)	6. (b)	7. (a)	8. (d)	29. (c)	10 ones = 10 ×1 = 10	
9. (a)	10. (c)	11. (b)	12. (b)		20 Tens = 20 × 10 = 200	
13. (d)	14. (d)	15. (d)	16. (a)		10 Ones more than 20 Tens = 200 + 10 = 210	
17. (b)	18. (c)	19. (d)	20. (c)		210 has least value in those options	
21. (a)	22. (a)	23. (a)	24. (a)			
25. (a)						
26. (c)	353267 = Three lakh fifty three thousand two hundred sixty seven			30. (c)		

LEVEL 2

1. **(a)**

2. **(a)** Since 8 × $\boxed{10000000}$ = 80000000

3. **(a)**

4. **(b)** As place value of 5 in 45321 is 5000

5. **(c)**

6. **(c)** As 98446 lies at the farthest distance from zero on the number line.

7. **(b)**

8. **(a)** As Face value of 5 in 765001 is 5.

9. **(a)**

10. **(d)** Since the product of the place values of two 2's in 102132 is 2000 × 2

11. **(a)**

12. **(b)** As 24 ones + 3 hundred + 15 tens = 24 + 300 + 150 = 474

13. **(a)** 14. **(c)** 15. **(a)** 16. **(c)**

17. **(d)** 18. **(d)**

19. **(c)** Since 500109 represent five lakhs one hundred and nine.

20. **(a)**

21. **(d)** As 12000 + 1200 + 120 + 12 = 13332.

22. **(d)**

23. **(a)**

24. **(c)** As 7400 546 = 7000000 + 400000 + 500 + 40 + 6

25. **(a)** Since 99999 + 1 = 100000, which is the smallest 6-digit number.

26. **(d)** 92700, 44000, 93000, 14620

27. **(d)** 2963 = 2 + 9 + 6 + 3 = 20
Hundred digit (6) is double of one's digit. (3)

28. **(d)**

29. **(c)** The number shown on the abscus is written as = 243715

30. **(a)**

31. **(d)**

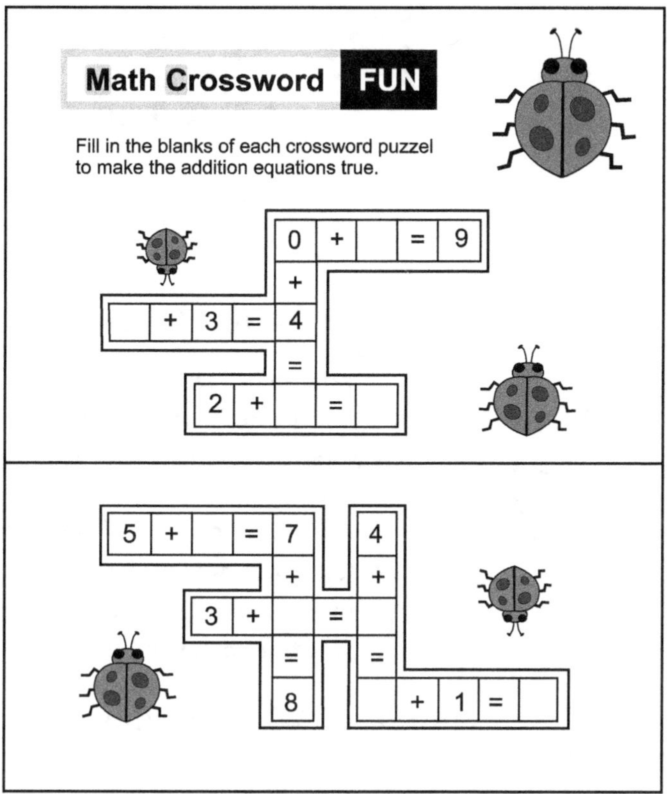

Clowning Around

Directions: Add and colour the picture using the colour code.

colour code

1	2	3	4	5	6	7	8	9	10
pink	white	black	brown	purple	green	blue	orange	yellow	red

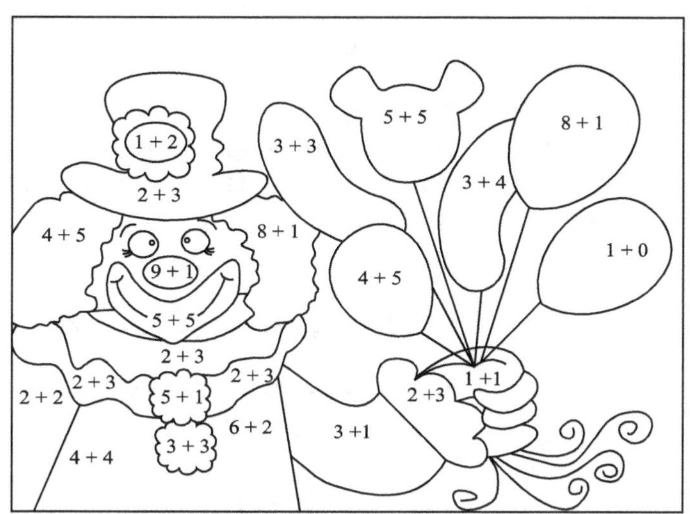

Addition

Example : If there are 30 boys and 12 girls in a class, then find the total number of students in the class.

Solution :

No. of boys = 30
No. of girls = 12
          +
Total Number = 42
of students in the class.

LEARNING OBJECTIVES

This lesson will help you to:—

❖ be able to find the sum of two numbers.
❖ be able to solve real life problems based on addition.
❖ explore various facts of addition.
❖ be able to define addition.
❖ be able to define the terminologies of addition.
❖ be able to explain the properties of addition.

QUICK CONCEPT REVIEW

WHAT IS ADDITION?

Combining two or more objects of same kind is known as addition. It is bringing two or more numbers (or things) together to make a new total. Addition is finding the total, or sum, by combining two or more numbers.

Some other names used in addition are Sum, Plus, Increase & Total.

TERMINOLOGY

Sum

The result obtained after addition is called sum. It is the result obtained after adding one number to another.

Addend

The numbers that are to be added are called addends.

ADDEND + ADDEND = SUM

For example: 50 + 20 = 70

Here, 50 = Addend
      20 = Addend
      70 = Sum

PROPERTIES OF ADDITION

1. **When we add 1 to any number, the answer is always its successor.**

   For Example: Tina had 1 fish in her fish tank.

   Her mom gave her another fish on her birthday.

   How many fish are there in all?

   There was 1 fish in the fish tank. One more is added to it.

   Therefore, total number of fishes in the fish tank
   $$= 1 + 1 = 2$$

2. **When we add zero to a number, the answer is the number itself.**

   That is, $29 + 0 = 29$

   Hence, we can say that when we add zero to a number, the answer is the number itself.

3. **If we change the order of addends while adding, the sum does not change.**

   For example: $25 + 34 = 59$

   Here, Addend 1 = 25

   Addend 2 = 34

   Sum = 59

   If we interchange the addends with each other, that is 34 becomes addend 1 & 25 becomes addend 2. The sum remains the same.

   That is, $34 + 25 = 59$

   Hence, we can say that if the order of the addends to be added is changed, the sum will remains the same.

DIFFERENT WAYS TO MAKE A NUMBER

Let us find out different ways to form the number 50.

All the petals of the flower represent ways to form the number 50. We can add many more petals to this flower.

Amazing Facts

❖ The sum is always greater than the numbers being added, except when one of the numbers being added is zero.

❖ If you add up the numbers 1 to 100. Consecutively ($1 + 2 + 3 + 4 + 5 + \dots$) the total is 5050.

❖ Opposite sides of a die always add up to seven (7).

Property of addition:

If three numbers are to be added, then any two of them can be added first and then the third number can be added to the result and we obtain the final answer.

For Example : $2 + (3 + 4) = (2 + 3) + 4$

or $2 + 7 = 5 + 4$

or $9 = 9$

Activity Time

❖ Add 4 more petals to the flower given below.

Example : Add 2 & 3 on a number line.

Solution :

So 2 + 3 = 5

ADDITION WITH NUMBER LINE

Example,
45 + 27 = ?

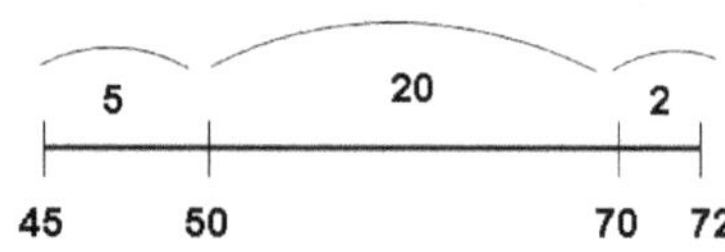

Break the smaller number as shown above and reach to the answer.

Step 1: 45+5 = 50

Step 2: 50+20 = 70

Step 3: 70+2 = 72

Therefore, 45 + 27 = 72

ADDITION WITHOUT REGROUPING

Lily went to the zoo, she found that there were 1163 animals & 824 birds. She wants to know that the total number of animals & birds in the zoo. Let us help her to do so.

Number of animals in the zoo = 1163

Number of birds in the zoo = 824

Total number of animals & birds in the zoo = 1163 + 824

We can also write this in columnar form as follows:

```
   Th  H  T  O
       1  1  6  3
   +      8  2  4
   ____________
```

Step 1: Start with ones column & proceed towards the left.

Adding 3 & 4 on ones column gives 7 as shown below:

```
   Th  H  T  O
       1  1  6  3
   +      8  2  4
   ____________
                7
```

Step 2: Now moving to the tens column, 6 + 2 = 8

```
   Th  H  T  O
       1  1  6  3
   +      8  2  4
   ____________
             8  7
```

Step 3: In the hundreds column, 1+8 = 9

```
Th H  T  O
   1  6  3
+  8  2  4
___________
   9  8  7
```

Step 4: Lastly, in the thousands column, bring 1 as it is.

```
Th H  T  O
 1 1  6  3
+  8  2  4
___________
 1 9  8  7
```

Hence, total number of animals & birds in the zoo = 1987.

This kind of addition is known as addition without regrouping. Now we will learn how to do addition with regrouping.

ADDITION WITH REGROUPING

In a month, 7125 men & 3799 women went to the beach. Find out the total number of people who visited the beach.

Number of men = 7125

Number of women = 3799

Total number of people = 7125 + 3799

Let us write it in column form:

```
Th H  T  O
 7 1  2  5
+3 7  9  9
___________
```

Step 1: Adding the digits on ones column, 5 + 9 = 14.

We will write 4 in the ones column & 1 will be regrouped to tens column as shown below:

```
Th H  T  O
         1
 7 1  2  5
+3 7  9  9
___________
         4
```

Step 2: In the tens column, add 1, 2, & 9.

1 + 2 + 9 = 12

Again 1 will be regrouped to hundreds column.

Example : Add 132 + 254 + 168 + 146 with suitable rearrangement

Solution:

We should add 132 with 168 and 254 with 146

So (132 + 168) + (254 + 146)

= 300 + 400

= 700

An Interesting
Poem on Addition

Add at a circus.
Come along with me.
Add at a circus.
Math is fun you see!
3 + 3 is 6; 8 + 2 is 10; 2 + 1 is 3.
Even clowns add. It's easy.
5 + 2 is 7; 10 + 10 is 20. 12 + 3 is 15;
3 + 1 is 4; 6 + 2 is 8
I love the circus! It was great!
Add at a circus.
Come along with me.
Add at a circus.
Math is fun you see!
No clowing around now.
You put in the answers.

Example :- Add the following :
456 + 1398 + 2456 + 789

Solution

```
  Th   H   T   O
            4   5   6
     +  1   3   9   8
        2   4   5   6
            7   8   9
     ─────────────────
        5   0   9   9
```

```
  Th   H   T   O
            1   1
        7   1   2   5
     +  3   7   9   9
     ─────────────────
                2   4
```

Step 3: 1+1+7 = 9 in the hundreds column.

```
  Th   H   T   O
            1   1
        7   1   2   5
     +  3   7   9   9
     ─────────────────
            9   2   4
```

Step 4: Moving to the thousands column, 7 + 3 = 10

```
  Th   H   T   O
            1   1
        7   1   2   5
     +  3   7   9   9
     ─────────────────
     1  0   9   2   4
```

Therefore, total number of people = 10924

This form of addition is known as addition with regrouping.

AMAZING ADDITION PATTERNS

A. Sum of three consecutive numbers differ by 3.

    1 + 2 + 3 = 6
    2 + 3 + 4 = 9
    3 + 4 + 5 = 12
    4 + 5 + 6 = 15 ……. .

B. Sum of 5 consecutive numbers differ by 5.

    1 + 2 + 3 + 4 + 5 = 15
    2 + 3 + 4 + 5 + 6 = 20
    3 + 4 + 5 + 6 + 7 = 25 ………. .

C. 1 + 2 + 3 + 4 + 5 + 6 + 7 + 8 + 9 + 10 = 55

    Sum of 1 to 10 = 55
    11 to 20 = 155
    21 to 30 = 255
    31 to 40 = 355…………

D. 1 + 3 = 4   (2 Addends × 2=4)
    1 + 3 + 5 = 9   (3 Addends × 3=9)

1 + 3 + 5 + 7 = 16   (4 Addends x 4=16)

1 + 3 + 5 + 7 + 9 = 25 ……. (5 Addends x 5=25)

E. 2 + 4 + 6 = 2 × 6 = 12

2 + 4 + 6 + 8 = 2 × (6 + 4) = 2 × 10 = 20

2 + 4 + 6 + 8 + 10 = 2 × (10 + 5) = 2 × 15 = 30

2 + 4 + 6 + 8 + 10 + 12 = 2 × (15 + 6) = 2 × 21 = 42

2 + 4 + 6 + 8 + 10 + 12 + 14 = 2 × (21 + 7) = 2 × 28 = 56

F. 3 + 6 = 3 × (1 + 2) = 3 × 3 = 9

3 + 6 + 9 = 3 × (1 + 2 + 3) = 3 × 6 = 18

3 + 6 + 9 + 12 = 3 × (1 + 2 + 3 + 4) = 3 × 10 = 30

3 + 6 + 9 + 12 + 15 = 3 × (1 + 2 + 3 + 4 + 5) = 3 × 15 = 45

G. 1 + 9 = 10

1 + 99 = 100

1 + 999 = 1000

1 + 9999 = 10000

1 + 99999 = 100000

Multiple Choice Questions

LEVEL 1

1. The sum is always ___________ than the numbers being added, except of the numbers being added is _________.
   - (a) greater, zero
   - (b) less, zero
   - (c) greater, one
   - (d) less, one

2. If we change the order of the numbers being added, the _________ does not change.
   - (a) sum
   - (b) difference
   - (c) multiplication
   - (d) division

3. 0 + 33 = ______ [Mental Mathematics]
   - (a) 0
   - (b) 33
   - (c) 34
   - (d) 30

4. If we add ___________ to any number, the sum remains the same.
   - (a) zero
   - (b) one
   - (c) two
   - (d) three

5. If we add _________ to any number, the sum is always its successor.
   - (a) zero
   - (b) one
   - (c) two
   - (d) three

6. 25 + 1 = ________
   [Mental Mathematics]
   - (a) 25
   - (b) 26
   - (c) 27
   - (d) 28

7. Addend + ______________ = ______________ .
   - (a) Addend, Sum
   - (b) Minuend, Sum
   - (c) Subtrahend, Sum
   - (d) Difference, Sum

8. Pick the odd one out.
   - (a) Sum
   - (b) Plus
   - (c) Increase
   - (d) Difference

9. On adding two numbers, the result obtained is called __________ .
   - (a) sum
   - (b) difference
   - (c) addend
   - (d) minuend

10. The numbers to be added are known as __________ .
   - (a) sum
   - (b) difference
   - (c) addend
   - (d) minuend

11. 25 + _____ = 26
(a) 0 (b) 1
(c) 2 (d) 3

12. 1 + 0 = _______
(a) 0 (b) 1
(c) 2 (d) 3

13. Pick odd one out.

[Mental Mathematics]
(a) 1 + 1 = 2 (b) 28 + 1 = 29
(c) 151 + 1 = 152 (d) 9005 + 0 = 9005

14. Pick odd one out. **[Mental Mathematics]**
(a) 5 + 5 (b) 8 + 2
(c) 6 + 4 (d) 5 + 4

15. Pick odd one out.
(a) Addend (b) Sum
(c) Total (d) Difference

16. 516 + ______ = 516 **[Mental Mathematics]**
(a) 0 (b) 1
(c) 2 (d) 516

17. 1005 + _____ = 1006 **[Mental Mathematics]**
(a) 0 (b) 1
(c) 2 (d) 1005

18. Simplify : 11 + 21 + 17 **[2015]**
(a) 94 (b) 49
(c) 39 (d) 32

19. 999 + 1 = _______.

[Mental Mathematics]
(a) 999 (b) 1
(c) 0 (d) 1000

20. 999 + 0 = _______ .

[Mental Mathematics]

(a) 999 (b) 0
(c) 1 (d) 1000

21. Election were held in a city in May 2000. The 4 candidates in election got 12,906, 13,545, 23,342 and 102 votes individually. Find the total number of votes polled. **[2019]**
(a) 48,985 (b) 49,598
(c) 94,985 (d) 49,895

22. Rizul had following 4 jars of marbles. How many total number of marbles Rizul had, when rounded off to nearest hundreds? **[2021]**

Jar 1 Jar 2 Jar 3 Jar 4

4375 1872 3488 1937
(a) 11600 (b) 11700
(c) 11680 (d) 12000

23. There are 4758 men, 3978 women and 2650 children in a village. What is the total population of the village? **[2021]**
(a) 11386 (b) 12466
(c) 10836 (d) 13478

24. Six years ago, Namita was 4 times as old as Maya. If Maya is 18 years old now, then find their total age after 10 years. **[2022]**
(a) 92 years (b) 82 years
(c) 112 years (d) 96 years

LEVEL 2

1. Match the following: **[Critical Thinking]**

	List I		List II
A.	Order Property	1.	5 + 1 = 6
B.	Property of One	2.	5 + 0 = 5
C.	Zero Property	3.	Greater than the addends except of the number added is zero
D.	The sum is always	4.	5 + 4 = 4 + 5 = 9

	A	B	C	D		A	B	C	D		A	B	C	D		A	B	C	D
(a)	4	1	2	3	(b)	4	1	3	2	(c)	1	4	2	3	(d)	4	3	2	1

2. P = 454658, Q = 400085, R = 408789. Which one of the following is the greatest? **[2011]**
   (a) P + R
   (b) Q + R
   (c) P + Q
   (d) All of these are equal

3. Find 3 different ways to make the number 99. **[Tricky]**
   (a) 99+0, 98+1, 90+9
   (b) 99+1, 98+2, 90+10
   (c) 99+0, 98+10, 90+1
   (d) 99+2, 98+11, 90+9

4. Fill in the gap: **[2013]**
   97 + 88 + 92 = 88 + _________ + 97.
   (a) 97
   (b) 88
   (c) 92
   (d) All of these

5. Find the values of A, B, C & D. **[Critical Thinking]**

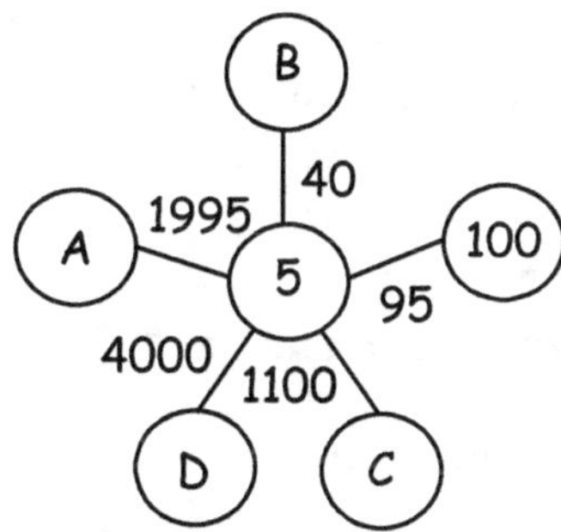

	A	B	C	D
(a)	2000	45	1105	4005
(b)	1995	40	1100	4000
(c)	1990	20	109	3995
(d)	1990	2	1095	3995

6. Which of the following is correct? **[2016]**
   (a) 500 + 31 = 503 + 1
   (b) 500 + 31 = 520 + 1
   (c) 500 + 31 = 50 + 31
   (d) None of these

7. Find the value of A, B, C & D. **[Tricky]**

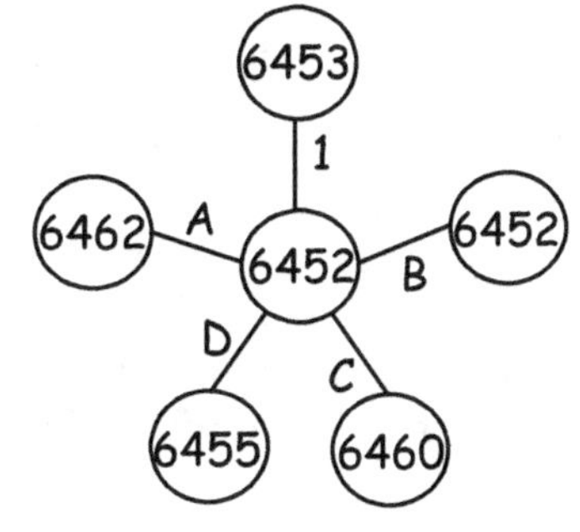

	A	B	C	D
(a)	10	0	8	3
(b)	0	10	18	30
(c)	0	10	80	3
(d)	10	10	8	3

8. Look at the problem given here.
   $\square = \triangle + 4$ **[2010]**
   If $\triangle = 7$, what is $\square$?
   (a) 3   (b) 7
   (c) 11   (d) 14

9. Fill in the blank:

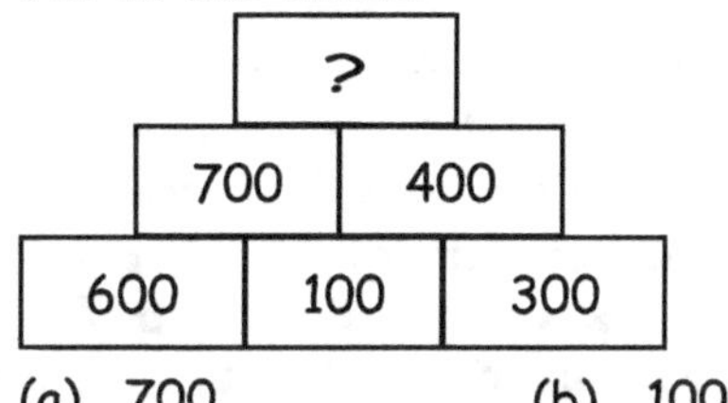

   (a) 700   (b) 1000
   (c) 1100   (d) 100

10. If $\square + \square + \square + \square + \square = 125$ and $\square = \stackrel{}{\bigstar} + 4$, then find the value of $\stackrel{}{\bigstar} + \stackrel{}{\bigstar} + \square + \square$. **[2015]**
    (a) 25   (b) 45
    (c) 50   (d) 92

11. Find A & B: **[Tricky]**

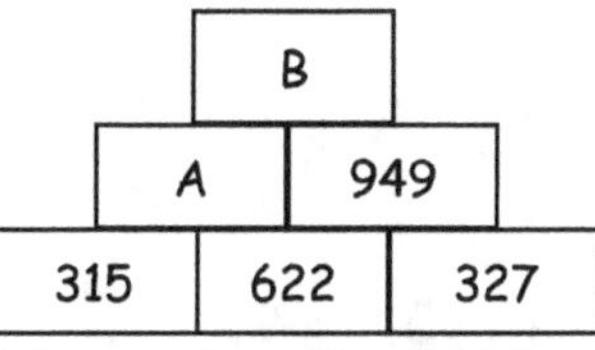

    (a) A = 937, B = 1886
    (b) A = 949, B = 937
    (c) A = 315, B = 2000
    (d) A = 500, B = 1000

12. The annual fees of Riya is ₹ 5372 & the annual fees of Rohan is ₹ 4352. What is their total fees altoghether? **[2008]**
    - (a) 9734
    - (b) 9724
    - (c) 9624
    - (d) 9825

13. Write different ways to make 3452 in all the arms of the starfish. **[Critical Thinking]**

- (a) 3452+1, 3451+0, 3450+2, 2000+1452, 3000+1
- (b) 3452+10, 3451+11, 3450+2, 2000+1452, 3000+23
- (c) 3452+0, 3451+1, 3450+2, 2000+1452, 3000+452
- (d) 3452+1, 3451+0, 3450+2, 2000+1452, 3000+ 234

14. A car travelled from town A to town B & then from town B to town C. The distance between town A & B is 4364 kms. & between B & C is 5473 kms. What is the total distance travelled by the car? **[2010]**
    - (a) 9834
    - (b) 6453
    - (c) 9837
    - (d) 5463

15. Find the values of A, B & C.

    [Critical Thinking]

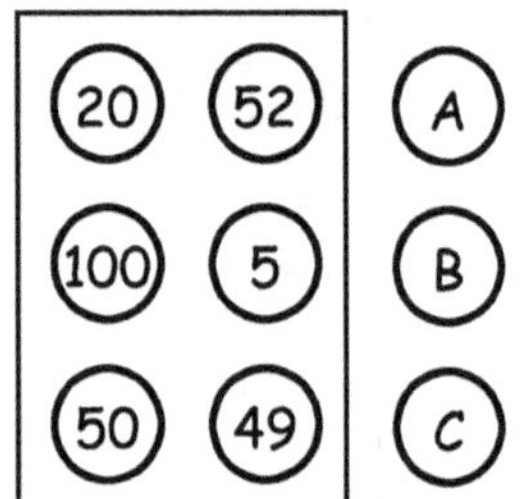

- (a) A = 77, B = 95, C = 99
- (b) A = 72, B = 105, C = 99
- (c) A = 20, B = 100, C = 50
- (d) A = 52, B = 5, C = 49

16. How many times 45 should be added to itself such that their sum becomes 270? **[2012]**
    - (a) 4
    - (b) 5
    - (c) 6
    - (d) 7

17. Read the statements carefully and tick the correct option. **[Critical Thinking]**

    Statement A: We use addition when we put two or more things together.

    Statement B: We use addition when we find how many things are left.
    - (a) Statement A is correct.
    - (b) Statement B is correct.
    - (c) Both are correct.
    - (d) Both are incorrect.

18. Identify the sum of first five prime numbers. **[2014]**
    - (a) 26
    - (b) 25
    - (c) 28
    - (d) 11

19. Tick the correct statement. **[Tricky]**

    Statement A: 999 + 0 = 999.

    Statement B: 999 + 1 = 1 + 999 = 1000.
    - (a) Statement A is correct.
    - (b) Statement B is correct.
    - (c) Both are correct.
    - (d) Both are incorrect.

20. Gia purchased a dress for ₹ 5473 & a pair of footwear for ₹ 2335. What is the total amount she spent? **[2009]**
    - (a) 8708
    - (b) 7808
    - (c) 7800
    - (d) 7353

21. Write different ways to make 2393 on all the arms of the octopus.

- (a) 2392+1, 2393+0........
- (b) 2392+0, 2393 +1........
- (c) 1000+123, 2312+1........
- (d) 123+1234, 2356+23.......

22. Samrat spent ₹ 8,762 to paint his house. He also spent ₹ 987 to repair the roof. What was the total amount Samrat spent to paint his house and repair the roof? [2011]
    (a) ₹ 7,775   (b) ₹ 9,749
    (c) ₹ 9,750   (d) ₹ 18,632

23. Fill in the correct places: [Tricky]

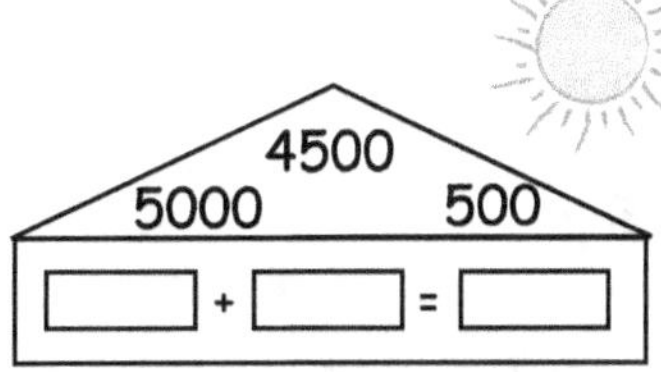

    (a) 5000 + 500 = 5500
    (b) 5000 + 500 = 5000
    (c) 500 + 4500 = 5000
    (d) 5000 – 500 = 4500

24. Find A & B:

	40	A
35	10	25
B	30	25

    (a) A = 50, B = 55
    (b) A = 25, B = 25
    (c) A = 10, B = 30
    (d) A = 25, B = 25

25. Add the following:
    23512+28975
    (a) 52000   (b) 23512
    (c) 26783   (d) 52487

26. Find A & B:

	A	5322
233	109	124
B	100	5198

    (a) A = 100, B =200
    (b) A = 209, B = 5298
    (c) A = 230, B = 123
    (d) A = 1243, B= 2445

27. On Tuesday, 28917 people watched the cricket test match. On Wednesday, 26625 people watched the match. On Thursday, the attendance was 31897. What was the total attendance for these three days? [2017]
    (a) 87500
    (b) 86700
    (c) 87439
    (d) 85000

28. Identify the addends & the sum. [Mental Mathematics]
    5674 + 6 = 5680
    (a) Addends = 5674 & 5680, Sum = 6
    (b) Addends = 5680 & 6, Sum = 5674
    (c) Addends = 5674 & 6, Sum = 5680
    (d) Addends = 5674, Sum = 5680

29. Add the following: 8084 + 2900
    (a) 10984
    (b) 10987
    (c) 10936
    (d) 10332

30. Read the statements carefully and choose the correct option.

    Statement A: The answer in addition is called sum.

    Statement B: The answer in addition is called difference.
    (a) A is correct.
    (b) B is correct.
    (c) Both are correct.
    (d) Both are incorrect.

31. Kunal is playing of darts. The dart board is divided into 3 sections having different points as shown in the figure. The score of Kunal is the sum of the paints he acquired after throwing 3 darts on the board, which of the following cannot be the score of Kunal? [2018]

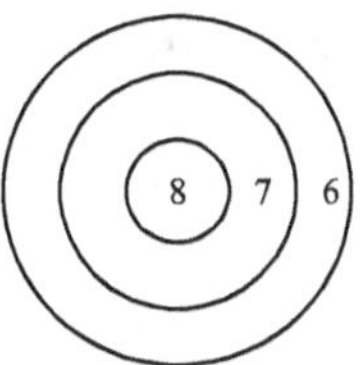

    (a) 22   (b) 23
    (c) 20   (d) 26

32. Find the value of [notebook] + [calendar], if + [notebook] + [notebook] + [notebook] + [notebook] + [notebook]

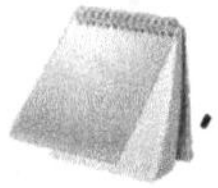

    + = 2700 and [notebook] – [calendar] = 428   [2020]

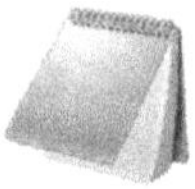

    (a) 652   (b) 540
    (c) 112   (d) 684

33. Arjun's weight is 34 kg 375 g. Kapil's weight is two times of Arjun's weight. What is the total weight of both of them?   [2020]
    (a) 103 kg 125 g   (b) 103 kg 375 g
    (c) 68 kg 750 g   (d) 98 kg 250 g

34. Mr Veer took 23 days of leave from office. If his last working days was 16th July, then on what date did he have to join office after leave?
    (a) 5th August   (b) 7th August
    (c) 9th August   (d) 8th August

35. If $\square$ = 1024, $\triangle$ = $\bigcirc\bigcirc\bigcirc$ and $\square$ – $\triangle$ = 208, then find the value of $\triangle$ + $\bigcirc$.   [2022]

    (a) 1024   (b) 1080   (c) 1084   (d) 1088

RESPONSE GRID

LEVEL 1

1. a b c d	2. a b c d	3. a b c d	4. a b c d	5. a b c d
6. a b c d	7. a b c d	8. a b c d	9. a b c d	10. a b c d
11. a b c d	12. a b c d	13. a b c d	14. a b c d	15. a b c d
16. a b c d	17. a b c d	18. a b c d	19. a b c d	20. a b c d
21. a b c d	22. a b c d	23. a b c d	24. a b c d	

LEVEL 2

1. a b c d	2. a b c d	3. a b c d	4. a b c d	5. a b c d
6. a b c d	7. a b c d	8. a b c d	9. a b c d	10. a b c d
11. a b c d	12. a b c d	13. a b c d	14. a b c d	15. a b c d
16. a b c d	17. a b c d	18. a b c d	19. a b c d	20. a b c d
21. a b c d	22. a b c d	23. a b c d	24. a b c d	25. a b c d
26. a b c d	27. a b c d	28. a b c d	29. a b c d	30. a b c d
31. a b c d	32. a b c d	33. a b c d	34. a b c d	35. a b c d

Solutions with Explanation

LEVEL 1

1.	(a)	2.	(a)	3.	(b)	4.	(a)
5.	(b)	6.	(b)	7.	(a)	8.	(d)
9.	(a)	10.	(c)	11.	(b)	12.	(b)
13.	(d)	14.	(d)	15.	(d)	16.	(a)

17. (b)

18. (b)   11 + 21 + 17 = 49

19. (d)   20. (a)

21. (d)   Total number of votes = 12,906 + 13,545 + 23,342 + 102 = 49895

22. (b)   Total number of marbles Rizul had = 4375 + 1872 + 3488 + 1937 = 11672
Rounded off to nearest hundred = 11700 marbles

23. (a)   Total population of village = Men + Women + Children
= 4758 + 3978 + 2650
= 11386

24. (a)   Present age of Maya = 18 years
6 years ago, Maya's age = 12 years
6 years ago, Namita was 4 times of Maya's age
So, Namita's age was = 12 × 4 = 48 years
Namita's present age = 54 years
After 10 years
Maya's age = 28 years
Namita's age = 64 years
Their total age after 10 years
= 28 + 64 = 92 years.

LEVEL 2

1. (a)

2. (a)   As P + R = 454658 + 408789 = 863447, which is the greatest

3. (a)

4. (c)   97 + 88 + 92 = 88 + 92 + 97

5. (a)

6. (d)   None of these

7. (a)

8. (c)   ☐ = 7 + 4 = 11

9. (c)

10. (d)   As ☐ = 25 and ☆ = 21
So, 21 + 21 + 25 + 25 = 92

11. (a)   12. (b)   13. (c)   14. (c)

15. (b)

16. (c)   As 45 + 45 + 45 + 45 + 45 + 45 = 270
So 6 times 45 must be added to get 270

17. (a)

18. (c)   As first 5 prime numbers are 2, 3, 5, 7, 11
So 2 + 3 + 5 + 7 + 11 = 28

19. (c)   20. (b)   21. (a)

22. (b)   As ₹8762 + ₹987 = ₹9749
So 21 + 21 + 25 + 25 = 92

23. (c)   24. (a)   25. (d)   26. (b)

27. (c)   As 28917 + 26625 + 31897 = 87439

28. (c)   29. (a)   30. (a)   31. (d)

32. (a)   Value of 5 Books = 2700
So, value of 1 Book = 540
1 Book - 1 calender = 428
1 calendar = 540 – 428 = 112
So, 1 Book + 1 Calender = 540 + 112 = 652

33. (a)   Arjun's weight = 34 kg 375 gm
Kapil's weight = 2 × 34.375 = 68.750 kg
So, Total weight of both of them = 34.375 kg + 68.750 kg = 103.125 kg = 103 kg 125 gm

34. (c)   Number of days for which leave taken by Mr. Veer = 23 days
His last working day = 16th july
After leave he had to join =
= 16th july + 23 days
= 16th july + 15 days of July + 8 days of Aug.
So, he will join on 9th August.

35. (d)

Maths Crossword Puzzle

Fill in the blanks of each crossword puzzle to make the subtraction equations true

Puzzle 1

74	−		=				−	12	=	
−				−		−				
	−		=	23		32	−		=	18
=				=		=				=
21		51	−	23	=					

Puzzle 2

				−	56	=	31			
−				−		−				−
34		87	−	44	=					79
=				=		=				=
65	−		=				−	13	=	

LEARNING OBJECTIVES

This lesson will help you to:—

- ❖ be able to find the difference between two numbers.
- ❖ be able to solve real life problems based on subtraction.
- ❖ explore various facts of subtraction.
- ❖ be able to define subtraction.
- ❖ be able to define the terminologies of subtraction.
- ❖ be able to explain the properties of subtraction.

QUICK CONCEPT REVIEW

WHAT IS SUBTRACTION?

Subtraction is taking away some objects from a given collection. It is taking one number away from another.

Some other names used in subtraction are Minus, Less, Difference, Decrease, Take Away, Deduct.

TERMINOLOGY

Difference

The result obtained after subtraction is called difference. It is the result obtained after subtracting one number from another.

Minuend

The number that is to be subtracted from is called minuend.

Subtrahend

The number that is to be subtracted is called subtrahend.

Real Life Example

- ❖ Subtraction is used in every sphere of our life. It is used in our daily activities like purchasing grocery, all monetary transactions like in banks etc.

> More on top ?????
>
> No need to stop.
>
> More on the floor ?????
>
> Go next door, get ten more.
>
> Numbers the same ??????
>
> Zero's the game.

Do You Know?

To get predecesser of a given number we subtract 1 from the number whose predecesser we have to find. For example, Predecesser of 8 is 8 – 1 = 7.

Amazing Fact

❖ The question given below can be solved with an amazing shortcut also.

5000 – 1832 = ?

5000 ⟶ 5000 - 1 ⟶ 4999

1832 ⟶ 1832 - 1 ⟶ -1831

$$\overline{3168}$$

Do You Know?

8 – 5 is not equal to 5 – 8 as 8 – 5 = 3 but 5 – 8 can not be solved at this stage.

MINUEND – SUBTRAHEND = DIFFERENCE

For example, 50 – 20 = 30

Here,   Minuend = 50

     Subtrahend = 20

      Difference = 30

PROPERTIES OF SUBTRACTION

1. When we subtract a number from itself, the answer is always zero.

   For example: 6884-6884 = 0

2. When we subtract zero from a number, the answer is the number itself.

   For example: Monty saw 9 mangoes on a mango tree. He wants to eat the mangoes but could not reach them. How many mangoes were left on the tree?

   There were 9 mangoes on the tree. Monty could not get any mango. It means still there were 9 mangoes on the tree.

   This can be written as 9 – 0 = 9

   Therefore, there were 9 mangoes left on the tree.

   Hence, we can say that when we subtract zero from a number, the answer is the number itself.

SUBTRACTION WITH NUMBER LINE

72 – 45 = ?

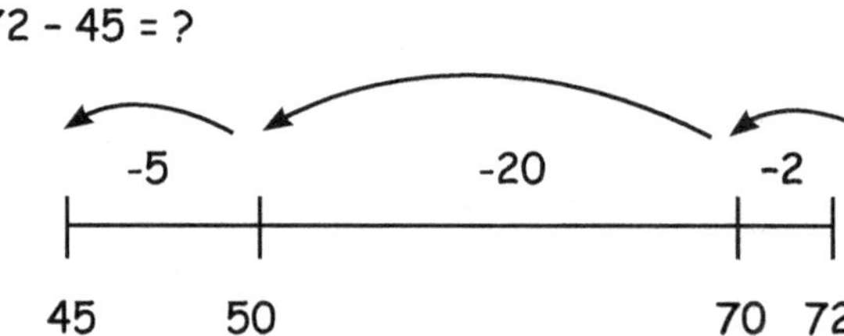

5 + 20 + 2 = 27

Therefore, 72 – 45 = 27

USES OF SUBTRACTION

1. **To find out how many are left:** In a singing competition, 25 students out 75 qualified for the next round? How many students were left unselected?

   Here we have to find the number of students who were left unselected. Whenever we have to find how many are left we use subtraction.

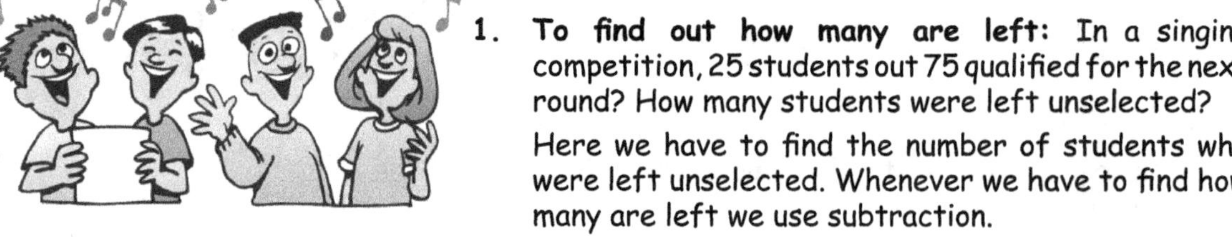

Therefore, number of students left unselected = Total number of students – Number of students selected = 75 – 25 = 50

2. **To compare groups:** A Bakery had 52 pastries & 95 cookies. How many more cookies are there than pastries?

 = 52    = 95

There are 2 groups:

(a) Pastries and

(b) Cookies

Now to compare the quantity of 2 groups, we will subtract the smaller group from the larger group.

This is shown as follows:

```
  9 5 cookies
 -5 2 pastries
  4 3 more cookies than pastries.
```

3. **To find what does not belong to a group:** Mrs. Ben has 15 dogs. Out of them 5 are pugs. Find out how many dogs are not pugs.

Total number of dogs = 15

Number of Pugs = 5

To find the number of dogs which do not belong to the group of pugs, we will subtract the number of pugs from total number of dogs.

Therefore, 15 – 5 = 10 dogs are not pugs.

Example: Fill in the blank to make the given statement true

19 + _______ = 25

Solution: Here 25 – 19 = 6

So 19 + <u>6</u> = 25

4. **To find what was taken away:** A farmer loaded a truck with 1129 apples. On the way, some apples fell on the road. On unloading, the farmer found that there are only 1000 apples. Find out how many apples fell from the truck.

Here we know the original number & the number which is left over. We need to find the number of apples taken away.

This can be written as follows:

| 1129 | – | ? | = | 1000 |

Therefore, the number of apples which fell from the truck are = 1129 – 1000 = 129

5. **To find how many more are needed:** A thirsty crow needs 1255 pebbles to put in the pot to raise the

water level. But he has only 255 pebbles. How many more pebbles does he need ?

<table>
<tr><td>225</td><td>+</td><td>?</td><td>=</td><td>1255</td></tr>
</table>

The number of pebbles required = 1255 – 255 = 1000 more pebbles.

SUBTRACTING FOUR DIGIT NUMBER

1. **Without Regrouping/Borrowing:** There are 2549 seats in a circus tent. 2138 people came to see the circus show. How many seats were left vacant?

   To find out the number of vacant seats we will use subtraction as follows:

   No. of vacant seats = Total no. of seats – no. of seats occupied by people.

   = 2549 – 2138

Th	H	T	O
2	5	4	9
– 2	1	3	8
0	4	1	1

   Therefore, 411 seats were left vacant.

2. **By Regrouping/Borrowing:** Out of 2138 people who came to see the circus, 1619 were adults. Find out how many children were there? (see the previous circus figure.)

   Total number of children = Total number of people – Total number of adults

   = 2138 – 1619

   This can also be written as:

Th	H	T	O
1	11	2	18
2	1	3	8
– 1	6	1	9
0	5	1	9

Circus

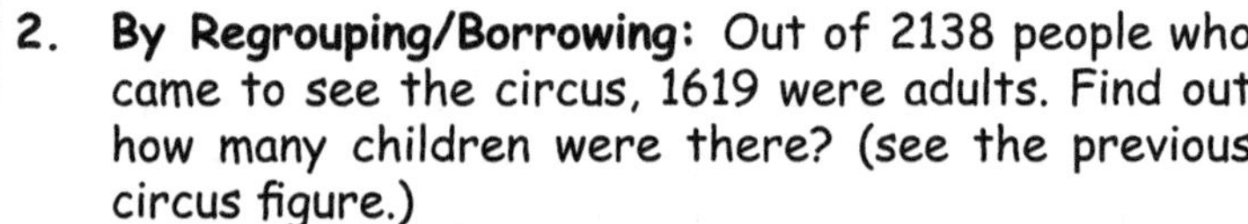

Addition Fact

We can get an addition fact from a given subtraction fact.

For example

37 – 12 = 25.

We can write the addition fact as 37 = 12 + 25

SUBTRACTING WITH ZEROS

5000 – 1832 = ?

OR

Th	H	T	O
5	0	0	0
– 1	8	3	2

There are not enough ones, tens or hundreds and we can't regroup from zero.

Therefore, we will make 0 into 10 & then regroup as shown below.

Reduce 5 by 1 and 5 becomes 4 & 0 becomes 10. Now reduce 10 by 1. 10 becomes 9 & 0 becomes 10. Repeat this process & subtract. The result is shown below.

```
    Th   H   T   O
    4    9   9
         1̶0̶ 1̶0̶ 10
    5̶    0̶   0̶   0
-   1    8   3   2
   ─────────────────
    3    1   6   8
   ─────────────────
```

Subtraction Facts

Subtraction facts from a given addition fact.

From a given addition fact, we can derive two subtraction facts.

For Example

27 + 19 = 46

We can write the 2 subtraction facts as 46 – 19 = 27

and 46 – 27 = 19

Some More Subtraction

Example :- (i) What should be subtracted from 1000 to get 999?

(ii) What should be subtracted from 105 to get the smallest three digit number?

Solution : (i) As 1000 – 1 = 999, So, 1 should be subtracted from 1000 to get 999

(ii) As 105 – 5 = 100

So, 5 is to be subtracted from 105 to get 100.

Multiple Choice Questions

LEVEL 1

1. ______________ is taking away some objects from a given collection. It is taking one number away from another.
   - (a) Addition
   - (b) Subtraction
   - (c) Multiplication
   - (d) Division

2. The result obtained after subtraction is called ____________.
   - (a) minuend
   - (b) subtrahend
   - (c) difference
   - (d) sum

3. ______________ is the number that is to be subtracted from.
   - (a) Minuend
   - (b) Subtrahend
   - (c) Difference
   - (d) Sum

4. Pick the odd one out.
   - (a) Minus
   - (b) Less
   - (c) Difference
   - (d) Sum

5. Find the Minuend: [Mental Mathematics]

   | ? | − | 5 | = | 45 |

   - (a) 50
   - (b) 40
   - (c) 15
   - (d) 100

6. When we subtract a number from itself, the answer is always __________.
   - (a) zero
   - (b) one
   - (c) two
   - (d) itself

7. Fill in the blank. [Mental Mathematics]

   | 115 | − | ? | = | 0 |

   - (a) 0
   - (b) 1
   - (c) 115
   - (d) 100

8. When we subtract __________ from a number, the answer is the number itself.
   - (a) zero
   - (b) one
   - (c) two
   - (d) itself

9. Fill in the blank. [Mental Mathematics]

   | 217 | − | ? | = | 217 |

   - (a) 0
   - (b) 1
   - (c) 2
   - (d) 217

10. Subtract using number line.

    95 – 59
    - (a) 36
    - (b) 37
    - (c) 38
    - (d) 38

11. Subtract using number line.

    1254 – 999
    - (a) 255
    - (b) 256
    - (c) 257
    - (d) 258

12. Solve the problem.

    | 15 | − | ? | = | 25 |

    - (a) 10
    - (b) 15
    - (c) 25
    - (d) 5

13. Solve using shortcut.

    8000 – 1584
    - (a) 6416
    - (b) 6400
    - (c) 1584
    - (d) 6410

14. Subtract:

    9000 – 1999
    - (a) 7000
    - (b) 7001
    - (c) 7002
    - (d) 7003

15. Subtract:

    3549 – 1234
    - (a) 2315
    - (b) 2316
    - (c) 2317
    - (d) 2318

16. Subtract:

    5643 - 2999
    - (a) 2644
    - (b) 2655
    - (c) 2614
    - (d) 2643

17. Saksham has 925 balls. 580 were basketballs and rest were cricket balls. He sold some cricket balls and found that he had 125 cricket balls left. How many cricket balls were sold? [2019]
    (a) 176 (b) 240
    (c) 125 (d) 220

18. Subtract 49876 (when rounded off to nearest thousands) from 95846 (when rounded off to nearest hundreds). [2020]
    (a) 45800 (b) 35700
    (c) 85000 (d) 46000

19. There were 2860 boys and 1840 girls in a school hall. 450 boys and 380 girls more than boys left the school hall. How many students were remained in the school hall? [2022]
    (a) 3250 (b) 3370
    (c) 3420 (d) 3550

20. Vinay gained 2 kg 775 g. What was his weight earlier, if he weighs 58 kg 215 g now? [2022]
    (a) 55 kg 440 g (b) 53 kg 430 g
    (c) 56 kg 460 g (d) 57 kg 470 g

21. A + B + 45896 = C + (d) If C + D = 96023 + B, find the value of (A) [2022]
    (a) 50120 (b) 50127
    (c) 30127 (d) 20127

LEVEL 2

1. Match the following: [Tricky]

List I		List II	
A.	Minuend	1.	5 – 4 = <u>1</u>
B.	Subtrahend	2.	<u>5</u> – 4 = 1
C.	Difference	3.	5 – <u>4</u> = 1

	A	B	C
(a)	2	3	1
(b)	1	2	3
(c)	3	2	1
(d)	1	3	2

2. Read the statements carefully and choose the correct option.

   Statement A: Minuend – Subtrahend = Difference

   Statement B: Minuend – Difference = Subtrahend

   (a) Statement A is true B is false.
   (b) Statement B is true A is false.
   (c) Both the statements are true.
   (d) Both the statements are false.

3. Find the Subtrahend:

   | 100 | – | ? | = | 90 |

   (a) 10 (b) 0
   (c) 90 (d) 1

4. What is 256 less than 5679? [2014]
   (a) 5835 (b) 5935
   (c) 5423 (d) 5635

5. Tick the correct option. [Tricky]
   A. 999 – 0 = 999
   B. 999 – 999 = 0
   (a) A is correct
   (b) B is correct
   (c) Both are correct
   (d) Both are incorrect

6. If L – 77 = M – 77, then which one of the following expression is correct? [2016]
   (a) L < M (b) L > M
   (c) L ≠ M (d) L = M

7. Tick the correct option.
   A. 812 – 0 = 0
   B. 812 – 812 = 0
   (a) A is correct
   (b) B is correct
   (c) Both are correct
   (d) Both are incorrect

8. 43 thousands less than 473743 is
   _________. [2013]
   (a) 43000
   (b) 430743
   (c) 443074
   (d) 437430

9. Tick the correct option.
   A. Subtraction is used to find out how many are left.
   B. Subtraction is used to find out the total amount.
   (a) A is correct
   (b) B is correct
   (c) Both are correct
   (d) Both are correct

10. To get the predecessor of 7 + 8, what should be subtracted from 21? [2015]
    (a) 1
    (b) 15
    (c) 7
    (d) 8

11. We use subtraction when we have to find out how many more to be _________ to get the given number.
    (a) added
    (b) subtracted
    (c) multiplied
    (d) divided

12. Gia has a book of 119 pages. She has read 59 pages. How many pages are left to be read?
    (a) 60
    (b) 59
    (c) 119
    (d) 58

13. Look at the numbers shown below. Subtract 2 from the 3rd number from the left. The answer is the same as the _________ number from the right. [2011]

    Left ③ ⑧ ⑦ ② ⑤ Right

    (a) 1st
    (b) 2nd
    (c) 3rd
    (d) 4th

14. Solve the problem.

    | 1524 | − | ? | = | 20000 |

    (a) 18476
    (b) 18756
    (c) 18746
    (d) 18776

15. What is the difference between the smallest 5-digit number and the greatest 4-digit number? [2013]

    (a) 3
    (b) 2
    (c) 1
    (d) 9

16. Find the values of A, B, C & D.
    [Critical Thinking]

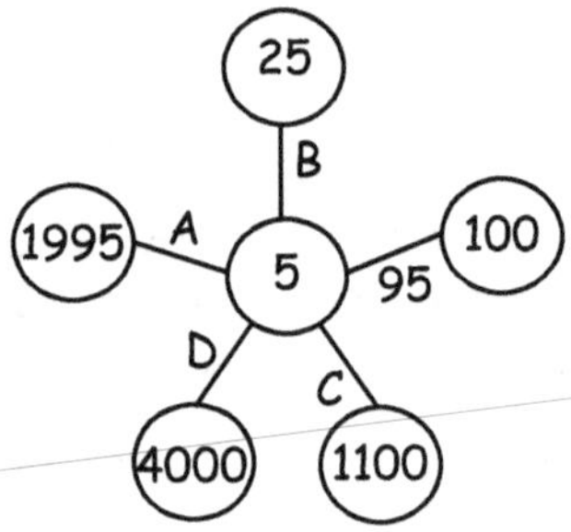

	A	B	C	D
(a)	1990	20	1095	3990
(b)	1990	20	1095	3995
(c)	1990	20	109	3995
(d)	1990	2	1095	3995

17. For a wedding the decorators have to fix 1250 flowers in the hall. If they had already fixed 985 flowers, how many more flowers do they have to fix? [2016]
    (a) 270
    (b) 265
    (c) 272
    (d) 358

18. Find the value of A, B, C & D.
    [Critical Thinking]

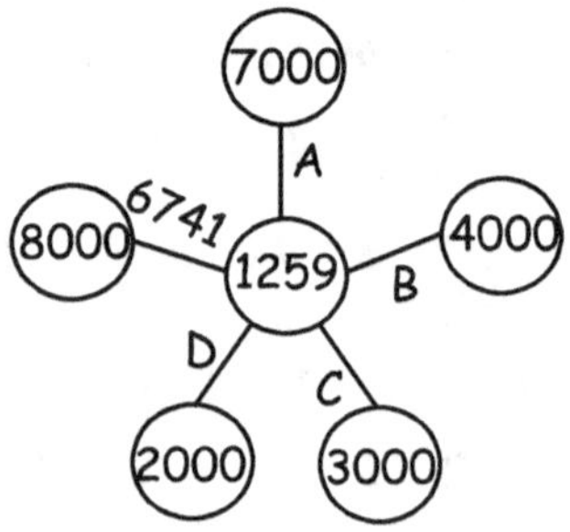

	A	B	C	D
(a)	5741	274	174	741
(b)	5741	2741	1741	741
(c)	574	274	1741	741
(d)	574	271	1741	741

19. Fill in the blank. **[Tricky]**

100	10	5
90	5	
?		

(a) 95   (b) 450

(c) 45   (d) 85

20. Find the value of A, B, & C: **[Tricky]**

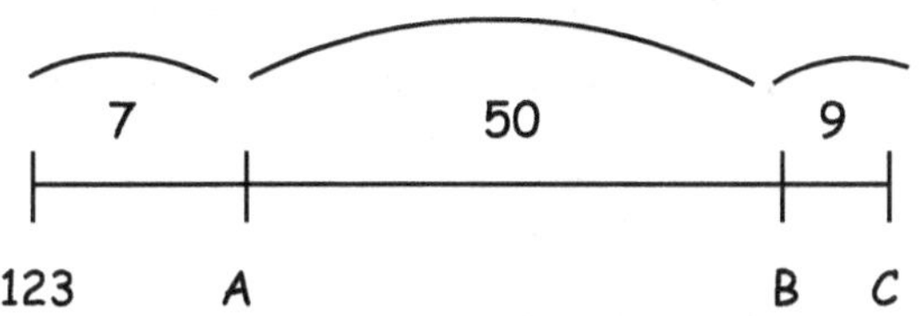

	A	B	C
(a)	130	180	189
(b)	123	180	189
(c)	130	150	189
(d)	130	180	180

21. A poultry farm sends 1647 eggs to the market in a van. On the way, 234 eggs broke. How many eggs were left in the van? **[2017]**

(a) 1413   (b) 1234

(c) 1647   (d) 234

22. Find A & B:

5000	1000	500
4000	A	
B		

(a) A = 500, B = 3000

(b) A = 5000, B = 3500

(c) A = 500, B = 3500

(d) A = 500, B = 1000

23. In the parking area, there were 2198 cars & 1212 bikes. How many more cars were there than bikes? **[2010]**

(a) 986   (b) 987

(c) 988   (d) 989

24. Find the missing numbers.

[Critical Thinking]

1900	100	25	10	5
1800	75	15	A	
B	C	D		
E	F			
G				

	A	B	C	D	E	F	G
(a)	5	1725	60	10	1665	50	1615
(b)	5	1725	60	10	1665	50	16
(c)	5	1725	60	10	1665	5	1615
(d)	5	1725	60	1	1665	50	1615

25. Match the following:

	List I		List II
A.	⑩ ⓪	1.	㊄
B.	㊅ ①	2.	⓪
C.	㉓ ㉓	3.	⑩

	A	B	C
(a)	3	1	2
(b)	3	2	1
(c)	1	2	3
(d)	2	1	3

26. Fill the missing numbers.

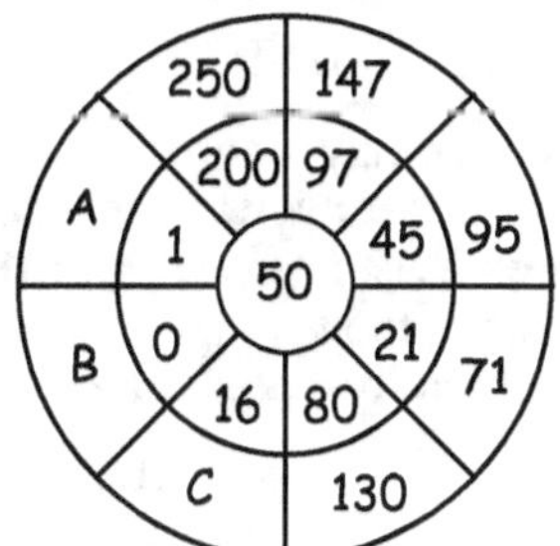

	A	B	C
(a)	51,	50,	66
(b)	50,	52,	67
(c)	71,	130,	95
(d)	250,	147,	95

27. What least number should be subtracted from the sum of 344 + 462 + 27 such that result becomes 0? [2011]

(a) 833 (b) 823
(c) 843 (d) 853

28. Match the following: [Tricky]

List I		List II	
A.	㊸ ⑪	1.	②
B.	(81) (79)	2.	㉚
C.	(52) ㉒	3.	㉜

	A	B	C
(a)	3	1	2
(b)	2	1	3
(c)	1	3	2
(d)	3	2	1

29. Find the value of A, B, C:

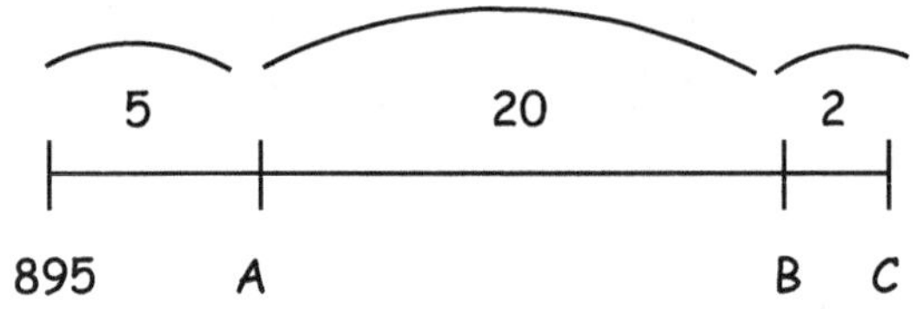

	A	B	C
(a)	90	920	922
(b)	900	920	922
(c)	900	92	922
(d)	900	920	92

30. Sharma family consumes 1000 kgs wheat in a year whereas, Verma family consumes 959 kgs of wheat in a year. How much more kgs. of wheat does Sharma family consume? [2008]

(a) 41 (b) 45
(c) 40 (d) 39

31. Fill in the correct places. [2009]

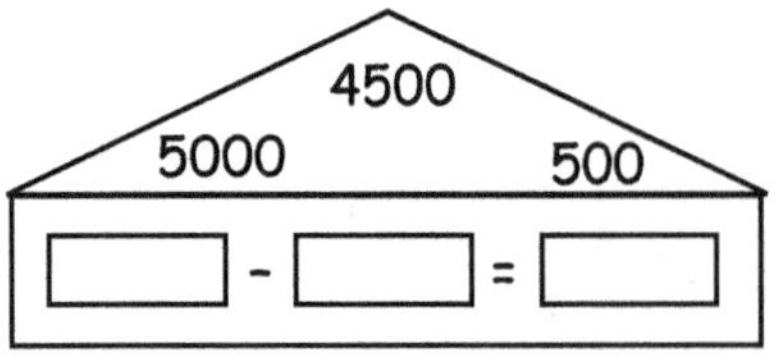

(a) 5000 - 500 = 500
(b) 5000 - 500 = 5000
(c) 4500 - 500 = 5000
(d) 5000 - 500 = 4500

32. Arwin has ₹ 565650 with him. He buys a house for ₹300000 and ₹25460 spend for other purposes. How much money left with him? [2012]

(a) ₹ 290190 (b) ₹ 230190
(c) ₹ 240190 (d) ₹ 241190

33. Fill in the missing numbers. [Tricky]

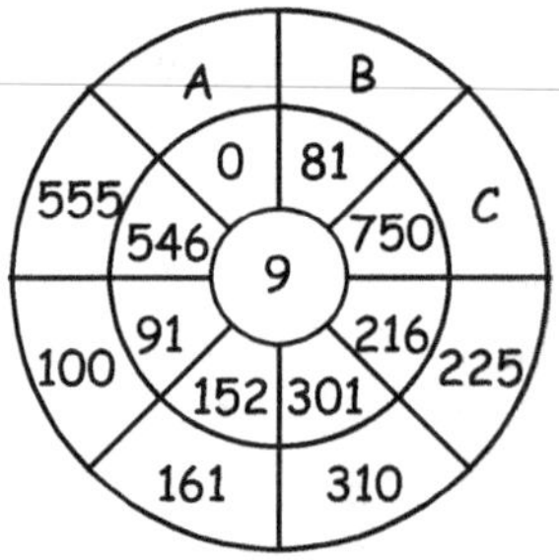

	A	B	C
(a)	9,	90,	759
(b)	10,	90,	790
(c)	9,	89,	789
(d)	9,	90,	900

34. Parking space in theatre P is for 79,407 cars, while the same in theatre Q is for 58,868 cars. How many more cars can be parked in theatre P than in theatre Q? [2015]

(a) 38,275 (b) 21,549
(c) 21,461 (d) 20,539

35. How many hundreds must be subtracted from 27683 to get 2783? [2018]

(a) 249 (b) 2400
(c) 20000 (d) 2000

36. Anjana has to cover 20 km 560 m distance. She walked 1 km 200 m. She covered 10 km 150 m by an auto and rest of the distance by car. How much distance did she cover by car? [2020]

(a) 9 km 21 m (b) 9 km 210 m
(c) 7 km 350 m (d) 7 km 300 m

37. A small-scale industry made 750 candles in a week. The candles were packed in set of 12 each. How many packets were made and how many candles were left behind respectively? **[2022]**

    (a) 62, 6   (b) 64, 6
    (c) 62, 8   (d) 63, 7

38. If ★ + ★ + ★ = 1275 and

    1000 – ★ = ⬤

    than ⬤ – ★ = ?   **[2022]**

(a) 270   (b) 310
(c) 150   (d) 370

39. The difference between 21 hundreds 5 tens 8 ones and the sum of 980 and 1405 is __________. **[2022]**

    (a) 2 hundreds + 7 ones
    (b) 2 tens + 7 tens + 1 ones
    (c) 2 hundreds + 2 tens + 7 ones
    (d) 2 None of these

40. Mr. Sharma has ₹52596, he buys a refrigerator worth ₹18946 and a television worth ₹30420. How much amount of money is left with him? **[2022]**

    (a) ₹3350   (b) ₹4320
    (c) ₹3230   (d) ₹3530

RESPONSE GRID

LEVEL 1

1. a b c d	2. a b c d	3. a b c d	4. a b c d	5. a b c d
6. a b c d	7. a b c d	8. a b c d	9. a b c d	10. a b c d
11. a b c d	12. a b c d	13. a b c d	14. a b c d	15. a b c d
16. a b c d	17. a b c d	18. a b c d	19. a b c d	20. a b c d
21. a b c d				

LEVEL 2

1. a b c d	2. a b c d	3. a b c d	4. a b c d	5. a b c d
6. a b c d	7. a b c d	8. a b c d	9. a b c d	10. a b c d
11. a b c d	12. a b c d	13. a b c d	14. a b c d	15. a b c d
16. a b c d	17. a b c d	18. a b c d	19. a b c d	20. a b c d
21. a b c d	22. a b c d	23. a b c d	24. a b c d	25. a b c d
26. a b c d	27. a b c d	28. a b c d	29. a b c d	30. a b c d
31. a b c d	32. a b c d	33. a b c d	34. a b c d	35. a b c d
36. a b c d	37. a b c d	38. a b c d	39. a b c d	40. a b c d

Solutions with Explanation

LEVEL 1

1. **(b)** Subtraction
2. **(c)** Difference
3. **(a)** Minuend
4. **(d)** Sum
5. **(a)** 50

   ? – 5 = 45

   Minuend = 5 + 45 = 50
6. **(a)** Zero
7. **(c)** 115

   115 – 115 = 0
8. **(a)** Zero
9. **(a)** 0

   217 – 0 = 217
10. **(a)**

    95 – 59 = 1 + 30 + 5 = 36
11. **(a)**

    1254 – 999 = 1 + 1000 + 54 = 255
12. **(a)** 15 + 10 = 25
13. **(a)**

    $$\begin{array}{r} 80\ 0\ 0 \\ 15\ 8\ 4 \end{array} \qquad \begin{array}{r} 8\ 0\ 0\ 0\ \text{-}1 \\ 1\ 5\ 8\ 4\ \text{-}1 \\ \hline \end{array} \qquad \begin{array}{r} 7\ 9\ 9\ 9 \\ \text{-}1\ 5\ 8\ 3 \\ \hline 6\ 4\ 1\ 6 \end{array}$$
14. **(b)** 7001

15. **(a)** 2315
16. **(a)** 2644
17. **(d)** Total number of cricket balls

    = 925 – 580 = 345

    Number of balls left = 125

    Thus, number of balls sold

    = 345 – 125 = 220
18. **(a)**
19. **(c)** Number of boys in hall = 2860

    Number of boys left the school

    = 450

    Remaining boys present in school

    = 2860 – 450 = 2410

    Number of girls in hall = 1840

    Number of girls left the school

    = 450 + 380 = 830

    Remaining girls present in school

    = 1010

    Total number of students remaining in the school hall

    = 2410 + 1010 = 3420
20. **(a)** Vinays weight at present

    = 58.215 kg

    gained weight = 2.775 kg

    So, Earlier weight of vinay

    = 58.215 – 2.775 = 55.440 kg

    So, 55kg 440 gm
21. **(b)**

LEVEL 2

1. **(a)**
2. **(c)**
3. **(a)** 10

   100 – ? = 90

   100 – 90 = 10

   Therefore, subtrahend = 10
4. **(c)** Since 5679 – 256 = 5423
5. **(c)** Both are correct
6. **(d)**
7. **(c)** Both are correct

8. **(b)** Since 473743 – 43000 = 430743

9. **(a)** A is correct.

10. **(c)** As predecessor of 7 + 8 = 15 – 1 = 14

So 21 – $\boxed{7}$ = 14

11. **(a)** Added

12. **(a)** 119 – 59 = 60 pages

13. **(a)** As 7– 2 = 5 which is 1st number from the right.

14. **(a)** 20000 – 1524 = 18476

15. **(c)** As 10000 – 9999 = 1

16. **(b)** A = 1990

B = 20

C = 1095

D = 3995

17. **(b)** As 1250 – 985 = 265

18. **(b)** A = 5741

B = 2741

C = 1741

D = 741

19. **(d)** 85

20. **(a)** A = 130, B = 180, C = 189

21. **(a)** 1413 eggs

22. **(c)** A = 500 , B = 3500

23. **(a)** 986 cars

24. **(a)** A = 5, B = 1725, C = 60, D = 10, E = 1665, F = 50, G = 1615

25. **(a)**

26. **(a)**

27. **(a)** As 344 + 462 + 27 = 833

So 833 must be subtracted to get O.

28. **(a)**

29. **(b)** A = 900, B = 920, C = 922

30. **(a)** 41 kgs.

31. **(d)** 5000 – 500 = 4500

32. **(c)** As ₹300000 + ₹25460 = ₹325460

So, ₹565650 – ₹325460 = ₹240190

33. **(a)**

34. **(d)** As 79407 – 58868 = 20539

35. **(a)** 27683 – 2783 = 24900

249 hundreds.

36. **(a)** Total distance = 20 km 560 mtr.

= 20.560 km

Distance covered by walking

= 1 km 200 m =1.2 km

Distance covered by auto

= 10 km 150 m = 10.150 km

Total Distance covered by walking and Auto = 1.2 km + 10.150 km = 11.350 km

Remaining distance

= 20.560 –11.350 = 9.210 km

= 9 km 210 meter

37. **(d)** Total number of candles = 750

Number of candles in each set = 12

So, total number of packets would be

$$= \quad 12\overline{)750}(62$$

$$\frac{72}{30}$$

$$\frac{24}{6}$$

Hence 62 packets were made and 6 candles were left after packing.

38. **(c)** Value of 3 stars = 1275

So value of 1 star= 1275/3 = 425

So, 1000 – 425   = 575

Value of 1 circle = 575

Then, 575 –425   = 150

39. **(c)** 21 Hundreds 5 tens 8 ones = 2158

Sum of 980 + 1405 = 2385

So, difference between them

= 2385 –2158 = 227

2 Hundreds + 2 Tens + 7 Ones

40. **(c)** Amount spent = ₹30420 + ₹18946

=₹49366

Remaining amount of money

Mr. Sharma has = ₹52596 – ₹49366

= ₹3230

Name ________________________

Multiplying without regrouping –2-digit top factors

Time Race

Multiply and see how fast you can finish the race.

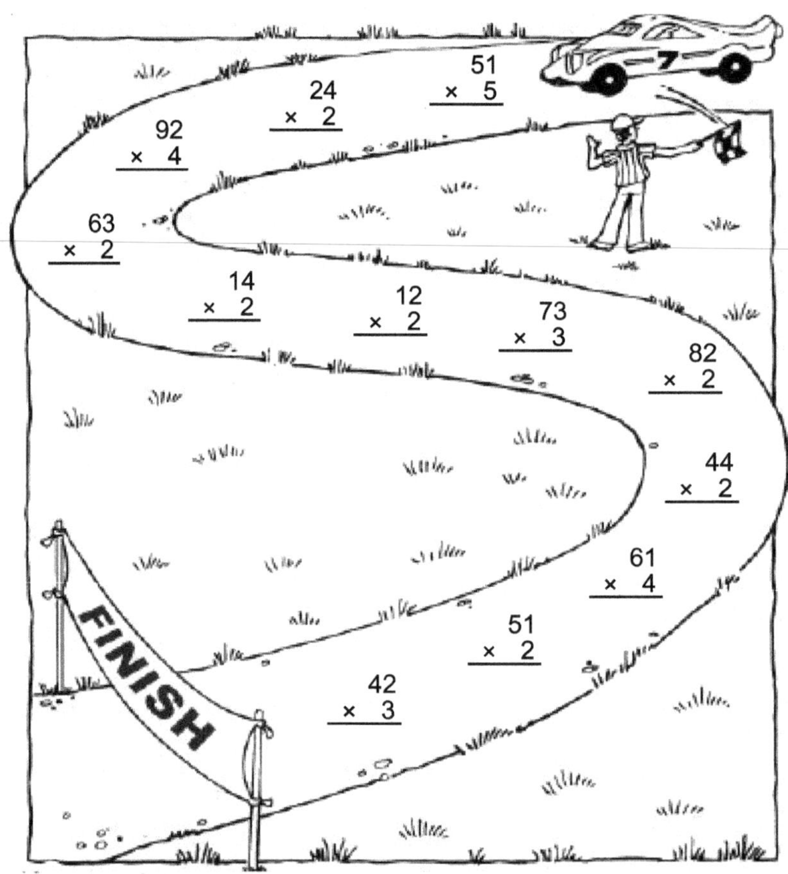

Three race cars raced around the track. Each race car completed 32 laps. How many laps in all did the race cars complete? Solve the problem on another piece of paper.

Multiplication:

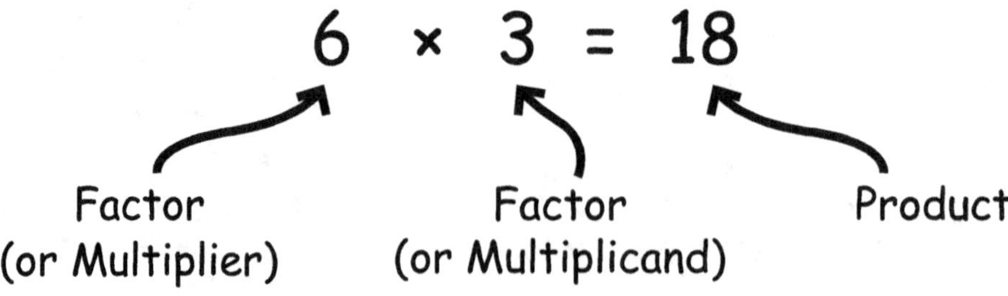

$$6 \times 3 = 18$$

Factor (or Multiplier)   Factor (or Multiplicand)   Product

5

Chapter

Multiplication

LEARNING OBJECTIVES

This lesson will help you to:—

- ❖ be able to find the product of two numbers.
- ❖ explore various facts of multiplication.
- ❖ be able to define the terminology of multiplication.
- ❖ be able to explain the properties of multiplication.

QUICK CONCEPT REVIEW

MULTIPLICATION

A hen laid 28 eggs & the chicks were born. She wants to distribute sweets to her friends & relatives. They have 20 families of friends & relatives.

She wants to give 6 sweets to each family. She started counting the number of sweets to be purchased from the market.

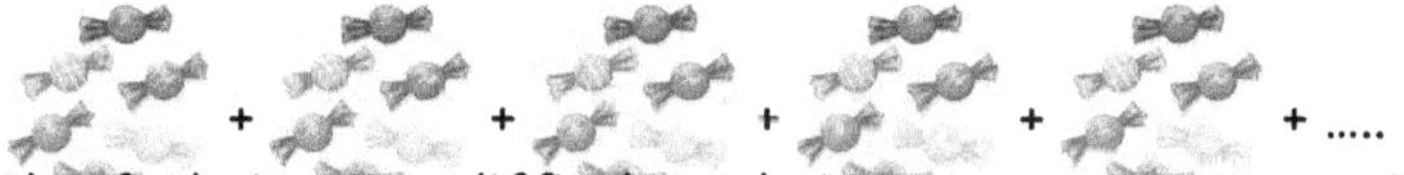

She finds it quite difficult and time consuming to count the total number of sweets to be purchased. Can you help her find out an easier way to do so?

6 sweets are to be distributed to each family and there are 20 families in all. So instead of adding 6 again and again 20 times, we can simply multiply 6 by 20. The answer will be the same in both the cases.

6 + 6 + 6 + 6 + 6 + 6 + 6 + 6 + 6 + 6 + 6 + 6 + 6 + 6 + 6 + 6 + 6 + 6 + 6 + 6 = 6 × 20 = 120 sweets.

Therefore, we can say that multiplication is a short form of repeated addition.

It is a mathematical operation that indicates how many times a number is added to itself.

Real Life Examples

Example : There are 5 kids in a family. If each kid gets 4 toffees, then find the number of toffees distributed in the family.

Solution : As 5 × 4 = 20

So, 20 toffees are distributed in the family.

Amazing Facts

❖ Multiplying two same numbers with 5 at ones place.

Example, 45 × 45 = ?

The last two digits of the answer will always be 25.

Now multiply 4 by the number that follows it, i.e.

(4 × 5 = 20)

Write the number in front of 25.   2025

Therefore, 45 × 45 = 2025.

❖ Multiplying by 11.

For multiplying any number by 11, just place the first and last digit as it is on their respective places and add the two digits and place the sum between the first and last digit.

Example,

```
              Th  H    T    O
11 × 11  =         1  (1+1)  1
                        = 1 2 1
25 × 11  =         2  (2+5)  5
                        = 2 7 5
124 × 11 = 1 (1+2) (2+4)   4
                        = 1 3 6 4
```

Do You Know?

Methods of multiplication were documented in the Egyptian, Greek, Indian and Chinese civilizations.

If you can multiply 9 × 3,

Say it with me.

27

If you can multiply 6 × 8,

You are great.

48

Multiplication is the process of finding the product of any two numbers.

TERMINOLOGY

When multiplication is considered as repeated addition:

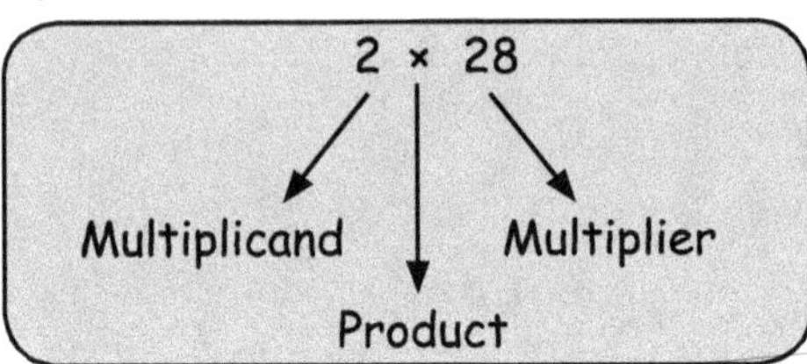

The number to be multiplied is called the multiplicand.

The number of multiples is called the multiplier.

When any two numbers are multiplied:

The numbers to be multiplied are called factors or multiplicands.

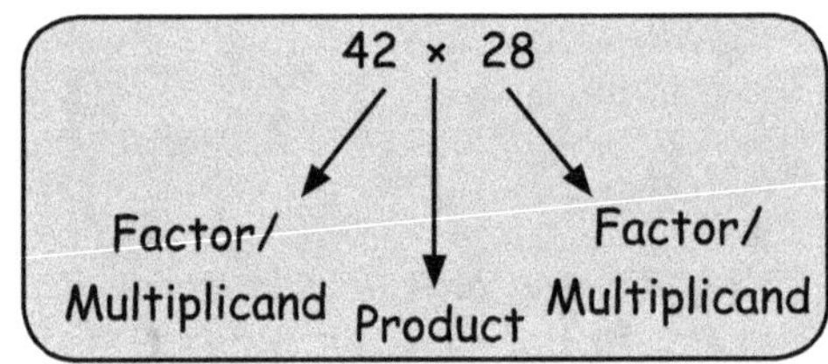

The result after multiplication is known as the product.

PROPERTIES OF MULTIPLICATION

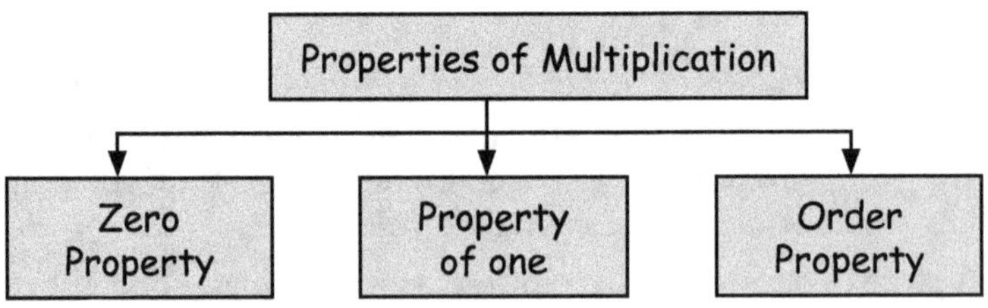

ZERO PROPERTY

When we multiply any number by 0, the answer is always 0.

For Example: 32 × 0 = 0

PROPERTY OF ONE

When we multiply any number by 1, the product is the number itself.

For Example: 32 × 1 = 32

ORDER PROPERTY

When two numbers are multiplied together, the product is the same regardless of the order of the multiplicands.
For Example: 4 x 2 = 2 x 4

BOX MULTIPLICATION

In Box multiplication method we break the two numbers to be multiplied in ones, tens & hundreds.

For Example: If we want to multiply 44 by 18, we will break 44 & 18.

44 becomes 40 tens & 4 ones and 18 becomes 10 tens & 8 ones. Now we can multiply the numbers easily & quickly as shown below:

44 × 18 = ?

	40	4		40	4
10	40 × 10	4 × 10	10	400	40
8	40 × 8	4 × 8	8	320	32

So, 44 × 18 = 400 + 320 + 40 + 32 = 792

MULTIPLICATION BY 10'S & 100'S

If we want to multiply any number by 10, we will just write 0 in ones place & then multiply the number by 1.

For Example:

	Th	H	T	O
2 x 10 =			2	0
32 x 10 =		3	2	0
432 x 10 =	4	3	2	0

Therefore, to multiply by 10, we write 0 at ones place & multiply the rest numbers.

If we want to multiply any number by 100, we move the digits two places to the left & write two zeros at the end.

For Example:

	Th	H	T	O
5 x 100 =		5	0	0
26 x 100 =	2	6	0	0

Try It!

Solution :
235 × 19 = 4465
and 235 × 10 = 2350
and 235 × 9 = 2115
So 235 × 10 + 235 × 9
= 2350 + 2115
= 4465
Yes, they both are equal.

Distributive Property of Multiplication Over Subtraction

If a, b, c are any three numbers,
then a × (b − c) = a × b − a × c.
For example: 57 × 8
can be solved as 57 × (10 − 2)
or 57 × 10 − 57 × 2
= 570 − 114 = 456

Example: Simplify using properties of multiplication.
111 × 9 + 111 × 2 − 111
Solution: 111 × 9 + 111 × 2 − 111
         =111 × (9 + 2 − 1)
         =111 × 10 =1110

Try It!

Example :- Simplify
692 × 8 × 0 × 15
Solution :- 692 × 8 × 0 × 15 = 0.
Example : Fill in the blanks.
(a) 892 × _________ = 892
(b) 5 × _________ = 40
(c) 187 × _________ = 0
Solution:
(a) 892 × <u>1</u> = 892
(b) 5 × <u>8</u> = 40
(c) 187 × <u>0</u> = 0

MULTIPLYING BY A TWO DIGIT NUMBER

Kitty wants to knit pullovers, if it takes 24 wool balls to make 1 pullover, how many wool balls are required to make 52 pullovers.

To find out the no. of wool balls required we will multiply the no. of pullovers to be made & the no. of balls required to make 1 pullover.

52 × 24 =?

Step 1	**Step 2**	**Step 3**
Multiply by ones.	Multiply by tens.	Add the products.
(52 × 4)	(52 × 20)	

```
   Step 1              Step 2              Step 3
     5 2                 5 2                 5 2
   × 2 4               × 2 4               × 2 4
   ─────               ─────               ─────
   2 0 8 (52×4)        2 0 8 (52×4)        2 0 8 (52×4)
                     1 0 4 0 (52×20)     +1 0 4 0 (52×20)
                     ───────────         ───────────
                                           1 2 4 8
                                         ───────────
```

MULTIPLYING BY A THREE DIGIT NUMBER

The process of multiplying a number by a three digit number is the same as multiplying by a two digit number as explained above.

SOME INTERESTING PATTERNS IN MULTIPLICATION

❖   15873 × 7 × 1 = 111111

       15873 × 7 × 2 = 222222

       15873 × 7 × 3 = 333333 and so on...

❖   37 × 3 × 1 = 111

       37 × 3 × 2 = 222

       37 × 3 × 3 = 333 and so on ...

❖   9 × 0 + 1 = 1

       9 × 1 + 2 = 11

       9 × 2 + 3 = 21

       9 × 3 + 4 = 31

       9 × 4 + 5 = 41 and so on ...

Multiple Choice Questions

LEVEL 1

Direction (Qs. 1 to 25): Choose the correct option.

1. Factor × Factor = ?
   (a) Product   (b) Multiplicand
   (c) Multiplier   (d) Square

2. Multiplication is the short form of repeated __________.
   (a) Multiplication   (b) Division
   (c) Addition   (d) Subtraction

3. 43 × 0 = ?
   (a) 43   (b) 0
   (c) 44   (d) 42

4. 66 × 1 = ?
   (a) 66   (b) 67
   (c) 65   (d) 0

5. 74 × 21 = 21 × __________.
           [Mental Mathematics]
   (a) 74   (b) 21
   (c) 1554   (d) 1

6. 543 × 10 = ?   **[Mental Mathematics]**
   (a) 5430   (b) 5400
   (c) 543   (d) 54300

7. 23 × 100 = ?   **[Mental Mathematics]**
   (a) 2300   (b) 23000
   (c) 230   (d) 23

8. 65 × __________ = 74 × 65
   (a) 65   (b) 74
   (c) 0   (d) 10

9. 11 × 11 = ?   **[Mental Mathematics]**
   (a) 111   (b) 121
   (c) 131   (d) 141

10. 25 × 25 = ?
    (a) 325   (b) 425
    (c) 525   (d) 625

11. Pick the odd one out: 5, 10, 15, 20, 24.
    (a) 5   (b) 15
    (c) 20   (d) 24

12. Pick the odd one out: 11, 22, 32, 44, 55.
    (a) 11   (b) 22
    (c) 32   (d) 44

13. 22 × 5 = ?
    (a) 100   (b) 105
    (c) 110   (d) 115

14. __________ × 5 = 50
            [Mental Mathematics]
    (a) 5   (b) 10
    (c) 15   (d) 20

15. 9 × 400 = ?   **[Mental Mathematics]**
    (a) 36   (b) 360
    (c) 3600   (d) 36000

16. 9 × 9 = ?   **[Mental Mathematics]**
    (a) 9   (b) 18
    (c) 81   (d) 99

17. 500 × 0 = ?   **[Mental Mathematics]**
    (a) 0   (b) 50
    (c) 500   (d) 5000

18. 7899 × 1 = ?   **[Mental Mathematics]**
    (a) 7900   (b) 7899
    (c) 7898   (d) 7890

19. 500 × 400 = ?   **[Mental Mathematics]**
    (a) 200   (b) 2000
    (c) 20000   (d) 200000

20. __________ × 12 = 96
    (a) 3   (b) 5
    (c) 8   (d) 9

21. 65 × 64 = ?
    (a) 4160   (b) 4225
    (c) 4165   (d) 4260

22. 28 × 50
    (a) 140   (b) 1440
    (c) 1400   (d) 1140

23. 966 × 20
    (a) 19320   (b) 1932
    (c) 1930   (d) 19300

24. $987 \times 9 = ?$
(a) 8888 (b) 8883
(c) 3888 (d) 8833

25. $796 \times 7 = ?$
(a) 5572 (b) 2257
(c) 5277 (d) 2527

26. A library has 312 racks of books. If each rack has 263 books, then how many total books are there? [2018]
(a) 92006 (b) 91846
(c) 81042 (d) 82056

27. Payal bought 12 boxes of cold drinks for a party. There were 19 cans in each box. How many total cans of cold drinks did she buy? [2019]
(a) 232 (b) 228
(c) 216 (d) 202

28. Deepak filled 17 L 450 mL of water in a tank every day. How much quantity of water did he fill in 7 days? [2020]
(a) 110 L 120 mL (b) 102 L 150 mL
(c) 150 L 122 L (d) 122 L 150 mL

29. 950 nuts are manufactured in a factory every day. How many nuts can be manufactured in 60 days? [2020]
(a) 57000 (b) 58000
(c) 60000 (d) 62000

30. Last year, Kartik celebrated his eighteenth birthday. This year his brother Swastik is twice as old as Kartik. How old will be Swastik in five years time? [2021]
(a) 47 years (b) 38 years
(c) 41 years (d) 43 years

31. 950 bags of cement are needed to build a house. How many bags of cement are needed to build 43 such houses? [2022]
(a) 44370 (b) 40850
(c) 41850 (d) 43950

LEVEL 2

1. Find the missing number with reference to the given image: [2017]

(a) 540 (b) 550
(c) 560 (d) 570

2. Match the following: [Critical Thinking]

	List I		List II
A.	Order Property	1.	$54 \times 1 = 54$
B.	Zero Property	2.	$32 \times 17 = 17 \times 32$
C.	Property of one	3.	$25 \times 0 = 0$
D.	Factor × Factor	4.	0
E.	98433×0	5.	Product

        A B C D E
(a) 2 3 1 5 4
(b) 1 2 3 4 5
(c) 2 1 3 4 5
(d) 1 2 3 5 4

3. Fill in the blanks: [Tricky]

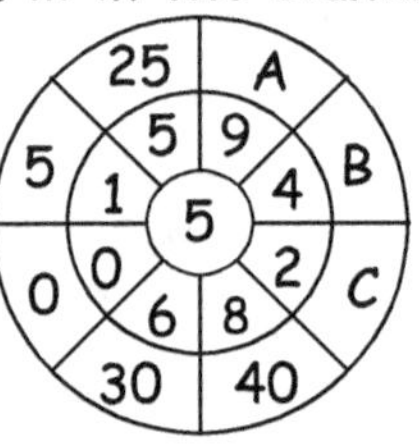

         A   B   C
(a) 45, 20, 10
(b) 45, 40, 30
(c) 45, 0, 10
(d) 45, 5, 10

4. Find the missing number. [Tricky]

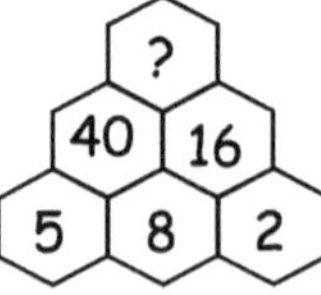

(a) 630
(b) 640
(c) 650
(d) 660

5. Fill in the blanks. **[2009]**

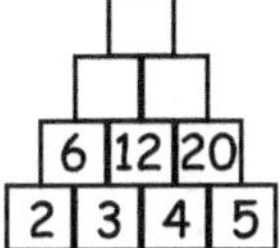

(a) 73, 24, 20000 (b) 6, 12, 20
(c) 72, 240, 17280 (d) 2, 3, 4

6. Fill in the blank spaces. **[Tricky]**

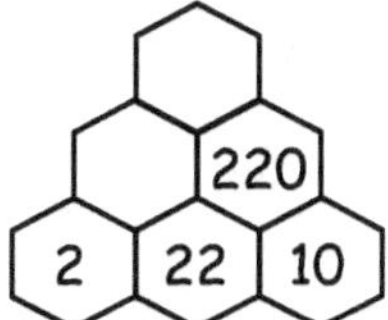

(a) 440, 9680 (b) 44, 9680
(c) 4400, 9680 (d) 22, 220

7. There are 70 crayons in each box. How many crayons are in 93 boxes?

(a) 6510 (b) 6520
(c) 6530 (d) 6540

8. Fill in the boxes as per the box multiplication method.

	20	9
20		
2		

(a) 400, 40, 180, 18
(b) 400, 400, 1800, 18
(c) 4000, 40, 180, 18
(d) 400, 40, 180, 180

9. Fill in the boxes as per the box multiplication method.

	400	20	9
10			
5			

(a) 400, 200, 200, 100, 90, 45
(b) 4000, 2000, 200, 100, 90, 45.
(c) 4000, 2000, 200, 10, 9, 4
(d) 4000, 200, 200, 10, 90, 45

10. Multiply using box multiplication method. 63 × 49

(a) 3086 (b) 3087
(c) 3088 (d) 3089

11. Multiply using box multiplication method.

233 × 65
(a) 15145 (b) 15115
(c) 15445 (d) 15454

12. What number should go in the blank to make the given number sentence true?**[2010]**

100 = 4 × _______ × 5
(a) 4 (b) 5
(c) 25 (d) 100

13. Fill in the blanks.

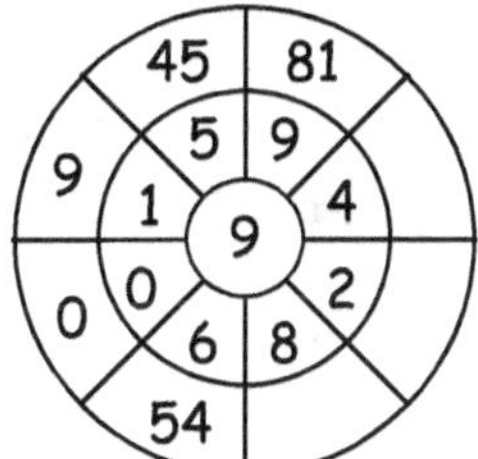

(a) 36, 18, 72
(b) 54, 0, 9
(c) 45, 81, 72
(d) 4, 2, 8

14. Which of the following is NOT equal to 84 × 47? **[2014]**

(a) 80 × 47 + 4 × 47
(b) 84 × 40 × 7
(c) 84 × 40 + 84 × 7
(d) 82 × 47 + 2 × 47

15. If 2 glasses of water is required to cook 1 glass of rice. Then how many glasses of water are required to cook 15 glasses of rice. **[Tricky]**

(a) 15 (b) 2
(c) 30 (d) 17

16. Insert the missing number. **[2016]**

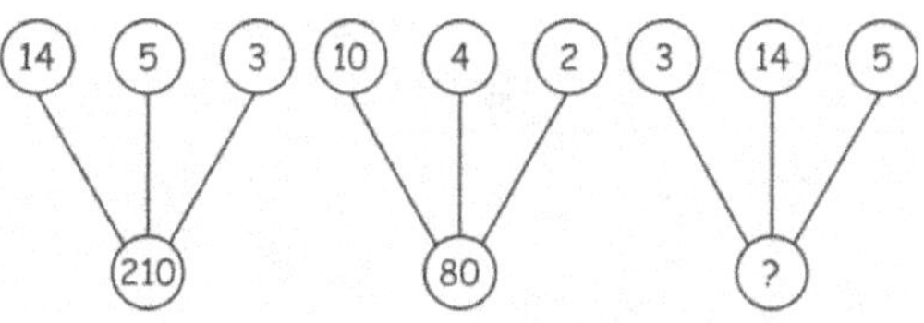

(a) 300 (b) 200
(c) 205 (d) 210

17. Match the following: [Critical Thinking]

	List I		List II
A.	1500 × 10	1.	1728
B.	2219 × 0	2.	105000
C.	4200 × 25	3.	9025
D.	95 × 95	4.	0
E.	96 × 18	5.	15000

           A B C D E
(a) 5 1 2 3 4
(b) 2 4 5 3 1
(c) 5 4 3 2 1
(d) 5 4 2 3 1

18. Which digit should come in place of ☐, so that following multiplication becomes correct? **[2015]**

$$
\begin{array}{r}
3\ \square\ 6 \\
\times\ \ \ \ 5 \\
\hline
1\ 9\ 8\ 0 \\
\hline
\end{array}
$$

(a) 5   (b) 8
(c) 6   (d) 9

19. Tom, Jack , Jenny & Lily have 250 Pokemon cards each. How many cards do they have in all?
(a) 1000   (b) 250
(c) 4   (d) 1100

20. 6 + 6 + 6 + _________ 45 times is equal to : **[2013]**
(a) 300   (b) 270
(c) 280   (d) 700

21. Find out the missing number: [Tricky]

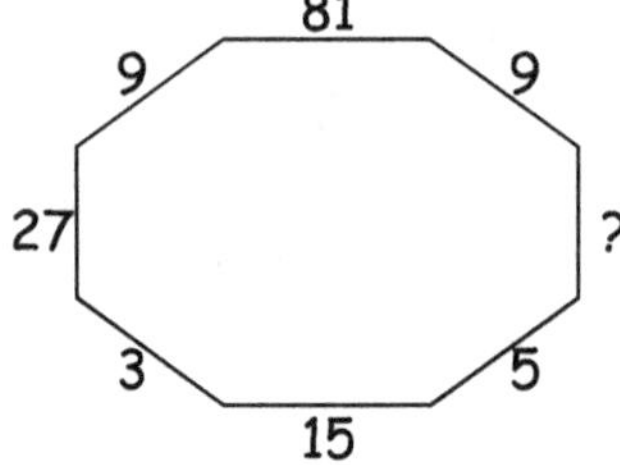

(a) 81   (b) 45
(c) 15   (d) 27

22. When 78456 is multiplied by A, we get 2510592. Find the value of A. **[2011]**
(a) 28   (b) 30
(c) 32   (d) 34

23. Find the missing number: **[Tricky]**

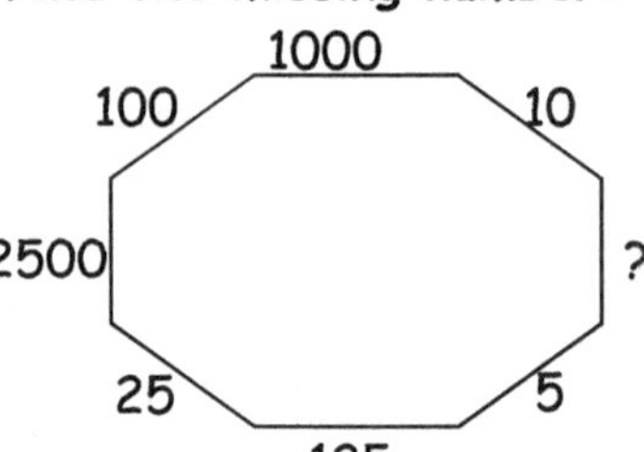

(a) 50   (b) 1000
(c) 125   (d) 2500

24. Solve the problem.

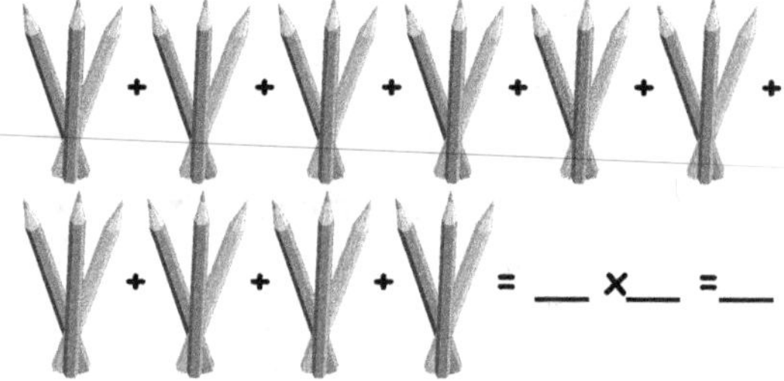

(a) 3 × 10 = 30   (b) 3 × 9 = 27
(c) 3 × 8 = 24   (d) 3 ×10 = 10

25. One dozen of apple cost ₹ 60, then what is the cost of 12 dozen of apples? **[2014]**
(a) ₹ 640   (b) ₹ 720
(c) ₹ 840   (d) ₹ 960

26. Match the following: **[Tricky]**

	List I		List II
A.	15873 × 7 × 1 =	1.	111
B.	9 × 2 + 3 =	2.	111111
C.	37 × 3 × 3 =	3.	21
D.	37 × 3 × 1 =	4.	333

      A B C D   A B C D
(a) 1 3 4 2   (b) 2 4 3 1
(c) 3 2 4 1   (d) 2 3 4 1

27. A cricket stadium has 456 rows with 200 seats in each row. How many seats are there in the stadium? **[2010]**
(a) 91200
(b) 91000
(c) 81200
(d) 90200

Direction (Qs. 28 to 30): Solve the given word problems and then choose the correct option.

28. Christine bought 6 boxes of erasers. Each box had 42 erasers. How many erasers does Christine have?
    (a) 522 erasers
    (b) 524 erasers
    (c) 252 erasers
    (d) 250 erasers

29. Max bought 6 bags of jellybeans. If each bag has 24 jellybeans, what is the total amount that he has ? [2008]
    (a) 124 jellybeans
    (b) 144 jellybeans
    (c) 114 jellybeans
    (d) 140 jellybeans

30. There are 6 shelves of books in class. If each shelf has 8 books on it, how many books are on the shelves?
    (a) 84
    (b) 48
    (c) 40
    (d) 80

31. There are 6665 students in a school. Each student contributed ₹ 53 for a society welfare programme. How much money the students contributed together? [2012]
    (a) ₹ 353245
    (b) ₹ 406575
    (c) ₹ 426575
    (d) ₹ 456575

32. The length of a square field is 480 m. Vishal runs 5 rounds around the field. Find the total distance ran by Vishal. [2012]
    (a) 2400 m
    (b) 960 m
    (c) 9600 m
    (d) 4800 m

33. Join the dots by multiplying the numbers & find out the last number. See what image appears. [Tricky]

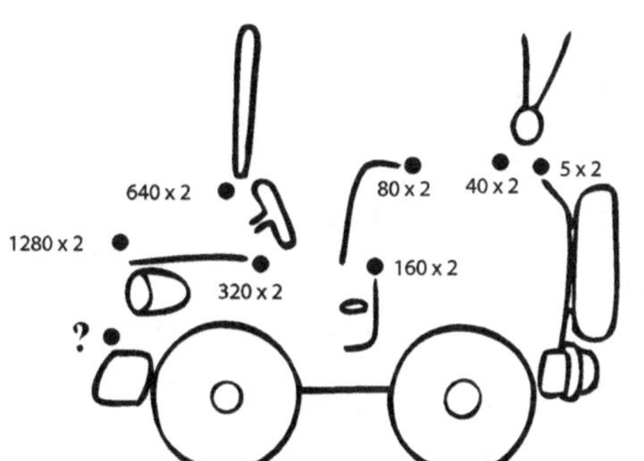

34. Mr. Das earns ₹ 9,876 per month. What would be his annual income? [2016]
    (a) ₹ 1,23,052
    (b) ₹ 1,11,082
    (c) ₹ 1,18,512
    (d) ₹ 1,25,432

35. Find the missing number. [2018]
    3 × 8 × 14 × 12 × ? = 126 × 288
    (a) 6
    (b) 9
    (c) 12
    (d) 8

36. Sonali had 78 boxes with 287 bangles in each box. If 1453 bangles were broken then how many unbroken bangles were there? [2018]
    (a) 21843
    (b) 20763
    (c) 22913
    (d) 20933

37. Fill in the blanks. [2018]
    • 4 groups of 9 is P less than 2 groups of 19.
    • 3 groups of 5 is Q more than 6 groups of 2.
    • 7 groups of 6 is R less than 9 groups of 6.
    • 8 groups of 8 is S more than 4 groups of 15.

	P	Q	R	S			P	Q	R	S
(a)	3	3	10	4		(b)	2	4	12	6
(c)	2	3	12	4		(d)	3	4	10	6

38. 20 chairs and 15 tables were purchased for a hotel. If each chair costs ₹ 110 and a table costs ₹235, then the total amount to be paid is _______. [2020]
    (a) ₹5725
    (b) ₹5000
    (c) ₹8250
    (d) ₹7359

39. Niharika has ₹1500. She wants to purchase 18 sacks of rice as shown. How much more money does she need? [2021]
    (a) ₹660
    (b) ₹560
    (c) ₹540
    (d) ₹650

40. Q is the smallest whole number which is greater than 99. Find the greatest possible whole number which is less than Q × Q **[2022]**
(a) 9801   (b) 10000
(c) 9899   (d) 9999

41. Find the vale of P – Q + R × S. **[2022[**

$$
\begin{array}{r}
1\,5\,\boxed{P} \\
\times\quad Q\,4 \\
\hline
\boxed{R}\,1\,6 \\
+\,1\,3\,8\,6\,0 \\
\hline
1\,4\,\boxed{S}\,7\,6 \\
\end{array}
$$

(a) 7   (b) 13   (c) 11   (d) 19

42. The product of number X and number Y is 2880. The difference of both numbers X and Y is 32. If both numbers are multiples of 8 then find the sum of numbers X and Y. **[2022]**
(a) 114   (b) 112   (c) 144   (d) 104

43. 76392 is 4882 more than ⭐. What is the difference between ⭐ and the product of 68 and 6? **[2022]**
(a) 71436   (b) 81200
(c) 71102   (d) 80866

44. In the multiplication given below letters A, B and C represent different digits. **[2022]**

$$
\begin{array}{r}
A\,A\,A\,A \\
\times\,7 \\
\hline
C\,B\,B\,B\,A \\
\end{array}
$$

If C = 3, then which one of the following can be true?
(a) 4A – 2B = 4   (b) 5A – 3B = 4
(c) 2A + B = 11   (d) A + 2B = 16

RESPONSE GRID

LEVEL 1

1. a b c d   2. a b c d   3. a b c d   4. a b c d   5. a b c d
6. a b c d   7. a b c d   8. a b c d   9. a b c d   10. a b c d
11. a b c d   12. a b c d   13. a b c d   14. a b c d   15. a b c d
16. a b c d   17. a b c d   18. a b c d   19. a b c d   20. a b c d
21. a b c d   22. a b c d   23. a b c d   24. a b c d   25. a b c d
26. a b c d   27. a b c d   28. a b c d   29. a b c d   30. a b c d
31. a b c d

LEVEL 2

1. a b c d   2. a b c d   3. a b c d   4. a b c d   5. a b c d
6. a b c d   7. a b c d   8. a b c d   9. a b c d   10. a b c d
11. a b c d   12. a b c d   13. a b c d   14. a b c d   15. a b c d
16. a b c d   17. a b c d   18. a b c d   19. a b c d   20. a b c d
21. a b c d   22. a b c d   23. a b c d   24. a b c d   25. a b c d
26. a b c d   27. a b c d   28. a b c d   29. a b c d   30. a b c d
31. a b c d   32. a b c d   33. a b c d   34. a b c d   35. a b c d
36. a b c d   37. a b c d   38. a b c d   39. a b c d   40. a b c d
41. a b c d   42. a b c d   43. a b c d   44. a b c d

Solutions with Explanation

LEVEL 1

1. **(a)** Product
2. **(c)** Addition
3. **(b)** 0, When we multiply any number by 0, the answer is always 0.
4. **(a)** 66

   When we multiply any number by 1, the product is the number itself.
5. **(a)** 74

   When two numbers are multiplied together, the product is the same regardless of the order of the multiplicands.
6. **(a)** 5430
7. **(a)** 2300
8. **(b)** 74 (Order Property)
9. **(b)** 121
10. **(d)** 625
11. **(d)** 24 (All the numbers are multiples of 5 except 24.)
12. **(c)** 32 (All the numbers are multiples of 11 except 32.)
13. **(c)** 110
14. **(b)** 10
15. **(c)** 3600
16. **(c)** 81
17. **(a)** 0
18. **(b)** 7899
19. **(d)** 200000
20. **(c)** 8

21. **(a)** 4160
22. **(c)** 1400
23. **(a)** 19320
24. **(b)**   **25. (a)**
26. **(d)** Total books = 312 × 263 = 82056
27. **(b)** Cans in 1 box = 19

   Cans in 12 boxes = 19 × 12 = 228
28. **(d)** Amount of water filled in tank per day = 17.450 L

   So total quantity of water in tank In a week = 7 ×17.450 L

   = 122.150 L

   = 122 L 150 ml
29. **(a)** Quantity of nuts manufactured in 1 day = 950

   Nuts manufactured in 60 days

   = 950 × 60 = 57,000 nuts
30. **(d)** Last Year kartik was = 18 years

   This year kartik is = 19 years old

   Swastik's Age this year = 2 × 19

   = 38 years

   In five years swastik will be = 38 + 5

   = 43 years.
31. **(b)** Number of bags of cement are needed to build a house = 950

   Total number of bags of cement bags needed to build 43 houses

   = 950 × 43

   = 40850

LEVEL 2

1. **(a)** 540
2. **(a)**   **3. (a)**
4. **(b)** 40 × 16 = 640
5. **(c)**
6. **(b)** 2 × 22 = 44

   22 × 10 = 220

   220 × 44 = 9680

7. **(a)** Total number of crayons

   = 70 × 93 = 6510
8. **(a)**   **9. (b)**
10. **(b)** 63 × 49 = 2400+120+540+27 = 3087
11. **(a)** 233 × 65 = 12000 + 1800 + 180 + 1000 + 150 + 15 = 15145
12. **(b)** Since 4 × <u>5</u> × 5 = 100

13. **(a)**

14. **(b)** As 84 × 47 ≠ 84 × 40 × 7

15. **(c)** Total number of glasses = 2 × 15 = 30

16. **(d)** Since 3 × 14 × 5 = 42 × 5 = 210

17. **(d)**

18. **(d)** As 396 × 5 = 1980

19. **(a)** Total number of cards = 250 × 4
= 1000

20. **(b)** As 6 × 45 = 270

21. **(b)** 9 × 9 = 81
9 × 3 = 27
3 × 5 = 15
5 × 9 = 45

22. **(c)** As 78456 × 32 = 2510592

23. **(a)** 10 × 5 = 50

24. **(a)** 3 × 10= 30

25. **(b)** As 60 × 12 = ₹720

26. **(d)** A → 2; B → 3, C → 4, D → 1

27. **(a)** Total number of seats
= 456 × 200 = 91200

28. **(c)** 252 erasers

29. **(b)**

30. **(b)** 48 books

31. **(a)** Since 6665 × 53 = ₹353245

32. **(a)** As 480 × 5 = 2400 m

33. **(b)** 2560 × 2 = 5120

34. **(c)** ₹9876 × 12 = ₹ 118512

35. **(b)** 9

36. **(d)** Unbroken bangles
= (78 × 287 – 1453) = 20933

37. **(c)** P = 2 Q = 3 R = 12 S = 4 [P = 2 × 19 - 4 × 9 = 2]

38. **(a)** Number of chairs   =   20
Cost of 1 chair   =   ₹110
Total cost of chairs =   20 × 110
= ₹2200
Number of tables   =   15
Cost of 1 table ₹235
Total cost of 15 tables
=   15 × ₹235 = ₹3525
Total Amount to be paid
=   ₹2200 + 3525 = ₹5725

39. **(a)** Total money = ₹ 1500
Value of 1 sack = ₹ 120
So value of 18 sacks = 120 × 18
= ₹ 2160
Money needed to purchase 18 sacks of Rice = ₹ 2160 – ₹ 1500
= ₹ 660

40. **(d)** Given, Q > 99
Q is the smallest whole number
So, Q = 100
Q × Q = 100 × 100 = 10000
Possible nearest whole number which is less than 10000 = 9999

41. **(d)**

	1.5	4
×	9	4
	6	16
+13	8	60
14	4	76

P – Q + R × S
= 4 – 9 + 6 × 4
= 4 – 9 + 24
= 19

42. **(b)** Product of X and Y = X × Y = 2880
Difference of X and Y = X – Y = 32
So, X × Y = 2880 and X – Y = 32
Let X = 72 and Y = 40
72 × 40 = 2880
X – Y = 72 – 40 = 32
So, the sum of X and Y = 72 + 40
= 112

43. **(c)** star + 4882 = 76392
∴ star = 76392 –4882
= 71510
Product of 68 and 6 = 68 × 6 = 408
Difference between star and product of 68 and 6 = 71510 – 408
= 71102

44. **(a)**

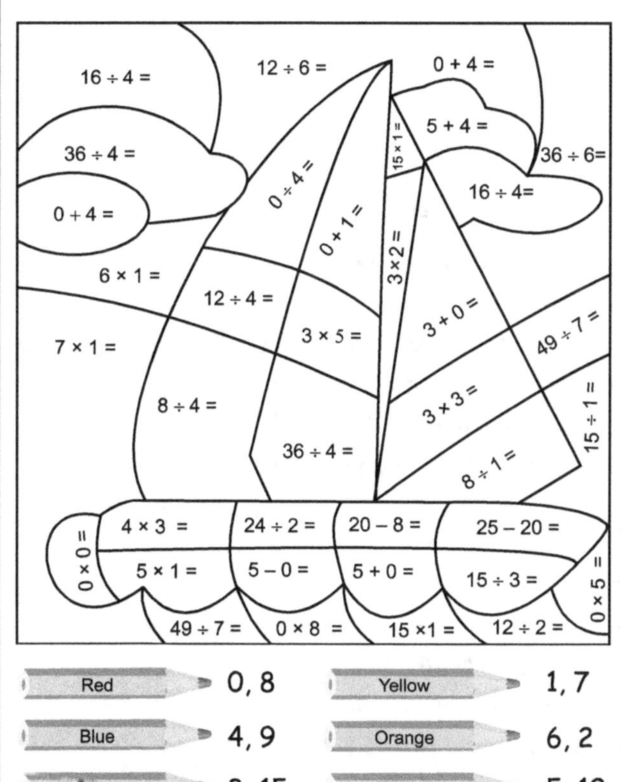

quotient

divisor ⟌ dividend

−x x x

remainder

Red	0, 8	Yellow	1, 7
Blue	4, 9	Orange	6, 2
Green	3, 15	Brown	5, 12

Remember that remainder is always less than the divisor.

For Example: $3\overline{)9}$ (3, -9, 0 , $3\overline{)8}$ (2, -6, 2 , $3\overline{)7}$ (2, -6, 1

So, when we divide by 3, remainders can be 0, 1 or 2 but never 3.

6
Chapter

Division

❖ Division is used in almost each and every sphere of our life. Division is used in daily household activities, shopping in a mall, eating pizza etc.

LEARNING OBJECTIVES

This lesson will help you to:—

❖ divide one number by another.

❖ be able to solve real life problems based on division.

❖ explore various facts of division.

❖ be able to define the terminology of division.

❖ be able to explain the properties of division.

QUICK CONCEPT REVIEW

What is DIVISION?

Division is splitting into equal parts or groups.

It is the result of "fair sharing".

When we share equally we divide.

Symbolically, we write it as follows:

$27 \div 9 = 3$

For example:

Kitty found 25 beautiful pearls on the seashore. She collected and brought all of them home. Now she wants to put them in jewellery boxes. She can put 5 pearls in one jewellery box.

She made 1 group of 5 pearls & put them in 1 jewellery box.

She put 5 more pearls in 2nd jewellery box.

❖ Division by zero is not defined. You cannot divide any number by zero. Let us take an example. You have 20 toffees which you want to distribute to your classmates but if everyone is absent and there are no classmates in your class, then to whom will you distribute the toffees.

She is left with some pearls, so she put 5 pearls in another jewelry box.

5 more in another jewellery box.

5 pearls in another box.

Example: How many 4's are there in

(a) 16   (b) 64   (c) 32

Solutions : (a) We know that

$16 \div 4 = 4$

So there are four 4's in 16.

(b) As $64 \div 4 = 16$

So, there are sixteen 4's in 64

(c) As $32 \div 4 = 8$

So, there are eight 4's in 32.

There are no more pearls left.

Kitty required 5 jewellery boxes to keep the pearls.

Therefore, we can say that 25 pearls put into equal groups of 5 each gives 5 groups.

OR

We can say that, 25 pearls divided by 5 pearls in 1 group gives 5 groups.

When we group equally, we divide.

Symbolically, we write it as,

$25 \div 5 = 5$

Hence, Division is splitting into equal parts or groups. It is separating or distributing something into parts.

TERMINOLOGY

Dividend

The number to be divided is called the dividend. It is the number you want to divide up.

For example: $12 \div 6 = 2$. Here 12 is to be divided by 6. Hence, 12 is the dividend.

Divisor

The number which divides the dividend is called the divisor. It is the number that we are dividing by.

For example: $12 \div 6 = 2$. Here 12 is to be divided by 6. Hence, 6 is the divisor.

Quotient

The result obtained after dividing one number by another is called quotient. It is the answer in division.

❖ The remainder must always be smaller than the divisor.

❖ You can check the answer by just following a simple rule-
(QUOTIENT X DIVISOR) + REMAINDER = DIVIDEND

❖ Any number divided by 10 gives the ones digit as remainder and the other digits as the quotient.

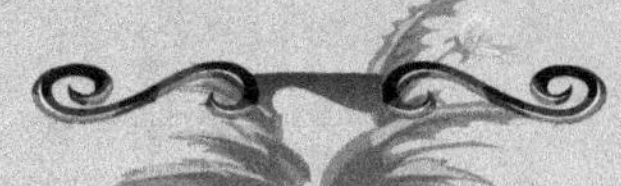

For example: 12 ÷ 6 = 2. Here 12 divided by 6 gives 2. Therefore, 2 is the quotient.

Remainder - ?

PROPERTIES OF DIVISION

Zero Property

(a) If zero is divided by any number, the answer is always zero.

For example: If we have zero number of chocolates to be divided amongst the students, then each will get zero chocolate.

0 ÷ 5 = 0

(b) If any number is divided by zero, then problem cannot be solved.

Property of one

If any number is divided by one, the answer is the number itself.

For example: Ram's family has gone to the market so he is alone at home. There are 9 cookies kept in the kitchen. How many cookies will Ram get to eat?

Here, Ram can eat all the 9 cookies as there is no one else to share the cookies.

Therefore, 9 cookies are to be divided amongst 1 person.

That is, 9 ÷ 1 = 9

Dividing a number by itself

If any number is divided by itself, the answer will always be one.

For Example: Ram's family is back at home. They have brought pizza for all of them. There are total 6 members in the family including Ram. The pizza is divided in 6 equal parts. How many parts will each member get?

6 equal parts are to be shared amongst 6 members.

That is, 6 ÷ 6 = 1.

Each member will get 1 part of pizza.

Therefore, we can say that any number divided by itself gives 1 as the quotient.

LONG DIVISION

Division can also be shown as follows:

$$\text{Divisor}\overline{\big)\text{Dividend}}^{\text{Quotient}}$$

For example: 9 ÷ 3 = 3

It can also be written as,

An Interesting Poem on Division

Division, division, division
A terribly easy decision,
Lets me just share,
My apple or pear,
With utter and perfect precision...
Here's some good words of advice,
I think I might say them all twice,
Learn each times table,
And you'll also be able,
To go and divide really nice...
Young laddie, it won't make things worse,
Division brings no type of cruse,
Repeated subtraction?
Break to a fraction?
Or multiply things in reverse?
Quotients are things that we find,
When division's how math problem's signed,
It has the math smarts,
To cut pies in parts,
The inverse of things we combined...

$$3 \,\overline{)\,\begin{array}{c} 9 \\ \hline 9 \\ 9 \\ \hline \times \end{array}}$$

To understand the concept of Long division, let us take another example,

$45 \div 5 = ?$

$$5 \,\overline{)\,\begin{array}{c} 9 \\ \hline 45 \\ 45 \\ \hline \times \end{array}}$$

Because $5 \times 9 = 45$

Digit on the tens place is less than the divisor (4 < 5). Therefore, we will write quotient on ones. This is called Long Division.

IMPERFECT DIVISION

We have already learnt that division can be shown in two ways.

But sometimes, it doesn't work perfectly.

It happens whenever we get remainder in division. Let us see what a remainder is.

There are 49 chocolates which have to be distributed amongst 9 friends. How many chocolates will each friend receive?

49 chocolates are to be shared equally amongst 9 friends.

That is, $49 \div 9$ or

$$9 \,\overline{)\,\begin{array}{c} \\ \hline 49 \end{array}}$$

Sometimes in division, we may not be able to equally group or share the objects.

Something is left over.

This leftover number is called the remainder.

Divisor ⟵ 9 $\overline{)}$ 5 ⟶ Quotient, 49 ⟶ Dividend, 45, 4 ⟶ Remainder

Let us have a look on another example:

$451 \div 6 = ?$

Try It!

Example : Find if 325 ÷ 25 is equal to 25 ÷ 325

Solution : 25) 325 (13
25
75
75
00

So 325 ÷ 25 = 13. But we cannot divide 25 by 325. So 325 ÷ 25 is not equal to 25 ÷ 325

Misconcept/Concept

Misconcept: Division is commutative, order does not matter.

Concept: Division is not commutative, order does matter.

```
    1 2 5 8
5 ) 6 2 9 0
   -5
    1 2
   -1 0
      2 9
    -  2 5
         4 0
    -    4 0
            ×
```

```
    2 4 2 6
2 ) 4 8 5 3
   -4
    0 8
   -  8
      0 5
    -    4
         1 3
    -    1 2
            1
```

```
      7 5
6 ) 4 5 1        (6 × 7 = 42)
   -4 2          (45 - 42 = 3)
    3 1          (6 × 5 = 30)
   -3 0          (31 - 30 = 1)
      1
```

Here, Quotient = 75 & Remainder = 1

CHECKING THE ANSWER

Let us check our answer of the above solved problem:

The trick is (Quotient × Divisor) + Remainder = Dividend

So, on the left hand side we have,

Quotient = 75

Divisor = 6

Remainder = 1

& on the right hand side we have

Dividend = 451

The answer would be correct if left hand side = Right hand side

Left hand side

(75 × 6) + 1 = 450 + 1 = 451

Right hand side

451

Left hand side = Right hand side = 451

Therefore, our answer is correct.

DIVIDING A 4 DIGIT NUMBER

Dividing a 4 digit number is just like dividing any other 3 digit number.

A school has organized a medical camp for 6290 students of the school. The students were divided in groups of 5 students in each group. Let us find out how many such groups will be formed.

Number of groups formed = Total number of students ÷ Number of students in 1 group

= 6290 ÷ 5 = ?

Here, Quotient = 1258 & Remainder = 0

Therefore, the number of groups formed = 1258

Let us have a look on another example.

$4853 \div 2 = ?$

Here, Quotient = 2426 & Remainder = 1

$$
\begin{array}{r}
89 \\
10\overline{)891} \\
-80\!\downarrow \\
\hline
91 \\
-\;90 \\
\hline
1
\end{array}
$$

DIVIDING A NUMBER BY 10

Let us find out $891 \div 10 = \underline{\quad\quad}$

To solve the above problem, we have an amazing shortcut. Let us have a look....

For example: $891 \div 10 = ?$

Here, Quotient = 89 & Remainder = 1

Now, $68 \div 10 = ?$

Quotient = 6 & Remainder = 8

$590 \div 10 = ?$

Quotient = 59 & Remainder = 0

Isn't it easy?

DIVIDING A NUMBER BY A 2 DIGIT NUMBER

45 students were selected for presenting the school exhibition. They were divided in groups of 15 students in each group to assign different departments. Let us find out how many such groups were formed.

$45 \div 15 = ?$ or $15\overline{)\quad 45\quad}$

When we divide any number by any 2 digit number, first of all, we will estimate the quotient.

$15\overline{)\quad 45\quad}$ rounds to $10\overline{)\quad 40\quad}$

To solve this, $10 \times 4 = 40$

Therefore, the quotient is 4.

Now, try this estimated quotient.

$15 \times 4 = 60 > 45$

$15 \times 3 = 45 = 45$

Finally,

$$
\begin{array}{r}
3 \\
15\overline{)\;45} \\
-45 \\
\hline
\times
\end{array}
$$

Therefore, Quotient = 3 & Remainder = 0

A pastry shop made 310 pastries which are to be packed in 24 boxes. How many pastries will each box contain?

Total number of 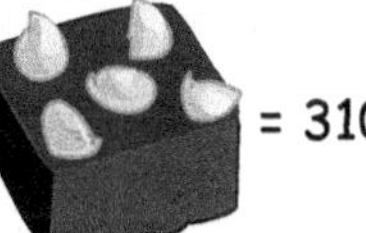 = 310

Try It!

Example : Divide 98765 by 12.
Solution:

$$
\begin{array}{r}
8230 \\
12\overline{)98765} \\
96\!\downarrow \\
\hline
27 \\
24\!\downarrow \\
\hline
36 \\
36\!\downarrow \\
\hline
005
\end{array}
$$

Quotient is 8230 and Remainder is 5.

Example : Divide 352 by 16.

Solution :
$$
\begin{array}{r}
16\overline{)352}(22 \\
32 \\
\hline
32 \\
32 \\
\hline
00
\end{array}
$$

Quotient is 22 & Remainder is 0.

Division by 10, 100 and 1000

Division by 10, 100, etc of numbers that are not divisible by 10, 100 etc.

Consider 529 ÷ 10

Since the divisor is 10, then the last digit (right most) of the dividend is remainder and the number formed by the remaining digits is quotient.

∴ Q = 52 and R = 9

Similarly

❖ If the divisor is 100, then last two digits of the dividend is remainder and remaining digits is quotient.

❖ If the divisor is 1000, then the last three digits of the dividend is remainder and the remaining digits is quotient.

Multiplication facts from a given division fact.

If 90 ÷ 30 = 3, then

30 × 3 = 90 and

3 × 30 = 90

Total number of  = 24

Number of pastries in 1 box = Total number of pastries ÷ Total number of boxes

$$= 310 \div 24$$

$$= 24 \overline{)310}$$

Here we have to divide the number by a 2 digit number.

Therefore, we will estimate the quotient first.

$$24 \overline{)310} \quad \text{rounds to} \quad 20 \overline{)300}$$

To solve this, 20 × 15 = 300

Therefore, the quotient is 15.

Now, try this estimated quotient.

$$24 \times 15 = 360 > 310$$

$$24 \times 14 = 336 > 310$$

$$24 \times 13 = 312 > 310$$

$$24 \times 12 = 288 < 310$$

Finally,

$$\begin{array}{r} 12 \\ 24 \overline{)\begin{array}{r} 310 \\ -288 \\ \hline 22 \end{array}} \end{array}$$

Therefore, Quotient = 12 & Remainder = 22.

INTERESTING PATTERNS IN DIVISION

As the dividend increases, the quotient also increases.

$$4 \div 2 = 2$$

$$40 \div 2 = 20$$

$$400 \div 2 = 200$$

$$4000 \div 2 = 2000$$

As the divisor increases, the quotient decreases.

$$4000 \div 2 = 2000$$

$$4000 \div 20 = 200$$

$$4000 \div 200 = 20$$

$$4000 \div 2000 = 2$$

Multiple Choice Questions

LEVEL 1

1. When we share equally we __________.
   (a) add   (b) subtract
   (c) multiply   (d) divide

2. The number to be divided is called the __________.
   (a) quotient   (b) divisor
   (c) dividend   (d) remainder

3. After dividing a number, the leftover is called __________.
   (a) quotient   (b) divisor
   (c) dividend   (d) remainder

4. When we group equally, we __________.
   (a) add   (b) subtract
   (c) multiply   (d) divide

5. __________ is separating or distributing something into parts.
   (a) Addition   (b) Subtraction
   (c) Multiplication (d) Division

6. When we get remainder, it is called __________.
   (a) imperfect division
   (b) perfect division
   (c) division
   (d) multiplication

7. __________ is the number that we are dividing by.
   (a) Dividend   (b) Divisor
   (c) Quotient   (d) Remainder

8. $8 \div 2 = 4$. Here, 4 is the __________.
   [Mental Mathematics]
   (a) quotient   (b) remainder
   (c) dividend   (d) divisor

9. If any number is divided by __________, the answer is the number itself.
   (a) zero   (b) one
   (c) two   (d) itself

10. Zero divided by any number (except zero) gives __________.
   (a) zero   (b) one
   (c) two   (d) three

11. Solve the problem:
    $2663 \div 7$
    (a) Q = 380, R = 3
    (b) Q = 380, R = 2
    (c) Q = 380, R = 1
    (d) Q = 383, R = 0

12. Estimate the quotient:
    [Mental Mathematics]
    $256 \div 45$
    (a) Q = 5   (b) Q = 4
    (c) Q = 3   (d) Q = 6

13. Solve the problem: **[2008]**
    $518 \div 61$
    (a) Q = 8, R = 31   (b) Q = 8, R = 30
    (c) Q = 8, R = 29   (d) Q = 9, R = 30

14. Find the quotient & remainder if any.
    $93 \div 39$
    (a) Q = 2, R = 15   (b) Q = 3, R = 15
    (c) Q = 1, R = 15   (d) Q = 15, R = 3

15. Solve the problem: **[2009]**
    $640 \div 80$
    (a) 10   (b) 9
    (c) 8   (d) 6

16. Solve the problem: **[Tricky]**
    $2944 \div 100$
    (a) Q = 44, R = 29   (b) Q = 29, R = 44
    (c) Q = 2, R = 944   (d) Q = 294, R = 4

17. Solve the problem: **[2010]**
    $891 \div 26$
    (a) Q = 34, R = 7   (b) Q = 32, R = 1
    (c) Q = 21, R = 8   (d) Q = 33, R = 9

18. Solve the problem: **[Tricky]**
    $451 \div 100$
    (a) Q = 45, R = 1   (b) Q = 4, R = 51
    (c) Q = 5, R = 1   (d) Q = 1, R = 51

19. Find the quotient and remainder when 1496 is divided by 20.   **[2013]**
    (a) Q = 74, R = 16   (b) Q = 74, R = 14
    (c) Q = 70, R = 15   (d) Q = 72, R = 16

20. Find the divisor, if dividend = 88, quotient = 12 & remainder = 4. **[2017]**
    (a) 7   (b) 8
    (c) 9   (d) 5

21. If the smallest 5-digit number formed by digits 8, 6, 0 and 4 (each digit must be used at least once) is divided by 12, then the quotient will be ________ **[2018]**
    (a) 3390   (b) 3309
    (c) 3339   (d) 3039

22. 22050 cartoons were to be transported in 90 trucks. How many cartoons could 1 truck carry. If each truck carries equal number of cartoons?   **[2019]**
    (a) 325   (b) 210
    (c) 245   (d) 320

23. If Saumya wants to pour whole water from jug into the glasses of 400 mL capacity, then how many glasses will she need?   **[2021]**

3L 200 mL

    (a) 7   (b) 8   (c) 6   (d) 9

24. 159 students went to the zoo. 84 of them were boys and the rest were girls. If the girls were grouped into groups of 5, then how many groups of girls were there?   **[2022]**
    (a) 15   (b) 25   (c) 16   (d) 17

25. Raj was facing the stadium. He makes a $\frac{3}{4}$ turn to his left. What will he be facing now?   **[2022]**

    (a) Railway station   (b) Home
    (c) School   (d) Stadium

LEVEL 2

1. State whether the following statement/s are correct/incorrect.
   Statement A: 12 ÷ 6 = 2, Here 12 = Quotient.   **[Critical Thinking]**
   Statement B: 25 ÷ 2 , Remainder = 1.
   (a) Only statement A is correct.   (b) Only statement B is correct.
   (c) Both are correct.   (d) Both are incorrect.

2. Match the following: **[Critical Thinking]**

	List I		List II
A.	If any number is divided by 1, the answer is the number itself.	1.	6 ÷ 6 = 1
B.	If any number is divided by itself, the answer is always 1.	2.	0 ÷ 6 = 0
C.	Any number cannot be divided by zero.	3.	6 ÷ 1 = 6
D.	Zero divided by any number gives zero.	4.	6 ÷ 0 = X

	A	B	C	D			A	B	C	D
(a)	4	3	2	1		(b)	3	1	4	2
(c)	1	2	3	4		(d)	3	1	2	4

3. Rahul has solved a division problem. Find out whether he has solved it correctly or not? [Mental Mathematics]

   $42 \div 8 ; Q = 5, R = 2$
   (a) It is correct
   (b) It is incorrect
   (c) Can't say
   (d) None of these

4. Which number will replace the question mark? [2016]

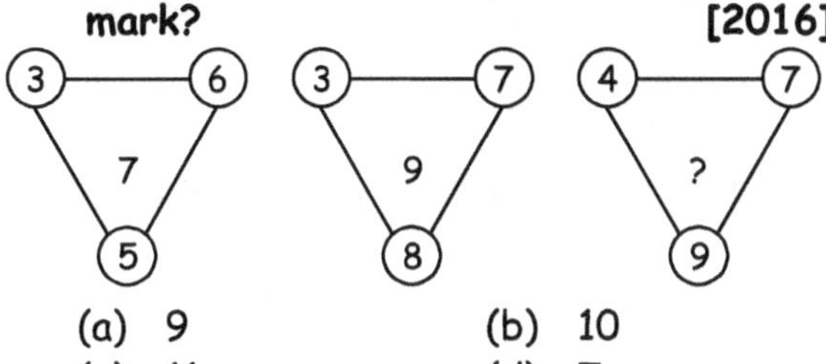

   (a) 9
   (b) 10
   (c) 11
   (d) 7

5. Match the following: [Tricky]

	List I		List II
A.	$99 \div 10$	1.	Q = 2716 R = 0
B.	$1251 \div 100$	2.	Q = 9 R = 9
C.	$5432 \div 2$	3.	Q = 12 R = 51
D.	$9817 \div 5$	4.	Q = 1963 R = 2

	A	B	C	D			A	B	C	D
(a)	2	3	1	4		(b)	1	2	3	4
(c)	4	3	2	1		(d)	2	3	4	1

6. A dozen has 12 units. How many dozens are there in 7044 units? [2008]
   (a) 587
   (b) 857
   (c) 590
   (d) 586

7. Fill in the blank spaces in anti clock wise:

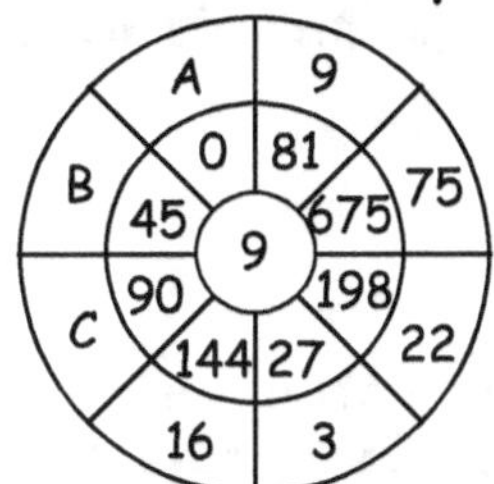

	A	B	C
(a)	0,	5,	10
(b)	0,	9,	0
(c)	9,	9,	9
(d)	0,	9,	90

8. What least number should be added to 69 so that it becomes divisible by 9? [2015]
   (a) 1
   (b) 2
   (c) 3
   (d) 5

9. Fill in the blank spaces in anti clock wise: [Mental Mathematics]

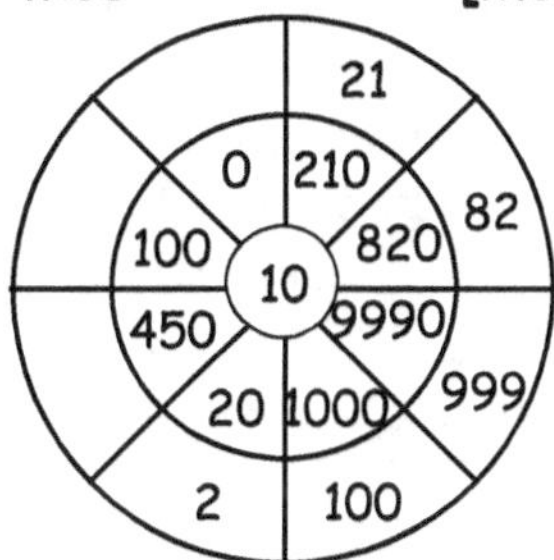

   (a) 0, 10, 45
   (b) 0,9,0
   (c) 9,9,9
   (d) 0,9,90

10. When X is divided by 16, the quotient is 256 and the remainder is 14, find the value of X. [2012]
    (a) 4110
    (b) 4010
    (c) 3910
    (d) 3810

11. Find the dividend if divisor = 21, quotient = 43 & remainder = 19. [2009]
    (a) 920
    (b) 922
    (c) 923
    (d) 924

12. Place the numbers in boxes.

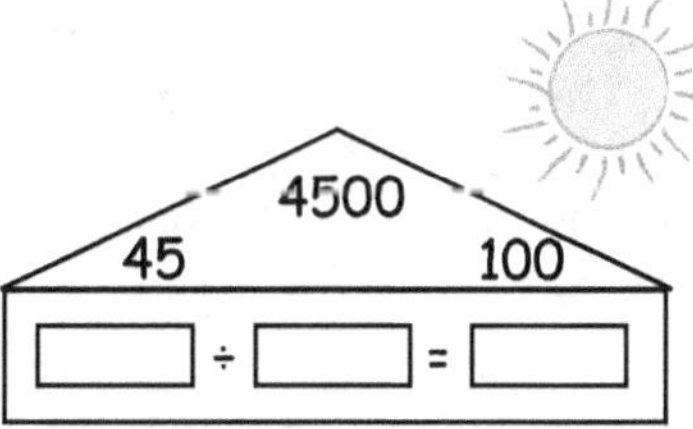

    (a) $4500 \div 45 = 100$ or $4500 \div 100 = 45$
    (b) $4500 \div 45 = 4500$ or $4500 \div 100 = 100$
    (c) $100 \div 45 = 4500$ or $100 \div 4500 = 45$
    (d) $45 \div 100 = 4500$ or $45 \div 4500 = 100$

13. Arwin earns ₹ 721 in a week. How much money does he earn in 16 days? [2014]
    (a) ₹ 1200
    (b) ₹ 1240
    (c) ₹ 1648
    (d) ₹ 1500

14. Find the length of 1 piece of rope. [Mental Mathematics]

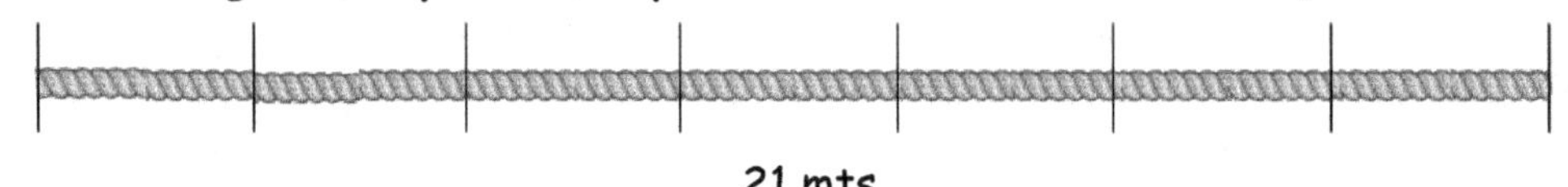

21 mts.

(a) 3 mts. (b) 7 mts. (c) 21 mts. (d) 10 mts.

15. Find the number of buses required to carry 20,625 passengers waiting at the bus stand for Haridwar, if each bus carries 165 passengers? [2011]
(a) 105 (b) 115
(c) 120 (d) 125

16. Fill in blanks in reference to the given image:

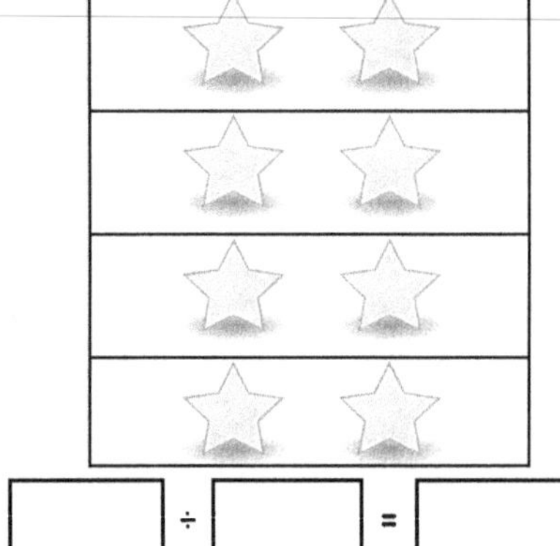

	÷		=	

(a) 8 ÷ 2 = 4 or 8 ÷ 4 = 2
(b) 4 ÷ 2= 8 or 2 ÷ 4 = 2
(c) 2 ÷ 4 = 8 or 4 ÷ 2 = 2
(d) 2 ÷ 8= 4 or 4 ÷ 8 = 2

17. Mala & Rozy plucked flowers to make garlands. They have 15 flowers to share amongst themselves. Find out how many flowers will be there in 1 garland?
(a) Q = 7, R=1

(b) Q = 1, R = 7

(c) Q = 2, R =7

(d) Q = 7, R = 2

18. There are a total of 516 trees in 6 parks. There are an equal number of trees in each park. Exactly how many trees are there in each park? [2011]
(a) 96 (b) 86
(c) 81 (d) 68

19. Find Q & R in the given image:

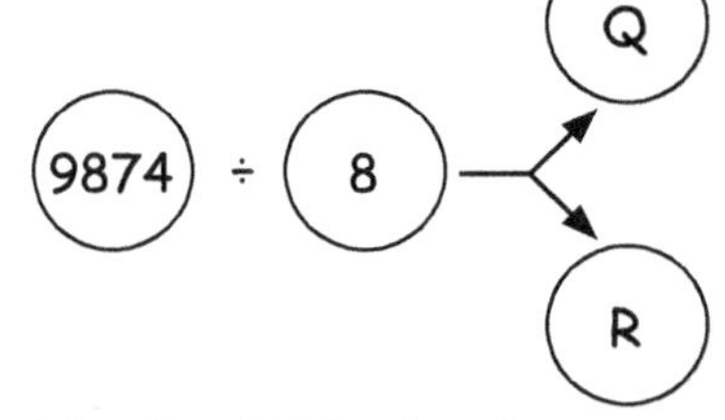

(a) Q = 1123 R = 3
(b) Q = 1223 R = 0
(c) Q = 1243 R = 1
(d) Q = 1234 R = 2

20. 4600 people were to be transported in 100 buses. How many people could 1 bus carry, if each bus carry equal number of people? [2014]
(a) 46 (b) 460
(c) 4500 (d) 200

21. There are 10 friends and 55 bananas. If the bananas are divided equally among the students, how many does each friend get?[Mental Mathematics]
(a) Q = 5, R = 3
(b) Q = 5, R = 2
(c) Q = 5, R = 5
(d) Q =1, R =5

22. 990 cold drink bottles are to be placed in crates. Each crate can hold 18 bottles. How many crates would be needed? [2015]
(a) 50 (b) 55
(c) 60 (d) 65

23. Tina wants to buy 1250 cookies for a party. If there are 5 cookies in each package, how many packages should Tina buy?
    (a) 240   (b) 250
    (c) 260   (d) 125

24. A farmer picked 823 tomatoes from his field and divided them equally into 36 bunches. How many tomatoes are in each bunch? Is there any tomato left out from packing?
    (a) Q = 22, R = 31
    (b) Q = 23, R = 32
    (c) Q = 21, R = 32
    (d) Q = 31, R = 22

25. An ice cream vendor had 220 cherries. He split the cherries evenly among 110 ice cream sundaes. How many cherries did the vendor put on each sundae? [2008]
    (a) 3   (b) 4
    (c) 2   (d) 5

26. A group of 1500 students wants to ride a roller coaster. If the cars on the roller coaster each hold 5 people. How many cars will the students need?
    (a) 200   (b) 300
    (c) 400   (d) 500

27. Complete the pattern.

    [Mental Mathematics]

    $4 \div 2 = 2$
    $\_\_\_ \div 2 = 20$
    $400 \div 2 = \_\_\_$
    $4000 \div 2 = \_\_\_$

    (a) 40, 200, 2000
    (b) 400, 20, 200
    (c) 4, 200, 200
    (d) 4000, 200, 2000

28. For the annual examination 1176 children were made to sit in 21 rooms. If every room had equal number of children, find the number of children sitting in one room. [2016]
    (a) 60   (b) 56
    (c) 54   (d) 42

29. Complete the pattern.

    $8000 \div 4 = 2000$
    $\_\_\_ \div 40 = 200$
    $8000 \div 400 = \_\_\_$
    $\_\_\_ \div 4000 = 2$

    (a) 8000, 20, 8000
    (b) 8000, 200, 8000
    (c) 8000, 2000, 8000
    (d) 800, 200, 800

30. Find the value of S × R − P + Q [2018]

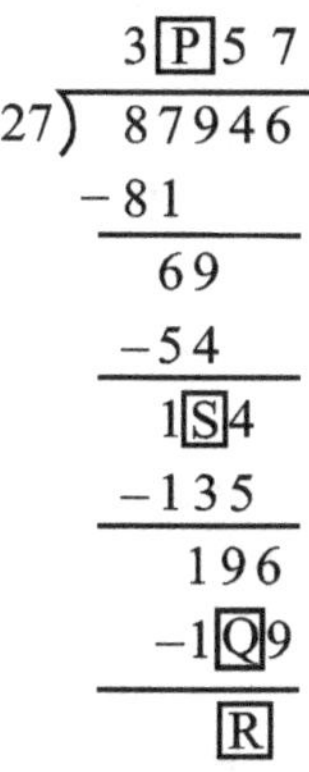

    (a) 41
    (b) 30
    (c) 32
    (d) 38

31. Vedika plans to read a book of 2470 pages. She reads 26 pages in 1 day. In how many days will she read the complete book, if she reads equal number of pages every day? (2021)
    (a) 94
    (b) 95
    (c) 85
    (d) 105

32. A typist can type 90 words in 180 seconds. Find the number of words she can type in 300 seconds, if she maintains a constants speed (2022)
    (a) 150
    (b) 175
    (c) 125
    (d) 200

RESPONSE GRID

LEVEL 1

1. a b c d   2. a b c d   3. a b c d   4. a b c d   5. a b c d
6. a b c d   7. a b c d   8. a b c d   9. a b c d   10. a b c d
11. a b c d   12. a b c d   13. a b c d   14. a b c d   15. a b c d
16. a b c d   17. a b c d   18. a b c d   19. a b c d   20. a b c d
21. a b c d   22. a b c d   23. a b c d   24. a b c d   25. a b c d

LEVEL 2

1. a b c d   2. a b c d   3. a b c d   4. a b c d   5. a b c d
6. a b c d   7. a b c d   8. a b c d   9. a b c d   10. a b c d
11. a b c d   12. a b c d   13. a b c d   14. a b c d   15. a b c d
16. a b c d   17. a b c d   18. a b c d   19. a b c d   20. a b c d
21. a b c d   22. a b c d   23. a b c d   24. a b c d   25. a b c d
26. a b c d   27. a b c d   28. a b c d   29. a b c d   30. a b c d
31. a b c d   32. a b c d

Solutions with Explanation

LEVEL 1

1. **(d)** divide
2. **(c)** dividend
3. **(d)** remainder
4. **(d)** divide
5. **(d)** Division
6. **(a)** imperfect division
7. **(b)** Divisor
8. **(a)** quotient
9. **(b)** one
10. **(a)** zero
11. **(a)** Q = 380, R = 3
    (380 × 7) + 3 = 2663
12. **(a)** 256 ÷ 45
    256 ÷ 45 rounds to 200 ÷ 40
    40 × 5 = 200
    So 45 × 5 = 225< 256

Therefore,

$$45\overline{)256}$$

        5
    45) 256
        -225
        ─────
         31

13. **(b)** Q = 8 , R = 30
14. **(a)**
15. **(c)** Q = 8 , R = 0
16. **(b)** Q = 29, R = 44
17. **(a)** Q = 34 , R = 7
18. **(b)** Q = 4, R = 51
19. **(a)** Q = 74, R = 16
20. **(a)** (Quotient × Divisor) + Remainder
    = Dividend
    (12 × D) + 4 = 88
    (12 × D) = 88 – 4

(12 × D) = 84

D = 84 ÷ 12 = 7

21. **(c)** Smallest 5 digit number = 40068

$$
\begin{array}{r}
3339 \\
12\overline{)\ 40068} \\
36 \\
\overline{40} \\
36 \\
\overline{46} \\
36 \\
\overline{108} \\
108 \\
\overline{\times\times}
\end{array}
$$

22. **(c)** Cartoons in 90 trucks = 22050

Cartoons in 1 truck = 22050 ÷ 90
= 245

23. **(b)** Quantity of water in jug = 3L 200 ml = 3200 ml

Capacity of 1 glass of water
= 400 ml

Number of glasses can be filled
from water in the jug $= \dfrac{3200}{400} = 8$

24. **(a)** Total students went to the Zoo
= 159

Number of boys = 84

Remaining students = 159 –84
= 75

Remaining students are girls

So, number of girls = 75

Number of girls in a group = 5

So, total number of group of girls

$= \dfrac{75}{5} = 15$

25. **(c)**

LEVEL 2

1. **(b)** B is correct.

2. **(b)**

3. **(a)** 42 ÷ 8

Q = 5, R = 2

L.H.S = (5 × 8) + 2 = 42

R.H.S = 42

Therefore, L.H.S. = R.H.S

The answer is correct.

4. **(b)** As 3 + 6 + 5 = 14, So 14 ÷ 2 = 7

Also 3 + 7 + 8 = 18, So 18 ÷ 2 = 9

So, 9 + 7 + 4 = 20, So 20 ÷ 2 = 10

5. **(a)**

6. **(a)** 7044 ÷ 12 = 587

7. **(a)**

8. **(c)** As 69 + 3 = 72

So 72 ÷ 9 = 8

9. **(a)**

10. **(a)** As (16 × 256) + 14
= 4096 + 14 = 4110

11. **(b)** (Quotient × Divisor) + Remainder
= Dividend

(43 × 21) + 19 = D

Therefore, Dividend = 922.

12. **(a)** 4500 ÷ 100 = 45

Or

4500 ÷ 45 = 100

13. **(c)** Earnings of 1 day = 721 ÷ 7 = ₹ 103

Earnings of 16 days = 103 × 16
= ₹ 1648

14. **(a)** Length of 1 Piece = 21 ÷ 7 = 3

15. **(d)** As 20625 ÷ 165 = 125

16. **(a)** 8 ÷ 2 = 4 or 8 ÷ 4 = 2

17. **(a)** Total flowers = 15

No. of garlands = 2

No. of flowers in 1 garland = 15 ÷ 2

Equal no. of flowers in 1 garland = 7

1 flower is left over.

18. **(b)** As 516 ÷ 6 = 86

19. **(d)**

20. **(a)** Since 4600 ÷ 100 = 46

21. **(c)** Each friend got = 55 ÷ 10

Q = 5 , R = 5

Each friend got 5 bananas & 5 bananas were left over.

22. **(b)** As 990 ÷ 18 = 55

23. **(b)**   No. of packages = 1250 ÷ 5
Answer = 250 packages

24. **(a)**   Number of tomatoes in 1 bunch
= 823 ÷ 36
31 tomatoes were left over.

25. **(c)**   No. of cherries on 1 ice cream
sundae = 220 ÷ 110 = 2

26. **(b)**   No. of cars required
= 1500 ÷ 5 = 300

27. **(a)**   Required pattern =

4 ÷ 2	=	2
40 ÷ 2	=	20
400 ÷ 2	=	200
4000 ÷ 2	=	2000

28. **(b)**   Since 1176 ÷ 21 = 56.

29. **(a)**   Required Pattern:

8000 ÷ 4	=	2000
8000 ÷ 40	=	200
8000 ÷ 400	=	20
8000 ÷ 4000	=	2

30. **(a)**   P = 2   S = 5   Q = 8   R = 7
5 × 7 – 2 + 8 = 41

31. **(b)**   Total Pages in the book = 2470 pages
Number of pages vedika reads in a day = 26 pages
Total days taken by vedika to read the book $= \dfrac{2470}{26}$
= 95 days

32. **(a)**   A typist can type 90 words in 180 seconds
Number of words typed in 1 second $= \dfrac{90}{180}$
So, total numer of words typed in 300 seconds $= \dfrac{90 \times 300}{180} = 150$

Finding Factors

Factors are numbers that you multiply together to get another number. For example, 2 multiplied by 4 equals 8. So 2 and 4 are the factors of 8.

Find the factors of the numbers given below. See the example.

10 = __2 × 5__   18 = __________

24 = __________   30 = __________

32 = __________   39 = __________

Find the missing factors

15 = 3 × ☐   21 = 3 × ☐

45 = 9 × ☐   42 = 7 × ☐

36 = 2 × 2 × 3 × ☐

60 = 2 × 3 × 2 × ☐

75 = 5 × 3 × ☐

Prime Number

a number that has only two factors:

1 and iteself

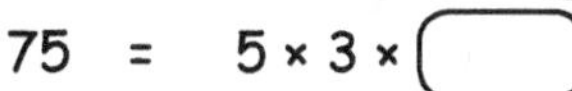

5

1   25

PRIME
PRime = I and ME!

Composite Number
a number that has more than two factors
(They create colorful factor rainbows!)

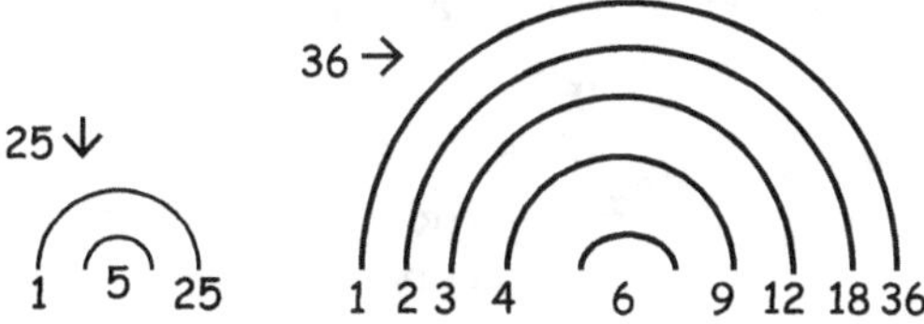

0 and 1 are neither prime nor composite.

7 Chapter | Multiples and Factors

❖ A number's composite factors are found by multiplying 2 or more prime factors.

For example: The composite factors of 18 (2 × 3 × 3) are 6 (2x3) and 9 (3 × 3).

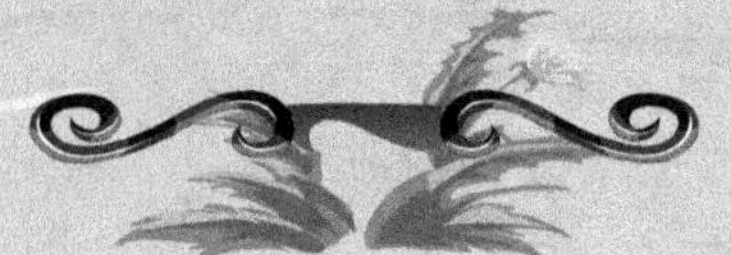

Example : Write the smallest common multiple of 2 and 3.

Solution : Smallest common multiple of 2 and 3 = 2 × 3 = 6

❖ Money can use the concept of factors. One can exchange a 100-rupee note by two 50-rupee notes (factors 2 and 50) or five 20- rupee note (factors 5 and 20).

LEARNING OBJECTIVES

This lesson will help you to:—

❖ understand the concept of factors.

❖ understand the concept of multiples.

❖ use factor tree to find the factors of a number.

❖ find prime numbers, factors and multiples of given number.

❖ apply factors and multiples to real life situations.

QUICK CONCEPT REVIEW

Factors are numbers that multiplies to get another number.

For example: 4 and 7 are multiplied to get 28, then 4 and 7 are factors of 28.

Multiples are product obtained by multiplying one number by another.

For example: 8 and 11 are multiplied to get 88, then 88 is a multiple of 8 and 11.

The factors (or multiples) that are common between 2 or more numbers are called common factors (or multiples) of given numbers.

PROPERTIES OF FACTORS AND MULTIPLES

❖ 1 is a factor of every number.

❖ Every number is a factor of itself.

❖ Every factor of a number is an exact divisor of that number.

❖ Every factor of a number is less than or equal to that number.

❖ Factors of a given number are finite.

❖ Every number is a multiple of itself.

❖ Every multiple of a number is greater than or equal to that number.

❖ The number of multiples of a given number is unlimited/infinite.

PRIME AND COMPOSITE NUMBERS

Prime numbers: A number having only two factors i.e., 1 and number itself is called prime number.

Example: 2, 3, 5, 7, 11, 19, 23, etc. are prime numbers.

> **Note:** 2 is the only even prime number.

Composite numbers: Numbers having more than two factors are called composite numbers.

Example: 4, 6, 9, 12, 15, 24, 25 etc. are composite numbers.

EVEN AND ODD NUMBERS

Even numbers: Numbers which are exactly divisible by 2 are called even numbers. These numbers end with 0, 2, 4, 6 or 8.

Example: 96, 60, 48, 34, 72 are even numbers.

Odd numbers: Numbers which are not exactly divisible by 2 are called odd numbers. These numbers end with 1, 3, 5, 7, 9.

Example: 27, 63, 31, 45, 57, are odd numbers.

Misconcept/Concept

Misconcept: Student might confuse between the concept of factors and multiples.

Concept: Explain factors come from dividing and multiples come from multiplying.

Misconcept: 1 is a prime number

Concept: 1 is not a prime number, 1 is neither composite nor prime.

Example : Write the smallest even common factor of 8 and 20.

Solution : $8 = 2 \times 2 \times 2$ and $20 = 2 \times 2 \times 5$. So, 2 is smallest even common factor of 8 and 20.

Multiple Choice Questions

LEVEL 1

Direction (Qs. 1 to 3): Look at the analogy carefully and choose the correct option.

1. **Up: Down:: Factor : ________ .**
   (a) Multiple　　　(b) Prime
   (c) Composite　　(d) Divide

2. **7 : 14:: 5: ________ .**
   (a) 21　　(b) 15
   (c) 28　　(d) 14

3. **________ : 9:: 4: 24 .**
   (a) 3　　(b) 2
   (c) 5　　(d) 7

4. **Which one of the following is a factor of 45 and not a multiple of 3?**
   [Mental Mathematics]
   (a) 5　　(b) 9
   (c) 15　　(d) 7

5. **Which one of the following is a multiple of 2 but not a factor of 8?**
   (a) 2　　(b) 8
   (c) 4　　(d) 6

6. **Which is odd one out? [Mental Mathematics]**
   (a) 26　　(b) 39
   (c) 65　　(d) 71

7. Which is odd one out?
   (a) 12   (b) 43
   (c) 24   (d) 18

8. What are the multiples of 16 between 40 and 90?
   (a) 48, 64, 80   (b) 44, 64, 80
   (c) 42, 66, 86   (d) 46, 68, 88

9. What is the seventh multiple of 9?
   [Mental Mathematics]
   (a) 81   (b) 56
   (c) 45   (d) 63

10. What is the eleventh multiple of 6?
    [Mental Mathematics]
    (a) 88   (b) 44
    (c) 66   (d) 55

11. What is the next number in the sequence?   **[Tricky]**
    2, 6, 18, 54……
    (a) 216   (b) 162
    (c) 108   (d) 165

12. You are thinking of a number that is a multiple of 7 and 12. What is the smallest number that you can think of?
    [Tricky]
    (a) 168   (b) 49
    (c) 84   (d) 36

13. Find all the factors of 12.   **[2016]**
    (a) 2, 3, 4, 6   (b) 1, 2, 3, 4, 6
    (c) 1, 2, 4, 6, 12   (d) 1, 2, 3, 4, 6, 12

14. What is the greatest length that is used to measure 8 m, 6 m and 14 m exactly?
    (a) 4 m   (b) 3 m
    (c) 6 m   (d) 2 m

15. Which of the following numbers has the least number of factors?   **[2014]**
    (a) 12   (b) 15
    (c) 13   (d) 20

16. Which of the following numbers has the least number of factors?
    (a) 66   (b) 106
    (c) 78   (d) 110

17. Find the total number of factors of 18.   **[2011]**

(a) Three   (b) Four
(c) Five   (d) Six

Direction (Qs. 18 to 30): Choose the correct option in the questions given below.

18. Which number below is a factor of 12?
    [2008]
    (a) 10   (b) 7
    (c) 5   (d) 6

19. Which number below is not a factor of 8?
    (a) 3   (b) 2
    (c) 1   (d) 8

20. Which one of the following options has all prime numbers?   **[2012]**
    (a) 2, 5, 9   (b) 5, 6, 11
    (c) 4, 5, 7   (d) 2, 3, 5

21. Which number below is a factor of 16?
    (a) 7   (b) 2
    (c) 6   (d) 3

22. Which of the following shows all the factors of 30?   **[2012]**
    (a) 1 2, 3, 5, 6, 10, 15, 30
    (b) 2, 3, 5, 6, 15, 30
    (c) 1, 2, 3, 5, 6
    (d) 1, 2, 5, 6, 15, 30, 60

23. Which number below is a factor of 21?
    [Mental Mathematics]
    (a) 5   (b) 2
    (c) 7   (d) 6

24. Which number below is a factor of 25?
    (a) 4   (b) 3
    (c) 2   (d) 5

25. Which number below is not a factor of 20?
    (a) 1   (b) 20
    (c) 8   (d) 4

26. Which number below is a factor of 18?
    [Mental Mathematics]
    (a) 10   (b) 2
    (c) 4   (d) 5

27. Which one of the following is the 12th multiple of 12?   **[2016]**
    (a) 124   (b) 444
    (c) 144   (d) 142

28. Which number below is not a factor of 14?   [Mental Mathematics]
(a) 14   (b) 2
(c) 7   (d) 6

29. Which number below is not a factor of 24?   [Mental Mathematics]
(a) 8   (b) 10
(c) 4   (d) 12

30. Which number below is a factor of 22?
     [2009]
(a) 2   (b) 3
(c) 6   (d) 5

31. Which of the following has the greatest number of factors?   [2020]
(a) 12   (b) 24
(c) 48   (d) 32

32. How many multiples of 15 are there in between 95 and 185?   [2021]
(a) 6   (b) 5
(c) 7   (d) 8

LEVEL 2

1. Match the following: [Critical Thinking]

	List I		List II
A.	First 4 multiples of 3	1.	6, 12, 18, 24
B.	First 4 multiples of 6	2.	5, 10, 15, 20
C.	First 4 multiples of 5	3.	10, 20, 30, 40
D.	First 4 multiples of 10	4.	3, 6, 9, 12

	A	B	C	D			A	B	C	D
(a)	1	2	3	4		(b)	4	1	2	3
(c)	2	3	1	4		(d)	4	2	3	2

2. Which number is a common factor of 42 and 70?   [2017]
(a) 7   (b) 10
(c) 21   (d) 8

3. Match the following: [Critical Thinking]

	List I		List II
A.	3 factors of 100 are	1.	4, 12, 16
B.	3 factors of 75 are	2.	2, 25, 50
C.	3 factors of 48 are	3.	3, 5, 15
D.	3 factors of 56 are	4.	7, 4, 8

	A	B	C	D			A	B	C	D
(a)	1	2	3	4		(b)	4	1	2	3
(c)	2	3	1	4		(d)	4	2	3	1

4. What is the sum of the first and second common multiples of 4 and 6?   [2013]
(a) 36   (b) 144
(c) 72   (d) 288

5. Read the statement carefully and choose the correct option with true/false.   [Critical Thinking]
(A) You get a multiple when a number is multiplies by another number.
(B) A factor is a number that is half of itself.
(C) 1 is a factor of every number.
(D) Every multiple is less or equal to the number.
(a) FTTF   (b) TFTF
(c) TFFT   (d) FTFT

6. Read the statement carefully and choose the correct option with true/false.   [2010, Tricky]
(A) 6 is multiple of 18.
(B) 24 is a multiple of 3.
(C) 5 is factor of 20.
(D) 88 is factor of 4.
(a) FTTF   (b) TFTF
(c) TFFT   (d) TTTT

7. Read the statement carefully and choose the correct option with true/false.
(A) 63, 77 and 81 are all multiples of 9.   [Critical Thinking]
(B) 49, 63 and 88 are all multiples of 7.
(C) 2, 5 and 8 are factors of 40.
(D) 3, 6 and 13 are factors of 234.
(a) FTFT
(b) TFTF
(c) TTFF
(d) FFTT

8. Which one of the following is common factor of 24 and 26?   [2013]
   (a) 1, 2   (b) 2, 3
   (c) 2, 3, 4   (d) All of these

9. From the list given below find how many numbers are factors of 125?

   2, 3, 5, 7, 25, 50, 100

   (a) 3   (b) 0
   (c) 1   (d) 2

10. From the list given below find how many of the numbers are multiples of 20?   [Tricky]

    12, 25, 40, 36, 80, 100, 110, 150

    (a) 3   (b) 0
    (c) 1   (d) 2

11. What defines the two circles A and B (including the common portion between A and B) in the following diagram? Choose the correct option.   [Tricky]

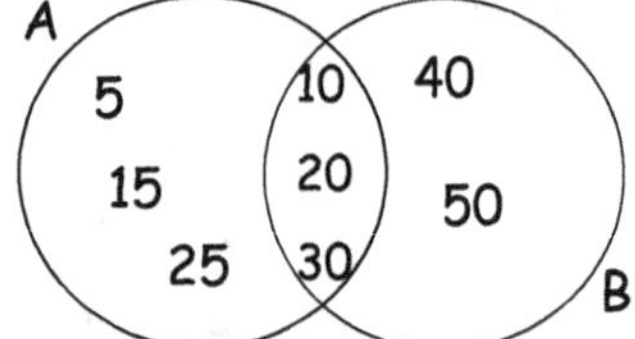

    (a) A: Multiples of 5; B: Multiples of 20
    (b) A: Multiples of 5; B: Multiples of 10
    (c) A: Multiples of 10; B: Multiples of 5
    (d) A: Multiples of 20; B: Multiples of 5

12. What defines the two circles A and B (including the common portion between A and B) in the following diagram? Choose the correct option.   [Tricky]

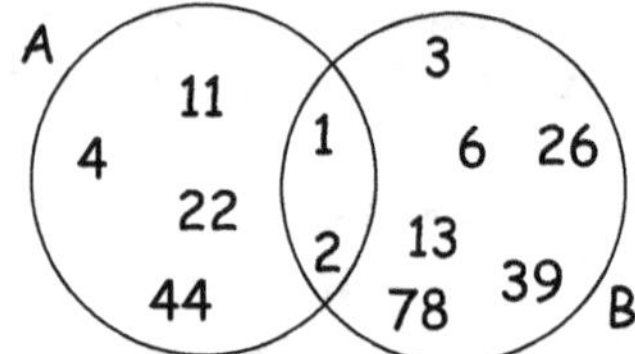

    (a) A: Factors of 24; B: Factors of 68
    (b) A: Factors of 78; B: Factors of 44
    (c) A: Factors of 66; B: Factors of 39
    (d) A: Factors of 44; B: Factors of 78

13. What is the next picture in the sequence?   [2008]

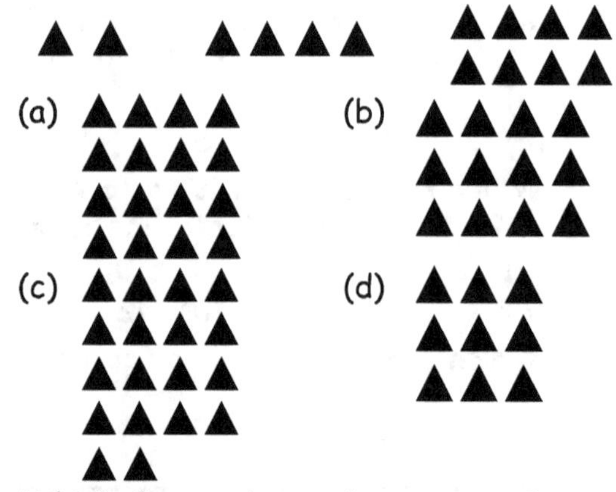

14. Which figure shows the correct factor tree for 24? [2010] [Critical Thinking]

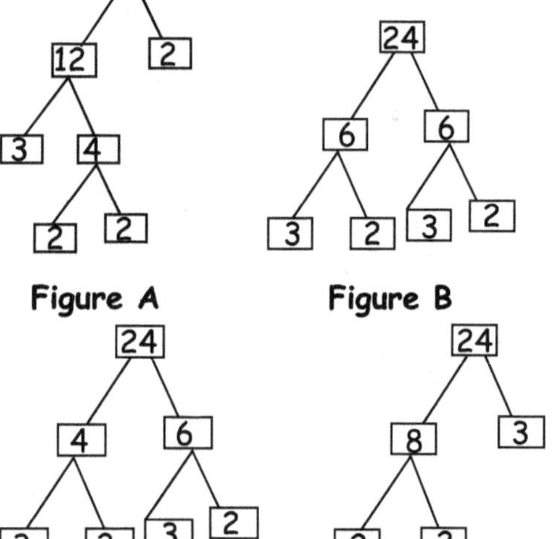

Figure A   Figure B

Figure C   Figure D

    (a) Figure A   (b) Figure B
    (c) Figure C   (d) Figure D

15. Which numbers complete the factor tree for 88?   [2008]

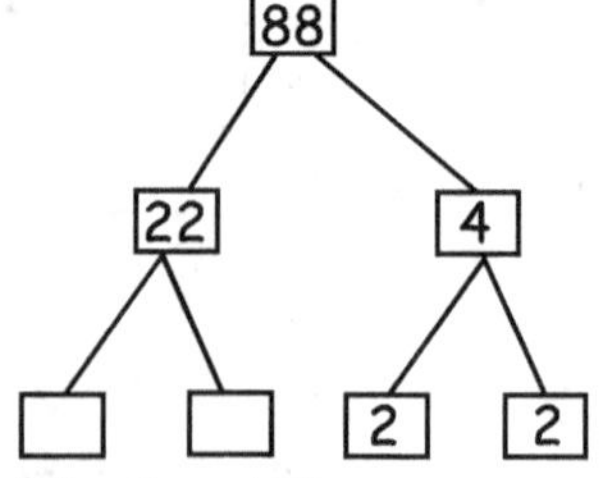

    (a) 4 and 11
    (b) 2 and 11
    (c) 4 and 12
    (d) 3 and 11

16. Which numbers complete the factor tree? **[2009]**

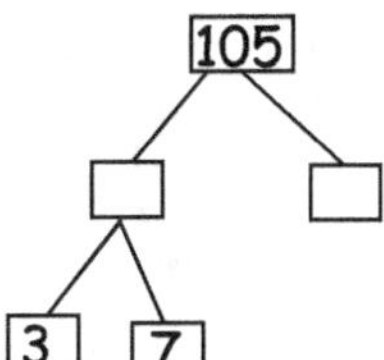

    (a) 21 and 4 (b) 5 and 42
    (c) 42 and 4 (d) 21 and 5

17. There are 50 students going for a field trip. The teacher thought of dividing the students in groups. Which of the following statements are true/false? **[Tricky]**

    A. The teacher can make groups of 5.
    B. The teacher can make groups of 10.
    C. The teacher can make groups of 6.
    D. The teacher can make groups of 7.
    (a) TTFF (b) FFTT
    (c) TFTF (d) FTFT

18. Suhana wants to buy flowers for her friends. She can buy roses in bunch of 7 flowers and carnations in bunch of 10 flowers. She wants to buy the same number of roses and carnations. What is the minimum number of flowers Suhana will need to buy?
    (a) 70 flowers (b) 140 flowers
    (c) 130 flowers (d) 80 flowers

19. Shikha has 45 green balls, 18 blue balls and 63 red balls. She wants to put them in bags with same number of each type of ball in each bag. How many bags will Shikha need? **[2009]**
    (a) 8 bags (b) 7 bags
    (c) 9 bags (d) 6 bags

20. Richa has 15 glasses and 45 cups. She is to put them in equal groups such that none of the glass or cup is left over. What is the maximum number of groups that Richa can make?
    (a) 15 (b) 3 (c) 5 (d) 10

21. Arnav wants to buy pencils and erasers. The pencils are available in the pack of 12 and the erasers are available in packs of 8. Arnav wants to buys the same number of pencils and erasers, what is the minimum number of pencils or erasers will Arnav buy? **[Tricky]**
    (a) 3 packs of pencils and 2 packs of erasers.
    (b) 2 packs of pencils and 3 packs of erasers.
    (c) 4 packs of pencils and 2 packs of erasers.
    (d) 2 packs of pencils and 4 packs of erasers.

22. Three alarm clocks ring the alarm at 3, 6 and 9 minutes respectively. In 60 minutes how many times will the clocks ring together? **[Tricky]**
    (a) 3 times (b) 2 times
    (c) 4 times (d) 1 time

23. Raj cycles 6 km at a time and Shiv cycles 8 at a time. At the end of a week they realize that they have cycled the same number of kilometers. What is the minimum number of kilometers they would have cycled?
    (a) 12 km (b) 32 km
    (c) 18 km (d) 24 km

24. Sia has 12 orange juice cans and 45 mango juice cans. She wants to distribute them among children equally so that no juice can is left. What will be the greatest number of children among whom Sia can distribute the juice cans? **[Critical Thinking]**
    (a) 4 (b) 5 (c) 3 (d) 9

25. Which shows the correct table of factors and product?

(a)

Factor		Factor		Product
4	×	3	=	16
7	×	7	=	42
5	×	11	=	55
8	×	9	=	63

(b)

Factor		Factor		Product
4	×	3	=	12
7	×	5	=	35
2	×	11	=	22
8	×	10	=	80

(c)

Factor		Factor		Product
4	×	3	=	12
7	×	5	=	45
2	×	11	=	22
6	×	6	=	30

(d)

Factor		Factor		Product
3	×	3	=	9
8	×	5	=	50
3	×	11	=	33
6	×	7	=	42

26. I am multiple of 23. I am an odd number and have 3 digits. I am also a multiple of 7. Who am I? [Tricky]
    (a) 161 (b) 207
    (c) 205 (d) 159

27. I am a factor of 45. I am single digit odd number. I am also a factor of 54. Who am I? [Tricky]
    (a) 7
    (b) 9
    (c) 5
    (d) 11

28. How many multiple of 10 are there from 20 to 150? [2015]
    (a) 13
    (b) 14
    (c) 15
    (d) 12

29. Every number is a ____(i)____ of 1. Every number except ____(ii)____ is a factor of itself. A factor of a number is either ____(iii)____ than or equal to that number. We can find factors by using ____(iv)____ 12 and 3 are ____(v)____ of 36. The numbers of multiples of a given number is ____(vi)____ .
    (a) (i) multiples   (ii) zero
        (iii) less   (iv) division
        (v) factors   (vi) unlimited
    (b) (i) factors   (ii) one
        (iii) greater   (iv) multiplication
        (v) multiples   (vi) limited
    (c) (i) multiples   (ii) one
        (iii) less   (iv) subtraction
        (v) divisors   (vi) countable
    (d) (i) factors   (ii) zero
        (iii) greater   (iv) addition
        (v) remainders   (vi) unlimited

Direction (Qs. 30 to 32): Factors of a number which are prime are called its prime factors. Factors of 36 are : 1, 2, 3, 4, 6, 9, 12, 18. Prime factors of 36 are: 2, 3. A number can be written as a product of its prime factors, e.g. 36 = 2 × 2 × 3 × 3. A factorization in which every factor is prime is called prime factorization of the number. Two numbers are co-prime if they have only 1 as the common factor. Based on the information given above answer the following questions.

30. Which one of the following shows the prime factorization of the number 48?
    (a) 48 = 4 × 4 × 3
    (b) 48 = 8 × 6
    (c) 48 = 2 × 2 × 2 × 2 × 3
    (d) 48 = 12 × 4

31. Which one of these are co-primes?
    (a) 24, 32
    (b) 18, 12
    (c) 9, 16
    (d) 60, 84

32. Prime numbers between 20 and 40 are
    (a) 23, 29, 31, 32
    (b) 23, 29, 31, 37
    (c) 21, 25, 27, 29
    (d) 33, 35, 37, 39

33. Match the following : [2014]

	A		B
A	Prime numbers	(i)	(5 & 8)
B	Co-primes	(ii)	(2 & 3)
C	Twin-primes	(iii)	(3 & 5)

    (a) A-i; B-ii, C-ii
    (b) A-ii, B-i, C-iii
    (c) A-ii, B-iii, C-i
    (d) A-i, B-iii, C-ii

34. Study the grid and answer the following question.

1	2	3	4	5	6	7	8	9	10
11	12	13	14	15	16	17	18	19	20
21	22	23	24	25	26	27	28	29	30
31	32	33	34	35	36	37	38	39	40
41	42	43	44	45	46	47	48	49	50
51	52	53	54	55	56	57	58	59	60
61	62	63	64	65	66	67	68	69	70
71	72	73	74	75	76	77	78	79	80
81	82	83	84	85	86	87	88	89	90
91	92	93	94	95	96	97	98	99	100

All the encircled numbers are the _________ numbers, and all the crossed out numbers are __________ numbers respectively.

(a) prime, co-prime

(b) prime, composite

(c) even, odd

(d) composite, prime

35. Find the greatest number that will divide 28 + x and 24 + x without leaving any remainder when x = 4. **[2011]**

(a) 1

(b) 2

(c) 4

(d) 14

36. The teacher gave 12 books a group of children and asked them to arrange them in different groups under some conditions like **[Tricky]**

A. Each group should have the same number of books.

B. No of books should be left over.

C. Each grouping should be different from the other.

This activity will help the children to understand the concept of

(a) Addition

(b) Subtraction

(c) Multiples and factors

(d) Measurements

37. All the multiples of 3, except 3, all the multiples of 5, except 5 and all the multiples of 7, except 7 are __________ **[Tricky]**

(a) even numbers

(b) composite numbers

(c) prime numbers

(d) co-prime

38. Read the following statements and identify the number.

[2016, Critical Thinking]

(i) I am a 2-digit even number.

(ii) I am a common multiple of both 6 and 7.

(iii) I have a total of 8 factors.

(a) 43   (b) 35

(c) 42   (d) 84

39. Multiply 8th multiple of 14 with 12th multiple of 19 and round off the answer to the nearest thousand. The final result is ________. **[2018]**

(a) 26000

(b) 25000

(c) 25600

(d) 25500

40. Find the sum of (3rd multiple of 11) and (the difference between common factors of 8 and 10). **[2019]**

(a) 42   (b) 36

(c) 34   (d) 32

41. Match the following and select the CORRECT option.   [2020]

Column I   Column II

P. The number of factors of 125 is ______.   (i) 5

Q. Common price factor of 15 and 50 is ______. (ii) 272

R. L.C.M. of (16, 34) is ______.   (iii) 14

S. H.C.F. of (98, 14) is ______.   (iv) 4

	P	Q	R	S			P	Q	R	S
(a)	(iv)	(i)	(ii)	(iii)		(b)	(i)	(ii)	(iv)	(iii)
(c)	(iv)	(i)	(iii)	(ii)		(d)	(i)	(ii)	(iii)	(iv)

42. Fill in the blanks and select the CORRECT option.   [2021]

- L.C.M. of 24 and 48 is _P .
- Number of factors of 124 is _Q .
- H.C.F. of 12 and 32 is _R .

	P	Q	R			P	Q	R
(a)	72	5	4		(b)	48	5	8
(c)	48	6	4		(d)	72	6	8

43. Which of the following is INCORRECT?   [2022]
(a) Every number is a multiple of itself
(b) Every number is not a multiple of 1.
(c) 20 is a multiple of 1.
(d) A multiple of a number can be greater than the number itself.

RESPONSE GRID

LEVEL 1

1. a b c d   2. a b c d   3. a b c d   4. a b c d   5. a b c d
6. a b c d   7. a b c d   8. a b c d   9. a b c d   10. a b c d
11. a b c d   12. a b c d   13. a b c d   14. a b c d   15. a b c d
16. a b c d   17. a b c d   18. a b c d   19. a b c d   20. a b c d
21. a b c d   22. a b c d   23. a b c d   24. a b c d   25. a b c d
26. a b c d   27. a b c d   28. a b c d   29. a b c d   30. a b c d
31. a b c d   32. a b c d

LEVEL 2

1. a b c d   2. a b c d   3. a b c d   4. a b c d   5. a b c d
6. a b c d   7. a b c d   8. a b c d   9. a b c d   10. a b c d
11. a b c d   12. a b c d   13. a b c d   14. a b c d   15. a b c d
16. a b c d   17. a b c d   18. a b c d   19. a b c d   20. a b c d
21. a b c d   22. a b c d   23. a b c d   24. a b c d   25. a b c d

26. a b c d   27. a b c d   28. a b c d   29. a b c d   30. a b c d
31. a b c d   32. a b c d   33. a b c d   34. a b c d   35. a b c d
36. a b c d   37. a b c d   38. a b c d   39. a b c d   40. a b c d
41. a b c d   42. a b c d   43. a b c d

Solutions with Explanation

LEVEL 1

1. **(a)** Example: 2 is a factor of 6 and 6 is a multiple of 2.

2. **(b)** Since, 14 is a multiple of 7; 15 is a multiple of 5.

∴ Required answer = 7 : 14 : : 5 : 15

3. **(a)** Since, 4 is a factor of 24 and 3 is a factor of 9.

∴ Answer = 3 : 9 : : 4 : 24

4. **(a)** Factors of 45: 1, 3, 5, 9, 15, 45

Multiples of 3: 3, 6, 9, 12, 15, 18.....

So, 5 is a factor of 45 but not a multiple of 3.

5. **(d)** Factors of 8: 1, 2, 4, 8

Multiples of 2: 2, 4, 6, 8, 10, 12.....

So, 6 is a multiple of 2 but not a factor of 8.

6. **(d)** 26, 39, and 65 are multiples of 13 whereas 71 is not a multiple of 13.

7. **(b)** 12, 249, and 18 are multiples of 6 whereas 43 is not a multiple of 6.

8. **(a)** 48, 64 and 80 are the multiples of 16 lies between 40 and 90.

16 × 3 = 48 ; 16 × 4 = 64 ; 16 × 5 = 80.

9. **(d)** 63 = 9 × 7

10. **(c)** 66 = 6 × 11

11. **(b)** The rule is to multiply each term by 3 to get the next term. So 54 × 3 = 162 is the next number in the sequence

12. **(c)** Multiples of 7: 7, 14, 21, 28, 35, 42, 49, 56, 63, 70, 77, 84, 91.......

Multiples of 12: 12, 24, 36, 48, 60, 72, 84, 96.....

Smallest number is 84 because 84 is minimum common multiple of 7 and 12.

13. **(d)** All the factors of 12 are 1, 2, 3, 4, 6, 12

14. **(d)** 8 = 2 × 2 × 2

6 = 2 × 3

14 = 2 × 7

Maximum length will be 2 m

15. **(c)** 13 has only 2 factors 1 and 13

16. **(b)** The factors of 106 are 1, 2, 53 and 106.

The factors of 78 are 1, 2, 3, 6, 13, 26, 39 and 78.

The factors of 110 are 1, 2, 5, 10, 11, 22, 55 and 110.

The factors of 66 are 1, 2, 3, 6, 11, 22, 33 and 66.

17. **(d)** There are 6 factors of 18, which are 1, 18, 2, 9, 3 and 6

18. **(d)**   **19.** **(a)**

20. **(d)** 2, 3, 5 are all prime numbers

21. **(b)**

22. **(a)** All the factors of 30 are 1, 2, 3, 5, 6, 10, 15, 30

23. **(c)**   **24.** **(d)**

25. **(c)**   **26.** **(b)**

27. **(c)** 12th multiple of 12 = 12 × 12 = 144

28. **(d)**   **29.** **(b)**

30. **(a)**

31. **(d)** 48 has the greatest number of factors

32. **(a)** 105, 120, 135, 150, 165, 180 = 6

LEVEL 2

1. **(b)**

2. **(a)** 7 is the common factor of 42 and 70.

3. **(c)**

4. **(a)** First and second common multiples of 4 and 6 are 12 and 24.
So, sum = 12 + 24 = 36

5. **(b)**

6. **(a)** FTTF; 6 is a factor of 18 and 88 is a multiple of 4.

7. **(d)** 63 (3x 3 x 7) and 81 (3 x 3 x 3 x 3) are multiples of 9 but 77 (7 x 11) is not a multiple of 9.
49 (7 x7) and 63 (7 x 3 x 3) are multiples of 7 but 88 (2 x 2 x 2 x 11) is not a multiple of 7.
2, 5 and 8 are factors of 40 (1 x 2 x 2 x 2 x 5)
3, 6 and 13 are factors of 234 (1 x 2 x 3 x 3 x 13)

8. **(a)** 1 and 2 common factors of 24 and 26

9. **(d)** 5 and 25 are factors of 125. Hence, only two numbers are factors of 125 from the given list.

10. **(a)** 40, 80 and 100 are multiples of 20. Hence we have only three numbers are multiples of 20 from the given list.

11. **(b)** In circle A 5, 10, 15, 20, 25, 30 are multiples of 5.
In circle B 10, 20, 30, 40, 50 are multiples of 10.

12. **(d)** In circle A 1, 2, 4, 11, 22, 44 are factors of 44.
In circle B 1, 2, 3, 6, 13, 26, 39, 78 are factors of 78.

13. **(a)** The rule is to multiply number of triangles in each term by 2 to get the number of triangles in the next term. So 8 x 2 = 16 triangles will be in the next picture.

14. **(a)** In Figure B, 24 = 4 x 6 and not 6 x 6.

In Figure C, 4 = 2 x 2 and not 3 x 2.
In Figure D, 8 = 2 x 2 x 2 and not 2 x 2.

15. **(b)** Since, 22 = 2 x 11 therefore 2 and 11 completes the factor tree.

16. **(d)** 3 x 7 = 21 and 21 x 5 = 105

17. **(a)** 50 divided by 5 means 10 students in each group.
50 divided by 10 means 5 students in each group.
50 divided by 6 means 8.3 students in each group. Not possible.
50 divided by 7 means 7.1 students in each group. Not possible.

18. **(a)** Number of roses Suhana can buy: 7, 14, 21, 28, 35, 42, 49, 56, 63, 70, 77,........
Number of carnations Suhana can buy : 10, 20, 30, 40, 50, 60, 70.......
Since, 70 is the common (minimum multiple).
∴ The minimum number of flowers she can buy are 70 + 70 = 140.

19. **(c)** 45 = 5 x 9
18 = 2 x 9
63 = 7 x 9
She will need 9 bags with 5 green balls, 2 blue balls and 7 red balls in each bag.

20. **(a)** 15 = 3 x 5
45 = 3 x 3 x 5
So the greatest common factor is 3 x 5 = 15. So Richa can make a maximum of 15 groups.

21. **(b)** Multiples of 8: 8, 16, 24, 32, 40......
Multiples of 12: 12, 24, 36, 48........
Minimum number of pencils or erasers bought is 24 i.e 2 packs of pencils and 3 packs of erasers.

22. **(a)** Multiples of 3: 3, 6, 9, 12, 15, 18, 21, 24, 27.....

Multiples of 6: 6, 12, 18, 24, 30......
Multiples of 9: 9, 18, 27......
The clocks ring in every 18 minutes together.

1st time the clock will ring in 18 minutes, then at 36 minutes and then at 54 minutes. So in 60 minutes the clocks will ring 3 times.

23. (d) Multiples of 6: 6, 12, 18, 24.........
Multiples of 8: 8, 16, 24, 32.........

The minimum common multiple is 24, so they would have cycled at least 24 km each i.e. Raj cycled 4 laps of 6 km and Shiv cycled 3 laps of 8 km.

24. (c) $12 = 2 \times 2 \times 3$
$45 = 3 \times 3 \times 5$

Since 3 is the common factor so the greatest number of children will be 3. Sia can distribute 4 orange juices each to 3 children and 15 mango juices each to 3 children.

25. (b)

26. (a) $23 \times 7 = 161$

27. (b) $45 = 5 \times 9$
$54 = 6 \times 9$
9 is a single digit odd number.

28. (b) Multiples of 10 from 20 to 150 are 20, 30, 40, 50, 60, 70, 80, 90, 100, 110, 120, 130, 140 and 150

29. (a)

30. (c) $48 = 2 \times 2 \times 2 \times 2 \times 3$ shows prime factorisation of 48 because every factor is prime.

31. (c) 9, 16 are co-primes
$9 = 3 \times 3$
$16 = 4 \times 4$

9 and 16 have only 1 as the common factor.

32. (b) 23, 29, 31, 37 are prime numbers.

33. (b) A → (ii), B → (i), C → (iii)

34. (b) Encircled numbers are prime and crossed out numbers composite.

35. (c) If $x = 4$, then $28 + x = 32$ and $24 + x = 28$, then 4 is the greatest number that divides 32 and 28 completely.

36. (c) Given activity is helpful to understand multiples and factors because 12 books can be arranged in groups having 1, 2, 3, 4, 6 and 12 books in each group.

37. (b) Composite numbers.
Numbers having three or more than 3 factors are called composite numbers.

38. (c) 42 is 2-digit even number and common multiple of 6 and 7. Factors of 42 are 1, 42, 2, 21, 3, 14, 6, 7.

39. (a) $8 \times 14 = 112$
$12 \times 19 = 228$
$112 \times 228 = 25536 \approx 26000$

40. (c) 3rd multiple of 11 = $3 \times 11 = 33$
Common factors of 8 and 10 are 2 and 1
Difference between Common factors of 8 and 10 = 2 – 1 = 1
Thus, required sum = 33 + 1 = 34

41. (a)

42. (c) LCM of 24 and 48 = 48
Number of factors of 124 = 6
(1, 2, 4, 31, 62, 124 = 6)
HCF of 12 and 32 = 4

43. (b) Every number is a a multiple of 1.

Rules for Fractions

Addition : (Same denominator)

$$\frac{A}{B} + \frac{C}{B} = \frac{A + C}{B}$$

Subtraction : (Same denominator)

$$\frac{A}{B} - \frac{C}{B} = \frac{A - C}{B}$$

Multiplication :

$$\frac{A}{B} \times \frac{C}{D} = \frac{AC}{BD}$$

Addition : (different denominator)

$$\frac{A}{B} + \frac{C}{D} = \frac{AD}{BD} + \frac{BC}{BD} = \frac{AD + BC}{BD}$$

Subtraction : (different denominator)

$$\frac{A}{B} - \frac{C}{D} = \frac{AD}{BD} - \frac{BC}{BD} = \frac{AD - BC}{BD}$$

Division

$$\frac{A}{B} \div \frac{C}{D} = \frac{A}{B} \times \frac{D}{C} = \frac{AD}{BC}$$

Name _____________   Date _____________

Sums of Fractions and Mixed Fractions Version 1

Direction : add the following fractions and mixed fractions for each problem.

1. $\dfrac{6}{7} + \dfrac{3}{7}$

2. $10\dfrac{10}{11} + \dfrac{7}{11}$

3. $\dfrac{1}{4} + 7\dfrac{1}{4}$

4. $4\dfrac{2}{3} + 7\dfrac{1}{3}$

5. $\dfrac{2}{9} + \dfrac{5}{9}$

6. $8\dfrac{1}{2} + \dfrac{1}{2}$

7. $2\dfrac{3}{8} + 3\dfrac{4}{8}$

8. $\dfrac{3}{6} + 11\dfrac{2}{6}$

9. $10\dfrac{7}{12} + \dfrac{2}{12}$

10. $\dfrac{2}{10} + \dfrac{9}{10}$

Fraction

A fraction is any part of a group, number or whole.

One circle has been cut in half.
A half is a fraction.
We write one half as

The top numbers is called the numerator — $\dfrac{1}{2}$ — It is the number of parts we have.

The botton number is called the denominator — It is the total number of parts the whole is divided into.

There are three main types of fractions.

Proper Fraction

$\dfrac{1}{2}$ numerator / denominator

The numerator is less than the denominator

$\dfrac{1}{4}$ $\dfrac{2}{3}$ $\dfrac{7}{10}$

Improper Fraction

$\dfrac{5}{2}$ numerator / denominator

The numerator is larger than or equal to the denominator.

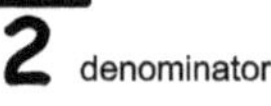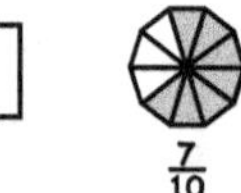

$\dfrac{4}{4}$ $\dfrac{5}{3}$ $\dfrac{7}{4}$

Mixed Fraction

Mixed fraction is written as a whole number with a proper fraction.

$2\dfrac{1}{2}$

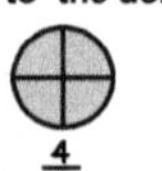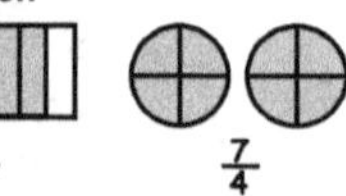

$2\dfrac{2}{3}$ $2\dfrac{3}{4}$

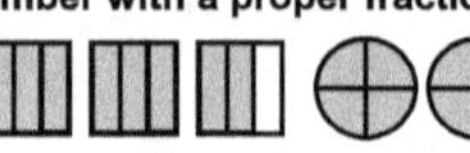

Chapter 8

Fractions

LEARNING OBJECTIVES

This lesson will help you to:—

- ❖ learn to identify half, one-fourth and three-fourth of a whole.
- ❖ learn and understand the meaning of $\frac{1}{3}$, $\frac{1}{4}$ and $\frac{2}{3}$.
- ❖ learn to appreciate the equivalence of $\frac{2}{4}$ and $\frac{1}{2}$ and of $\frac{2}{2}$, $\frac{3}{3}$ and $\frac{4}{4}$ and 1.
- ❖ study about the numerator and denominator of a fraction.
- ❖ learn about mixed fractions.
- ❖ study about addition and subtraction of fractions.

QUICK CONCEPT REVIEW

Whole Number: Whole Numbers are simply the numbers 0, 1, 2, 3, 4, 5, … (and so on). They're not fractions, they are not decimals, they are simply whole numbers.

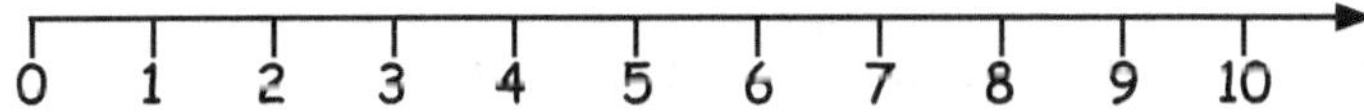

No Fractions!

Fraction: A fraction is a part of a whole.

Fraction= Numerator / Denominator.

TYPES OF FRACTION

There are three types of fraction:

- ❖ **Proper Fraction:** These are those fractions where numerator is smaller than the denominator.
- ❖ **Improper Fraction:** These are those fractions where numerator is larger than the denominator.

Real Life Examples

- ❖ Sharing food is a good way to introduce various concepts about fractions. For example, using a chocolate bar and dividing it into pieces.
- ❖ Measurements during baking uses fractions such as one fourth of a cup of milk or half a spooonful of sugar etc.

Like Fractions

Those fractions which have the same denominator are like fractions.

For example :

$\frac{11}{15}$, $\frac{13}{15}$ and $\frac{2}{15}$

are like fractions as they have the same denominator.

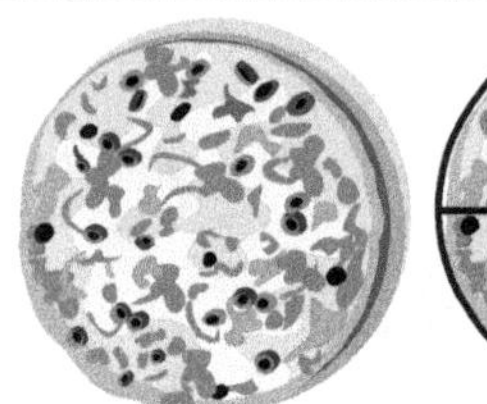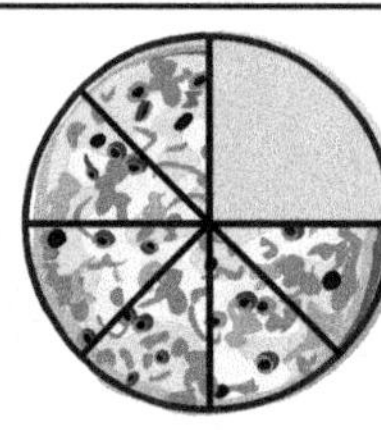

$$= 1 + \frac{3}{4} = \frac{4+3}{4} = \frac{7}{4}$$

Whole Number $2\frac{1}{3}$ — Numerator / Denominator

❖ **Mixed Fractions**

❖ A Mixed Fraction is a whole number and a proper fraction combined.
Ex. $1\frac{2}{3}$, $2\frac{3}{5}$ etc.

❖ For everyday use, people understand mixed fractions better: Example: It is easier to say "I ate $2\frac{1}{4}$ sausages", than "I ate $\frac{9}{4}$ sausages".

Proper Fraction	Improper Fraction	Mixed Fraction
Smaller → 3 / Larger → 5	Larger (or equal) → 9 / Smaller (or equal) → 5	$2\frac{1}{3}$

Numerator: The upper part of fraction that represents the number of parts you have.

Denominator: The lower part of fraction that represents the number of parts the whole is divided into.

Half ($\frac{1}{2}$)

❖ It is two parts of a whole.
❖ It has 1 as Numerator and 2 as Denominator.
❖ It is the simplest form.
❖ It is a proper fraction.

One-fourth ($\frac{1}{4}$)

❖ It is four parts of a whole.
❖ It has 1 as Numerator and 4 as Denominator.
❖ It is a proper fraction.

Two-third ($\frac{2}{3}$)

❖ It is one - third part minus the whole.
❖ It is greater than $\frac{1}{3}$ part.
❖ It is a proper fraction.
❖ It has 2 as Numerator and 3 as Denominator.

Three-fourth ($\frac{3}{4}$)

❖ It is one fourth part minus the whole.
❖ It is greater than $\frac{1}{4}$.
❖ It is a proper fraction.
❖ It has 3 as Numerator and 4 as Denominator.

Equivalent fractions :

Some fractions may look different, but are really the same, for example:

Try It!

Example : Write the following fractions in ascending order
$\frac{11}{4}$, $\frac{11}{5}$ and $\frac{11}{6}$

Solutions : If numerator is same in the given fractions then we look at denominators. The fractions with largest denominator will be the smallest of all and fraction with smallest denominator will be the largest of all. So, in ascending order $= \frac{11}{6}$, $\frac{11}{5}$ and $\frac{11}{4}$.

$$\frac{4}{8} \quad = \quad \frac{2}{4} \quad = \quad \frac{1}{2}$$

(Four-eighths)   (Two-quarters)   (One-half)

❖ The equivalent fraction is obtained by multiplying/ dividing the numerator and denominator by a same number.

❖ $\dfrac{2}{2} = \dfrac{3}{3} = \dfrac{4}{4} = \dfrac{5}{5} = \dfrac{6}{6} = \dfrac{7}{7} \ldots\ldots = \dfrac{1}{1} = 1.$

CONVERTING IMPROPER FRACTIONS TO MIXED FRACTIONS

To convert an improper fraction to a mixed fraction, follow these steps:

1. Divide the numerator by the denominator.
2. Write down the whole number answer.
3. Then write down any remainder above the denominator.

Addition and Subtraction of Fractions

Addition/Subtraction when the denominator is same : You can add/subtract fractions easily if the bottom number (the denominator) is the same.

Example:

$$\frac{5}{8} \quad + \quad \frac{1}{8} \quad = \quad \frac{6}{8} \quad = \quad \frac{3}{4}$$

Addition/Subtraction when the denominator is different: When the denominator is not same, then we need to make the denominator same. The denominator can be made same by the following two methods:

❖ Common Denominator
❖ Least Common Multiple

Common Denominator: This method involves multiplying the given denominators together.

Example: $\dfrac{1}{3} + \dfrac{1}{6} = ?$

Multiplying the current denominators 3 and 6 we get, $3 \times 6 = 18$. Now instead of having 3 or 6 totals, we will have 18.

Thus, $\dfrac{6}{18} + \dfrac{3}{18} = \dfrac{9}{18}$

❖ The word "fraction" originates from the Latin word, "fractus", which means broken.

❖ Only improper fractions can be converted into mixed numbers.

❖ The bricks that were used to build the great bath in Indus valley civilization were in perfect $4:2:1$ ratio.

❖ Fractions were firstly used in the Indus Valley civilization, followed by the Egyptians and the Greeks.

❖ The Egyptians wrote numbers (based on tens) alongside pictures called hieroglyphs.

For example: $\dfrac{1}{3} + \dfrac{1}{15}$ would be represented as shown below:

Notice the man's feet is pointing towards the direction of writing (from left to right). When the feet pointing toward the direction of writing means add. Otherwise, it means subtract. In this case, it is pointing towards the direction of writing.

Also notice that there is a shape that looks like an open mouth (the ellipse). It refers to a fraction.

Misconcept/Concept

Misconcept: The fractions with numerator other than 1 are greater than 1.

Concept: You can't have a fraction that is bigger than one.

Misconcept: The bigger the number on the bottom, the bigger the fraction.

Concept: This is not true. The smaller the number on the denominator, the bigger will be the fraction. For example: $\frac{1}{2}$ is bigger than $\frac{1}{6}$.

Do You Know?

Converting a Mixed fraction onto improper fraction

For example: $4\,\frac{2}{3}$

$$= \frac{4 \times 3 + 2}{3}$$

$$= \frac{12 + 2}{3} = \frac{14}{3}$$

So, whole number part of mixed fraction is multiplied to denominator and numerator is added to get the numerator of final improper fraction.

Example : Convert $\frac{32}{5}$ into mixed fraction.

Solution:

So, $\frac{32}{5} = 6\,\frac{2}{5}$

Least Common Multiple: In the above example, 18 is a relatively larger number. Instead of using the common denominator way, we can also opt for least common multiple.

Here is how to find out:

$\frac{1}{3}$ List the multiples of 3: 3, **6**, 9 , 12, 15, 18, 21.....

$\frac{1}{6}$ List the multiples of 6: **6**, 12, 18, 24, 30, 36......

Then find the smallest number that is the same. The answer is 6, and that is the least common multiple.

❖ When we multiply top and bottom of $\frac{1}{3}$ by 2 we get $\frac{2}{6}$.

❖ $\frac{1}{6}$ already has a denominator of 6.

The question now looks like:

$$\frac{2}{6} + \frac{1}{6} = \frac{3}{6}$$

❖ Last step is to simplify the fraction (if possible). In this case $\frac{3}{6}$ is simpler as $\frac{1}{2}$.

Thus, the steps followed are:

1. Find the least common multiple of the denominators (which is called the Least Common Denominator).
2. Change each fraction (using equivalent fractions) to make their denominators the same as the least common denominator.
3. Then add (or subtract) the fractions.

MULTIPLICATION OF FRACTIONS

There are 3 simple steps to multiply fractions
1. Multiply the top numbers (the numerators).
2. Multiply the bottom numbers (the denominators).
3. Simplify the fraction if needed.

DIVISION OF FRACTIONS

There are 3 simple steps to divide fractions:
1. Turn the second fraction (the one you want to divide by) upside-down

   (this is now a reciprocal).
2. Multiply the first fraction by that reciprocal.
3. Simplify the fraction (if needed).

Multiple Choice Questions

LEVEL 1

1. Pick the odd one out.
   (a) $\dfrac{3}{8}$ (b) $\dfrac{4}{9}$
   (c) $\dfrac{6}{13}$ (d) $\dfrac{21}{5}$

2. Write $\dfrac{31}{8}$ as a mixed number.
   (a) 4 (b) $4\dfrac{7}{8}$
   (c) $3\dfrac{1}{8}$ (d) $3\dfrac{7}{8}$

3. A fraction A/B = 1, when
   [Mental Mathematics]
   (a) A>B
   (b) A<B
   (c) A=B
   (d) None of these

4. Express 400ml as a fraction of 1L.
   [Mental Mathematics]
   (a) $\dfrac{4}{10}$ (b) $\dfrac{3}{10}$
   (c) $\dfrac{5}{10}$ (d) $\dfrac{7}{10}$

5. Pick the odd one out.
   (a) $\dfrac{2}{5}$ (b) $\dfrac{3}{5}$
   (c) $\dfrac{8}{20}$ (d) $\dfrac{6}{15}$

6. Which two fractions are equivalent?
   (a) $\dfrac{5}{2}$ and $\dfrac{2}{5}$ (b) $\dfrac{4}{3}$ and $\dfrac{8}{6}$
   (c) $\dfrac{1}{4}$ and $\dfrac{2}{4}$ (d) $\dfrac{2}{3}$ and $\dfrac{1}{3}$

7. Simplify : $\dfrac{6}{9} \times \dfrac{6}{3}$ **[2015]**
   (a) $\dfrac{3}{4}$ (b) $\dfrac{4}{3}$
   (c) $\dfrac{1}{3}$ (d) $\dfrac{1}{4}$

8. Choose the incorrect option from the following:
   (a) $\dfrac{1}{2} = \dfrac{4}{8}$ (b) $\dfrac{1}{2} = \dfrac{6}{12}$
   (c) $\dfrac{1}{3} = \dfrac{5}{10}$ (d) $\dfrac{1}{3} = \dfrac{5}{15}$

9. Convert $12\dfrac{3}{11}$ into the improper fraction. **[2011]**
   (a) $\dfrac{121}{27}$ (b) $\dfrac{135}{11}$
   (c) $\dfrac{141}{11}$ (d) $\dfrac{111}{11}$

10. Evaluate $5\dfrac{2}{3} - 3\dfrac{1}{2} =$ **[Mental Mathematics]**
    (a) 2 (b) $2\dfrac{7}{6}$
    (c) $2\dfrac{1}{6}$ (d) $1\dfrac{2}{5}$

11. Convert the improper fraction $\dfrac{518}{27}$ into a mixed fraction. **[2012]**
    (a) $5\dfrac{19}{27}$ (b) $27\dfrac{19}{5}$
    (c) $19\dfrac{5}{27}$ (d) $27\dfrac{5}{19}$

12. Reduce the fraction to its lowest form: 9/15.
    (a) $\dfrac{3}{5}$ (b) $\dfrac{5}{3}$
    (c) $\dfrac{3}{15}$ (d) $\dfrac{5}{9}$

13. How many minutes are there in $\dfrac{2}{3}$ of an hour? **[Mental Mathematics]**
    (a) 40 minutes (b) 50 minutes
    (c) 60 minutes (d) 20 minutes

14. What will be the equivalent fraction of $\dfrac{3}{7}$ with denominator 63?
    (a) $\dfrac{21}{63}$ (b) $\dfrac{28}{63}$
    (c) $\dfrac{27}{63}$ (d) $\dfrac{25}{63}$

15. Which of the following numbers are arranged in ascending order?   [2018]

    (a) $\dfrac{7}{12}, \dfrac{8}{12}, \dfrac{10}{12}, \dfrac{9}{12}, \dfrac{11}{12}$

    (b) $\dfrac{3}{7}, \dfrac{4}{7}, \dfrac{5}{7}, \dfrac{8}{7}, \dfrac{10}{7}$

    (c) $\dfrac{11}{14}, \dfrac{10}{14}, \dfrac{8}{14}, \dfrac{6}{14}, \dfrac{3}{14}$

    (d) $\dfrac{15}{19}, \dfrac{13}{19}, \dfrac{10}{19}, \dfrac{7}{19}, \dfrac{9}{19}$

16. Mohan reaches school by a school bus in $\dfrac{3}{8}$ hours. If he walks to school it takes him $\dfrac{3}{4}$ hours. How much more time does it take him to walk to school than to go by bus?   [2019]

    (a) $\dfrac{5}{8}$ hours   (b) $\dfrac{3}{8}$ hours

    (c) 4 hours   (d) $\dfrac{9}{8}$ hours

17. Manoj reads $\dfrac{8}{9}$ of a book. If there are total 1431 pages in the book, then how many pages are left to be read?   [2020]

    (a) 140   (b) 113
    (c) 159   (d) 195

18. Find the missing number.   [2021]

    (a) 2
    (b) 3
    (c) 6
    (d) 4

19. Harshit won exactly $\dfrac{3}{5}$ of the ribbons for 1"place. Which of the following could be the group of ribbons Harshit won?   [2021]

(a) 

(b)

(c) 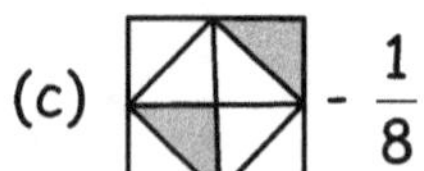

(d)

20. Select the correct sign to make the expression true.   [2022]

$$\dfrac{3}{4} + \dfrac{1}{6} - \dfrac{3}{7} \ \square \ \dfrac{1}{3} + \dfrac{17}{28}$$

    (a) >
    (b) <
    (c) =
    (d) Can't be determined

21. There were 1800 girls and 960 boys in a hall. An hour later, $\dfrac{7}{10}$ of the girls left the hall. How many children were in the hall after an hour?   [2022]

    (a) 1800   (b) 1500
    (c) 1700   (d) 1900

22. Select the CORRECT option for shaded fraction.   [2022]

    (a) $-\dfrac{5}{10}$ (b) $-\dfrac{4}{6}$

    (c) $-\dfrac{1}{8}$ (d) $-\dfrac{4}{9}$

23. Ankush had 500. He spent $\dfrac{1}{4}$ of the money. How much amount of money is left with him?   [2022]

    (a) ₹325   (b) ₹375
    (c) ₹125   (d) ₹295

LEVEL 2

1. If $\dfrac{1}{3} + \dfrac{1}{6} + \dfrac{1}{12} = X$, then $X + \dfrac{17}{12} = ?$

   (a) 4   (b) 3
   (c) 2   (d) 1

2. Write down the fraction of the coloured portion. [Mental Mathematics]

   (a) $\dfrac{7}{5}$ (b) $\dfrac{5}{7}$

   (c) $\dfrac{7}{12}$ (d) $\dfrac{5}{12}$

   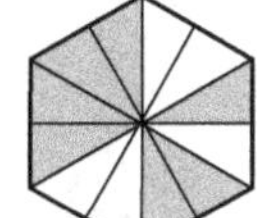

3. It takes Julia 1/2 hour to wash, comb her hair and put on her clothes, and 1/4 hour to have her breakfast. How much time does it take Julia to be ready for school?

   (a) $\dfrac{3}{4}$ hour   (b) $\dfrac{5}{4}$ hour

   (c) $\dfrac{2}{4}$ hour   (d) 1 hour

4. Big Chilli Pepper Restaurant uses the hottest peppers in its 3 Alarm Chilli. It accepts only best peppers from the produce market. Write a fraction that shows what part of this group of peppers that will be accepted.

   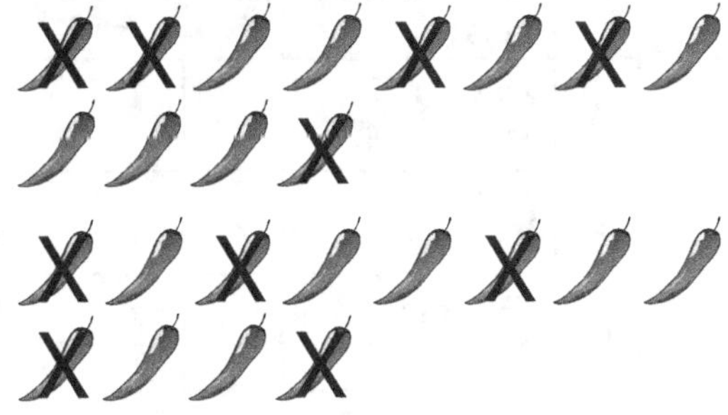

   (a) $\dfrac{7}{12}$ (b) $\dfrac{5}{12}$

   (c) $\dfrac{7}{24}$ (d) $\dfrac{5}{24}$

5. If $\dfrac{3}{4} = \dfrac{18}{d}; \dfrac{5}{8} = \dfrac{25}{e}; \dfrac{9}{11} = \dfrac{f}{66}; \dfrac{7}{8} = \dfrac{g}{64}.$

   [Critical Thinking]

List I		List II	
A.	d	1.	56
B.	e	2.	54
C.	f	3.	40
D.	g	4.	24

      A **B** **C** **D**

(a) 4   3   2   1
(b) 1   2   4   3
(c) 2   3   1   4
(d) 3   1   2   4

Direction (Qs. 6 to 11): Evaluate the following questions

6. $\dfrac{2}{5} \times \dfrac{3}{4} \times \dfrac{5}{8}$ [Mental Mathematics]

   (a) $\dfrac{3}{8}$ (b) $\dfrac{3}{7}$

   (c) $\dfrac{3}{16}$ (d) $\dfrac{6}{20}$

7. $\dfrac{3}{8} \times \dfrac{7}{10} \times \dfrac{5}{12}$ [Mental Mathematics]

   (a) $\dfrac{7}{64}$ (b) $\dfrac{7}{81}$

   (c) $\dfrac{21}{64}$ (d) $\dfrac{105}{84}$

8. $\left[2\dfrac{1}{2}\right] / \left[3\dfrac{3}{4}\right]$

   (a) $\dfrac{8}{75}$ (b) $1\dfrac{1}{2}$

   (c) $\dfrac{2}{3}$ (d) $9\dfrac{3}{8}$

9. $\left[\dfrac{3}{8}\right] / \left[\dfrac{5}{12}\right]$ [Mental Mathematics]

   (a) $1\dfrac{1}{9}$ (b) $\dfrac{5}{32}$

   (c) $\dfrac{4}{5}$ (d) $\dfrac{9}{10}$

10. $\left[\dfrac{15}{4}\right] / \left[\dfrac{5}{9}\right]$

    (a) $6\dfrac{3}{4}$ (b) $2\dfrac{1}{12}$

    (c) $\dfrac{12}{25}$ (d) $\dfrac{4}{27}$

11. $\left[\frac{2}{15}\right]/\left[\frac{3}{5}\right]$

    (a) $\frac{2}{11}$ (b) $\frac{2}{25}$

    (c) $4\frac{1}{2}$ (d) $\frac{2}{9}$

12. Out of 20 people in a line for ice cream, one-quarter want vanilla. How many people want vanilla ice cream?   [2008]

    (a) 5 people   (b) 4 people
    (c) 6 people   (d) 8 people

13. Of the 8 students in Mrs. Barr's art class, six-eighths are in sixth grade. How many sixth graders are in Mrs. Barr's art class?

    (a) 1   (b) 8
    (c) 6   (d) 5

14. Which one of the following is a set of equivalent fractions?   [2014]

    (a) $\left[\frac{1}{95}, \frac{3}{190}\right]$ (b) $\left[\frac{5}{95}, \frac{15}{190}\right]$

    (c) $\left[\frac{17}{95}, \frac{51}{285}\right]$ (d) $\left[\frac{5}{110}, \frac{15}{150}\right]$

15. Of the 16 students on a field trip to a museum, one-fourth brought their lunch. How many students did not brought their lunch?

    (a) 4   (b) 12
    (c) 6   (d) 10

16. In the figure given below two arms intersect each other. Fill in the blank with correct number so that the sum of each arm is the same.   [2016]

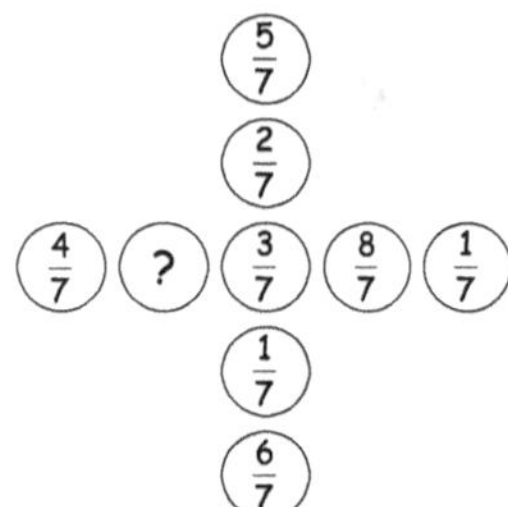

    (a) $\frac{5}{7}$ (b) $\frac{3}{7}$

    (c) $\frac{1}{7}$ (d) $\frac{2}{7}$

17. There are 12 berries in a bowl on the counter. Two-sixths of them are raspberries. How many raspberries are in the bowl?   [Tricky]

    (a) 5   (b) 8
    (c) 4   (d) 6

18. What number should go in the box to make the statement true?   [2010]

    $$\frac{1}{2} = \frac{\Box}{8}$$

    (a) 8   (b) 6
    (c) 4   (d) 2

19. Jaya counted 8 students in the choir. Three-quarters of the students have brown hair. How many students in the choir have brown hair?

    (a) 4 students   (b) 5 students
    (c) 6 students   (d) 7 students

20. Which list shows the fractions in order from the greatest to the least?

    [2011, Tricky]

    (a) $\frac{7}{10} > \frac{7}{9} > \frac{7}{8}$ (b) $\frac{7}{9} > \frac{7}{8} > \frac{7}{10}$

    (c) $\frac{7}{8} > \frac{7}{9} > \frac{7}{10}$ (d) $\frac{7}{10} > \frac{7}{8} > \frac{7}{9}$

21. Match the following: [Critical Thinking]

List I		List II	
A.	$\left(\frac{3}{7}\right)/\left(\frac{5}{14}\right)$	1.	2
B.	$\left(\frac{1}{4}\right)/\left(\frac{1}{8}\right)$	2.	7
C.	$(8)/\left[1\frac{1}{7}\right]$	3.	$\frac{26}{9}$
D.	$\left[3\frac{1}{4}\right]/\left[1\frac{1}{8}\right]$	4.	$\frac{6}{5}$

	A	B	C	D
(a)	1	3	2	4
(b)	2	1	3	4
(c)	4	1	2	3
(d)	1	2	3	4

22. Which of the following is/are false? [Tricky]

A. $\frac{5}{3}$ is an improper fraction.

B. $\frac{3}{8}$ is a proper fraction.

C. $2\frac{3}{5}$ is a mixed fraction

(a) A, B
(b) B, C
(c) C, A
(d) None of these

23. Find the like fraction from below ________. [2013]

$$\frac{3}{8}, \frac{5}{7}, \frac{6}{12}, \frac{4}{9}, \frac{5}{8}, \frac{7}{11}, \frac{5}{17}, \frac{4}{19}$$

(a) $\frac{5}{8}$ and $\frac{3}{8}$
(b) $\frac{4}{9}$ and $\frac{4}{19}$
(c) $\frac{6}{12}$ and $\frac{7}{11}$
(d) $\frac{5}{7}$ and $\frac{5}{17}$

24. If the shaded area has a value of $\frac{1}{3}$, what is the value of the whole shape? [Critical Thinking]

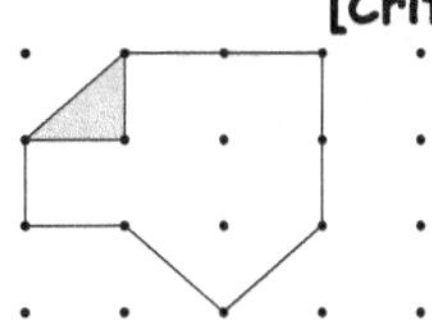

(a) $\frac{12}{5}$
(b) $\frac{13}{3}$
(c) $\frac{13}{4}$
(d) $\frac{13}{5}$

25. Mrs. Edwards bought a large pizza. A large pizza has 12 slices. If her daughter, Andrea, ate two slices, what fraction of the pizza was left? [2009]

(a) $\frac{5}{6}$
(b) $\frac{6}{5}$
(c) $\frac{2}{3}$
(d) $\frac{3}{5}$

26. Paul put 20 flowers in a vase on the table. Two-tenths are yellow roses. How many yellow roses are in the vase?

(a) 4 yellow roses
(b) 8 yellow roses
(c) 2 yellow roses
(d) 12 yellow roses

27. To have $a + 1\frac{3}{4} = 2$, a must be equal to [2009]

(a) $\frac{1}{8}$
(b) $\frac{1}{4}$
(c) $\frac{2}{4}$
(d) $\frac{1}{3}$

28. If $A = \frac{1}{4}$, $B = \frac{2}{7}$ and $C = \frac{1}{3}$, then [Critical Thinking]

1. A>B
2. B<C
3. A<C

Which of the statements are true?

(a) 1, 2
(b) 2, 3
(c) 3, 1
(d) 1, 2, 3

29. What fraction is the shaded part? [2010]

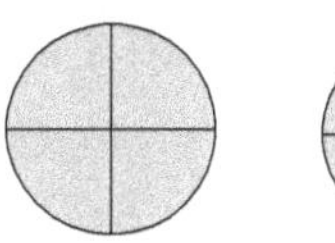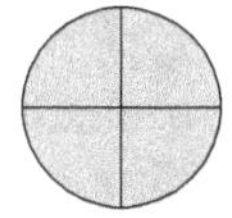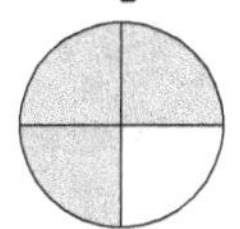

(a) 2
(b) $1\frac{1}{2}$
(c) $2\frac{3}{4}$
(d) $1\frac{3}{4}$

30. Four-sevenths of the 70 crayons Daya and Chaaya were using were broken. How many crayons were broken? [2010]

(a) 28 crayons
(b) 40 crayons
(c) 48 crayons
(d) 25 crayons

Direction (Qs. 31 and 32): Study the diagram and answer the following questions.

31. What is the fraction of lit bulbs?

(a) $\frac{4}{8}$
(b) $\frac{4}{7}$
(c) $\frac{4}{16}$
(d) $\frac{16}{7}$

32. What is the fraction of diffused bulbs?

    (a) $\dfrac{5}{7}$ (b) $\dfrac{3}{28}$

    (c) $\dfrac{12}{7}$ (d) $\dfrac{3}{7}$

33. What fraction of boxes in the given grid are red in colour.   [2010]

    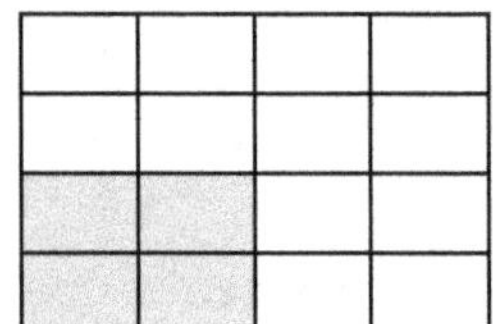

    (a) $\dfrac{1}{4}$ (b) $\dfrac{1}{8}$

    (c) $\dfrac{4}{8}$ (d) $\dfrac{1}{16}$

34. Billy ate $1\dfrac{1}{4}$ pizzas and John ate $1\dfrac{2}{3}$ pizzas. How much more pizza did John eat than Billy?

    (a) $\dfrac{2}{3}$ (b) $\dfrac{5}{12}$

    (c) $\dfrac{1}{4}$ (d) $\dfrac{7}{12}$

35. Robert and Davison walked past 15 cars in the parking garage. Two-thirds of the cars had bumper stickers. How many of those cars had bumper stickers?   [2011]

    (a) 3 cars   (b) 6 cars
    (c) 2 cars   (d) 10 cars

36. If $3\dfrac{3}{4} + 2\dfrac{5}{6} = x\dfrac{y}{z}$, then   [Tricky]

    (a) $x = 6, y = 12, z = 7$
    (b) $x = 12, y = 7, z = 6$
    (c) $x = 6, y = 7, z = 12$
    (d) None of these

37. If $x = \dfrac{5}{12}$, $y = \dfrac{17}{24}$, $z = \dfrac{11}{18}$, then

    [Critical Thinking]

    A. x, z, y are in ascending order.
    B. y, z, x are in descending order.
    Which of the statement is true?

    (a) A
    (b) B
    (c) A and B
    (d) Neither A nor B

38. The total number of children in a class is 40. 7 children were absent on Monday. What fraction of the class was present on Monday?   [2015]

    (a) $\dfrac{7}{40}$ (b) $\dfrac{33}{40}$

    (c) $\dfrac{40}{7}$ (d) $\dfrac{40}{33}$

39. David, Mary, and Khalid are among 18 people waiting for the bus. Seven-ninths of them have an umbrella. How many people waiting for the bus have an umbrella?   [Tricky]

    (a) 12 people   (b) 9 people
    (c) 7 people   (d) 14 people

Direction (Qs. 40 and 41): Read the following information and answer the given questions.

In Mr. Nussbaum's class, $\dfrac{1}{6}$ of all students have blonde hair, $\dfrac{2}{6}$ of all students have brown hair, and $\dfrac{3}{6}$ of all students have black hair.

40. What fraction of students have either blond or brown hair?

    (a) $\dfrac{1}{4}$ (b) $\dfrac{1}{2}$

    (c) $\dfrac{1}{3}$ (d) $\dfrac{1}{6}$

41. What fraction of students have black or blonde hair?

    (a) $\dfrac{2}{5}$ (b) $\dfrac{2}{7}$

    (c) $\dfrac{2}{6}$ (d) $\dfrac{2}{3}$

42. Aiyana put 8 plates in the cupboard. One-half of them are blue. How many blue plates are in the cupboard?

    (a) 4 blue plates   (b) 6 blue plates
    (c) 8 blue plates   (d) 2 blue plates

43. If $A = \dfrac{3}{10} + \dfrac{7}{15}$; $B = \dfrac{5}{9} + \dfrac{7}{12}$ then

    [Tricky]

    (a) $A = B$ (b) $A > B$
    (c) $A < B$ (d) None of these

44. Who among the following students made the CORRECT statement?

    [2016, Critical Thinking]

Samrath : $\dfrac{2}{9}$ and $\dfrac{4}{18}$ are equivalent fractions.

Kavleen : Two fractions are equivalent when they have same denominators.

Mohit : Two fractions are equivalent when they have same value.

(a) Samrath and Kavleen
(b) Kavleen and Mohit
(c) Samrath and Mohit
(d) All are correct.

45. Which of the following options has the same shaded fraction as the unshaded fraction of given figure. **[2018]**

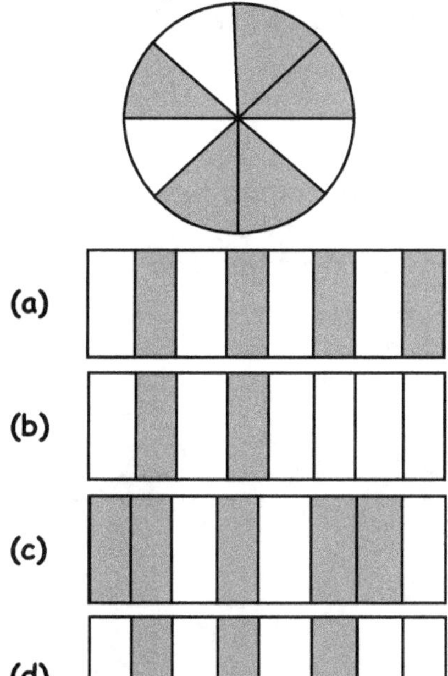

46. Fill in the blanks:

- There were 40 children at a party, 14 of them were boys. <u>P</u> fraction of children were girls.

- Cost of a teddy bear is $\dfrac{2}{3}$ of the cost of a doll. If cost of the teddy bear is ₹114, then cost of the doll is ₹ <u>Q</u>.

- Difference between $3\dfrac{1}{4}$ and $2\dfrac{3}{8}$ is <u>R</u>.

- If $x+\dfrac{5}{12}=\dfrac{7}{6}$, then x = <u>S</u>. **[2018]**

	P	Q	R	S
(a)	$\dfrac{7}{20}$	76	$\dfrac{5}{8}$	$\dfrac{1}{4}$
(b)	$\dfrac{13}{20}$	76	$\dfrac{7}{8}$	$\dfrac{1}{4}$
(c)	$\dfrac{7}{20}$	171	$\dfrac{5}{8}$	$\dfrac{3}{4}$
(d)	$\dfrac{13}{20}$	171	$\dfrac{7}{8}$	$\dfrac{3}{4}$

47. Which of the following shows $\dfrac{9}{8}-\dfrac{5}{8}$ shaded part? **[2020]**

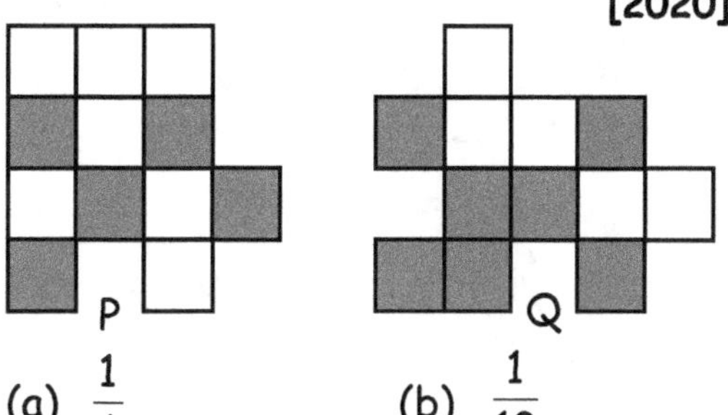

(a)   (b)   (c)   (d)

48. Find the difference between the shaded fractions of the given figures. **[2020]**

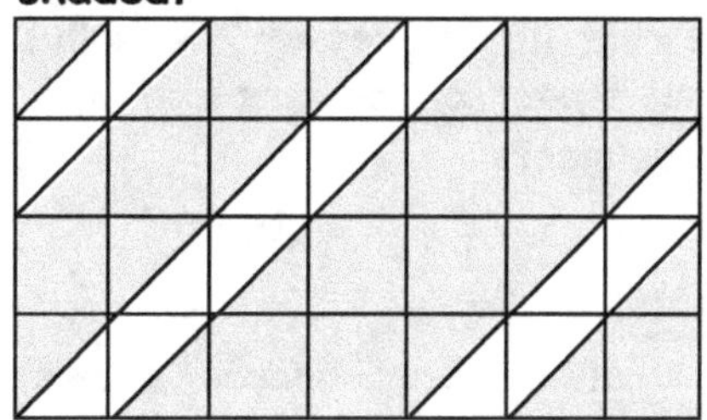

(a) $\dfrac{1}{6}$ (b) $\dfrac{1}{12}$

(c) $\dfrac{1}{4}$ (d) $\dfrac{1}{3}$

49. What fraction of the given figure is shaded? **[2021]**

(a) $\dfrac{1}{2}$ (b) $\dfrac{4}{7}$

(c) $\dfrac{3}{7}$ (d) $\dfrac{5}{7}$

50. Kaushal spent $\dfrac{5}{10}$ of his monthly salary on house rent, $\dfrac{3}{10}$ on groceries and saved the rest. What fraction of his salary was saved in a month? **[2021]**

    (a) $\dfrac{7}{10}$

    (b) $\dfrac{3}{10}$

    (c) $\dfrac{3}{5}$

    (d) $\dfrac{1}{5}$

51. Find the sum of the shaded fractions of the given figures. **[2021]**

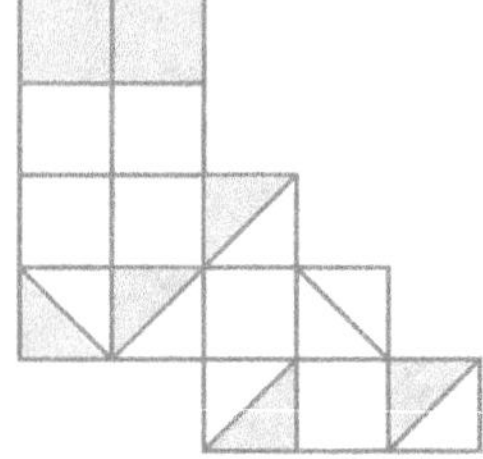 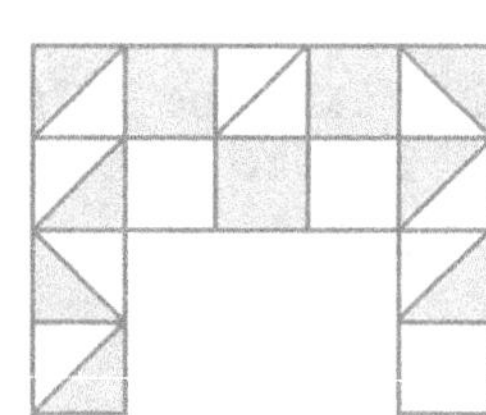

    (a) $\dfrac{5}{7}$

    (b) $\dfrac{6}{7}$

    (c) $\dfrac{4}{7}$

    (d) $\dfrac{3}{7}$

52. Divya baked 255 cookies. She packed $\dfrac{2}{5}$ of them into boxes of 6 equally and the rest into boxes of 3 equally. How many boxes of cookies did she pack altogether? **[2022]**

    (a) 65

    (b) 68

    (c) 63

    (d) 67

53. The given bar graph shows the number of children in all the families staying in Beverly Apartments. **[2022]**

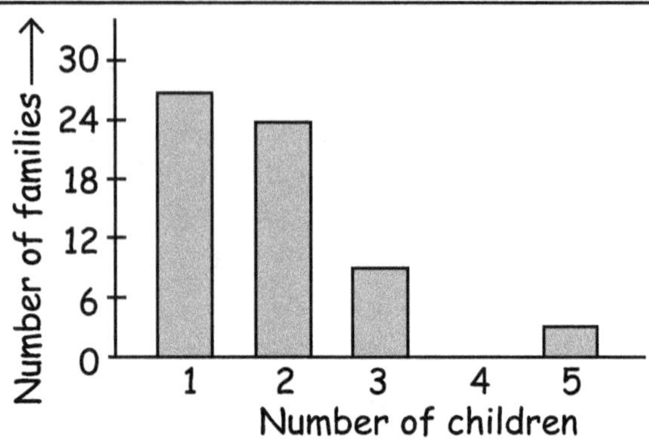

The number of families which have _________ children is $\dfrac{1}{3}$ of the number of families which have 1 child. **[2022]**

    (a) 2

    (b) 3

    (c) 4

    (d) 5

54. Find the difference between the fractions representing the shaded parts of the given figures. **[2022]**

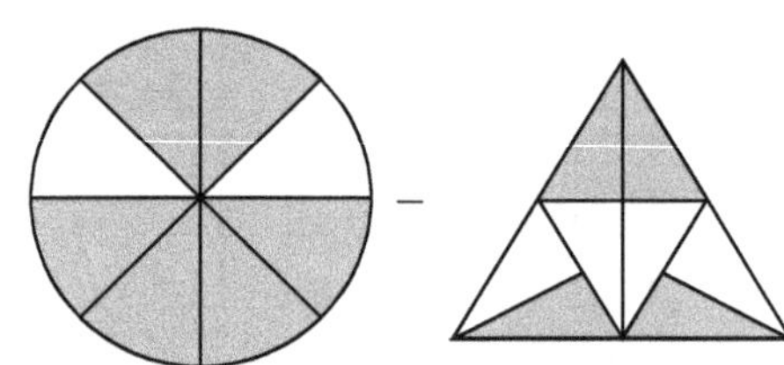

    (a) $\dfrac{1}{8}$

    (b) $\dfrac{3}{8}$

    (c) $\dfrac{1}{4}$

    (d) $\dfrac{1}{2}$

55. In which one of the following figures, the fraction represented by shaded parts is more than the fraction represented by shaded parts in 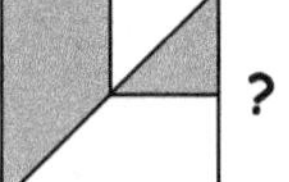 ? **[2022]**

    (a) 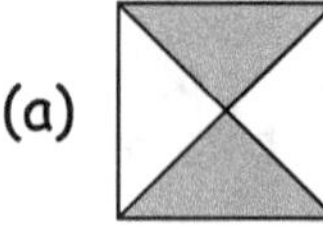

    (b) 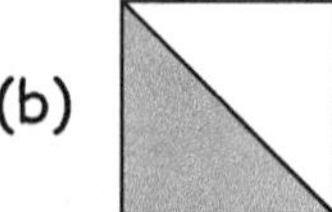

    (c) 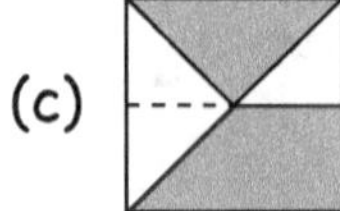

    (d) 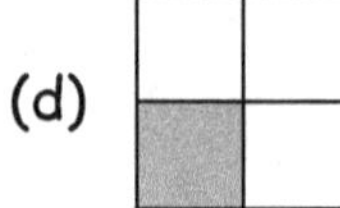

56. Find the odd one out. [2022]

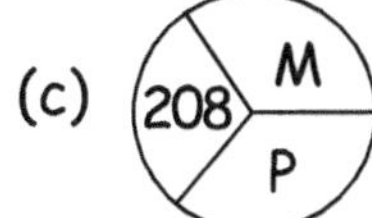

(a) 88 H K (b) 84 L H (c) 208 M P (d) 380 S T

57. Identify the number which will replace the question mark(?)? [2022]

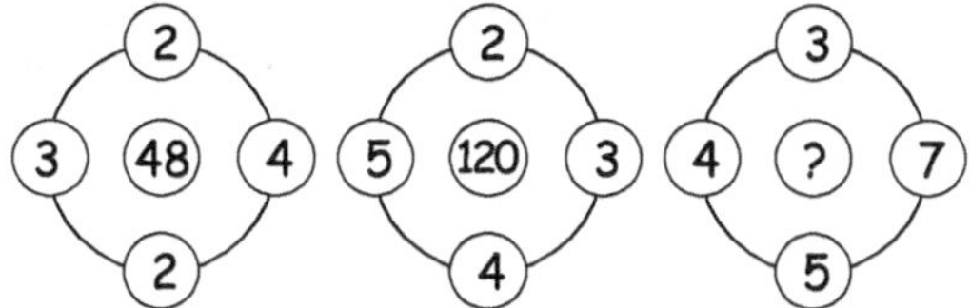

(a) 386 **(b)** 420
(c) 428 **(d)** 468

58. Decimal number for the fraction represented by the unshaded parts of the given figure is: [2022]

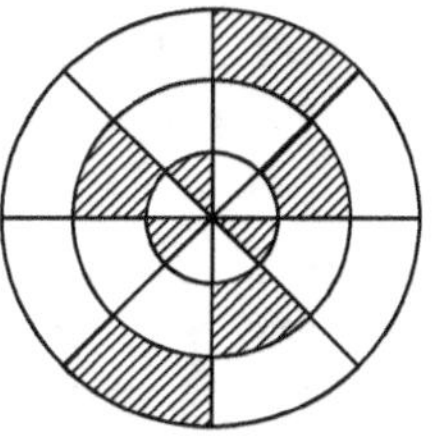

(a) 0.250 **(b)** 0.500
(c) 0.375 **(d)** 0.625

RESPONSE GRID

LEVEL 1

1. a b c d   2. a b c d   3. a b c d   4. a b c d   5. a b c d
6. a b c d   7. a b c d   8. a b c d   9. a b c d   10. a b c d
11. a b c d   12. a b c d   13. a b c d   14. a b c d   15. a b c d
16. a b c d   17. a b c d   18. a b c d   19. a b c d   20. a b c d
21. a b c d   22. a b c d   23. a b c d

LEVEL 2

1. a b c d   2. a b c d   3. a b c d   4. a b c d   5. a b c d
6. a b c d   7. a b c d   8. a b c d   9. a b c d   10. a b c d
11. a b c d   12. a b c d   13. a b c d   14. a b c d   15. a b c d
16. a b c d   17. a b c d   18. a b c d   19. a b c d   20. a b c d
21. a b c d   22. a b c d   23. a b c d   24. a b c d   25. a b c d
26. a b c d   27. a b c d   28. a b c d   29. a b c d   30. a b c d
31. a b c d   32. a b c d   33. a b c d   34. a b c d   35. a b c d
36. a b c d   37. a b c d   38. a b c d   39. a b c d   40. a b c d
41. a b c d   42. a b c d   43. a b c d   44. a b c d   45. a b c d
46. a b c d   47. a b c d   48. a b c d   49. a b c d   50. a b c d
51. a b c d   52. a b c d   53. a b c d   54. a b c d   55. a b c d
56. a b c d   57. a b c d   58. a b c d

Solutions with Explanation

LEVEL 1

1. **(d)** $\frac{21}{5}$ is the odd one out since it is the only improper fraction given in the options.

2. **(d)** When we divide 31 by 8, we get 7 as remainder and 3 as dividend, thus the mixed fraction would be Dividend + Remainder/Divisor
$$= 3 + \frac{7}{8} \text{ or } 3\frac{7}{8}.$$

3. **(c)** $\frac{A}{B} = 1$ only when both the numerator and the denominator are same i.e. A = B.

4. **(a)** 1 litre= 1000 ml. 400 ml as a fraction of 1 L $= \frac{400}{1000} = \frac{4}{10}$

5. **(b)** $\frac{2}{5} = \frac{6}{15} = \frac{8}{20}$. Thus $\frac{3}{5}$ is the odd one out.

6. **(b)** $\frac{4}{3}$ and $\frac{8}{6}$ are equivalent fractions. When we simplify $\frac{8}{6}$, we get $\frac{4}{3}$.

7. **(b)** As $\frac{6}{9} \times \frac{6}{3} = \frac{6 \times 6}{9 \times 3} = \frac{36}{27} = \frac{4}{3}$

8. **(c)** $\frac{1}{3}$ is not equivalent to $\frac{5}{10}$. $\frac{5}{10}$ on simplification is equivalent to $\frac{1}{2}$.

9. **(b)** $12\frac{3}{11} = \frac{12 \times 11 + 3}{11} = \frac{135}{11}$

10. **(c)** $5\frac{2}{3} - 3\frac{1}{2} = \frac{17}{3} - \frac{7}{2} = \frac{13}{6} = 2\frac{1}{6}$

11. **(c)** $\frac{518}{27} = 19\frac{5}{27}$

12. **(a)** The lowest form of the fraction is $\frac{3}{5}$. Since both these numbers are divisible by 3, when divided yield the fraction $\frac{3}{5}$.

13. **(a)** Number of minutes in 1 hour = 60, Minutes in $\frac{2}{3}$ of 1 hour
$$= \frac{2}{3} \times 60 = 40 \text{ minutes.}$$

14. **(c)** The equivalent fraction of $\frac{3}{7} = \frac{\square}{63}$. When we multiply 7 by 9 we get 63, thus multiplying the numerator be 9 too, we get 27. Thus the equivalent fraction will be $\frac{27}{63}$.

15. **(b)** $\frac{3}{7}, \frac{4}{7}, \frac{5}{7}, \frac{8}{7}, \frac{10}{7}$

16. **(b)** Difference $= \left(\frac{3}{4} - \frac{3}{8}\right)$ hours
$$= \frac{6-3}{8} = \frac{3}{8} \text{ hours}$$

17. **(c)** Total pages in a book = 1431

Portion of book completed $\frac{8}{9}$

book $= 1431 \times \frac{8}{9}$
$$= 1272$$

Remaining pages = 1431 – 1272
(left to be read) = 159 pages

18. **(a)** $6 \times 3 = 18$
$3 \times 2 = 6$

19. **(a)**

20. **(b)** $\frac{3}{4} + \frac{1}{6} - \frac{3}{7} \ \square \ \frac{1}{3} + \frac{17}{28}$

$\frac{22}{24} - \frac{3}{7} \ \square \ \frac{79}{28}$

$\frac{85}{168} \ \square \ \frac{79}{84}$

$\frac{41}{84} < \frac{79}{84}$

21. **(b)** Boys in a hall = 960
Girls in a hall = 1800

$\frac{7}{10}$ of the total number of girls

$$= \frac{7 \times 1800}{10} = 1260$$

Remaining number of girls in a hall
$$= 1800 - 1260 = 540$$
Total number of remaining students
$$= 960 + 540 = 1500$$

22. **(a)**

LEVEL 2

1. **(c)** We have $X = \frac{1}{3} + \frac{1}{6} + \frac{1}{12} = \frac{7}{12}$; Now
$$X + \frac{17}{12} = \frac{7}{12} + \frac{17}{12} = \frac{24}{12} = 2.$$

2. **(c)** Number of colored triangles = 7. Total triangles = 12.

Fraction of colored triangles = $\frac{7}{12}$.

3. **(a)** Time taken by Julia to be ready for school = $\left(\frac{1}{2} + \frac{1}{4}\right)$ hour = $\frac{3}{4}$ hour.

4. **(a)** $\frac{7}{12}$. Number of accepted chilies = 14; Total chilies = 24, Fraction of accepted chilies = Number of accepted chilies/Total chilies
$$= \frac{14}{24} = \frac{7}{12}.$$

5. **(a)**

6. **(c)** $\frac{2}{5} \times \frac{3}{4} \times \frac{5}{8} = \frac{3}{16}$. [Hint: first multiply any two fractions and then multiply its product with the third number]

7. **(a)** $\frac{3}{8} \times \frac{7}{10} \times \frac{5}{12} = \frac{7}{64}$

$$\left[\frac{7}{10} \times \frac{5}{12} = \frac{7}{24}; \frac{7}{24} \times \frac{3}{8} = \frac{7}{64}\right].$$

8. **(c)** $[2\frac{1}{2}] / [3\frac{3}{4}] = [\frac{5}{2}] / [\frac{15}{4}]$
$$= \frac{5}{2} \times \frac{4}{15} = \frac{2}{3}.$$

9. **(d)** $[\frac{3}{8}] / [\frac{5}{12}] = \frac{3}{8} \times \frac{12}{5} = \frac{9}{10}.$

10. **(a)** $[\frac{15}{4}] / [\frac{5}{9}] = \frac{15}{4} \times \frac{9}{5} = \frac{27}{4}$. Converting it into mixed fraction, we get $6\frac{3}{4}$.

11. **(d)** $[\frac{2}{15}] / [\frac{3}{5}] = \frac{2}{15} \times \frac{5}{3} = \frac{2}{9}.$

23. **(b)** Total money Ankash had = ₹500

Money spent $= \frac{1}{4}$ of total money
$$= ₹500 \times \frac{1}{4} = ₹125$$
Remaining money ₹500 – ₹125
$$= ₹375$$

12. **(a)** People who want vanilla ice-cream = Number of people in the line × Fraction of people wanting vanilla ice-cream = $20 \times \frac{1}{4} = 5.$

13. **(c)** Number of sixth graders in Mrs. Barr's art class = total students × fraction of students in sixth class
$$= 8 \times \frac{6}{8} = 6.$$

14. **(b)** $\frac{17}{95} = \frac{17 \times 3}{95 \times 3} = \frac{51}{285}$

15. **(b)** Number of students who did not brought their lunch = total number of students – number of students who got their lunch.

Number of students who brought their lunch = total students × fraction
$$= 16 \times \frac{1}{4} = 4.$$
Number of students who did not brought their lunch = 16 - 4 = 12.

16. **(c)** As $\frac{5}{7} + \frac{2}{7} + \frac{3}{7} + \frac{1}{7} + \frac{6}{7} = \frac{17}{17}$

So $\frac{4}{7} + \frac{1}{7} + \frac{3}{7} + \frac{8}{7} + \frac{1}{7} = \frac{17}{7}$

∴ Answer is $\frac{1}{7}$.

17. **(c)** Number of raspberries in the bowl = Total berries × fraction of raspberries
$$= 12 \times \frac{2}{6} = 4.$$

18. **(c)** $\frac{1}{2} = \frac{1 \times 4}{2 \times 4} = \frac{4}{8}$. So answer is 4.

19. **(c)** Students with brown hair = Number of students × fraction of students with brown hair = $8 \times \frac{3}{4} = 6.$

20. **(c)** $\dfrac{7}{8} > \dfrac{7}{9} > \dfrac{7}{10}$ is order from the greatest to the least.

21. **(c)**

22. **(d)** All the statements are true.

23. **(a)** $\dfrac{5}{8}$ and $\dfrac{3}{8}$ are like fractions.

24. **(b)** There are 13 halves in this shape. $13 \times \dfrac{1}{3} = \dfrac{13}{3}$.

25. **(a)** Number of pieces in pizza = 12, Pieces eaten = 2; pieces left = 12 - 2 = 10, Fraction of pieces left = $\dfrac{10}{12} = \dfrac{5}{6}$.

26. **(a)** Total number of yellow roses in the vase= Number of roses in the vase × fraction of yellow roses = $\dfrac{2}{10} \times 20 = 4$.

27. **(b)** $a + 1\dfrac{3}{4} = 2$; $a = 2 - 1\dfrac{3}{4} = 2 - \dfrac{7}{4} = \dfrac{8-7}{4} = \dfrac{1}{4}$.

28. **(b)** As it can be seen that $A = \dfrac{1}{4}$, $B = \dfrac{2}{7}$, $C = \dfrac{1}{3}$. Arranging these in the ascending order, we get $C > B > A$ i.e $\dfrac{1}{3} > \dfrac{2}{7} > \dfrac{1}{4}$. Thus the two options viz. B < C and A < C are correct.

29. **(c)** Two circles are fully shaded whereas third circle is shaded $\dfrac{3}{4}$. Thus total shaded portion is $2 + \dfrac{3}{4} = 2\dfrac{3}{4}$.

30. **(b)** Broken crayons = Total crayons × Fraction of broken crayons = $\dfrac{4}{7} \times 70 = 40$.

31. **(b)** Total number of bulbs = 28; Number of lit bulbs = 16; Fraction of lit bulbs = $\dfrac{16}{28}$ or $\dfrac{4}{7}$.

32. **(d)** Total number of bulbs = 28; Number of diffused bulbs = 12; Fraction of diffused bulbs = $\dfrac{12}{28}$ or $\dfrac{3}{7}$.

33. **(a)** Number of boxes in the grid = 16. Number of red boxes = 4. Thus fraction of red coloured boxes = $\dfrac{4}{16}$ or $\dfrac{1}{4}$.

34. **(b)** Pizza eaten by Billy = $1\dfrac{1}{4} = \dfrac{5}{4}$; Pizza eaten by John = $1\dfrac{2}{3} = \dfrac{5}{3}$. Fraction of Pizza eaten more by John than Billy = $\dfrac{5}{3} - \dfrac{5}{4} = \dfrac{5}{12}$.

35. **(d)** Number of Cars with bumper stickers = Total number of cars × fraction of cars with bumper stickers = $15 \times \dfrac{2}{3} = 10$.

36. **(c)** $3\dfrac{3}{4} + 2\dfrac{5}{6} = \dfrac{15}{4} + \dfrac{17}{6}$ $= 45 + \dfrac{34}{12} = \dfrac{79}{12} = 6\dfrac{7}{12}$.

37. **(a)** $\dfrac{5}{12} > \dfrac{11}{18} > \dfrac{17}{24}$. These are arranged according to the ascending order.

38. **(b)** $\dfrac{33}{40}$ is the fraction of the class present on Monday.

39. **(d)** People waiting for the bus having an umbrella = Total number of people × Fraction of people with umbrella = $18 \times \dfrac{7}{9} = 14$.

40. **(b)** Students having either blond or brown hair = Number of students with blond hair + Number of students with brown hair = $\dfrac{1}{6} + \dfrac{2}{6} = \dfrac{3}{6} = \dfrac{1}{2}$.

41. **(d)** Fraction of students have black or blonde hair = Number of students with black hair + Number of students with blonde hair = $\dfrac{3}{6} + \dfrac{1}{6} = \dfrac{4}{6} = \dfrac{2}{3}$.

42. **(a)** Number of blue plates in the cupboard = Total plates × fraction of blue plates = $8 \times \dfrac{1}{2} = 4$.

43. **(c)** $A = \dfrac{3}{10} + \dfrac{7}{15} = \dfrac{23}{30}$; $B = \dfrac{41}{36}$. Clearly it can be seen that $A < B$.

44. **(c)**   **45.** **(d)**

46. **(d)** Girls $= \dfrac{26}{40} = \dfrac{13}{20}$

Cost of doll $= 114 \times \dfrac{3}{2} = 171$

$3\dfrac{1}{4} - 2\dfrac{3}{8} = \dfrac{7}{8}$

$x = \dfrac{7}{6} - \dfrac{5}{12} = \dfrac{9}{12} = \dfrac{3}{4}$

47. **(b)** $\dfrac{9}{8} - \dfrac{5}{8} = \dfrac{4}{8} = \dfrac{1}{2}$

Option B's figure is half shaded

48. **(a)** Shaded fraction of figure P $= \dfrac{5}{12}$

Shaded fraction of figure Q $= \dfrac{7}{12}$

Difference between the shaded fractions of both the figures

$= \dfrac{7}{12} - \dfrac{5}{12} = \dfrac{2}{12} = \dfrac{1}{6}$

49. **(d)** Shaded area of Figure.

Number of fully shaded squares = 12

Number of half shaded squares = 16

So, Total number of shaded squares $= 12 + \dfrac{16}{2} = 20$

Total number of square in figure = 28

So shaded area of figure

$= \dfrac{20}{28} = \dfrac{5}{7}$

50. **(d)** Salary spent on house rent $= \dfrac{5}{10}$

Salary spent on groceries $= \dfrac{3}{10}$

Total spend salary

$= \dfrac{5}{10} + \dfrac{3}{10} = \dfrac{8}{10}$

Salary saved salary in month

$= 1 - \dfrac{8}{10} = \dfrac{2}{10} = \dfrac{1}{5}$

51. **(d)** Fully shaded squares = 5

half shaded squares = 14

Total shaded squares

$= 5 + \dfrac{14}{2} = 12$

Total squares in both figures = 14 + 14 = 28

So shaded fraction of the given

figures $= \dfrac{12}{28} = \dfrac{3}{7}$

52. **(b)** Total number of cookies = 255

215 of total cookies

$= \dfrac{2}{5} \times 255 = 102$

Number of boxes of 6 cookies

each $= \dfrac{102}{6} = 17$

Remaining cookies

$= \dfrac{3 \times 255}{5} = 153$

Number of boxes of 3 cookies

each $= \dfrac{153}{3} = 51$

Total number of boxes packed = 17 + 51 = 68

53. **(b)** The number of families which have 1 child = 27

Let the families with 1 child are represented by A

The number of families which have 3 children = 9

Let the families with 3 children are represented by B

Family B is 1/3 of family A

So, The number of families which have 3 children is 1/3 of the number of families which have 1 child.

54. **(c)**

55. **(c)**

56. **(b)**

57. **(b)**

58. **(c)**

$$3.8 - 1.26$$

$$
\begin{array}{r}
3.80 \\
-\ 1.26 \\
\hline
\end{array}
$$

← Stick a zero in there so you can do your borrowing (regrouping)!

$$
\begin{array}{r}
3.8^{7}10 \\
-\ 1.26 \\
\hline
2.54
\end{array}
$$

$$3.21 + 4.5$$

Line up the decimal point...

$$
\begin{array}{r}
3.21 \\
+\ 4.5 \\
\hline
7.71
\end{array}
$$

Add as usual!

and just drag the decimal point straight down!

9 Chapter

Decimals

LEARNING OBJECTIVES

This lesson will help you to:—

* study about the concept of decimals.
* study about the conversion of a fraction into a decimal.
* learn to compare the fractions.
* study about the basic mathematical functions of decimals.

QUICK CONCEPT REVIEW

What are decimals?

* Decimals are also a way of expressing whole numbers like fractions and percentage.
* Decimals are used in situations which require more precision than whole numbers can provide. Three and one-fourth dollars is an amount between 3 dollars and 4 dollars. We use decimals to write this amount as $3.25.
* A decimal may have both a whole-number part and a fractional part. The whole-number part of a decimal is those digits to the left of the decimal point. The fractional part of a decimal is represented by the digits to the right of the decimal point. The decimal point is used to separate these parts.
* Decimal is denoted by a small dot (.)

  Examples:

decimal	whole-number part	fractional part
3.25	3	25
4.172	4	172
0.168	0	168

PLACE VALUE AND DECIMALS

millions	hundred thousands	ten thousands	thousands	hundreds	tens	ones	and	tenths	hundredths	thousandths	ten-thousandths	hundred-thousandths	millionths
					5	7	.	4	9				

❖ The zeros before the whole part and the zeros after the decimal part of a decimal number do not matter.

$$\cancel{0}\cancel{0}\cancel{0}\cancel{0}\cancel{0}\cancel{0}\cancel{0}\cancel{0}\cancel{0}\cancel{0}\cancel{0}\cancel{0}345.65\cancel{0}\cancel{0}\cancel{0}\cancel{0}\cancel{0}\cancel{0}\cancel{0}\cancel{0}\cancel{0}\cancel{0}\cancel{0}\cancel{0}\cancel{0}\cancel{0}\cancel{0}\cancel{0}\cancel{0}$$

❖ Decimal numbers are written according to some rules. The decimal rules are also consistent with normal whole numbers. A decimal number can be thought of as two numbers plus together. The first number is the whole part, and the other one is the decimal part. Therefore 3.45 is 3 plus with .45.

The leading zeros

Let's look at a normal whole number: 345

Hundreds	Tens	Units(ones)
3	4	5

We can break the number up to see how the number 345 is constructed.

The construction of a number 345 actually means

3 of 100s + 4 of 10s + 5 of ones.

Now imagine extending this number 345 to show some hidden numbers. These numbers have been taken away because they have no real value at all

Thousands	Hundreds	Tens	Units(ones)
0	3	4	5

Similarly the construction of the number 0345 is

0 of 1000s + 3 of 100s + 4 of 10s + 5 of ones.

Amazing Fact

❖ When we add two decimal numbers, the answer will have the same number of decimal digits as the given decimal numbers.

Try It!

Example : Convert $\dfrac{31}{5}$ into a decimal.

Solution :
$$5)\overline{31}\,(6.2$$
$$\underline{30}$$
$$10$$
$$\underline{10}$$
$$00$$

So, $\dfrac{31}{5} = 6.2$

We can see that 0 of 1000s means zero. So we do not count the number of 0s leading a number.

The trailing zeros after the decimal part of a decimal number.

Let's look at this number 0.650

Decimal Point	Tenths /10th	Hundredth /100th	Thousandths /1000th
0	6	5	0

The construction of this decimal part of a decimal number means

6/10 + 5/100 + 0/1000.

We can see that 0 out of 1000 is nothing. So we can ignore this 0. What it means is that 0.65 is the same as 0.650.

Similarly 0.6500 is the same as 0.65 because it means

6/10 + 5/100 + 0/1000 + 0/10000.

ADDITION AND SUBTRACTION OF DECIMALS

To add decimal numbers

1. Put the numbers in a vertical column, aligning the decimal points.

2. Add each column of digits, starting on the right and working left. If the sum of a column is more than ten, "carry" digits to the next column on the left.

3. Place the decimal point in the answer directly below the decimal points in the terms.

Let's look at an example:

123 + 0.0079 + 43.5 =

To add these numbers, first arrange the terms vertically, aligning the decimal points in each term. Don't forget, for a whole number like the first term, the decimal point lies just to the right of the ones column. You can add zeroes to the right of the decimal point to make it easier to align the columns. Then add the columns working from the right to the left, positioning the decimal point in the answer directly under the decimal points in the terms.

```
  123.0000
    0.0079
+  43.5000
  166.5079
```

```
7)10  .142857
   7
  30
  28
  20
  14
  60
  56
  40
  35
  50
  49
   1
```

We see that 142857 will repeat again and again.

So $\frac{1}{7}$ = 0.142857142857.....

= $0.\overline{142857}$

(where '-' represent repetition of digits).

To subtract decimal numbers:

1. Put the numbers in a vertical column, aligning the decimal points.

2. Subtract each column, starting on the right and working left. If the digit being subtracted in a column is larger than the digit above it, "borrow" a digit from the next column to the left.

3. Place the decimal point in the answer directly below the decimal points in the terms.

4. Check your answer by adding the result to the number subtracted. The sum should be equal to the first number.

Here's a subtraction example:

27.583 − 0.2 =

To subtract these numbers, first arrange the terms vertically, aligning the decimal points in each term. You can add zeroes to the right of the decimal point, to make it easier to align the columns. Then subtract the columns working from the right to the left, putting the decimal point in the answer directly underneath the decimal points in the terms. Check your answer by adding it to the second term and making sure it equals the first.

$$\begin{array}{r} 27.5\,8\,3 \\ -\ \ 0.2\,0\,0 \\ \hline 27.3\,8\,3 \\ \hline \end{array}$$

Note: To add (or subtract) decimals, always fill empty place values with zeros so that all of the numbers have the same number of decimal places.

CONVERTING FRACTIONS INTO DECIMALS

Fractions and decimals are two different ways to show the same values: parts of wholes.

Step 1: Find a number you can multiply by the bottom of the fraction to make it 10, or 100, or 1000, or any 1 followed by 0s.

Step 2: Multiply both top and bottom by that number.

Step 3: Then write down just the top number, putting the decimal point in the correct spot. (one space from the right hand side for every zero in the bottom number.)

Try It!

Example : Convert the following into decimals without actual division.

(a) $\dfrac{1}{5}$ (b) $\dfrac{3}{20}$ (b) $\dfrac{7}{125}$

Solution :

(a) $\dfrac{1}{5} = \dfrac{1 \times 20}{5 \times 20} = \dfrac{20}{100} = 0.20$

(b) $\dfrac{3}{20} = \dfrac{3 \times 5}{20 \times 5} = \dfrac{15}{100} = 0.15$

(c) $\dfrac{7}{125} = \dfrac{7 \times 8}{125 \times 8} = \dfrac{56}{1000} = 0.056$

Example : Convert $\dfrac{3}{5}$ into decimal.

Step 1 $= \dfrac{3 \times 2}{5 \times 2}$

Step 2 $= \dfrac{6}{10}$

Step 3 $= 0.6$

CONVERTING DECIMALS INTO FRACTIONS

Step 1: Write down the decimal divided by 1, like this: decimal/1.

Step 2: Multiply both top and bottom by 10 for every number after the decimal point. (For example, if there are two numbers after the decimal point, then use 100, if there are three then use 1000, etc.)

Step 3: Simplify (or reduce) the fraction.

For example : Convert 0.36 into fraction

$$\text{Step 1} = \frac{0.36}{1}$$

$$\text{Step 2} = \frac{0.36 \times 100}{1 \times 100}$$

$$\text{Step 3} = \frac{36}{100}$$

$$= \frac{9}{25}$$

ROUNDING OF DECIMALS

1. Find the place value you want (the "rounding digit") and look at the digit just to the right of it.

2. If that digit is less than 5, do not change the rounding digit but drop all digits to the right of it.

3. If that digit is greater than or equal to five, add one to the rounding digit and drop all digits to the right of it.

4. If you're dealing with a decimal number, drop all of the digits following the rounding digit.

Try It!

Example : Round off the following decimals to second place of decimal.

(a) 0.278

(b) 0.195

(c) 0.872

Solutions:

(a) 0.278 = 0.28 as third place is 8, greater than 5;

So 7 becomes 8

(b) 0.195 = 0.20 as last digit is 5. So 9 gets increased by 1. Hence 0.19 becomes 0.20

(c) 0.872 = 0.87 as third place digit is 2. So, 7 remains 7 only.

Hence 0.872 = 0.87.

Example: Convert 0.45 as fraction in lowest terms.

Solution : $0.45 = \frac{45}{100} = \frac{9}{20}$

So, $\frac{9}{20}$ is in lowest terms.

Example : Which of the following decimals has the greatest value.

0.30, 0.300, 0.4, 0.03

Solution : 0.4 has the greatest value.

Multiple Choice Questions

LEVEL 1

1. (1.2 - 0.6) is equal to
   [Mental Mathematics]
   (a) (2.7-2.1) (b) (5.2-4.5)
   (c) (7.3-6.5) (d) (5.0-4.3)

2. Why do we write the zero in 0.2?
   (a) To remind us that the number is less than one.
   (b) To remind us that the number is more than one.
   (c) Because it has no value.
   (d) None of these.

3. Which of the following is equal to $\dfrac{5}{100}$?
   [Mental Mathematics]
   (a) 5 (b) 0.5
   (c) 0.05 (d) 0.005

4. Add : 32.6 + 12.6 + 41.8 **[2015]**
   (a) 45 (b) 87
   (c) 54 (d) 78

5. 7/10 : 0.7 :: _____ : 0.07
   [Mental Mathematics]
   (a) 7/10 (b) 7/100
   (c) 0.7 (d) 7/1000

6. Find the sum of 2.03, 3.205 and 6.3
   [2012]
   (a) 12.145 (b) 14.265
   (c) 12.225 (d) 11.535

Direction (Qs. 7 and 8): Using the digits given write down the smallest and largest number possible to two decimal places without putting 0 in the tens or tenths column.
   [Repeatition not allowed]

7. 0 2 3 4 **[Tricky]**
   (a) Largest: 43.02 , Smallest:02.34
   (b) Largest: 43.02 , Smallest:20.34
   (c) Largest: 43.20, Smallest: 02.43
   (d) Largest: 04.23, Smallest: 02.34

8. 3 4 7 9 **[Tricky]**
   (a) Largest: 97.34 , Smallest:34.79
   (b) Largest: 97.43 , Smallest:34.79
   (c) Largest: 79.34 , Smallest:34.97
   (d) Largest: 97.34, Smallest: 43.79

9. Identify the correct option. **[2014]**
   (a) 14.7 = 14.3 (b) 14.7 < 14.3
   (c) 14.7 > 14.3 (d) Both (b) and (c)

10. Fill in the missing numbers to complete the pattern: **[Mental Mathematics]**
    4.4, _____, 4.8,_____,5.2, 5.4
    (a) 4.5,5 (b) 4.7, 5.1
    (c) 4.6, 5 (d) 4.5,5.1

11. Evaluate: 17.6 + 94/10 **[2009]**
    (a) 24 (b) 37
    (c) 27 (d) 25

12. Write 0.97 as a fraction.
    (a) 97/100 (b) 97/10
    (c) 97/1000 (d) 97/10000

13. Solve the problem: $25\dfrac{7}{10} - 12\dfrac{8}{10}$
    (a) 12.9 (b) 11.9
    (c) 13.9 (d) 12.5

14. If a decimal has only one digit after the decimal point, it is measuring in
    (a) tenths (b) hundredths
    (c) thousandths (d) units

15. Solve the problem: **[2010]**
    $92.1 - 15\dfrac{6}{10}$
    (a) 76.5 (b) 76
    (c) 77 (d) 76.8

16. Fill in the missing numbers to complete the pattern: **[Mental Mathematics]**
    _____, 2.00, 2.02, 2.04,_____,2.08
    (a) 1.8, 2.06 (b) 1.98, 2.06
    (c) 1.8, 2.60 (d) 1.9, 2.05

17. 1000 + 500 + 60 + 9 +3/10 + 4/1000 + 6/10000 is the expanded form of
    (a) 1569.3046　　(b) 1569.346
    (c) 1569.0346　　(d) 1569.3460

18. Write 0.039 as a fraction.　[2009]
    (a) 39/100　　(b) 39/1000
    (c) 3.9/10　　(d) 39/900

19. How many times 1.25 be added to make 10.　[2018]
    (a) 8　　(b) 12.5
    (c) 4　　(d) 5

20. What should be added to 90.468 to make a century?　[2019]
    (a) 9.532　　(b) 1.323
    (c) 10.452　　(d) 8.345

21. Which one of the following decimals should be subtracted from 73.234 to get a resulting decimal 57.096?[2022]
    (a) 16.138
    (b) 15.948
    (c) 15.968
    (d) 16.218

22. Atul distributed ₹126 among his eight friends equally. How much money did each of his friends get?　[2022]
    (a) ₹15.75　　(b) ₹13.50
    (c) ₹14.75　　(d) ₹16.25

LEVEL 2

1. Match the following:　[Tricky]

	List I		List II
A.	0.62	1.	62/10
B.	6.2	2.	62/1
C.	0.062	3.	62/100
D.	62	4.	62/1000

```
       A  B  C  D           A  B  C  D
(a)    3  1  4  2    (b)    2  3  4  1
(c)    1  3  2  4    (d)    4  2  1  3
```

2. What sign makes the sentence true?
   973/1000 ____ 0.175
   (a) >
   (b) <
   (c) =
   (d) None of these

3. What sign makes the sentence true?　[2008]
   818/1000 ____ 0.8
   (a) >
   (b) <
   (c) =
   (d) None of these

4. Five swimmers are entered into a competition. Four of the swimmers have had their turns. Their scores are 9.8 s, 9.75 s, 9.79 s, and 9.81 s. What score must the last swimmer get in order to win the competition?

   (a) Greater than 9.75 sec
   (b) Lesser than 9.75 sec
   (c) Greater than 9.81 sec
   (d) Lesser than 9.81 sec

Direction (Qs. 5 to 7): Choose the option in the given questions such that they are arranged in the ascending order.

5. 5.25, 15.3, 5.87, 5.78, 5.2
   (a) 5.2 < 5.25 < 5.78 < 5.87 < 15.3
   (b) 5.2 < 5.87 < 5.78 < 5.25 < 5.2
   (c) 5.25 > 5.2 > 5.78 > 5.87 > 15.3
   (d) 15.3 < 5.87 < 5.78 < 5.25 < 5.2

6. 7.765, 7.675, 6.765, 7.756, 6.776
   (a) 7.765 < 7.675 < 7.756 < 6.776 < 6.765
   (b) 6.765 < 6.776 < 7.675 < 7.756 < 7.765
   (c) 7.675 < 7.756 < 7.765 < 6.776 < 6.765
   (d) 7.756 < 7.765 < 6.776 < 6.765 < 7.675

7. 1.5, 1.375, 1.4, 1.3, 1.35, 1.425 **[Tricky]**
  (a) 1.375 < 1.35 < 1.3 < 1.425 < 1.4 < 1.5
  (b) 1.5 < 1.4 < 1.3 < 1.425 <1.375 < 1.35
  (c) 1.3 < 1.35 < 1.375 < 1.4 < 1.425 < 1.5
  (d) 1.425 < 1.375 < 1.4 < 1.3 < 1.5 <1.35

8. Match the following: **[Tricky]**

List I (Fraction)		List II (Decimal)	
A.	1/4	1.	0.50
B.	1/2	2.	0.20
C.	1/8	3.	0.25
D.	1/5	4.	0.125

	A	B	C	D			A	B	C	D
(a)	2	3	4	1		(b)	3	1	4	2
(c)	1	2	3	4		(d)	3	1	2	4

9. Look at the calculations carefully and choose the correct answer. **[Critical Thinking]**

  Statement A: 0.34 = 0.340

  Statement B: 345 = 3450
  (a) Only A is true.
  (b) Only B is true.
  (c) Both A and B are true.
  (d) Both A and B are false.

10. Round off 57.6 to the nearest unit.
  (a) 57   (b) 58
  (c) 57.5   (d) 60

11. Bob has $5.86. He wants to buy a CD costing $9.99. How much does he need ?
  (a) $4.13   (b) $14.38
  (c) $5.38   (d) $5.13

12. Choose the correct expanded form for 650.28.   **[2013]**
  (a) $60 + 50 + \dfrac{20}{10} + \dfrac{8}{100}$

  (b) $600 + 50 + \dfrac{2}{10} + \dfrac{8}{100}$

  (c) $60 + 500 + \dfrac{2}{100} + \dfrac{8}{10}$

  (d) $600 + 50 + 0 + \dfrac{2}{100} + \dfrac{8}{1000}$

13. What should be added to 78.3056 to make it 93?   **[2017]**
  (a) 14.6859   (b) 14.2596
  (c) 14.6944   (d) 14.8756

14. Identify the value of 1+0.1+0.01+0.001
  (a) 1.03   (b) 1.003 **[2014]**
  (c) 1.110   (d) 1.111

15. The train leaving platform 1 at 14:25 pm will arrive at 16:07 pm. How long will the train take?
  (a) 1 hour 42 minutes
  (b) 2 hours 35 minutes
  (c) 2 hours 12 minutes
  (d) 1 hours 22 minutes

16. Identify the correct expanded form of $\boxed{256.13}$.   **[2016]**
  (a) $250 + 6 + \dfrac{1}{100} + \dfrac{3}{1000}$

  (b) $200 + 50 + 6 + \dfrac{1}{10} + \dfrac{3}{100}$

  (c) $200 + 50 + 6 + \dfrac{1}{10} + \dfrac{3}{100}$

  (d) $200 + 50 + 6 + \dfrac{1}{10} + \dfrac{3}{100}$

17. A play station game cost ₹29.99, but the price went down by ₹4.75. How much does it cost now?
  (a) ₹26.25   (b) ₹34.74
  (c) ₹25.24   (d) ₹32.24

18. The value of fuel is ₹ 67.6. The price went up by 36 paise. What is the new price?
  (a) ₹ 103.96   (b) ₹ 103.60
  (c) ₹ 67.24   (d) ₹ 67.96

19. The gift shop is 15.6 kilometres east of the bicycle shop and 44.5 kilometres west of the party supply store. The grocery store is 50.2 kilometres south of the gift shop.
  Which is closer to the gift shop?

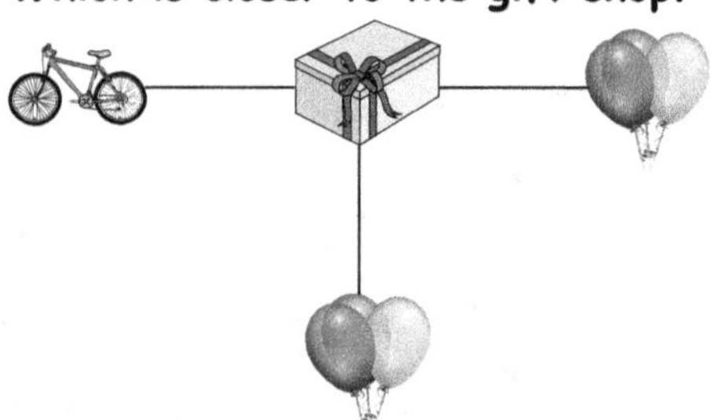

(a) Bicycle shop
(b) Grocery shop
(c) Party supply store
(d) All are at equal distance

20. The garbage dump is 24.3 miles west of the flower shop. The bakery is 43.2 miles east of the flower shop. The bakery is 26.1 miles west of the radio tower.

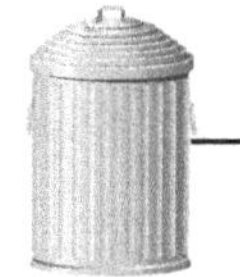
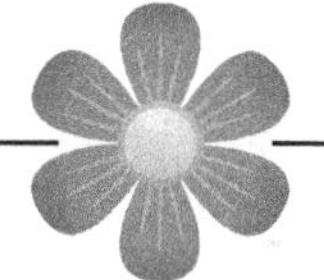
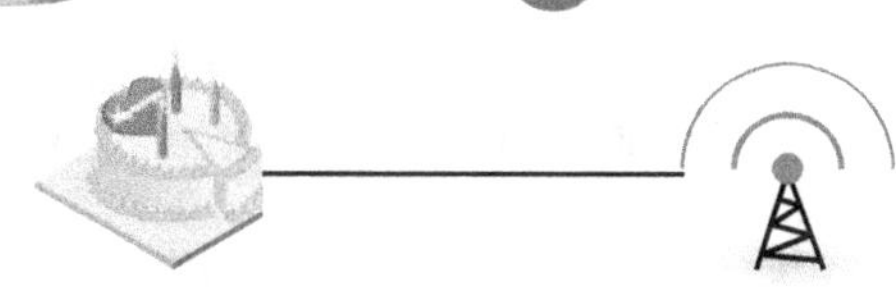

How far apart are the bakery and the garbage dump?
(a) 93.6 miles   (b) 68.6 miles
(c) 67.5 miles   (d) 69.3 miles

21. Professor Rogers measured the composition of gases in a sample. The sample contained 0.6 litres of oxygen, 0.7 litres of nitrogen, and 0.1 litres of carbon dioxide. What was the total volume of Professor Rogers's sample?
(a) 1.4 litres   (b) 1.3 litres
(c) 0.14 litres   (d) 0.104 litres

22. Which one of the following options is same as $50 + \dfrac{2}{10} + \dfrac{3}{1000}$? **[2015]**
(a) 50.23   (b) 50.023
(c) 50.203   (d) 50.0203

Direction (Qs. 23 to 26): Evaluate the following decimals by applying the rules of addition and subtraction.

23. If X = 3.7 + 2.95; Y = 8.7 + 3.999; Z = 10, Then X + Y + Z is equal to **[2008]**
(a) 26.548   (b) 29.345
(c) 29.349   (d) 38.356

24. A = 201.4 − 132.68, B = 11.62 − 6.068, then A − B **[2009]**

(a) 63.168   (b) 34.151
(c) 66.123   (d) 62.398

25. If 3.7 + 4.96 + 13.578 + 12.1347 = Y, then Y + 99 is
(a) 130.3589   (b) 132.3721
(c) 133.3727   (d) 132.1278

26. If 15 + 2.094 + 3.62 = X, then X + 2.05 =
(a) 22.764   (b) 21.456
(c) 28.635   (d) 22.358

27. Which one of the following is not true? **[2012]**
(a) 345.32456 and 356563.46645 are like decimals.
(b) 0.023 and 0.00023 are unlike decimals.
(c) 4.50 and 0.45 are equivalent decimals.
(d) All of these

28. Match the following: **[Critical Thinking]**

	List I		List II
A.	Fifty-six hundredths	1.	13.04
B.	One hundred and six tenths	2.	19.078
C.	Nineteen and seventy-eight thousandths	3.	100.6
D.	Thirteen and four hundredths	4.	0.56

     A B C D   A B C D
(a) 2 3 1 4   (b) 4 3 2 1
(c) 1 2 3 4   (d) 4 1 2 3

29. Yoshi measured the rainfall each day for a science lesson. He measured 0.3 centimetres on Monday, 0.9 centimetres on Tuesday, and 0.9 centimetres on Wednesday. How many centimetres of rain did Yoshi measure in all? **[2010]**
(a) 2.1 cm   (b) 2.1 m
(c) 2.5 cm   (d) 0.25 cm

30. Wayne hung out with his friends last Saturday. First, they drove 7.8 kilometres to go play miniature golf.

From there, they drove 7.1 kilometres to go to a baseball game. Then they drove 5.8 kilometres to the park. How many kilometres did Wayne and his friends drive in all?

(a) 21 cm
(b) 20.7 km
(c) 0.27 cm
(d) 2.7 cm

31. A jewellery maker ordered 9.7 kilograms of gold, 6.5 kilograms of silver, and 3.6 kilograms of copper. How many kilograms of metal did the jewellery maker order in all?   [2009]

(a) 19.8
(b) 0.19
(c) 24.6
(d) 21.3

32. Match the following: [Tricky]

List I		List II	
A.	3.7 + 2.99	1.	6.001
B.	0.47 + 3.3	2.	4.19
C.	0.5 +3.69	3.	3.77
D.	3.47 +2.531	4.	6.69

	A	B	C	D			A	B	C	D
(a)	4	3	2	1		(b)	2	3	1	4
(c)	1	2	3	4		(d)	3	1	4	2

33. During a snowstorm last winter, Harry measured the snowfall each day. It snowed 0.6 centimetres on Monday, 0.9 centimetres on Tuesday, and 0.9 centimetres on Wednesday. How many centimetres of snow did Harry measure in all?   [Tricky]

(a) 0.29 cm
(b) 2.4 cm
(c) 2.9 cm
(d) 3.4 cm

34. Write the GREY coloured blocks in the decimal form.

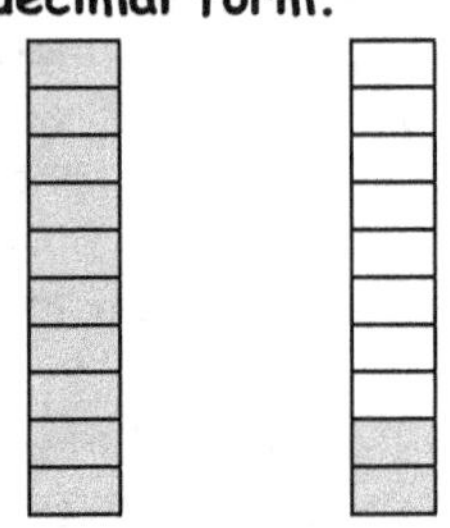

(a) 1.2
(b) 12.0
(c) 0.12
(d) 12.2

35. Write the shaded portion in the decimal form.   [2008]

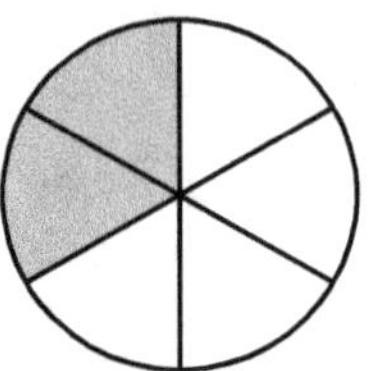

(a) 0.333
(b) 0.6
(c) 10.3
(d) 3.3

36. What number must be subtracted from 82 to obtain 72.693.

(a) 9.307
(b) 0.930
(c) 9
(d) 9.42

37. What is nine units and five tenths in decimals?

(a) 95
(b) 0.95
(c) 9.5
(d) 9.05

38. I have one unit and seven tenths. Write this number in decimals.   [Tricky]

(a) 17
(b) 1.7
(c) 7.1
(d) 0.17

39. B is 125.254 less than A and C is equal to the sum of A and B. If A = 5440.211. Find the value of A + B + C.   [2012, Tricky]

(a) 2151.0336
(b) 21510.336
(c) 21512.336
(d) 21010.336

40. Match the following: [Critical Thinking]

	List I		List II
A.	14-2.9	1.	13.907
B.	25 – 12.09	2.	11.1
C.	36 – 22.009	3.	13.991
D.	46 - 32.093	4.	12.91

	A	B	C	D			A	B	C	D
(a)	2	1	3	4		(b)	1	3	4	2
(c)	2	4	3	1		(d)	3	2	4	1

41. How many tens, units and tenths are there in 75.6?

(a) 7 tens, 5 units and 6 tenths
(b) 7 tens, 6 units and 5 tenths
(c) 6 tens, 5 units and 7 tenths
(d) 5 tens, 7 units and 6 tenths

42. P and Q are two decimals. If P=8.003+0.1 and Q=6.3+2.01 which one of the following is true?   [2011]
    (a) P > Q
    (b) P < Q
    (c) P = Q
    (d) All of these

43. Find the sum of place value of 2 in 2624.572.   [2019]
    (a) 6000
    (b) 2020.002
    (c) 2000.002
    (d) 2020

44. Mrs Sharma bought 225 m 18 cm of cloth from shop P, 212 m 20 cm of cloth from shop Q and 140 m 5 cm of cloth from shop R. What is the total length of cloth she bought from all the shops?   [2021]
    (a) 597 m 43 cm
    (b) 477 m 48 cm
    (c) 577 m 43 cm
    (d) 497 m 48 cm

45. Subhra bought 12 m of cloth to make 3 pairs to pants and 2 shirts. If she used 2.7 m of cloth to make each pair of pants and 1.9 m to make each shirt, then how much cloth was left? [2022]
    (a) 10 m
    (b) 10 cm
    (c) 100 cm
    (d) 11 m

46. The distance from city A to city B is 56 km 750 m; from city B to city is 33 km 225 m and from city C to city D is 50 km 175 m. Find the distance from city A to city D, if one has to go through cities B and C.   [2022]
    (a) 160 km 650 m
    (b) 130 km 250 m
    (c) 150 km 140 m
    (d) 140 km 150 m

RESPONSE GRID

LEVEL 1

1. a b c d   2. a b c d   3. a b c d   4. a b c d   5. a b c d
6. a b c d   7. a b c d   8. a b c d   9. a b c d   10. a b c d
11. a b c d   12. a b c d   13. a b c d   14. a b c d   15. a b c d
16. a b c d   17. a b c d   18. a b c d   19. a b c d   20. a b c d
21. a b c d   22. a b c d

LEVEL 2

1. a b c d   2. a b c d   3. a b c d   4. a b c d   5. a b c d
6. a b c d   7. a b c d   8. a b c d   9. a b c d   10. a b c d
11. a b c d   12. a b c d   13. a b c d   14. a b c d   15. a b c d
16. a b c d   17. a b c d   18. a b c d   19. a b c d   20. a b c d
21. a b c d   22. a b c d   23. a b c d   24. a b c d   25. a b c d
26. a b c d   27. a b c d   28. a b c d   29. a b c d   30. a b c d
31. a b c d   32. a b c d   33. a b c d   34. a b c d   35. a b c d
36. a b c d   37. a b c d   38. a b c d   39. a b c d   40. a b c d
41. a b c d   42. a b c d   43. a b c d   44. a b c d   45. a b c d
46. a b c d

Solutions with Explanation

LEVEL 1

1. **(a)** The difference between 1.2 and 0.6 is 0.6. In the options, the numbers 2.7 and 2.1 have the difference equal to 0.6.

2. **(a)** Zero as prefix before the decimal indicates that the number is smaller than 1.

3. **(c)** 5/100. The hundred in the denominator shows the hundredth place value. Which will be equal to 0.05

4. **(b)** As 32.6 + 12.6 + 41.8 = 87.0

5. **(b)** As the fraction 7/10 is equal to 0.7 in decimal form. Similarly 0.07 in decimal form can be written as 7/100 in fraction form. Thus 7/10: 0.7::7/100: 0.07.

6. **(d)** As 2.03 + 3.205 + 6.3 = 11.535

7. **(b)** The numbers are 0, 2, 3, 4. The largest out of these numbers are 4 and 3. The smaller numbers are 0 and 2. Arranging the numbers in descending order up to two decimal places, we have the largest number as 43.02, when arranging in ascending order, we get the smallest number as 20.34.

8. **(b)** The numbers are 3, 4, 7 and 9. The largest out of these numbers are 7 and 9. The smaller numbers are 3 and 4. Arranging the numbers in descending order up to two decimal places, we have the largest number as 97.43, when arranging in ascending order, we get the smallest number as 34.79.

9. **(c)** 14.7 > 14.3 is correct

10. **(c)** 4.4, ___, 4.8, ___, 5.2, 5.4. By studying the pattern we can see that the previous number is smaller than the next by 0.2. Thus by adding 0.2 to 4.4 and 4.8 respectively, we get 4.6 and 5 to complete the decimal chain.

11. **(c)** $17.6 + 9\dfrac{4}{10} = 17.6 + \dfrac{94}{10} = 17.6 +9.4 = 27.$

12. **(a)** There are two digits after the decimal point representing the tenth and the hundredth respectively. Thus $\dfrac{97}{100}$ is the correct answer.

13. **(a)** $25\dfrac{7}{10} - 12\dfrac{8}{10} = \dfrac{257}{10} - \dfrac{128}{10} = 25.7 - 12.8 = 12.9.$

14. **(a)** According to the place value system, after decimal point to the right is tenth place.

15. **(a)** $92.1 - 15\dfrac{6}{10} = 92.1 - \dfrac{156}{10} = 92.1 - 15.6 = 76.5.$

16. **(b)** ___, 2.00, 2.02, 2.04, ___, 2.08. By studying the pattern we can see that the previous number is smaller than the next by 0.02. Thus by adding 0.02 to 2.04 and subtracting 0.02 from 2.00, we get 1.98 and 2.06 to complete the decimal chain.

17. **(a)** $1000 + 500 + 60 + 9 + \dfrac{3}{10} + \dfrac{4}{1000} + \dfrac{6}{10000} = 1569.3046$ by using the place value system.

18. **(b)** 0.039 has tenth, hundredth and thousandth on the right side of the decimal indicating $\dfrac{39}{1000}$.

19.	**(a)**	$1.25 \times 8 = 10$	**21.**	**(a)**	
20.	**(a)**	Required number = 100 – 90.468 = 9.532	**22.**	**(a)**	

LEVEL 2

1. **(a)**

2. **(a)** 973/1000 ____ 0.175 ; 0.973 >0.175

3. **(a)** 818/1000 ____ 0.8 ; 0.818 >0.8

4. **(b)** The least score is 9.75. Thus for coming at fifth position, the swimmer must score less than 9.75.

5. **(a)** $5.2 < 5.25 < 5.78 < 5.87 < 15.3$

6. **(b)** $6.765 < 6.776 < 7.675 < 7.756 < 7.765$

7. **(c)** $1.3 < 1.35 < 1.375 < 1.4 < 1.425 < 1.5$

8. **(b)**

9. **(a)** Only A is true. 0.34 is equal to 0.340 because the zero after the decimals in the end does not hold any significance.

10. **(b)** The next unit near to 57.6 is 58 because the tenth place after the decimal point is greater than 5.

11. **(a)** Money with Bob =$5.86. Cost of CD= $9.99, more money required by Bob= $9.99- =$5.86 =$ 4.13.

12. **(b)** As $650.28 = 600 + 50 + \dfrac{2}{10} + \dfrac{8}{100}$

13. **(c)** To know what should be added to 78.3056 so as to obtain 93, we must subtract 78.3056 from 93. Thus 93-78.3056= 14.6944.

14. **(d)** As $1 + 0.1 + 0.01 + 0.001 = 1.111$

15. **(a)** The train leaving platform 1 at 14.25 pm will arrive at 16.07 pm in 1 hour 42 minutes.

16. **(d)** Since $256.13 = 200 + 50 + 6 + \dfrac{1}{10} + \dfrac{3}{100}$

17. **(c)** Present cost of play station = ₹29.99, decrement in price = ₹4.75.

New price = ₹(29.99 – 4.75) = ₹25.24.

18. **(d)** Old price = ₹ 67.6, increment in price = 36 paise or ₹ 36/100 = ₹ 0.36. Thus new price = ₹ 67.6 + ₹ 0.36 = ₹ 67.96

19. **(a)** Distance between gift shop and bicycle shop= 15.6 km; Distance between gift shop and party supply shop= 44.5 km; Distance between gift shop and grocery shop=50.2 km. As it can be clearly seen, the distance between gift shop and bicycle shop is the least which means they are nearest.

20. **(c)** Distance between garbage and bakery = Distance between bakery and flower shop + Distance between flower shop and garbage = 43.2 + 24.3 =67.5 miles.

21. **(a)** The total volume of Professor Rogers's sample= Quantity of oxygen + nitrogen + carbon dioxide = 0.6 +0.7 + 0.1 =1.4 litres.

22. **(c)** $50 + \dfrac{2}{10} + \dfrac{3}{1000} = 50.203$

23. **(c)** X= 3.7 + 2.95; Y = 8.7 + 3.999; Z = 10 ; X =6.65 , Y= 12.699; X + Y + Z = 6.65 + 12.699 + 10 = 29.349.

24. **(a)** A= 201.4 – 132.68, B = 11.62 – 6.068; Solving this we get A = 68.72 and B=5.552; Then A–B = (68.72-5.552)= 63.168.

25. **(c)** 3.7 + 4.96 + 13.578 + 12.1347 = Y; Y =34.3727; Y +99 = 34.3727 + 99 =133.3727.

26. **(a)** 15 + 2.094 + 3.62 = X, X= 20.714. Then X +2.05 = 20.714 + 2.05 = 22.764.

27. **(c)** 4.50 and 0.45 are equivalent fractions is false

28. **(b)**

29. **(a)** Rain measured by Yoshi - Rainfall measured on Monday + Tuesday + Wednesday =0.3 centimetres, 0.9 centimetres +0.9 centimetres = 2.1 centimetres.

30. **(b)** Distance covered by Wayne and his friends = (7.8 + 7.1 + 5.8) kilometres = 20.7 kms.

31. **(a)** Amount of metal ordered by the jewellery maker = Kilograms of gold + silver + copper = 9.7+6.5+3.6= 19.8.

32. **(a)**

33. **(b)** Total snowfall measured by Harry= Snowfall on Monday + Snowfall on Tuesday + Snowfall on Wednesday = 0.6 +0.9 +0.9 = 2.4 cms.

34. **(a)** There are two blocks. Each block is divided into ten parts. Block I is fully shaded. But block 2 has only 2 parts shaded. Thus we have 1 whole and 2/10 part covered which is equal to 1 +2/10 =1+0.2 = 1.2.

35. **(a)** There are 6 parts in the pie. 2 are shaded. Thus total shaded part is 2/6 which when divided yields 0.333.

36. **(a)** To obtain the number that must be subtracted from 82 to get 72.693, we can subtract 72.693 from 82. By doing so, we get 82-72.693 = 9.307.

37. **(c)** Unit number is placed on the left of the decimal whereas tenth is placed on the immediate left. Thus nine units and five tenths in decimals is equal to 9.5.

38. **(b)** Unit number is placed on the left of the decimal whereas tenth is placed on the immediate left. Thus 1 unit and 7 tenth is equal to 1.7.

39. **(b)** B = A – 125.254 = 5440. 211 – 125. 254
= 5314.957
C = A + B = 10755.168
So, A + B + C = 21510.336

40. **(c)**

41. **(a)** 75.6 = 7 tens, 5 units and 6 tenths.

42. **(b)** P = 8.003 + 0.1 = 8.103
Q = 6.3 + 2.01 = 8.31
So P < Q

43. **(b)** 2000 + 20 + 0.002 = 2020.002

44. **(c)** Cloths bought from shop P = 225 m 18 cm = 225.18 cm
Cloths bought from shop Q = 212 m 20 cm = 212.20 cm
Cloths bought from shop R = 140 m 5 cm = 240.05 cm
Total length of cloth = 225.18
= + 212.20
+140.05
____
577.43

45. **(b)** Total length of cloth =12
cloth used in making 3 pairs of pants = 3 × 2.7 = 8.1 m
cloth used in making 2 shirts = 2 ×1.9 = 3.8 m
Total needed cloth = 8.1 + 3.8 = 11.9 m
Remaining cloth = 12.0 – 11.9 = 0.1 m = 10 cm.

46. **(d)** The distance from city A to B = 56.750 km
city B to C = 33.225 km
city C to D = 50.175 km

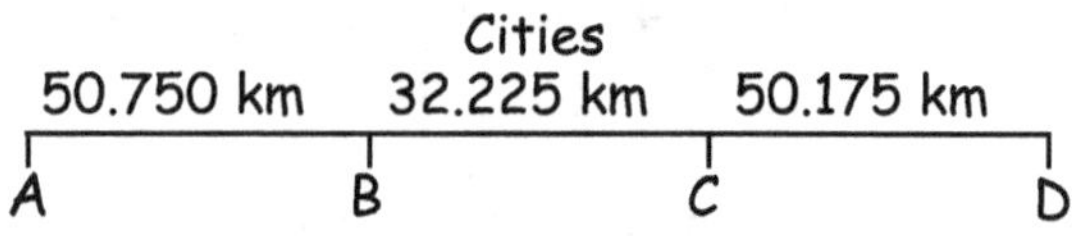

The distance from city A to D
= 56.750 +33.225 + 50.175
= 140.150 km
= 140 km 150 m

LENGTH

Metric	Customary
1 kilometre = 1000 metres	1 mile = 1760 yards
1 metre = 100 centimetres	1 mile = 5280 feet
1 centimetre = 10 millimetres	1 yard = 3 feet
	1 foot = 12 inches

CAPACITY AND VOLUME

1 Litre = 1000 millilitres	1 gallon = 4 quarts
	1 gallon = 128 fluid ounces
	1 quart = 2 pints
	1 pint = 2 cups
	1 cup = 8 fluid ounces

MASS AND WEIGHT

Metric	Customary
1 kilogram = 1000 grams	1 ton = 2000 pounds
1gram = 1000 milligrams	1 pound = 16 ounces

TIME

1 year = 365 days

1 year = 12 months

1 year = 52 weeks

1 week = 7 days

1 day = 24 hours

1 hour = 60 minutes

1 minute = 60 seconds

10
Chapter

Measurement

LEARNING OBJECTIVES

This lesson will help you to:—

❖ revise standard units of length like millimetre, centimetre and metre.

❖ choose appropriate standard unit of length.

❖ measure objects using standard unit of length.

❖ convert metre into centimetre.

❖ introduce standard units of weight like gram (gm) and kilogram (kg).

❖ choose appropriate standard unit of weight.

❖ weigh objects using standard units.

❖ convert the units of weight.

❖ introduce standard units of volume like litre (L).

❖ choose appropriate capacity of a container using standard unit of volume.

❖ convert the units of volume.

QUICK CONCEPT REVIEW

LENGTH

The standard unit for measuring length is 'metre'. The length of cloth, the height of a wall, the height of a tree, the distance between two objects are all measured in metres. Carpenters use measuring tape for making furniture, cloth merchant use a meter rod for measuring the length of clothes, measuring tape is also used by tailors, masons etc. Metre is also used to measure small distances.

Conversion of units

100 centimetres = 1 metre

100 cm = 1 m

We write 'm' for metre and 'cm' for centimetre. Smaller lengths are measured in centimetres. Sometimes smaller lengths are measured in decimetres. It is written as dm and is equal to 10 centimetres.

10 centimetres = 1 decimetres

10 decimetres = 1 metre

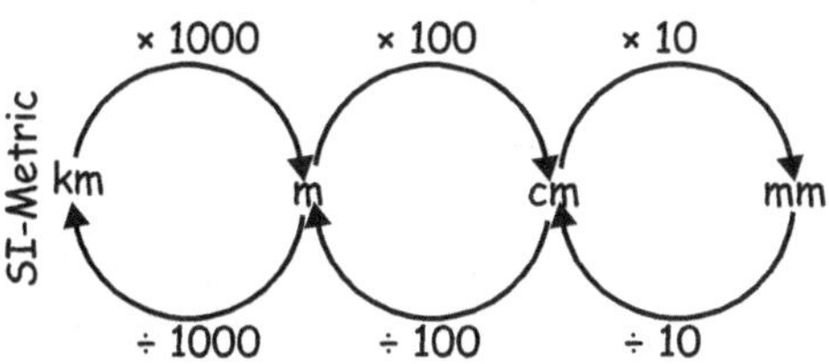

Rule 1: Multiply to change larger units to smaller units.

Rule 2: Divide to change smaller units to larger units.

Shortcut to Problem Solving for Length

❖ Always start from '0' while using measuring instruments.

❖ Millimetre (mm) and centimetre (cm) are used to measure small objects.

❖ Metre (m) is used to measure large objects.

❖ Metre (m) and kilometre (km) are used to measure large distances.

❖ Always convert the length of given objects into same unit of length before solving them.

Historical preview

❖ It was the Greeks who developed the "foot" as their fundamental unit of length. It was based on an actual measurement of Hercules' foot.

❖ The French created a standard unit of measurement called the metric system in 1790. This is today's international system of unit for measurement.

❖ The gram was originally defined in 1795.

❖ The litre was introduced in France in 1795.

❖ Litre was named after a French wine merchant, Claude Emile Jean-Baptiste Litre.

❖ The word litre is derived from an older French unit, the 'litron'.

❖ Archimedes discovered volume of solid objects using volume of water.

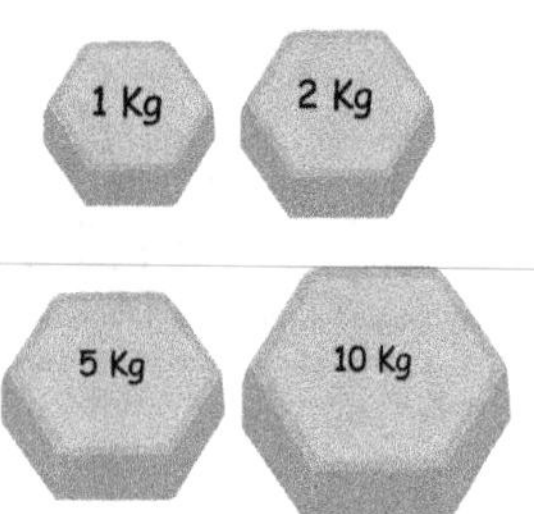

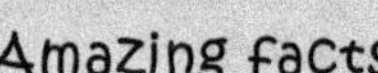

Amazing facts

- You can measure your height using inches (inch) and feet (ft) also.
- One metre (m) is same as 100 centimetres (cm).
- One kilometre is same as 1000 meters (m).
- One kilogram (kg) is same as 1000 grams (gm).
- The adult human brain weighs about 1300-1400 gm.
- The body mass index (BMI) gauges your weight in relation to height.
- The base word litre is often spelled differently based on geography; liter is the favored spelling in American English, while litre is used more often in European English.

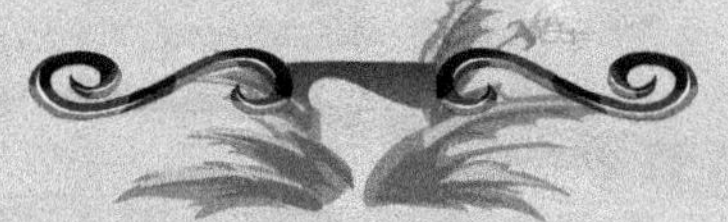

WEIGHT

The standard unit for measuring mass or weight is a kilogram. We weigh things in kilograms. Lighter objects and smaller quantities of things are weighed in grams. We write kilogram as Kg and gram as g.

1 kilogram = 1000 grams

Or

1kg = 1000 g

We use balance and weights to weigh things.

Shortcut to Problem Solving for weight

- ❖ Always start from '0' while using weighing balance.
- ❖ Gram (gm) is used to weigh lighter objects.
- ❖ Kilogram (kg) is used to measure heavier objects.
- ❖ Always convert the weight of given objects into same unit of weight before adding or subtracting them.

VOLUME (CAPACITY)

The capacity of a container is the maximum amount of liquid which it can hold. The standard unit for measuring capacity is 'litre'. We measure liquids like water, milk and oil in litres. Small amounts of liquids like medicine are measured in millilitres. We write litre as 'L' and millilitre as 'mL'.

1 litre = 1000 millilitres

Or

1 l = 1000 mL

Shortcut to Problem Solving for Volume

- ❖ Always use a container of capacity 1 litre to find the capacity of other containers.
- ❖ To find the volume a liquid, just pour it to a container with a measuring scale marked on it.
- ❖ Millilitre is used to measure less quantity of liquids.
- ❖ Litre is used to measure greater quantity of liquids.
- ❖ Always convert the volume of given liquids into same unit of volume before adding or subtracting them.

Multiple Choice Questions

LEVEL 1

1. Chimpy has drawn some lines on the wall. Estimate which line is the longest among the following lines.

   (a) ⟵⟶ (b) ⟵⟶ (c) ⟵⟶ (d) ⟵⟶

2. Peenu has written following statements about the metric unit she would use to measure some objects. Find the incorrect sentence among the following sentences:

   [Tricky]

   A: Centimetre is used to measure the length of a pencil.

   B: Kilometre is used to measure distance from one city to another.

   C: Metre is used to measure depth of a bucket.

   D: Metre is used to measure height of a tree.

   (a) B (b) C (c) D (d) A

Direction (Q. 3): Billu has made two lists of objects. Find the odd one among them.

3. List of objects whose length would be measured using centimetre unit.

   [Mental Mathematics]

   (a) (b) (c) (d)

4. A carpenter was putting up a shelf. The shelf needed to be 86 cm long but the piece of wood he had was 1 m and 26 cm long. His saw was 33 cm long. How much did he have to cut off the piece of wood to make it fit?

   (a) 40 cm (b) 43 cm (c) 50 cm (d) 53 cm

5. If 1 metre : 100 centimetre :: then 1 kilometre : ? **[Mental Mathematics]**

   (a) 100 metre (b) 100 centimetre (c) 1000 metre (d) 1000 centimetre

Direction (Q. 6): Add the following capacities:

6. 25 L 850 mL and 19 L 390 mL.

   (a) 45 L 240 mL. (b) 46 L 245 mL (c) 40 L 240 mL (d) 45 L 290 mL

7. Three large containers of water, each holding 15 L 500 mL, are poured in a water tank. How much water is in the tank? **[2008]**

   (a) 46 L 500 mL (b) 45 L 500 mL (c) 45 L 200 mL (d) 46 L 200 mL

8. A container has 2550 mL of water. How many litres and millilitres of water is in the container? **[Mental Mathematics]**

   (a) 2 L 500 mL (b) 2 L 525 mL (c) 2 L 505 mL (d) 2 L 550 mL

9. A jar can hold 4 L 250 mL honey. How much honey will be needed to fill 4 jars? **[2009]**

   (a) 16 litres (b) 15 litres (c) 17 litres (d) 17 L 250 mL

10. If the cost of 1 litre of a cough syrup is ` 480.40, find the cost of 500 mL. **[2010]**
    (a) ₹ 200.40   (b) ₹ 220.40   (c) ₹ 260.40   (d) ₹ 240.20

11. Rashmi needs 6 containers which can hold 15 L 600 mL oil. Find the capacity of each container. **[2009]**
    (a) 2 L 500 mL   (b) 2 L 600 mL   (c) 3 L 200 mL   (d) 2 L 100 mL

12. A barrel contains 20L 175 ml of oil. The barrel is emptied into 25 cans equally. Each can will hold _______ of oil. **[2018]**
    (a) 812 ml   (b) 917 ml   (c) 807 ml   (d) 87 ml

13. A jeweller made 4 gold ornaments weighing 14 g 200 mg, 15 g 900 mg, 9 g 700 mg and 5 g 900 mg. What is the total weight of the four ornaments? **[2019]**
    (a) 43 g 600 mg   (b) 25 g 500 g   (c) 45 g 700 mg   (d) 45 g 900 mg

14. The price of 1 kg of apples is twice that of 1 kg of guav(a) Prisha bought 3 kg of guavas and 2 kg of apples. If the price of 1 kg of guava is ₹40 then how much did she spend on buying the fruits? **[2022]**
    (a) ₹200   (b) ₹240   (c) ₹280   (d) ₹320

LEVEL 2

1. Sunny is learning about metric unit of length. He wrote following sentences in his notebook. Write true/false for the following sentences. **[Mental Mathematics]**
    A: There are 100 centimetres in a metre.
    B: There are 100 metres in a kilometre.
    C: Centimetre is a larger unit than kilometre.
    D: Metre is a smaller unit than centimetre.
    (a) T F T F   (b) F F F T   (c) T F F F   (d) F T F T

2. Complete the passage given below:
    Teepu is 25 years old. He loves driving. One day he went out for a drive in his car. After driving for 12 km, he stopped for something to eat. He then drive for another 26 km. He checked his car's fuel and realized that for _______(A)_______ km he has used 2 litres of petrol. His car was running out of fuel so he went to a petrol pump which was 8 km away and filled his car's tank with 3 litres of petrol. He checked his car's metre and realized that he has driven _______(B)_______ km from his house to the petrol pump. He then decided to drive back to his home and eventually arrived home at 8:00 pm which was _______(C)_______ km away from the petrol pump. He then told his mother that he drive _______(D)_______ km throughout the day.
    A : (a) 36 (b) 37 (c) 38 (d) 39
    B : (a) 45 (b) 46 (c) 47 (d) 48
    C : (a) 48 (b) 47 (c) 46 (d) 45
    D : (a) 89 (b) 90 (c) 91 (d) 92

3. Find the length of LM in the given figure. **[2016]**
    (a) 5 cm
    (b) 8 cm
    (c) 9 cm
    (d) 3 cm

4. Manku is a monkey. He loves drinking coconut water. One day while playing he saw a coconut tree which was 372 centimetres high. He wanted to get on top of the coconut tree but he couldn't jump at 372 centimetres high to reach upto the coconuts. So, he brought a stool which was 2 metres high. Look at the picture given below and determine how long does Manku needs to jump after climbing up the stool.
   (a) 1 metres   [Mental Mathematics]
   (b) 2 metres
   (c) 150 centimetres
   (d) 172 centimetres

5. What is the total length of the pole in centimeters if 30 cm long part of the pole is buried in the ground?   [2016]
   (a) 331 cm
   (b) 340 cm
   (c) 310 cm
   (d) 280 cm

6. Capacity of which groups of pots is correct to 1000 mL ?   [2016]

   (a) 400 mL, 400 mL, 400 mL
   (b) 500 mL, 500 mL, 500 mL
   (c) 300 mL, 300 mL, 300 mL
   (d) 500 mL, 250 mL, 250 mL

7. Convert 15 km 200 m into metres.   [2012]
   (a) 15200 m   (b) 17000 m   (c) 15020 m   (d) 15002 m

8. Arrange the objects given below in the order of length smallest to longest.
   A.   B.   C.   D.
   (a) A C D B   (b) C A D B   (c) C A B D   (d) A D C B

9. How many inches are in a foot and a half?   [2015]
   (a) 12   (b) 18   (c) 9   (d) 3

10. Meera is decorating her room using different sizes of ribbons. Arrange the ribbons given below from longest to shortest.
    A.   B.
    C.   D.
    (a) C D B A   (b) C D A B   (c) D C B A   (d) C A D B

11. Which group of buckets can hold more than 1000 mL of water together?   [2017]

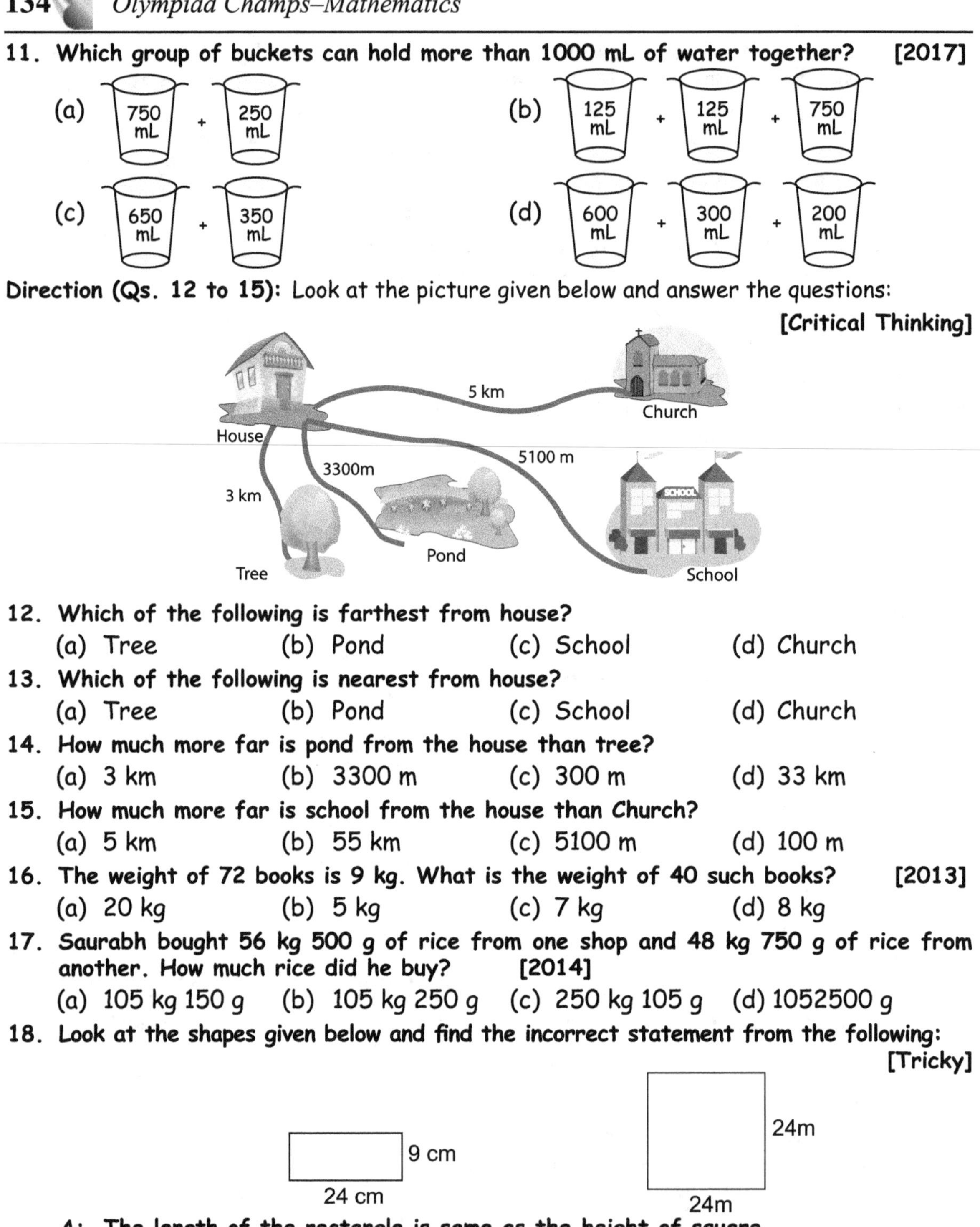

(a) ⬚ + ⬚   (b) ⬚ + ⬚ + ⬚

(c) ⬚ + ⬚   (d) ⬚ + ⬚ + ⬚

Direction (Qs. 12 to 15): Look at the picture given below and answer the questions:

[Critical Thinking]

12. Which of the following is farthest from house?
    (a) Tree   (b) Pond   (c) School   (d) Church

13. Which of the following is nearest from house?
    (a) Tree   (b) Pond   (c) School   (d) Church

14. How much more far is pond from the house than tree?
    (a) 3 km   (b) 3300 m   (c) 300 m   (d) 33 km

15. How much more far is school from the house than Church?
    (a) 5 km   (b) 55 km   (c) 5100 m   (d) 100 m

16. The weight of 72 books is 9 kg. What is the weight of 40 such books?   [2013]
    (a) 20 kg   (b) 5 kg   (c) 7 kg   (d) 8 kg

17. Saurabh bought 56 kg 500 g of rice from one shop and 48 kg 750 g of rice from another. How much rice did he buy?   [2014]
    (a) 105 kg 150 g   (b) 105 kg 250 g   (c) 250 kg 105 g   (d) 1052500 g

18. Look at the shapes given below and find the incorrect statement from the following:

[Tricky]

9 cm
24 cm
24m
24m

A: The length of the rectangle is same as the height of square.
B: The height of square is more than the height of rectangle.
C: The length of square is same as the height of square.
D: The height of rectangle is less than the length of rectangle.
    (a) D   (b) C   (c) B   (d) A

19. Anuj's weight is 64 kg and his sister is $1\frac{1}{4}$ times to his weight. What is the total weight of both of them? **[2013]**

    (a) 109 kg   (b) 102 kg   (c) 112 kg   (d) 144 kg

20. Distance between your house and your neighbour's house : ? : : Distance between your house and your school : kilometre

    (a) kilometre   (b) centimetre   (c) millimetre   (d) metre

21. The capacity of a small container is 380 mL and the capacity of a big container is 1250 mL. If Aakash uses 8 small containers and 1 big container of water to fill up an empty tank, then what is the capacity of the tank? **[2012]**

    (a) 3750 mL   (b) 4290 mL   (c) 3040 mL   (d) 4190 mL

Direction (Qs. 22 and 23): Look at the diagram given below and answer the questions :

22. Which is the longest wire?
    (a) B   (b) C   (c) D   (d) A

23. Which is the shortest wire?
    (a) B   (b) C   (c) D   (d) A

24. Sneha has 4 m 30 cm of cloth. If she needs only 2 m 70 cm of cloth to make a dress, then how much cloth will remain after making the dress? **[2014]**
    (a) 2 m 60 cm   (b) 1 m 60 cm   (c) 1 m 30 cm   (d) 5 m 60 cm

25. Shikha has $\frac{22}{3}$ m of green ribbon and Priya has $\frac{7}{3}$ m of yellow ribbon. Who has more ribbon and by how much? **[2015]**

    (a) Shikha, 5 m   (b) Priya, 5 m   (c) Shikha, 7 m   (d) Priya, 7 m

26. Hariya Wants to weigh some fruits in his weighing balance. What weight of fruits should be added to balance the scale. **[Critical Thinking]**

    A:

    (a) 400 g   (b) 500 g   (c) 600 g   (d) 700 g

Raghu is making a list of items which will weigh in grams and kilograms. Find the odd one among them.

27. Objects which will weigh in kilograms.

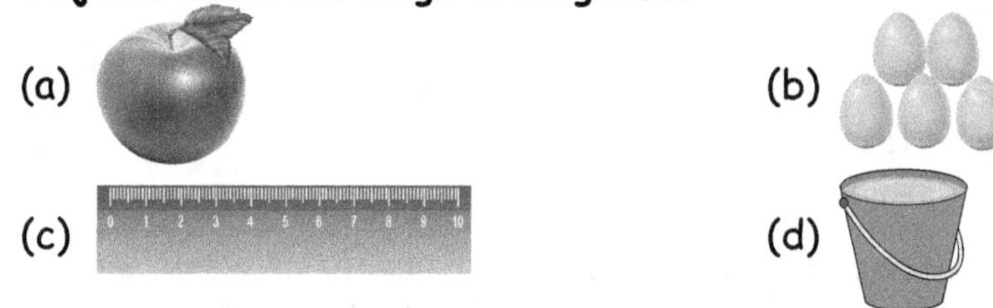

(a)

(b)

(c)

(d)

Direction (Qs. 28 to 31): Read the passage given below and answer the questions that follow:

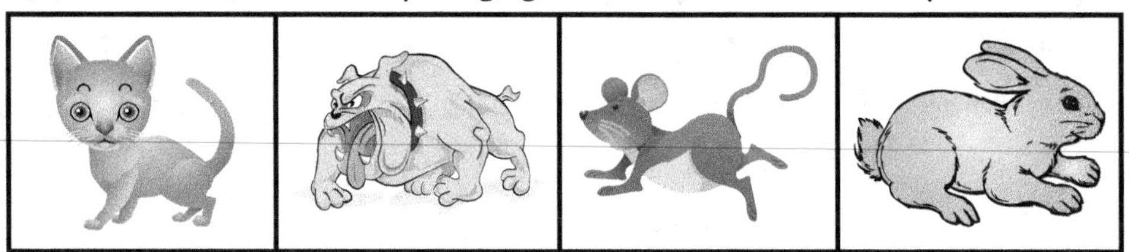

Chintu loves pets. He has four pets – a dog, a cat, a rabbit and a mouse. His veterinary doctor asked him to keep a record of the weight of his pets. One day he decided to note down the weight of his pets. He noted that his dog is 950 g heavier than his cat whose weight is 7 kg and his rabbit is 1 kg 200 g lighter than his cat. He also noted that his mouse weigh 275 g only.

28. How much does Chintu's dog weigh?
    (a) 957 g   (b) 7950 g   (c) 9507 g   (d) 7 kg

29. How much does Chintu's rabbit weigh?
    (a) 5600 g   (b) 5700 g   (c) 5800 g   (d) 5900 g.

30. Which pet is the heaviest?
    (a) Dog   (b) Cat   (c) Rabbit   (d) Mouse

31. If pin : grams :: ? : kilograms
    (a) paper   (b) book   (c) pencil   (d) study table

32. Parul want to match the following objects with their weights. Match the lists given below to help Parul.

	List I		List II
A.		1.	3 kg
B.		2.	18 g
C.		3.	100 g
D.		4.	90 kg

	A	B	C	D
(a)	2	4	3	1
(b)	2	4	1	3
(c)	1	3	4	2
(d)	1	3	2	4

33. Roli has made a list of objects with their weights. Find the incorrect statement among the following: **[Critical Thinking]**

    A: Weight of a packet of biscuit is about 100 g.

    B: Weight of a bottle of jam is about 500 g.

    C: Weight of a bottle of tomato ketchup is about 1 kg.

    D. Weight of 7 eggs is about 2 kg.

    (a) B   (b) C   (c) D   (d) A

34. Jalebi aunty is making kheer in her kitchen. Complete the chart given below to know about the ingrediants she is using in the recipe.

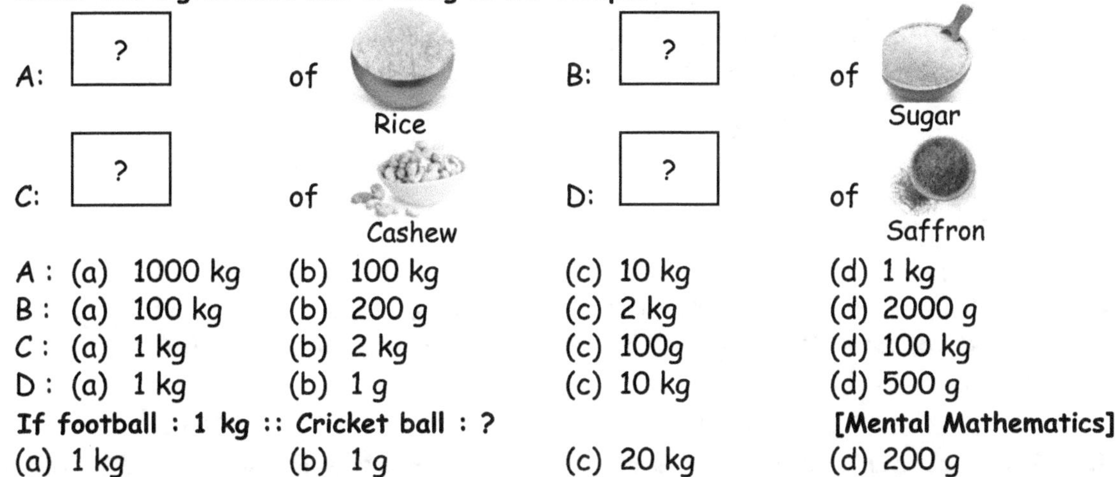

    A : (a) 1000 kg   (b) 100 kg   (c) 10 kg   (d) 1 kg

    B : (a) 100 kg   (b) 200 g   (c) 2 kg   (d) 2000 g

    C : (a) 1 kg   (b) 2 kg   (c) 100g   (d) 100 kg

    D : (a) 1 kg   (b) 1 g   (c) 10 kg   (d) 500 g

35. If football : 1 kg :: Cricket ball : ?   **[Mental Mathematics]**

    (a) 1 kg   (b) 1 g   (c) 20 kg   (d) 200 g

36. Lucky wrote some sentences about weight of some people. Write true/false for the following: **[Critical Thinking]**

    A: Weight of a new born baby is 100 kg.

    B: Weight of a man is about 7g.

    C: Weight of a girl is about 1000 kg.

    D: Weight of a woman is about 60 kg.

    (a) T F F F   (b) F F F T   (c) F F T F   (d) F T F F

37. Look at the pictures given below and find the weight to balance it.

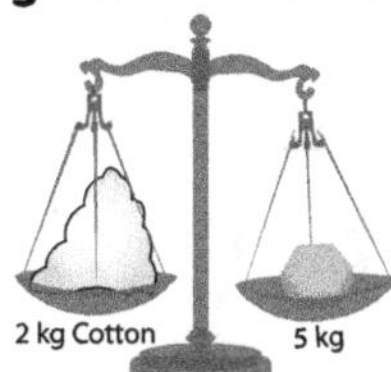

    (a) 1 kg Cotton   (b) 2 kg Cotton

    (c) 3 kg Cotton   (d) 4 kg Cotton

38. Annu aunty has made a list of objects with their weights. Find the incorrect among the following: [Critical Thinking]

    A: Weight of a mug full of coffee is about 450 g.

    B: Weight of a thread roll is about 2 kg.

    C: Weight of a letter is about 5 g.

    D: Weight of a pair of chappals is about 200 g.

    (a) D (b) C (c) B (d) A

39. A water tank contains 9800365 litres water. 456876 litres water is replaced by 9864 cubic stones. Find the remaining amount of water in the tank. [2011]

    (a) 8976590 litres (b) 9544356 litres (c) 9343489 litres (d) 9324326 litres

40. Look at the pictures given below and find the weight of the objects using numbers (0–9) only. [Tricky]

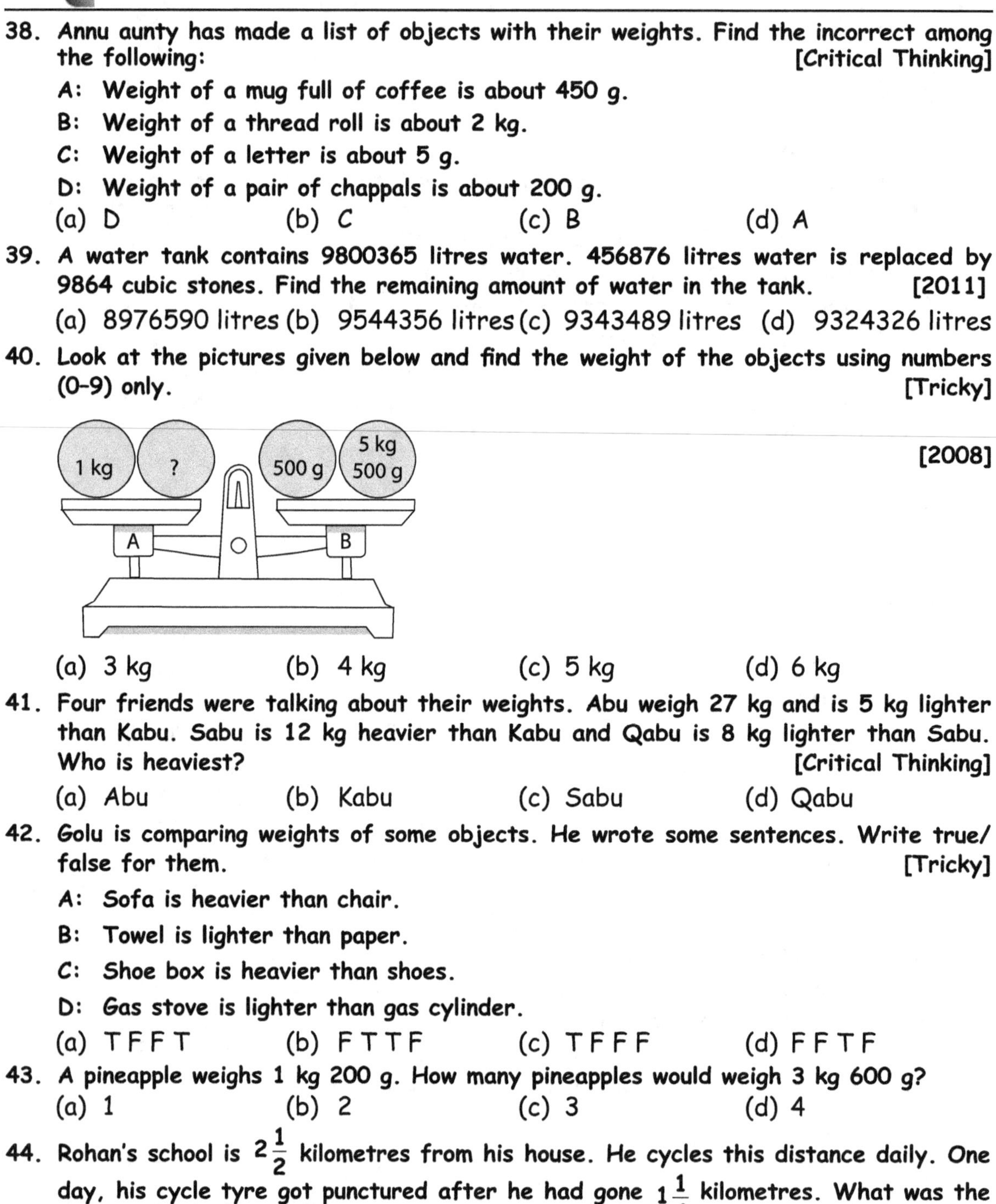

[2008]

    (a) 3 kg (b) 4 kg (c) 5 kg (d) 6 kg

41. Four friends were talking about their weights. Abu weigh 27 kg and is 5 kg lighter than Kabu. Sabu is 12 kg heavier than Kabu and Qabu is 8 kg lighter than Sabu. Who is heaviest? [Critical Thinking]

    (a) Abu (b) Kabu (c) Sabu (d) Qabu

42. Golu is comparing weights of some objects. He wrote some sentences. Write true/false for them. [Tricky]

    A: Sofa is heavier than chair.

    B: Towel is lighter than paper.

    C: Shoe box is heavier than shoes.

    D: Gas stove is lighter than gas cylinder.

    (a) T F F T (b) F T T F (c) T F F F (d) F F T F

43. A pineapple weighs 1 kg 200 g. How many pineapples would weigh 3 kg 600 g?

    (a) 1 (b) 2 (c) 3 (d) 4

44. Rohan's school is $2\frac{1}{2}$ kilometres from his house. He cycles this distance daily. One day, his cycle tyre got punctured after he had gone $1\frac{1}{4}$ kilometres. What was the distance he had to walk? [2014]

    (a) $1\frac{3}{4}$ km (b) $2\frac{1}{2}$ km (c) $3\frac{3}{4}$ km (d) $1\frac{1}{4}$ km

45. Complete the passage given below:

    Ladoo is a cute boy. He was very thin when he was in class 1. His weight has 20 kg. His mother started giving him healthy foods. After 6 months he gained ______

(A)______ kg and his weight become 32 kg. After 1 year, he gained ______(B)______ kg and his weight became 45 kg. He became very fat so he started exercising. After few months he lost ______(C)______ kg and his weight became 31 kg. Then he decided to maintain his weight and lost another ______(D)______ kg and so that he could keep his weight as 27 kg. Now he is normal not too fat and not too thin.

A : (a) 10   (b) 11   (c) 12   (d) 13
B : (a) 10   (b) 11   (c) 12   (d) 13
C : (a) 11   (b) 12   (c) 13   (d) 14
D : (a) 4   (b) 5   (c) 6   (d) 7

46. Read the statement and choose the correct option.   **[Critical Thinking]**

Statement A : Large quantities are measured in millilitres, whereas small quantities are measured in litres.

Statement B : Kerosene oil, petrol, milk etc., are measured in litres.

(a) Statement A is right B is wrong.   (b) Statement B is right A is wrong.
(c) Both the statements are right.   (d) Both the statements are wrong.

47. How many pieces of ribbon, measuring 45 cm each, can be cut from a roll of ribbon measuring 15 m 75 cm?   **[2016]**

(a) 45   (b) 35   (c) 65   (d) 77

48. Aakash had 34 kg 975 g of sugar. After packing it equally into 6 packets of equal weight, he was left with 8 kg 725 g of sugar. How much sugar was there in each packet?   **[2018]**

(a) 4 kg 375 g   (b) 3 kg 475 g   (c) 3 kg 725 g   (d) 4 kg 725 g

49. Study the given figures carefully and find the weight of   **[2018]**

(a) 400 g   (b) 200 g   (c) 100 g   (d) 300 g

50. 500 poles were erected along one side of a straight road. Two poles were 5 m apart. What is the distance between the first pole and the last pole?   **[2020]**

(a) 2 km 90 m

(b) 3 km 495 m

(c) 2 km 500 m

(d) 2 km 495 m

51. If the cost of 12 notebooks is ₹288 and the cost of 9 pens is ₹135, then what will be the cost of 2 pens and 5 notebooks?   [2022]

    (a) ₹138   (b) ₹150   (c) ₹142   (d) ₹123

RESPONSE GRID

LEVEL 1

1. a b c d	2. a b c d	3. a b c d	4. a b c d	5. a b c d
6. a b c d	7. a b c d	8. a b c d	9. a b c d	10. a b c d
11. a b c d	12. a b c d	13. a b c d	14. a b c d	

LEVEL 2

1. a b c d	2. a b c d	3. a b c d	4. a b c d	5. a b c d
6. a b c d	7. a b c d	8. a b c d	9. a b c d	10. a b c d
11. a b c d	12. a b c d	13. a b c d	14. a b c d	15. a b c d
16. a b c d	17. a b c d	18. a b c d	19. a b c d	20. a b c d
21. a b c d	22. a b c d	23. a b c d	24. a b c d	25. a b c d
26. a b c d	27. a b c d	28. a b c d	29. a b c d	30. a b c d
31. a b c d	32. a b c d	33. a b c d	34. a b c d	35. a b c d
36. a b c d	37. a b c d	38. a b c d	39. a b c d	40. a b c d
41. a b c d	42. a b c d	43. a b c d	44. a b c d	45. a b c d
46. a b c d	47. a b c d	48. a b c d	49. a b c d	50. a b c d
51. a b c d				

Solutions with Explanation

LEVEL 1

1. **(b)** The longest line is (b). Therefore, the answer is option (b).

2. **(b)** Since, depth of a bucket would measure in centimetres so, statement C is incorrect.

3. **(d)** Since, length of t-shirt would measure in centimetre. So, the odd one is t-shirt.

4. **(a)** The length of the wood = 1 m and 26 cm = 126 cm.
Length of shelf = 86 cm.
Length he needs to cut off = 126 cm – 86 cm = 40 cm.

5. **(c)** As 1 kilometre = 1000 metre.

6. **(a)**   **7.** **(a)**   **8.** **(d)**   **9.** **(c)**   **10.** **(d)**   **11.** **(b)**

12. **(c)** Each can oil = $\dfrac{20000+175}{25} = \dfrac{20175}{25}$ = 807 ml

13. **(c)** Total weight of the ornaments = 14 g 200 mg + 15 g 900 mg + 9 g 700 mg + 5 g 900 mg
= 45 g 700 mg

14. **(c)**

LEVEL 2

1. **(c)** Since, there are 100 centimetres in a metre. So, A is true.
   Since, there are 1000 metres in a kilometre, so, B is false.
   Since, centimetre is a smaller unit than kilometre, so, C is false.
   Since, metre is a larger unit than centimetre, so, D is false.
   Therefore, the answer is option (c) T F F F.

2. **A :** (c) Since, 12 km + 26 km = 38 km.
   B : (b) Since, 12 km + 26 km + 8 km = 46 km.
   C : (c) Since, he travelled for 12 km + 26 km + 8 km = 46 km
   D : (d) Since, he travelled for 46 km on one side so, total distance he travelled throughout the day becomes 2 times 46 km = 2 × 46 km = 92 km.

3. **(d)** LM = 12 – 4 – 5 = 3 cm.

4. **(d)** The height of tree = 372 cm
   Height of stool = 2 m = 200 cm
   Height of jump Manku needs to make = 372 cm – 200 cm = 172 cm.

5. **(b)** Total length of pole = 3.1 m + 30 cm = 310 cm + 30 cm = 340 cm.

6. **(d)** 1000 mL = 500 mL + 250 mL + 250 mL

7. **(a)** 15 km 200 m = 15000 m + 200 m = 15200 m

8. **(b)** The order of objects from length smallest to longest will be
   Match stick   —   Pencil box   —   Book   —   Table
        C   A   D   B
   Therefore, the answer is option (c) C A D B.

9. **(b)** As 1 foot = 12 inches
   So 1 foot and a half = 12 + 6 inches = 18 inches

10. **(b)** The answer is option (b) C D A B.

11. **(d)** As 600 mL + 30 mL + 200 mL = 1100 mL which is greater than 1000 mL.

12. **(c)** Since, the school is 5100 m = 5 km 100 m away from house so it is farthest of all from house.

13. **(a)** Since, tree is 3 km away from house, so it is nearest of all from house.

14. **(c)** The distance of pond from house = 3300 m.
   The distance of tree from house = 3 km = 3000 m.
   The distance pond is more far than tree from house = 3300 m – 3000 m = 300 m.

15. **(d)** The distance of school from house = 5100 m.
   The distance of Church from house = 5 km = 5000 m.
   The distance of school is more far than Church from house = 5100 m – 5000 m = 100 m

16. **(b)** Weight of 72 books = 9 kg
   Weight of 40 books = $\dfrac{9}{72}$ × 40 = 5 kg

17. **(b)** 56 kg 500 g + 48 kg 750 g = 105 kg 250 g

18. **(d)** Since, the length of rectangle is 24 cm and the length of square is 24 m, so the length of rectangle is less than the length of square. So, statement A is incorrect.

19. **(d)** Total weight = $64 + 1\dfrac{1}{4}$ of $64 = 64 + \dfrac{5}{4} \times 64$
   $= 64 + 80 = 144$ kg.

20. **(d)**   The distance between your house and your neighbour's house will be in metres.
21. **(b)**   Capacity of tank = 8 × 380 + 1250 = 3040 + 1250 = 4290 mL.
22. **(a)**   The longest wire is B.
23. **(c)**   The shortest wire is D.
24. **(b)**   4 m 30 cm – 2 m 70 cm = 1 m 60 cm
25. **(a)**   Shikha, 5 m
26. **(d)**   A: Since, 1 kg = 1000 g. The weight of fruits to be added = 1000 g – 300 g = 700 g.
27. **(d)**   Since, a bucket full of water would weigh in kilograms.
28. **(b)**   Weight of cat   = 7 kg
             Weight of dog   = 7 kg + 950 g = 7950 g
             Therefore, the answer is option (b) 7950 g.
29. **(c)**   Weight of cat   = 7 kg = 7000 g
             Weight of rabbit = 7000 g – 1200 g = 5800 g.
             Therefore, the answer is option (c) 5800 g.
30. **(a)**   The heaviest pet is dog. Therefore, the answer is option (a) dog.
31. **(d)**   Since, study table would weigh in kilograms. Therefore, the answer is option (d) study table.
32. **(b)**
33. **(c)**   Since, weight of 7 eggs would be less than 500g so it would be less than 2 kg. So, statement D is incorrect.
34. **A:**   1 kg of rice ⟶ option (d)
    B: 200 g of sugar ⟶ option (b)
    C: 100 g of cashewnuts ⟶ option (c)
    D: 1 g of saffron ⟶ option (b)
35. **(d)**   Cricket ball would weigh about 200 g.   Therefore, the answer is option (d) 200 g.
36. **(b)**
37. **(c)**   Since 5 kg = 2 kg + ⬭ 3 kg
             Therefore, the answer is option (c) 3 kg.
38. **(c)**   Since, weight of a thread roll is about 2g and not 2 kg. So, statement B is incorrect.
39. **(c)**   As 9800365 – 456876 = 9343489 litres
40. **(c)**   5 kg 500g + 500g = 6 kg
             ∴   6 kg – 1 kg = 5 kg
             Therefore, the answer is option (c) 5 kg.
41. **(c)**   Weight of Abu = 27 kg
             Weight of Kabu = 27 kg + 5 kg = 32 kg
             Weight of Sabu = 32 kg + 12 kg = 44 kg
             Weight of Qabu = 44 kg – 8 kg = 36 kg
             ∴   The heaviest is Sabu.
42. **(a)**
43. **(c)**   Weight of 1 pineapple = 1 kg 200g = 1200g
             ∴   Weight of 3 pineapples = 3 × 1200g = 3600g = 3 kg 600g

44. **(d)** $\quad 2\frac{1}{2} - 1\frac{1}{4} = \frac{5}{2} - \frac{5}{4} = 1\frac{1}{4}\,km$

45. A: **(c)** 32 kg – 20 kg = 12 kg

   B: **(d)** 45 kg – 32 kg = 13 kg

   C: **(d)** 45 kg – 31 kg = 14 kg

   D: **(a)** 31 kg – 27 kg = 4 kg

46. **(b)**

47. **(b)**

48. **(a)** Packed sugar = 34 kg 975 g – 8 kg 725 g = 26 kg 250 g

$$\text{Each packet sugar} = \frac{26\,kg\,250g}{6} = 4\,kg\,375\,g$$

49. **(b)**

50. **(d)**

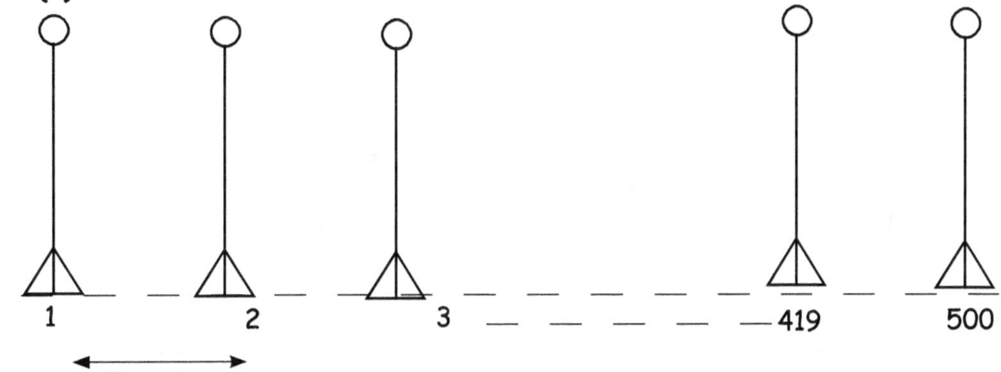

   distance between first pole and the last pole = 499 × 5
   = 2495 m
   = 2 km 495 m

51. **(b)**

Conversion of Money

1. Circle the coins to make 5 rupees. Cross out the coins you do not use.

2. Convert the following amount of money into paise.

a.

b.

11

Chapter

Money

❖ You and your friends go to bakery to purchase a cake and give money to shopkeeper. If you do not have exact amount as is the cost of cake then shopkeeper will give change back.

❖ You were given several coins and paper notes of different denominations and you are being asked to count the total money present

❖ In ancient days before money was invented, the barter system was used.

❖ Barter is a system of exchange by which goods or services are directly exchanged for other goods or services without using a medium of exchange, such as money.

LEARNING OBJECTIVES

This lesson will help you to:—

❖ overview of money and its use.

❖ convert Rupees to Paise.

❖ analyze situations to enable addition, subtraction, multiplication and division of money.

❖ enable a child to count the money.

❖ uses operations to find totals, change, multiple costs and unit cost.

❖ estimates roughly the totals and total cost.

❖ real life examples to help in better understanding of Rupees and Paisa.

QUICK CONCEPT REVIEW

❖ What is money? Money is any object or record that is generally accepted as payment for goods and services.

❖ The unit of currency in India is Rupees and 1 Rupee = 100 Paisa

  ➢ 10 coins of 10 Paisa make one Rupee

  ➢ 2 coins of 50 Paisa make one Rupee

  ➢ 4 coins of 25 Paisa make one Rupee

❖ Few important currencies of the world are United State Dollars ($), UK Pound Sterling and Euro.

❖ The paper based notes available in India are of ₹ 2000, ₹ 500, ₹ 200 ₹ 100, ₹ 50, ₹ 20, ₹ 10, ₹ 5 as shown below:

❖ The coins available in India are of ₹ 10, ₹ 5, ₹ 2 and ₹ 1, as shown below:

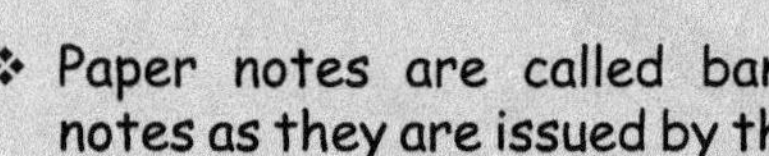
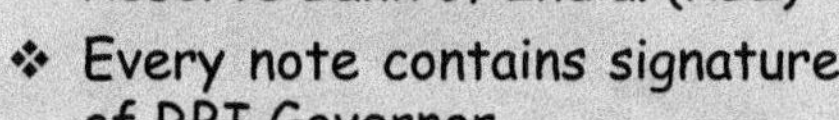
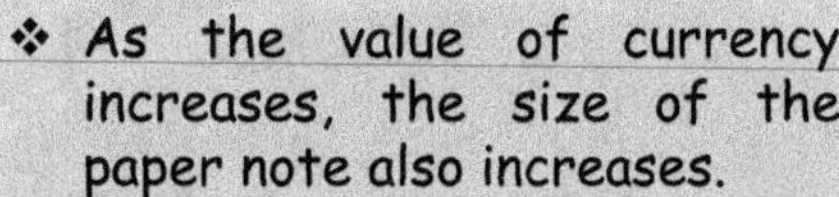
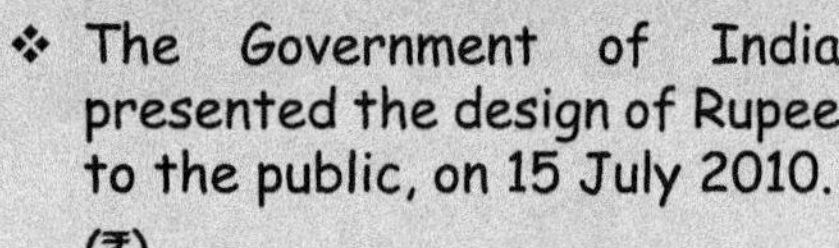

Amazing Facts

❖ Paper notes are called bank notes as they are issued by the Reserve Bank of India. (RBI)

❖ Every note contains signature of RBI Governor.

❖ As the value of currency increases, the size of the paper note also increases.

❖ The Government of India presented the design of Rupee to the public, on 15 July 2010. (₹)

❖ Following are the notes and coins which are not used anymore:

❖ When one goes for purchase to market and gives more money than the price of material, then the shopkeeper will return the money back. That returned money is known as change.

For example: You go to market to purchase a chocolate. The cost of the chocolate was ₹ 8 but you had ₹ 10 note. You gave ₹ 10 note and the shopkeeper returned you ₹ 2 as a change.

❖ You have learnt how to use operations to find totals, change, multiple costs and unit cost.

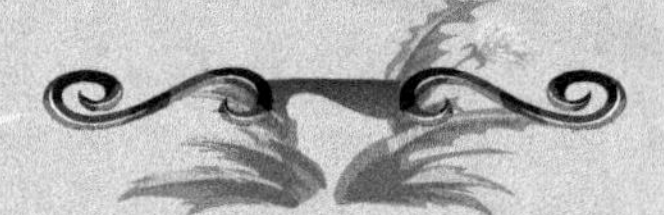

Misconcept/Concept

Misconcept: If a paper note is mutilated or torn, then you lose money as you feel that it cannot be used as no shopkeeper is ready to take it.

Concept: Mutilated notes can be tendered at all bank branches for and exchange obtained. Payment of exchange value of mutilated notes is governed by the Reserve Bank of India (Note Refund) Rules and one can get full / half / no value depending on the condition of the note.

Multiple Choice Questions

LEVEL 1

1. Sameer went to purchase cricket kit and gave to cashier two coins of ₹ 5, four notes of ₹ 10, three notes of ₹ 50 and two notes of ₹ 500. If the price of cricket kit was ₹ 1162, the change that he would have got back is _______.

   (a) ₹ 38 (b) ₹ 15 (c) ₹ 30 (d) ₹ 32

2. Kiran bought 5 cookies all of which were having equal price. If the total amount paid by her was ₹ 33, what was the price of 1 cookie?

   (a) ₹ 5 (b) ₹ 5.50 (c) ₹ 6.00 (d) ₹ 6.60

Direction (Qs. 3 to 7): Consider the prices of these items below to answer questions.

Apple:	₹ 180 per Kg
Pen:	₹ 8 per piece
Eraser:	₹ 5 for 2 erasers
Chocolate:	₹ 15 for 3 chocolates

3. Ram wants to buy half Kg apples and one chocolate. The total amount he needs to pay is: **[Mental Mathematics]**

   (a) ₹ 85 (b) ₹ 95 (c) ₹ 90 (d) ₹ 105

4. If Abhay wants to buy one pen and 3 erasers, how much he needs to pay?

   (a) ₹ 13 (b) ₹ 15 (c) ₹ 15.50 (d) ₹ 16.25

5. One kg apples can be bought for ₹ 180 and two chocolates can be brought for ₹ 7.50. This statement is _____. **[Mental Mathematics]**

   (a) True (b) False

   (c) Insufficient information (d) None of these

6. If Mohit has ₹ 122 and he wants to buy as many chocolates he can with this amount. The maximum number of chocolates that he can buy is:

   (a) 15 (b) 20 (c) 24 (d) 30

Direction (Qs. 7 to 10): Consider the following scenario to answer questions.

Priya and Payal are two friends and one day they decided to go to shopping together. Priya had ₹ 1500 and Payal had ₹ 2000 with them. Priya purchased shoes for ₹ 550, a skirt for ₹ 275 and a movie DVD for ₹ 50. Payal purchased top for ₹ 250, a bag for ₹ 480, a book for ₹ 115 and a tennis racket for ₹ 500.

7. What is the total money spent by Priya and Payal together in shopping?

   (a) ₹ 2220 (b) ₹ 2170 (c) ₹ 1720 (d) ₹ 880

8. The amount left with Payal after shopping is ______.

   (a) ₹ 540 (b) ₹ 550 (c) ₹ 555 (d) ₹ 655

9. On the way back to home, Priya purchased a toy for his little brother worth ₹ 99. Now, how much money is left with her?

    (a) ₹ 426   (b) ₹ 476   (c) ₹ 526   (d) ₹ 626

10. If the amount left with Payal is to be divided equally into 5 parts, what will be amount of one part?

    (a) ₹ 108   (b) ₹ 110   (c) ₹ 111   (d) ₹ 131

11. Convert ₹ 2465.25 into paise.   [2013]

    (a) 246525 paise   (b) 2465250 paise

    (c) 24652500 paise   (d) 246525000 paise

12. Identify the correct options :   [2014]

    (a) ₹ 1 = 100 paise   (b) 1 paise = ₹ 0.01

    (c) ₹ 7.50 = 750 paise   (d) All of these

13. Arrange the following amounts of money in descending order.

| ₹ 20.50 | ₹ 31.75 | ₹ 11.25 | ₹ 51.05 | ₹ 13.50 | ₹ 14.55 |

    (a) ₹ 31.75 > ₹ 51.05 > ₹ 20.50 > ₹ 14.55 > ₹ 13.50 > ₹ 11.25

    (b) ₹ 51.05 < ₹ 31.75 < ₹ 20.50 < ₹ 14.55 < ₹ 13.50 < ₹ 11.25

    (c) ₹ 51.05 > ₹ 31.75 > ₹ 20.50 > ₹ 14.55 > ₹ 13.50 > ₹ 11.25

    (d) ₹ 51.05 > ₹ 31.75 > ₹ 20.50 > ₹ 14.55 > ₹ 11.25 > ₹ 13.50

14. Arrange the following amounts of money in ascending order.   [2009]

| ₹ 275 | ₹ 175 | ₹ 225 | ₹ 250 | ₹ 575 | ₹ 150 | ₹ 100 | ₹ 75 | ₹ 510 |

    (a) ₹ 575 < ₹ 510 < ₹ 275 < ₹ 250 < ₹ 225 < ₹ 175 < ₹ 150 < ₹ 100 < ₹ 75

    (b) ₹ 75 < ₹ 100 < ₹ 125 < ₹ 175 < ₹ 225 < ₹ 250 < ₹ 475 < ₹ 510 < ₹ 575

    (c) ₹ 75 < ₹ 100 < ₹ 150 < ₹ 175 < ₹ 250 < ₹ 225 < ₹ 275 < ₹ 510 < ₹ 575

    (d) ₹ 75 < ₹ 100 < ₹ 150 < ₹ 175 < ₹ 225 < ₹ 250 < ₹ 275 < ₹ 510 < ₹ 575

Direction (Qs. 15 and 16): Consider the following scenario to answer the questions.

The sum of money with Rohan and Rahul is equal to money with Pooja. The total money with all three of them is ₹ 150.

15. How much money is present with Pooja?

    (a) ₹ 35   (b) ₹ 50   (c) ₹ 60   (d) ₹ 75

16. The amount of money present with Rahul is _____.

    (a) ₹ 25

    (b) ₹ 40

    (c) ₹ 75

    (d) Data insufficient. Cannot be determined

Direction (Qs. 17 to 19): Consider the following scenario to answer the questions.

Five friends Simran, Aruna, Shalini, Rashmi and Kiran went together to see the football match. The amount of money that they had is represented by the figure below. The height of each tower represents the amount of money they had.

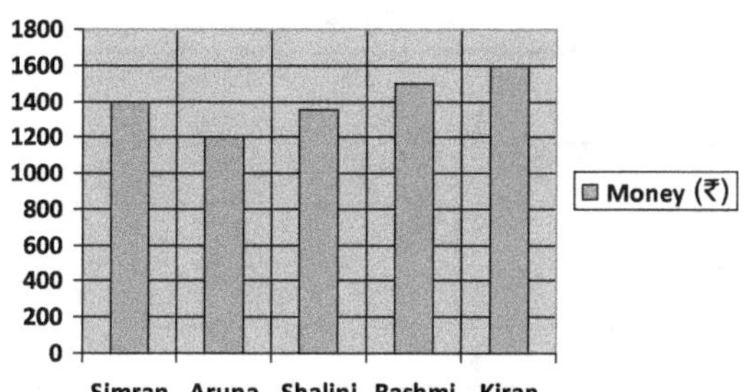

17. Who has the highest amount of money with her?

(a)   Kiran   (b)   Rashmi   (c)   Aruna   (d)   Simran

18. The difference between the highest and lowest amount of money is _____ .

(a)   ₹ 150   (b)   ₹ 200   (c)   ₹ 400   (d)   ₹ 250

19. Consider the following four statements.   [Critical Thinking]

A.   Aruna had the maximum amount of money.

B.   Total sum of money with Simran, Aruna and Kiran is ₹ 4200.

C.   Simran had the least amount of money.

D.   Difference between money of Simran and Aruna is ₹ 200.

Which of the following is correct where T stands for TRUE and F Stands for FALSE?

	A	B	C	D
(a)	T	F	F	T
(b)	F	T	F	T
(c)	F	T	T	F
(d)	T	F	T	F

20. ₹ 7 and 7 paise is written as :   [2014]

(a)   ₹ 7.7   (b)   ₹ 0.77   (c)   ₹ 7.07   (d)   ₹ 77

21. Add the following :   [2014]

₹ 54.89 + ₹ 32.00 + 745 paise

(a)   ₹ 9434   (b)   ₹ 794.34   (c)   ₹ 94.34   (d)   ₹ 943.40

22. The movie tickets of 8 people cost ₹ 1000. What will be the cost of 24 tickets?   [2014]

(a)   ₹ 300   (b)   ₹ 5000   (c)   ₹ 3000   (d)   ₹ 4500

23. How much money should be added to ₹ 25.70 to make ₹ 53.41?   [2012]

(a)   ₹ 27.51   (b)   ₹ 37.71   (c)   ₹ 17.71   (d)   ₹ 27.71

24. If 3 pens cost ₹ 15, how much do 5 pens cost?   [2012]

(a)   ₹ 25   (b)   ₹ 10   (c)   ₹ 15   (d)   ₹ 20

25. Which one of the following is true for ₹ 25.63?   [2012]

(a)   ₹ 25 and 63 paise   (b)   ₹ 2563

(c)   ₹ 256 and 3 paise   (d)   ₹ 2 and 63 paise

26. Rishi had ₹ 7295. He spent ₹ 2105 on shopping, ₹ 1223 on travelling and ₹ 1500 on movie. How much money is left with him now? **[2019]**

    (a) ₹ 2467   (b) ₹ 3105   (c) ₹ 2400   (d) ₹ 2050

LEVEL 2

1. Match the following: **[Tricky]**

	List I		List II
A.	₹ 65 ÷ ₹ 5	1.	₹ 13.50
B.	₹ 11.75 + ₹ 2.25	2.	₹ 13
C.	₹ 15.25 – ₹ 1.75	3.	₹ 6
D.	12 × 50 paisa	4.	₹ 14.50
E.	₹ 14.75 – 25 paisa	5.	₹ 14

	A	B	C	D	E
(a)	2	3	5	4	1
(b)	2	5	1	3	4
(c)	3	4	5	2	1
(d)	3	5	4	1	2

2. Yuvika is very fond of reading books. Once she bought books for ₹ 465 and she paid ₹ 500 to the bookstore, which expression shows the correct amount of change that she will get back?

    (a) ₹ 500 + ₹465   (b) ₹500 – ₹465   (c) ₹500 ÷₹ 465   (d) ₹500 ×₹ 465

3. Christina has ₹ 235 more than the money Jack has. If Jack has ₹ 200, how much money do they have together? **[2012]**

    (a) ₹ 625   (b) ₹ 635   (c) ₹ 630   (d) ₹ 650

4. At a local fair in Delhi, Katrina had ₹ 500 to spend. She spent ₹ 140 on video games, ₹ 45 on large popcorn and ₹ 15 on small lemonade. How much money is left with Katrina? **[2011]**

    (a) ₹ 300   (b) ₹ 150   (c) ₹ 200   (d) ₹ 130

Direction (Qs. 5 to 7): Consider the following picture to answer questions.

5. The total amount of money shown in the figure is _____.　　　[Mental Mathematics]

    (a) ₹ 2665　　　　(b) ₹ 2605　　　　(c) ₹ 2650　　　　(d) ₹ 2550

6. If ₹ 100 and ₹ 5 notes are removed from the picture and the remaining money is divided among 4 children, each child will get ₹ _____.　　　[Mental Mathematics]

    (a) 675　　　　　(b) 640　　　　　(c) 600　　　　　(d) 660

7. If two notes of ₹ 5, three notes of ₹ 10 and four notes of ₹ 50 are added to these notes, then the total amount of money will be ______.

    (a) ₹ 2720　　　　(b) ₹ 2905　　　　(c) ₹ 1855　　　　(d) ₹ 1775

8. Shikhar needs to buy a birthday present for his niece costing ₹ 545. He has some notes of ₹ 100, ₹ 20, ₹ 10 and coins of Re 1, 50p and 25p. Which of the following combination of notes and coins will help him in birthday present?

    [Critical Thinking/ Tricky]

    (a) 5 notes of ₹ 100, 1 notes of ₹ 20, 2 notes of ₹ 10, 4 coins of Re 1, 3 coins of 50p & 4 coins of 25p.

    (b) 4 notes of ₹ 100, 4 notes of ₹ 20, 2 notes of ₹ 10, 10 coins of Re 1, 20 coins of 50p & 10 coins of 25p.

    (c) 4 notes of ₹ 100, 5 notes of ₹ 20, 4 notes of ₹ 10, 2 coins of Re 1, 3 coins of 50p & 4 coins of 25p.

    (d) 5 notes of ₹ 100, 1 notes of ₹ 20, 2 notes of ₹ 10, 3 coins of Re 1, 2 coins of 50p & 4 coins of 25p.

9. Garima had ₹ 42700 in the bank. She put in another ₹ 250. How much more money must she put in, if she wants to have a sum of ₹ 60000?　　　[2013]

    (a) ₹ 17800　　　　(b) ₹ 17050　　　　(c) ₹ 14080　　　　(d) ₹ 10480

10. Ajay buys a piggy bank. He has 52 one rupee coins, 26 fifty paise coins and 32 twenty-five paise coins. How much money does he have?　　　[2013]

    (a) ₹ 74　　　　　(b) ₹ 73　　　　　(c) ₹ 68　　　　　(d) ₹ 80

Direction (Qs. 11 to 14): Consider the following story to answer questions.

In ancient times, there was a king named Vikramaditya who was very kind and helpful for poor people of his kingdom. He decided to remove poverty from his kingdom. He gave an order to his ministers to find poor people in his kingdom. They found 1000 poor people in the kingdom. So King appointed Ramsingh, Vikrant and Jaysingh from his ministers to come up with idea of removing poverty. Vikrant suggested that king should distribute ₹ 25 as one time allowance and ₹ 5 per month for 11 months. Jaysingh suggested that king should distribute rice and wheat worth ₹ 50 and also give ₹ 20 every 6 months for 2 years. Ramsingh suggested that king should distribute ₹ 75 to each person in the kingdom as a one-time allowance.

11. What will be the total expenses of King Vikramaditya if he decides to go with advice of Jaysingh?

    (a) ₹ 70000　　　　(b) ₹ 130000　　　　(c) ₹ 100000　　　　(d) ₹ 140000

12. How much amount per person will be distributed by king if he goes with advice of Vikrant?

    (a) ₹ 25   (b) ₹ 55   (c) ₹ 80   (d) ₹ 100

13. Whose suggestion will lead to the least expenses for the king Vikramaditya?

    (a) Vikrant   (b) Jaysingh   (c) Ramsingh   (d) None of these

14. Which of the following statement is NOT true?

    (a) Vikrant suggested to distribute ₹ 80000 to the people of kingdom.

    (b) Amount suggested by Jaysingh is greater than amount suggested by Ramsingh.

    (c) Total expenses if King decides to go by Vikrant's advice will be ₹ 55000.

    (d) Total expenses if King decides to go by Ramsingh's advice will be ₹ 75000.

15. To decorate a banquet hall, 354 electric bulbs were bought. If the cost of each bulb is ₹ 28, what is the total cost of 354 electric bulbs?   **[2015]**

    (a) ₹ 9912   (b) ₹ 7660   (c) ₹ 4944   (d) ₹ 9940

16. Rohan's father returned from foreign trip and he brought with him some currencies like 10 notes of 20 US Dollars, 5 notes of 10 UK pounds. If the price of 1 US Dollar = ₹ 50 and price of 1 UK pound = ₹ 80, then the total amount in rupees that he has is _______

    (a) ₹ 14000   (b) ₹ 12000   (c) ₹ 10000   (d) ₹ 4000

17. Sohan's father needs to pay ₹ 4000 for Sohan's quarterly school fees. He has the following amount with him. How much more amount father needs so that he can pay ₹ 4000 as quarterly fees?   **[2009]**

    • 1 note of ₹ 2000   • 2 notes of ₹ 500

    • 4 notes of ₹ 100   • 7 notes of ₹ 50

    • 3 notes of ₹ 20

    (a) ₹ 150   (b) ₹ 590   (c) ₹ 250   (d) ₹ 190

Direction (Qs. 18 and 19): Consider the following scenario to answer questions.

A family of four i.e. father, mother and two children went to visit zoo and took ₹ 1000 with them. The cost of zoo tickets is ₹ 50 per adult and ₹ 20 per child. They spent ₹ 200 for food and ₹ 50 to purchase bananas for monkeys. On returning back, father lost ₹ 110 from his purse.

18. What is the total amount the family spent during zoo visit?

    (a) ₹ 320   (b) ₹ 390   (c) ₹ 400   (d) None of these

19. While returning back, father lost ₹ 110 from his purse. What is the amount left with father after the zoo visit?

    (a) ₹ 420   (b) ₹ 480   (c) ₹ 500   (d) ₹ 650

20. Mohini is very fond of collecting different kinds of currencies both coins and paper notes. She has coins of 10p, 25p, 50p, Re 1, ₹ 5, ₹ 10 and notes of ₹ 5, ₹ 10, ₹ 20, ₹ 50 and ₹ 100. What is the total amount of money with her?

    (a) ₹ 195.75   (b) ₹ 201.85   (c) ₹ 200.75   (d) ₹ 200.85

21. I went for a journey with ₹ 32700. On the first day I spent ₹ 12350, on the second day ₹ 5980, and on the third day ₹ 10798. How much money do I have now? [2016]

    (a) ₹ 3500   (b) ₹ 3672   (c) ₹ 3572   (d) ₹ 4672

22. Raj needs to buy an ice-cream worth ₹ 10. He has some coins of 25p, 50p and Re 1. Which of the following combination of coins will help him in buying the ice-cream?   [2010]

    (a)   8 coins of 25p, 6 coins of 50p & 6 coins of Re 1.

    (b)   2 coins of 25p, 12 coins of 50p & 4 coins of Re 1.

    (c)   8 coins of 25p, 4 coins of 50p & 5 coins of Re 1.

    (d)   4 coins of 25p, 8 coins of 50p & 5 coins of Re 1.

23. Sumit went to watch a Hokey match in the stadium and carried ₹ 2000 with him. He paid ₹ 400 for the ticket and a cap for ₹ 50. Inside the stadium he bought a cold drink for ₹ 30. At the end of match, he donated ₹ 100 to the charity club maintained by stadium officials. The amount of money left with him is _____. [2009]

    (a) ₹ 1420   (b) ₹ 1380   (c) ₹ 1350   (d) ₹ 1290

24. Harish has 23 coins of 25 paise, 4 coins of 50 paise and one ₹ 10 note. Find the amount Harish has?   [2011]

    (a) ₹ 17.75   (b) ₹ 17.40   (c) ₹ 17.57   (d) All of these

25. If (bicycle) + (teddy bear) + (teddy bear) = ₹1986; (teddy bear) + (doll) = ₹2385 and (bicycle) + (bicycle)

    = ₹684, then find the cost of (doll)   [2018]

    (a) ₹1563   (b) ₹1060   (c) ₹1480   (d) ₹1673

26. Which of the following options have the greatest sum?   [2022]

    (a) 50 notes of ₹20, 12 notes of ₹10, 30 coins of ₹5

    (b) 3 notes of ₹100, 10 coins of ₹5

    (c) 12 notes of ₹100, 10 notes of ₹10

    (d) 50 notes of ₹10, 60 coins of ₹2, 80 coins of ₹1

RESPONSE GRID

LEVEL 1

1. a b c d   2. a b c d   3. a b c d   4. a b c d   5. a b c d
6. a b c d   7. a b c d   8. a b c d   9. a b c d   10. a b c d
11. a b c d   12. a b c d   13. a b c d   14. a b c d   15. a b c d
16. a b c d   17. a b c d   18. a b c d   19. a b c d   20. a b c d
21. a b c d   22. a b c d   23. a b c d   24. a b c d   25. a b c d
26. a b c d

LEVEL 2

1. a b c d   2. a b c d   3. a b c d   4. a b c d   5. a b c d
6. a b c d   7. a b c d   8. a b c d   9. a b c d   10. a b c d
11. a b c d   12. a b c d   13. a b c d   14. a b c d   15. a b c d
16. a b c d   17. a b c d   18. a b c d   19. a b c d   20. a b c d
21. a b c d   22. a b c d   23. a b c d   24. a b c d   25. a b c d
26. a b c d

Solutions with Explanation

LEVEL 1

1. (a) Amount given to cashier = $2 \times ₹\,5 + 4 \times ₹\,10 + 3 \times ₹\,50 + 2 \times ₹\,500$

= $₹\,10 + ₹\,40 + ₹\,150 + ₹\,1000$

= $₹\,1200$

Price of cricket kit is ₹ 1162

So, change to be returned back = ₹ 1200 – ₹ 1162 = ₹ 38.

2. (d) Cost of 5 cookies = ₹ 33

Cost of 1 cookie = 33/ 5 = ₹ 6.60

3. (b) Cost of 1 kg apples = ₹ 180

Cost of half kg apples = 180/ 2 = ₹ 90

Cost of 3 chocolates = ₹ 15

Cost of 1 chocolate = 15/ 3 = ₹ 5

So, Cost of half kg apples + 1 chocolate = ₹ 90 + ₹ 5 = ₹ 95

Hence, Ram needs to pay = ₹ 95.

4. (c) Cost of 1 pen = ₹ 8

Cost of 2 erasers = ₹ 5

Cost of 1 eraser = ₹ 5 / 2 = ₹ 2.50

Cost of 3 erasers = ₹ 2.50 × 3 = ₹ 7.50

Cost of 1 pen + 3 erasers = ₹ 8 + ₹ 7.50 = ₹ 15.50.

5. (b) One kg apples can be brought at ₹ 180 (given)

Let us see cost of 2 chocolates now

Cost of 3 chocolates = ₹ 15

Cost of 1 chocolate = 15 / 3 = ₹ 5

Cost of 2 chocolates = ₹ 5 × 2 = ₹ 10

Hence this statement is false.

6. (c) Cost of 1 chocolate = ₹ 5

For ₹ 122, number of chocolates = 122 / 5 = 24 + remainder 2

Ignore the remainder part

So, Maximum number of chocolates he can brought = 24.

7. **(a)** Money spent by Priya = ₹ 550 (shoes) + ₹ 275 (skirt) + ₹ 50 (movie DVD) = ₹ 875

Money spent by Payal = ₹ 250 (top) + ₹ 480 (bag) + ₹ 115 (book) + ₹ 500 (tennis racket) = ₹ 1345

The total money spent by Priya and Payal together = ₹ 875 + ₹ 1345 = ₹ 2220.

8. **(d)** Money present with Payal initially = ₹ 2000

Money spent by Payal = ₹ 250 (top) + ₹ 480 (bag) + ₹ 115 (book) + ₹ 500 (tennis racket) = ₹ 1345

Money left with Payal = ₹ 2000 - ₹ 1345 = ₹ 655.

9. **(c)** Money present with Priya initially = ₹ 1500

Money spent by Priya = ₹ 550 (shoes) + ₹ 275 (skirt) + ₹ 50 (movie DVD) = ₹ 875

Additional money spent to purchase a toy by Priya = ₹ 100

Total money spent by Priya = 875 + 99 = ₹ 974

Money left with Priya = ₹ 1500 - ₹ 974 = ₹ 526.

10. **(d)** Money left with Payal = ₹ 655

This is to be divided equally into 5 parts

So, one part amount will be = 655 / 5 = ₹ 131.

11. **(a)** ₹ 2465.25 = 246525 paise

12. **(d)** All of these

13. **(c)** ₹ 51.05 > ₹ 31.75 > ₹ 20.50 > ₹ 14.55 > ₹ 13.50 > ₹ 11.25

14. **(d)** ₹ 75 < ₹ 100 < ₹ 150 < ₹ 175 < ₹ 225 < ₹ 250 < ₹ 275 < ₹ 510 < ₹ 575

15. **(d)** Pooja has money equal to both Rahul and Rohan together, which means that Pooja has half of the total money.

So, money present with Pooja = ₹ 150 / 2 = ₹ 75.

16. **(d)** According to the question only given information is that ,Rohan and Rahul has money equal to Pooja = ₹ 75.

But there is no information to make out that how much both of these individually has.

Hence, data provided in question is not sufficient to answer this question.

17. **(a)** Largest tower is of Kiran who has ₹ 1600, hence highest amount is with Kiran

18. **(c)** Highest amount = ₹ 1600 (with Kiran)

Lowest amount = ₹ 1200 (with Aruna)

Difference = ₹ 1600 - ₹ 1200 = ₹ 400.

19. **(b)** Let's check all statement one by one.

Aruna had the maximum amount of money

Maximum amount is with Kiran = ₹ 1600, Hence statement (A) is false .

Total sum of money with Simran, Aruna and Kiran is ₹ 4200

Sum of money with Simran, Aruna and Kiran = ₹ 1400 + ₹ 1200 + ₹ 1600 = ₹ 4200. Hence statement (B) is true.

Simran had the least amount of money

Least amount is with Aruna = ₹ 1200, Hence statement (C) is false.

Difference between money of Simran and Aruna is ₹ 200

Difference between money of Simran and Aruna = ₹ 1400 - ₹ 1200 = ₹ 200. Hence statement (D) is true.

20. **(c)** ₹ 7 and 7 paise = ₹7.07

21. **(c)** ₹54.89 + ₹32.00 + 745 p = ₹94.34.

22. **(c)** Cost of 24 tickets = ₹1000 × 3 = ₹3000

23.	**(d)**	As 53.41 – 25.70 = ₹ 27.71	= ₹ 2105 + ₹ 1223 + ₹ 1500

23. **(d)** As 53.41 – 25.70 = ₹ 27.71

24. **(a)** Cost of 5 pens = $\dfrac{15}{3} \times 5$ = ₹ 25.

25. **(a)** ₹ 25.63 = ₹ 25 and 63 paise

26. **(a)** Rishi had ₹7295

Total money spent

= ₹ 2105 + ₹ 1223 + ₹ 1500

= ₹ 4828

Money left = ₹ 7295 - ₹ 4828

= ₹2467

LEVEL 2

1. **(b)** A.   ₹ 65 / 5 = ₹ 13

B.   ₹ 11.75 + ₹ 2.25 = ₹ 14

C.   ₹ 15.25 – ₹ 1.75 = ₹ 13.50

D.   12 × 50 paisa = ₹ 12 × ₹ 0.50 = ₹ 6

E.   ₹ 14.75 - 25 paisa = ₹ 14.75 - ₹ 0.25 = ₹ 14.50

Hence, Option (B) is correct.

2. **(b)** Change she will get back

= ₹ 500 - ₹ 465 = ₹ 35.

3. **(b)** Total money = ₹ 435 + ₹ 200

= ₹ 635

4. **(a)** ₹500 – (₹ 140 + ₹45 + ₹15) = ₹300

5. **(a)** Total money = ₹ 2000 + ₹ 500 + ₹ 100 + ₹ 50 + ₹ 10 + ₹ 5 = ₹ 2665

6. **(b)** If ₹ 100 and ₹ 5 notes are removed, then remaining money

= ₹ 2000 + ₹ 500 + ₹ 50 + ₹ 10 = ₹ 2560

This is to be divided equally among 4 children

So, each child will get = 2560 / 4 = ₹ 640.

7. **(b)** If two notes of ₹ 5, three notes of ₹ 10 and four notes of ₹ 50

Money added = 2 × ₹ 5 + 3 × ₹ 10 + 4 × ₹ 50 = ₹ 240

Total money now = Previous amount + added amount

= ₹ 2665 + ₹ 240

= ₹ 2905.

8. **(d)** Let's check all option one by one

In Option (a),

Total amount = 5 × ₹ 100 + 1× ₹ 20 + 2× ₹ 10 + 4 × ₹ 1 + 3× ₹ 0.50 + 4 × ₹ 0.25

= ₹ 500 + ₹ 20 + ₹ 20 + ₹ 4 + ₹ 1.50 + ₹ 1

= ₹ 546.50, this not right combination.

In option (b),

Total amount = 4 × ₹ 100 + 4 × ₹ 20 + 2× ₹ 10 + 10 × ₹ 1 + 20× ₹ 0.50 + 10 × ₹ 0.25

= ₹ 400 + ₹ 80 + ₹ 20 + ₹ 10 + ₹ 10 + ₹ 2.50

= ₹ 522.50, this is not right combination.

In option (c),

Total amount = 4 × ₹ 100 + 5 × ₹ 20 + 4× ₹ 10 + 2 × ₹ 1 + 3× ₹ 0.50 + 4 × ₹ 0.25

= ₹ 400 + ₹ 100 + ₹ 40 + ₹ 2 + ₹ 1.50 + ₹ 1

= ₹ 544.50, this not right combination.

In option (d),

Total amount = 5 × ₹ 100 + 1 × ₹ 20 + 2 × ₹ 10 + 3 × ₹ 1 + 2 × ₹ 0.50 + 4 × ₹ 0.25

= ₹ 500 + ₹ 20 + ₹ 20 + ₹ 3 + Re 1 + Re 1

= ₹ 545, this is right combination.

Hence with option (d), Shikhar can buy the birthday present.

9. **(b)** 60000 – (42700 + 250) = ₹17050

10. **(b)** ₹ 73

11. **(b)** Jaysingh advised to distribute rice and wheat worth ₹ 50 and also give ₹ 20 every 6 months for 2 years.

There are 1000 people in king's kingdom.

So, Cost of rice and wheat = ₹ 50 × 1000 = ₹ 50,000

If ₹ 20 to be distributed every 6 months, it means money distributed 2 times in a year. So in 2 years amount distributed 4 times.

Per person amount = ₹ 20 × 4 = ₹ 80

For 1000 people, amount to be distributed = ₹ 80 × 1000 = ₹ 80,000

So, total expenses of king in this case = ₹ 50,000 + ₹ 80,000 = ₹ 1,30,000.

12. (c) Vikrant suggested that king should distribute ₹ 25 as one time allowance and ₹ 5 per month for 11 months

Total amount per person = ₹ 25 + 5 × 11 = ₹ 25 + ₹ 55 = ₹ 80.

13. (c) Going by Jaysingh's advice, king's expenses = ₹ 130000 (as found in Q20)

Going by Vikrant's advice, kings expenses per person = ₹ 80

For 1000 people, king's expenses = ₹ 80 × 1000 = ₹ 80000

Ramsingh suggested that king should distribute ₹ 75 to each person in the kingdom as a one-time allowance.

In this case, king's expenses = ₹ 75 × 1000 = ₹ 75000

Least of these is ₹ 75000

Hence, Ramsingh's advice will lead to least expenses for king.

14. (c) We know from Q21 that the total expenses if King decides to go by Vikrant's advice will be ₹ 80000

Hence statement (c) is NOT true.

15. (a) ₹ 354 × 28 = ₹9912

16. (a) Price of 1 US Dollar = ₹ 50 (given)

Price of 1 UK pound = ₹ 80 (given)

Amount with Rohan's father = 10 notes of 20 US Dollars + 5 notes of

10 UK pounds
= (10 × 20 × 50) + (5 × 10 × 80)
= ₹ 10000 + ₹ 4000
= ₹ 14000.

17. (d) Amount present with Sohan's father:

• 1 note of ₹ 2000 = 1 × ₹ 1000
= ₹ 2000

• 2 notes of ₹ 500 = 2 × ₹ 500
= ₹ 1000

• 4 notes of ₹ 100 = 4 × ₹ 100
= ₹ 400

• 7 notes of ₹ 50 = 7 × ₹ 50
= ₹ 350

• 3 notes of ₹ 20 = 3 × ₹ 20 = ₹ 60

Sum = ₹ 2000 + ₹ 1000 + ₹ 400 +

₹ 350 + ₹ 60 = ₹ 3810

Sohan's father needs to pay ₹ 4000 for fees

So, more money he requires

= ₹ 4000 - ₹ 3810 = ₹ 190.

18. (b) Total amount spent = Tickets of 2 adults + tickets of 2 children + cost of food + cost of bananas

= 2 × ₹ 50 + 2 × ₹ 20 + ₹ 200 + ₹ 50

= ₹ 100 + ₹ 40 + ₹ 200 + ₹ 50 = ₹ 390.

19. (c) Initially money father had = ₹ 1000

Total amount spent during zoo visit = ₹ 390

Also, father lost from his purse = ₹ 110

So, remaining amount with father = ₹ 1000 - ₹ 390 - ₹ 110 = ₹ 500.

20. (b) Total amount with Mohini = ₹ 100 + ₹ 50 + ₹ 20 + ₹ 10 + ₹ 5 + ₹ 10 + ₹ 5 + Re 1 + ₹ 0.50 + ₹ 0.25 + ₹ 0.10 = ₹ 201.85

21. **(c)** ₹3572 is left

22. **(d)** Let's check all option one by one:

In option (a), 8 coins of 25p, 6 coins of 50p & 6 coins of Re 1

Total amount = 8x ₹ 0.25 + 6 x ₹ 0.50 + 6 x Re 1

= ₹ 2+ ₹ 3 + ₹ 6 = ₹ 11 ,it is not a right combination.

In option (b), 2 coins of 25p, 12 coins of 50p & 4 coins of Re 1

Total amount = 2x ₹ 0.25 + 12 x ₹ 0.50 + 4 x Re 1

= ₹ 0.50 + ₹ 6 + ₹ 4 = ₹ 10.50 , it is not a right combination

In option (c), 8 coins of 25p, 4 coins of 50p & 5 coins of Re 1

Total amount = 8x ₹ 0.25 + 4 x ₹ 0.50 + 5 x Re 1

= ₹ 4 + ₹ 2 + ₹ 5 = ₹ 11, it is not a right combination.

In option (d), 4 coins of 25p, 8 coins of 50p & 5 coins of Re 1

Total amount = 4 x ₹ 0.25 + 8 x ₹ 0.50 + 5 x Re 1

= Re 1 + ₹ 4 + ₹ 5

= ₹ 10, it is a right combination.

Hence, Raj can buy ice-cream with money in option (d).

23. **(a)** Money with Sumit = ₹ 2000

Money spent by him = ₹ 400 (ticket) + ₹ 50 (cap) + ₹ 30 (cold drink) + ₹ 100 (charity)

= ₹ 580

Money left with him = ₹ 2000 - ₹ 580 = ₹ 1420.

24. **(a)** As 23 × 25p + 4 × 50 p + 1000 p

= 1775 p = ₹ 17.75

25. **(a)** 1 cycle cost $= \dfrac{684}{2} = 342$

1 Teddy bear cost

$= \dfrac{1986 - 342}{2} = \dfrac{1644}{2} = 822$

∴ 1 Doll cost = 2385 – 822 = ₹1563

26. **(c)**

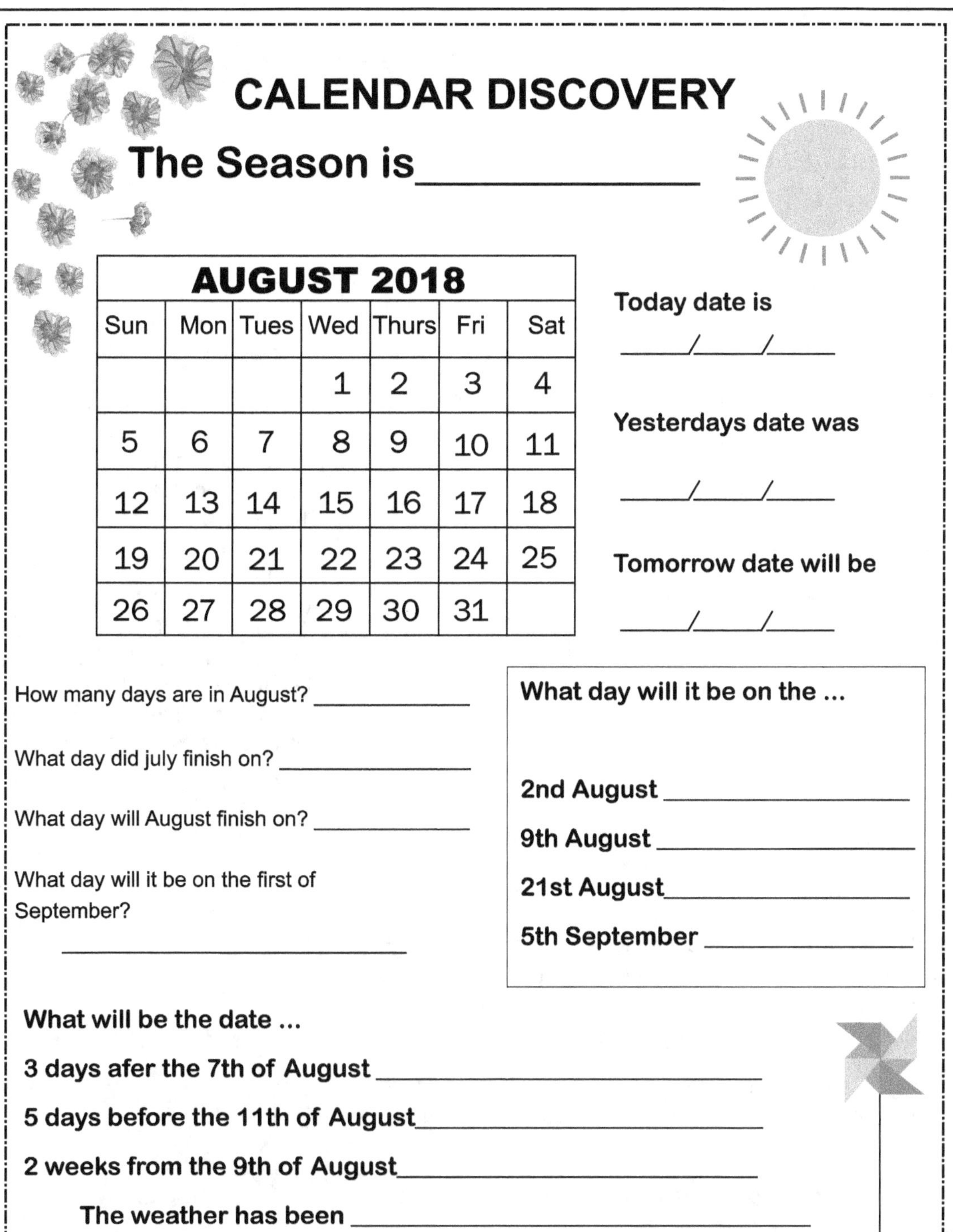

CALENDAR DISCOVERY

The Season is________________

AUGUST 2018

Sun	Mon	Tues	Wed	Thurs	Fri	Sat
			1	2	3	4
5	6	7	8	9	10	11
12	13	14	15	16	17	18
19	20	21	22	23	24	25
26	27	28	29	30	31	

Today date is

______/______/______

Yesterdays date was

______/______/______

Tomorrow date will be

______/______/______

How many days are in August? ______________

What day did july finish on? ________________

What day will August finish on? ______________

What day will it be on the first of September?

____

What day will it be on the ...

2nd August __________________

9th August ____________________

21st August___________________

5th September _______________

What will be the date ...

3 days afer the 7th of August ____________________________

5 days before the 11th of August____________________________

2 weeks from the 9th of August____________________________

The weather has been ________________________________

12 Chapter

Time and Calendar

LEARNING OBJECTIVES

This lesson will help you to:—

- ❖ learn about measurement of time (hour and minutes).
- ❖ identify the duration of day and night.
- ❖ study calendar with dates and days.
- ❖ express time, using the terms, 'a.m.' and 'p.m.'

QUICK CONCEPT REVIEW

Don't we talk about time all the time like:

Time to take a bath.

Time to eat food.

Time to sleep.

Wake up time.

So," What is time?"

Just like you have length to measure your garden, height to measure how tall you are, weight for the mass of your body, time is a measure for events. Events that are happening now or that had happened before.

Like length, weight or height have units, Time also has units and those are years, months, weeks, days, hours, minutes and seconds.

To measure with hours, minutes and seconds we use clock. In a day we have 24 hours.

> ❖ In ancients times people used to tell the time by watching the position of sun in the sky. They invented Obelisks (slender, tapering, four-sided monuments) which were built as early as 3500 B.C. Obelisks were special because they used moving shadows to tell about the time. Later on Egyptians modified it and made Sundials.

CLOCK AND TIME

A clock dial has 60 small divisions. These divisions show minutes or seconds. There are 12 numerals marked from 1 to 12 on clock face which are at an equal distances. 5th division is marked with 1, 10th division with 2 and so are 15th, 20th, 25th, 30th, 35th, 40th, 45th, 50th, 55th, and 60th divisions marked with 3, 4, 5, 6, 7, 8, 9, 10, 11 and 12 respectively. These divisions, generally shown with longer lines than other divisions, represent hours (see the clock dial given)

The minute hand takes 60 seconds in moving from one division to next division. This is known as 1 minute.

60 seconds = 1 minute.

The minute hand takes 5 minutes in reaching from one marked numeral to next marked numeral. And in completing one full revolution it takes 60 minutes. This is called one hour.

60 minutes = 1 hour

An hour hand moves from one numeral to next numeral in 60 minutes.

Further we have seconds hand which takes 1 minute to complete one round. 60 seconds = 1 minute

There are few examples for you –

2: 00

2:15

2:30

2:45

CALENDAR

There is a way of measuring time in months, weeks or days and that is called a calendar. We have 12 months namely January, February, March, April, May, June, July, August, September, October, November and December. Some months have 30 days and some have 31 days. February is a month where we have 28 days but every leap year we have February with 29 days. To remember that which month has got 30 and 31 days we can use this poem.

30 days have September,

April, June and November,

All the rest have 31,

Excepting February alone.

Which only has but 28 days clear

and 29 in each leap year.

Further 7 days makes a week. Name of the days are- Sunday, Monday, Tuesday, Wednesday, Thursday, Friday and Saturday.

A poem for the days of the week:

Monday's child is fair of face

Tuesday's child is full of grace

Wednesday's child is full of cheer

Thursday's child is sweet and dear

Friday's child is loving and kind

Saturday's child is happy all the time

Sunday's child is honest and true

But the sweetest child belongs to you.

Amazing Fact

❖ Months of the Year : Have you ever looked at the calendar and wondered where the names of the months came from? The origins of our calendar came from the old Roman practice of starting each month on a new moon. The Roman book - keepers would keep their records in a ledger called a "kalendarium" and this is where we get the word - Calendar.

Leap Year:

Every fourth year is called as a leap year. The year divisible by 4 is a leap year. Every year has 52 Mondays, Tuesdays, Wednesdays etc.

The 365th day of a normal year can be Monday or Tuesday or Wednesday, etc. Leap year has 364 + 2 days. So 52 weeks + 2 days = 366 days = leap year.

Example :- If today is Wednesday then what day was day before yesterday?

Solution. If today is Wednesday, then yesterday was Tuesday and day before yesterday was Monday.

Multiple Choice Questions

LEVEL 1

Direction (Qs. 1 to 8): Solve the word problems given below and then choose the correct option.

1. **Pick the odd one out.**
   (a) January　　(b) July　　(c) May　　(d) November

2. **Pick the odd one out.**　　　　　　　　　　　　**[Mental Mathematics]**
   (a) 24 hours　(b) 1 day　(c) 1440 minutes　(d) 60 seconds

3. **What does AM stands for?**
   (a) After noon　(b) Before noon　(c) Midnight　(d) None of these

4. **When do you wish your parents good night?**
   (a) After noon　(b) Night　(c) Evening　(d) None of these

5. **2:00 : 14:00 pm :: ______ : 20:00 pm.**　　　　**[Mental Mathematics]**
   (a) 6:00　(b) 8:00　(c) 7:00　(d) 9:00

6. **3 hrs 33 min = ________ min.**
   (a) 333　(b) 210　(c) 213　(d) 180

7. **How many weeks are there in 1 year?**　　　　　　　　　**[2010]**
   (a) 55　(b) 53　(c) 51　(d) 52

8. **p.m. means:**
   (a) post meridian　(b) post noon　(c) pre noon　(d) none of these

9. **The time from 12 mid night to 12 noon is noted as:**
   (a) a.m.　(b) p.m.　(c) midnight　(d) day

10. **The difference between 7 hours 25 min and 3 hrs 45 min is:**
    (a) 4 hrs 15 min　(b) 4 hrs 65 min　(c) 3 hrs 40 min　(d) 4 hrs 45 min

11. **The month with neither 31 days nor 30 days is:**　　　　**[2009]**
    (a) February　(b) April　(c) November　(d) December

12. **The number of weeks in 147 days are:**　　　　　　　**[2008]**
    (a) 27　(b) 21　(c) 23　(d) 22

13. **Pick the odd one out.**　　　　　　　　　　　　**[Mental Mathematics]**
    (a) September　(b) April　(c) June　(d) December

14. **Alison took 54 minutes to walk to school. Her brother took 18 minutes less to walk to the same school. How long did it take Alison's brother to walk to school?**
    (a) 30 min　(b) 36 min　(c) 38 min　(d) 35 min

15. **How many minutes should be added to the time shown by the clock to make it quarter past four?**　　　　　　　**[2012]**

    (a) 10 minutes

    (b) 15 minutes

    (c) 25 minutes

    (d) 30 minutes

16. Find the difference in the time shown by the following watches.   [2013]

    (a)   1000 sec
    (b)   1100 sec
    (c)   1200 sec
    (d)   1300 sec

17. Tina and Carl are traveling to New York City. Tina's plane arrives at 8:00 A.M. Carl's plane arrives 2 hours and 30 minutes later. What time does Carl's plane arrive?
    (a)   8:30 A.M.   (b)   9:30 A.M.   (c)   10:30 A.M.   (d)   11:30 A.M.

18. Which of the following is a leap year?   [2016]
    (a)   1994   (b)   1900   (c)   2016   (d)   1800

19. How many days will be there in 2 non-leap years?   [2014]
    (a)   734   (b)   732   (c)   730   (d)   365

20. Convert 6 hours and 30 minutes into minutes.   [2015]
    (a)   603 minutes   (b)   306 minutes   (c)   390 minutes   (d)   690 minutes

21. Amanda started reading a book at 5:40   [2017, Tricky]
    Amanda read her book for three hours. What time did she finish reading?

    (a)   7:30`   (b)   8:40   (c)   8:30   (d)   9:40

22. Benjamin walked to school, this morning, at (Refer to the above Fig. A)
    It took Benjamin twenty minutes to walk to school. What time did Benjamin arrive at school?

    (a)   6:05

    (b)   6:00

    (c)   5:55

    (d)   6:55   Fig A

23. The TV show Kyle watched ended at (Refer to the above Fig. A)
    Kyle watched thirty minute TV show. What time did the TV show begin?
    (a)   6:10   (b)   5:10   (c)   6:15   (d)   5:15

24. School starts in the morning at (Refer to the above Fig. A)
    The third grade class eats lunch six hours after school starts. Grace is in the third grade. What time is Grace's lunch?
    (a)   12:30   (b)   10:40   (c)   11:40   (d)   12:40

25. It is now 11:30 a.m. Where will the hour hand be pointing 1 hour later?   [2011]
    (a)   Between 11 and 12   (b)   Between 12 and 1
    (c)   At 12   (d)   At 1

26. Sheela reached the library at 12:05. The bus ride to the Library lasted 45 minutes. At what time did she board the bus?   [2013]
    (a)   11:20 a.m.   (b)   12:50 a.m.   (c)   11:20 p.m.   (d)   12:50 p.m.

Direction (Qs. 27 to 31): Answer the following questions based on the calendar.

JANUARY 2012

SUN	MON	TUE	WED	THU	FRI	SAT
1	2	3	4	5	6	7
8	9	10	11	12	13	14
15	16	17	18	19	20	21
22	23	24	25	26	27	28
29	30	31				

27. **Republic Day falls on which day?**
    (a) Wednesday   (b) Thursday   (c) Friday   (d) Sunday

28. **On what day was the New Year celebrated?**
    (a) Sunday   (b) Monday   (c) Saturday   (d) Tuesday

29. **Numbers of weekdays in the calendar are?**
    (a) 22   (b) 28   (c) 26   (d) 25

30. **Numbers of weekend days in the calendar are?**
    (a) 10   (b) 11   (c) 9   (d) 5

31. **How many holidays are there in this month? [Weekends are holidays also count Republic day]**
    (a) 10   (b) 9   (c) 11   (d) 12

32. **How many days are there from 21st April to 17th May?** [2016]
    (a) 24   (b) 28   (c) 27   (d) 26

33. **A race competition started at 11:45 a.m. and finished at 1:35 p.m. How long did the competition last?** [2017]
    (a) 1 hour
    (b) 1 hours and 20 minutes
    (c) 2 hours
    (d) 1 hour and 50 minutes

34. **Depending upon the time taken by each, find the odd one out.** [Tricky]
    (a) Julia worked on her chores from 3:15 P.M. until 4:00 P.M.
    (b) The music performance began at 7:50 P.M. It ended at 8:35 P.M.
    (c) They baby slept from 9:30 P.M. until 10:45 P.M.
    (d) Mary went to work at 9:07 A.M. She got home at 9:52 A.M.

35. **00:01: First minute of the day :: ______ : Last minute of the day.**
    (a) 12:59   (b) 24:59   (c) 23:59   (d) 24:00

36. **John took 1 h 35 min to drive from Town A to Town B. Jason started from Town A at the same time but arrived in Town B 38 min later. How long did it take Jason to drive from Town A to Town B?**
    (a) 2 hours 18 min   (b) 2 hours 13 min   (c) 2 hours 15 min   (d) 1 hours 18 min

37. **The Cahill family is going to see a movie at 5:50 PM. It is 11:20 AM right now. How long do they have to wait to see the movie?**
    (a) 5 hour, 20 min
    (b) 6 and a half hours
    (c) 6 hours
    (d) 6 hours 20 minutes

38. **Julia slept from 9:00 PM until 7:00 AM. She had a bad dream and could not sleep from 2:45 AM until 3:30 AM. How many hours did she sleep?** [2008, Tricky]
    (a) 10 and half an hours
    (b) 11 hours 45 minutes
    (c) 9 hours 15 minutes
    (d) 9 hours 45 minutes

39. Bobby left school at 2:15 PM. He walked to the library to work on his homework. It took 15 minutes to walk to the library. Bobby's father picked him up at the library one hour after he arrived. What time did Bobby's father pick him up?

    (a)   2:30   (b)   3:15   (c)   3:30   (d)   3:45

40. A reading contest in the library begins on July 6. The contest ends exactly 2 weeks later.

2013						JULY
SUNDAY	MONDAY	TUESDAY	WEDNESDAY	THURSDAY	FRIDAY	SATURDAY
	1	2	3	4	5	6
7	8	9	10	11	12	13
14	15	16	17	18	19	20
21	22	23	24	25	26	27
28	29	30	31			

    On what day will the reading contest end?

    (a)   July 13   (b)   July 20   (c)   July 21   (d)   July 27

41. Today is Monday. After 61 days, it will be:

    (a)   Wednesday   (b)   Saturday   (c)   Tuesday   (d)   Thursday

42. Gautam wakes up at 6:15 a.m. takes 45 minutes to get dressed, 12 minutes to eat breakfast and 20 minutes to reach school. At what time does he reach the school?   **[2014]**

    (a)   7:30 a.m.   (b)   7:32 a.m.   (c)   7:28 a.m.   (d)   7:35 a.m.

43. If a bus can travel 20 km in 20 minutes, how much distance will it cover in 3 hours.

    (a)   120 km   (b)   140 km   (c)   160 km   (d)   180 km **[2011]**

44. Sneha went for playing at 3:15 p.m. and returned home 1 hour 15 minutes later. Which of the following clocks shows the time she came back home?   **[2019]**

(a) 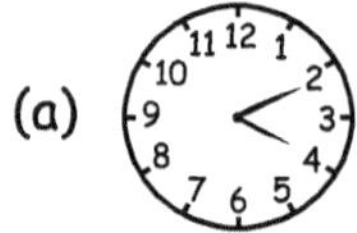   (b) 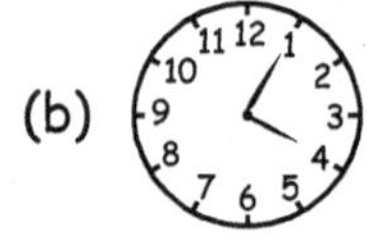   (c) 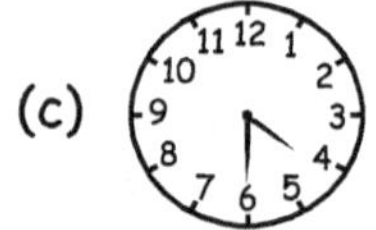   (d) 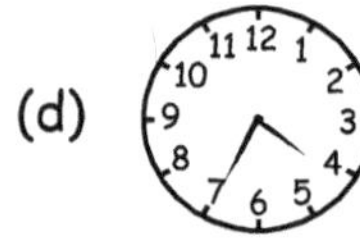

LEVEL 2

1.   Match the following:

	List I		List II
A.	2:15 – 3:00	1.	4:20 – 4:45
B	5:06 – 5:18	2.	9:40 – 9:55
C.	3:00 – 3:25	3.	8:00 – 8:45
D.	6:10 – 6:25	4.	7:02 – 7:14

	A	B	C	D
(a)	3	4	1	2
(b)	1	2	3	4
(c)	4	3	1	2
(d)	3	1	2	4

2. **Match the following:**

List I		List II	
A.	17:30	1.	4 pm
B.	22:00	2.	7:30 pm
C.	16:00	3.	10:00 pm
D.	19:30	4.	5:30 pm

	A	B	C	D
(a)	3	1	2	4
(b)	2	3	1	4
(c)	4	3	1	2
(d)	1	3	4	2

3. **Match the following:**   [Critical Thinking]

List I		List II	
A.	4	1.	Number of days in the month of February in the leap year.
B.	28	2.	Number of months with 31 days.
C.	7	3.	Number of month with 30 days.
D.	29	4.	Number of days in February.

	A	B	C	D
(a)	1	2	4	3
(b)	3	4	2	1
(c)	4	2	3	1
(d)	2	3	1	4

4. **Match the following:**   [Tricky]

List I		List II	
A.	$\frac{1}{2}$ hour	1.	60 minutes
B.	24 hour	2.	60 seconds
C.	1 hour	3.	1 day
D.	1 minute	4.	30 minutes

	A	B	C	D
(a)	4	3	1	2
(b)	2	1	3	4
(c)	3	2	4	1
(d)	1	2	3	4

5. **How many days are there from 21st March to 17th April?**   [2016]
   (a)   27 days   (b)   28 days   (c)   29 days   (d)   31 days

6. **Express $\frac{5}{12}$ of a day in hours.**   [2013, Tricky]
   (a)   2 hours   (b)   10 hours   (c)   12 hours   (d)   22 hours

7. **Aditya spent 25 minutes on his homework last night. He started it at 5:50pm. What time did he finish his homework?**   [Mental Mathematics]
   (a)   5:15   (b)   6:15   (c)   5:10   (d)   6:10

8. The cricket match started at 8:00pm. Each half was 45 minutes. What time did the first half end? **[Mental Mathematics]**
   (a) 8:45pm   (b) 9:30pm   (c) 8:35 pm   (d) 9:05pm

9. The school holiday starts in three weeks. School is open 5 days a week. How many school days are left until the holiday?
   (a) 25 days   (b) 21 days   (c) 15 days   (d) 20 days

10. Christine wanted to travel around the world. She worked out that the trip would take her five years. How many months would that be?
    (a) 15 months   (b) 65 months   (c) 60 months   (d) 52 month

11. It takes 12 minutes to bathe a dog at Dr. Kumar's Dog Home. How long would it take to bathe 10 dogs? **[Mental Mathematics]**
    (a) 100 minutes   (b) 3 hrs.   (c) 60 minutes   (d) 120 minutes

12. Sally walked one mile in 17 minutes. How long would it take her to walk three miles at the same speed? **[Mental Mathematics]**
    (a) 51 min   (b) 50 min   (c) 49 min   (d) 49 min

13. Maureen started her homework at 7.20 p.m. She finished it at 8.05 p.m. How long did she take to do her homework? **[Mental Mathematics]**
    (a) 40 min   (b) 45 min   (c) 50 min   (d) 55 min

14. A chess game started at 10.20 a.m. and ended at 12.30 p.m. How long did the game last?
    (a) 2 hours 10 min   (b) 2 hours   (c) 2 hours 20 min   (d) 1 hour 50 min

15. The flight from Chennai to Dubai took off at 4:45 hours. It landed at Dubai at 9:15 hours. How long was the flight? **[2015]**
    (a) 4 hrs. 50 mins.   (b) 3 hrs. 55 mins.   (c) 4 hrs. 30 mins.   (d) 4 hrs. 10 mins.

16. Sonika went to her friend's house at 1:15 p.m. Her father told her to be back home in 1 hour and 45 minutes. What time does Sonika needs to be at home? **[2016]**
    (a) 2:00 p.m.   (b) 2:30 p.m.   (c) 2:45 p.m.   (d) 3:00 p.m.

Direction (Qs. 17 to 21): I am standing with my friends in front of a movie theatre. We are deciding on which movies we must watch. Answer the following word problems.

17. 'Mitilda' plays at 7:10. It is now quarter to seven. How long before the movie starts?
    (a) 25 minutes   (b) 35 minutes
    (c) 1 hour 10 minutes   (d) 15 minutes

18. It takes 30 minutes to drive to the movie theater. 'Home Alone, Part-1' begins playing at ten after 1. What is the latest you can leave home?
    (a) 12: 50   (b) 12:30   (c) 12:40   (d) 12:55

19. Terminator begins at 2:35. It ends at 4:05. How long is the movie?
    (a) 1 hour 05 minutes   (b) 1 hour 20 minutes
    (c) 1 hour 30 minutes   (d) 1 hour 40 minutes

20. You and your friend meet at the movie theater to see 'Dabang'. You arrive at 5:40. Your friend arrives at 6:12. How long did you wait for your friend to arrive?
    (a) 22 minutes   (b) 1 hour 32 minutes
    (c) 32 minutes   (d) 28 minutes

21. Toy story begins at 5:20. It is 1 hour and 50 minutes long.
    What time does the movie end?
    (a) 7:10   (b) 7: 00   (c) 6:50   (d) 7:40

Direction (Qs. 22 to 24): Study the calendar below and answer the following questions.

November 2010						
S	M	T	W	T	F	S
31	1	2	3	4	5	6
7	8	9	10	11	12	13
14	15	16	17	18	19	20
21	22	23	24	25	26	27
28	29	30	1	2	3	4
5	6	7	8	9	10	11

22. You are going on holiday for 3 weeks starting on the 11th November, what day do you come back on?

    (a)   Wednesday   (b)   Thursday   (c)   Friday   (d)   Saturday

23. You are going on holiday on the 23rd November for 10 days what date and month will you come back?

    (a)   3 December   (b)   2 December   (c)   3 November   (d)   4 December

24. What is the date 3 weeks after 13th November?

    (a)   11 December   (b)   4 December   (c)   26 November   (d)   27 November

Direction (Qs. 25 to 27): The given table shows the time schedule of the arrival and departure times of train at different destinations along its route. Study the table and answer the questions.

Destination	Arrival	Departure
Central	___________	08:30
Apple Country	09:20	09:35
Santa Park	12:05	12:15
Fairy Land	13:00	14:00
Blue Lake	16:10	16:25
Candy Street	18:00	___________

25. How long does it take to travel from Apple Country to Santa park?

    (a)   2 hrs 25 min   (b)   2 hrs 30 min   (c)   2 hrs 35 min   (d)   3 hrs 25 min

26. How long does it take to travel from Apple Country to Fairy Land?

    (a)   3 hrs 50 min   (b)   3 hrs 25 min   (c)   3 hrs 35 min   (d)   3 hrs 55min

27. How long does it take to travel from Santa Park to Candy Street?

    (a)   5 hrs 15 min   (b)   5 hrs 30 min   (c)   5 hrs 45 min   (d)   6 hrs 15 min

28. A train which was scheduled to arrive at Nizamuddin station got 1 hour 25 min late. It leaves the station after 15 minutes and reaches Jaipur station at 9 : 45 p.m. after 8 hours 35 mins of Journey. Find its scheduled time to arrive at Nizamuddin station. **[2018]**

    (a) 10 : 30 a.m.   (b) 11:30 a.m.   (c) 11:20 a.m.   (d) 11:50 a.m.

29. Shivam's flight to Canada departs at 11:15 p.m. He has to check at the airport terminal 1 hour 45 minuts earlier. The journey to the terminal takes 50 min. He needs 30 min to get dressed and 15 minutes to have his dinner. At what time should he start preparing for his trip? **[2018]**

    (a) 6: 55 p.m.   (b) 8:05 p.m.   (c) 7:55 p.m.   (d) 8:25 p.m.

30. **What is the weight of marble P?** [2021]

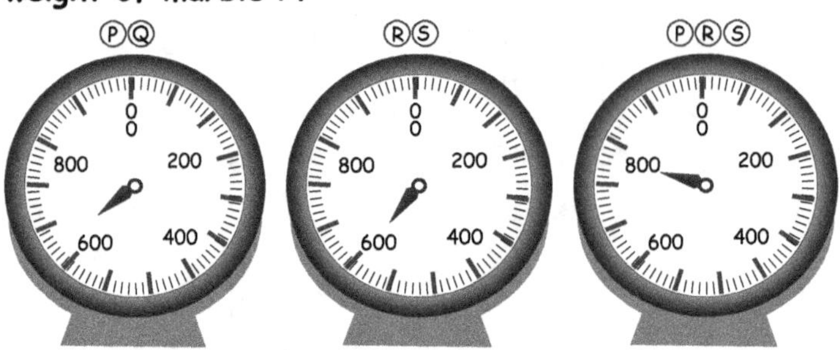

(a) 300 g　　　　　　　　　(b) 250 g

(c) 240 g　　　　　　　　　(d) 350 g

31. A shopping mall closes at 10:30 p.m. Its operating hours is 10 hours and 45 minutes. What time does the shopping mall open? [2022]

(a) 11:45 a.m.　　　　　　　(b) 11:25 a.m.

(c) 12:45 p.m.　　　　　　　(d) 12:25 p.m.

RESPONSE GRID

LEVEL 1

1. a b c d	2. a b c d	3. a b c d	4. a b c d	5. a b c d
6. a b c d	7. a b c d	8. a b c d	9. a b c d	10. a b c d
11. a b c d	12. a b c d	13. a b c d	14. a b c d	15. a b c d
16. a b c d	17. a b c d	18. a b c d	19. a b c d	20. a b c d
21. a b c d	22. a b c d	23. a b c d	24. a b c d	25. a b c d
26. a b c d	27. a b c d	28. a b c d	29. a b c d	30. a b c d
31. a b c d	32. a b c d	33. a b c d	34. a b c d	35. a b c d
36. a b c d	37. a b c d	38. a b c d	39. a b c d	40. a b c d
41. a b c d	42. a b c d	43. a b c d	44. a b c d	

LEVEL 2

1. a b c d	2. a b c d	3. a b c d	4. a b c d	5. a b c d
6. a b c d	7. a b c d	8. a b c d	9. a b c d	10. a b c d
11. a b c d	12. a b c d	13. a b c d	14. a b c d	15. a b c d
16. a b c d	17. a b c d	18. a b c d	19. a b c d	20. a b c d
21. a b c d	22. a b c d	23. a b c d	24. a b c d	25. a b c d
26. a b c d	27. a b c d	28. a b c d	29. a b c d	30. a b c d
31. a b c d				

Solutions with Explanation

LEVEL 1

1.	**(d)**	**2.**	**(d)**	**3.**	**(b)**	**4.**	**(b)**
5.	**(b)**	**6.**	**(c)**	**7.**	**(d)**		

8. **(a)** (post meridian) **9.** **(a)** (a.m.)

10. **(c)** 3 hrs 40 min **11.** **(a)** **12.** **(b)** **13.** **(d)**

14. **(b)**

15. **(c)** As 3 : 50 + 25 minutes = 4 : 15

16. **(c)** 20 minutes = 20 × 60 sec = 1200 sec.

17. **(c)**

18. **(d)** 2016 is a leap year

19. **(c)** 2 non - leap years = 2 × 365 days = 730 days

20. **(c)** 6 hours and 30 minutes = 6 × 60 minutes + 30 minutes = 390 minutes

21.	**(b)**	**22.**	**(b)**	**23.**	**(b)**	**24.**	**(c)**

25. **(b)** Between 12 and 1

26. **(a)** 12 :05 – 45 minute = 11:20 am

27.	**(b)**	**28.**	**(a)**	**29.**	**(a)**	**30.**	**(c)**

31. **(a)**

32. **(c)** There are 27 days from 21 April to 17 May.

33. **(d)** Time from 11:45 am to 1:35 pm is 1 hour and 50 minutes.

34.	**(c)**	**35.**	**(c)**	**36.**	**(b)**	**37.**	**(b)**
38.	**(c)**	**39.**	**(c)**	**40.**	**(b)**		

41. **(b)** Each day of the week is repeated after 7 days.
So, after 63 days, it will be Monday.
After 61 days, it will be Saturday.

42. **(b)** 7 : 32 am.

43. **(d)** In 20 minutes, bus travels 20 km.
3 hours = 3 × 60 minutes
= 180 minutes
∴ Bus travels in 180 minutes = 20 × 9 = 180 km

44. **(c)** Sneha went for playing at 3:15 p.m.
She returned home at (3 hours 15 minutes + 1 hour 15 minutes) = 4 hours 30 minutes.

LEVEL 2

1.	**(a)**	**2.**	**(c)**	**3.**	**(b)**	**4.**	**(a)**

5. **(b)** There are 28 days from 21th march to 17th April.

6. **(b)** $\dfrac{5}{12}$ of a day $= \dfrac{5}{12} \times 24$ hours = 10 hours

7.	**(b)**	**8.**	**(a)**	**9.**	**(c)**	**10.**	**(c)**
11.	**(d)**	**12.**	**(a)**	**13.**	**(b)**	**14.**	**(a)**

15. (c)   9:15 – 4:45 = 4 hrs 30 minutes

16. (d) **17. (a)** **18. (c)** **19. (c)**

20. (c) **21. (a)** **22. (b)** **23. (a)**

24. (b) **25. (b)** **26. (b)** **27. (c)**

28. (b) Total time = 1 hr 25 min + 15 min + 8 h 35 min

= 9 hr. 75 min. = 10 hr. 15 min.

Scheduled arrive time = 11 : 30 a.m.

29. (c) Total time

= 1 hr. 45 min. + 50 min. + 30 min. + 15 min.

= 1 hr. 140 min.

= 3 hr. 20 min.

Start preparing time = 7:55 p.m.

30. (b) Weight of Marbles (P + Q) = 650 g

Weight of Marbles (R + S) = 600 g

Weight of Marbles (P + R + S) = 850 g

So weight of Marble P = (P + R + S) – (R + S)

= (850 – 600) g

= 250 g

31. (a) Shopping mall operating hours = 10 Hours 45 minutes

Shopping mall closing time = 10:30 pm = 22:30 pm

So, opening time of shopping mall

= 22: 30 –10:45 = 11: 45 Hrs

13 CHAPTER FOREWORD

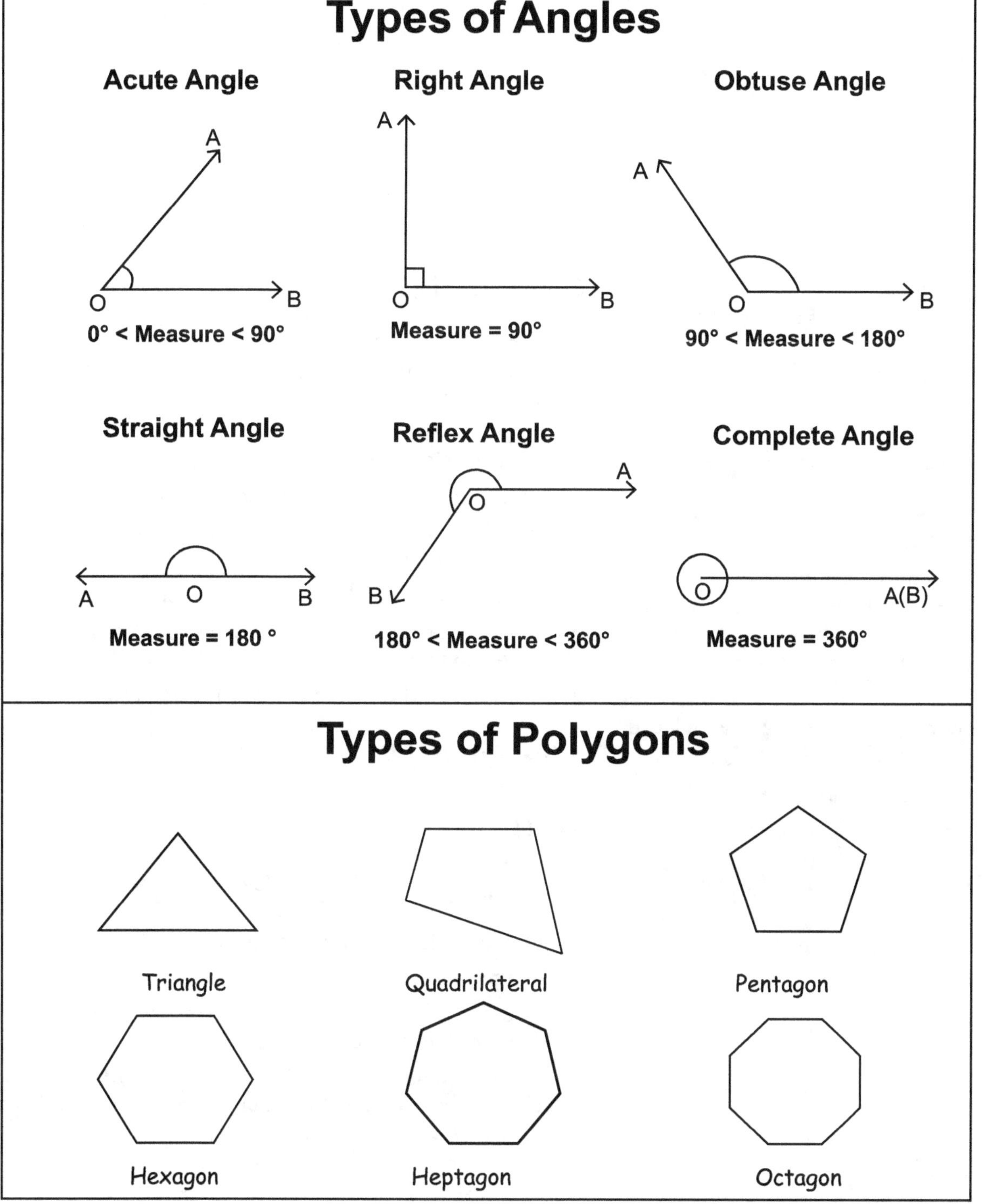

Types of Angles

Acute Angle

$0° <$ Measure $< 90°$

Right Angle

Measure $= 90°$

Obtuse Angle

$90° <$ Measure $< 180°$

Straight Angle

Measure $= 180°$

Reflex Angle

$180° <$ Measure $< 360°$

Complete Angle

Measure $= 360°$

Types of Polygons

Triangle

Quadrilateral

Pentagon

Hexagon

Heptagon

Octagon

Chapter 13 — Geometry

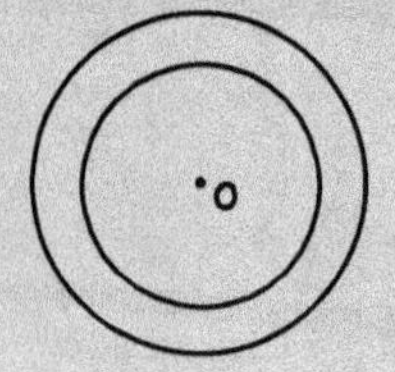

LEARNING OBJECTIVES

This lesson will help you to:—

- ❖ understand two dimensional and three-dimensional geometrical figures.
- ❖ learn about line symmetry, symmetrical and asymmetrical shapes.
- ❖ determine the number of line of symmetry.
- ❖ identify the different types of triangles on the basis of sides and angles.
- ❖ understand the different kinds of angles.
- ❖ learn about the angle sum properties of triangle and quadrilateral.
- ❖ know about the terms related to the circle.

QUICK CONCEPT REVIEW

CIRCLE

- ❖ A circle is a closed figure formed by points equidistant from a fixed point.
- ❖ Every circle has a fixed centre.
- ❖ The perimeter of the circle is called its circumference.
- ❖ The distance between the centre and any point on the circle is called its radius.
- ❖ A line segment passing through the centre of the circle, whose end points lie on the circle is called the diameter of the circle.

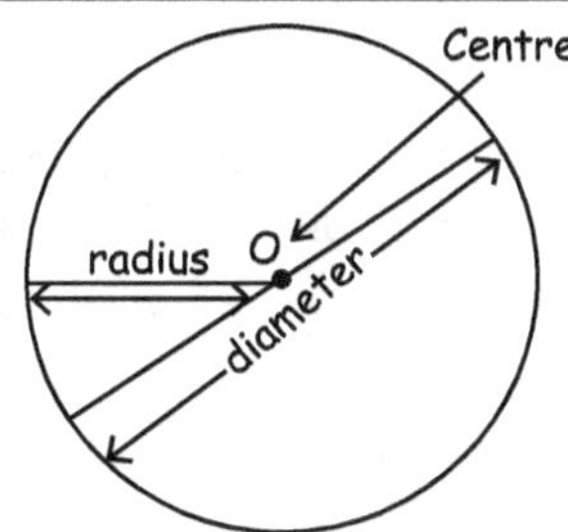

* The diameter of a circle is twice the radius.

* A line segment whose end points lie on the circle is called a chord.

* The diameter is the longest chord of a circle.

* Any part of a circle is called an arc.

* If an arc represents half of the circle it is a semi-circle.

ANGLE

* Two rays with a common end point form an angle. It is denoted by $\angle$.

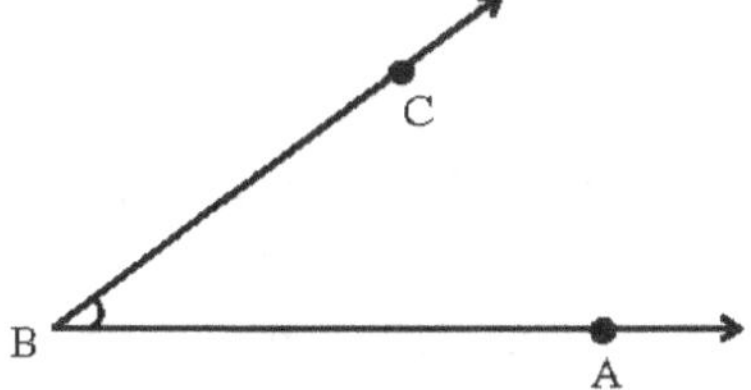

* The common end point is known as the vertex of the angle.

* The rays forming an angle are called the arms or sides of the angle.

* Angles measures in degrees.

* An angle whose measure is between 0° and 90° is called an acute angle.

* An angle whose measure is 90° is called a right angle.

* An angle whose measure is more than 90° but less than 180° is called an obtuse angle.

* An angle whose measure is 180° is called a straight angle and whose measure is 360° is called whole angle. It is also called complete angle.

* An angle whose measure is more than 180° but less than 360° is called a reflex angle.

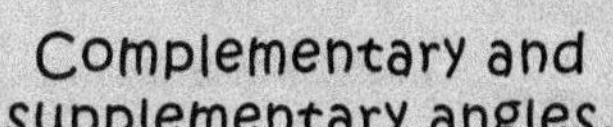

Complementary and supplementary angles.

Two angles whose sum is 90° are called as Complementary angles.

For example: 30° and 60° are complementery angles.

Two angles whose sum is 180° are called as Supplementary angles.

For example: 60° and 120° are supplementary angles.

Naming an Angle

There are two ways of naming an angle.

For example,

$\angle$ABC can be named

a) by its vertex as $\angle$B,

b) by the line segment forming the arms of the angle with a common point at the center as $\angle$ABC or $\angle$CBA

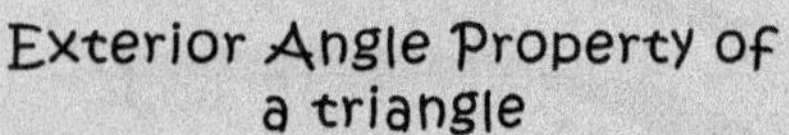

Exterior Angle Property of a triangle

Exterior angle of a triangle is equal to its sum of interior opposite angles.

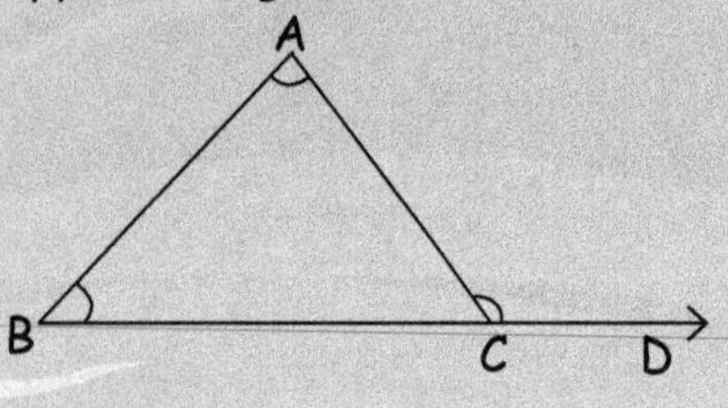

So,

∠ACD = ∠BAC + ∠ABC

as ∠ACD is exterior angle and ∠BAC and ∠ABC are its interior opposite angles.

A TRIANGLE

❖ A triangle is a closed figure having three sides, three vertices and three angles. It is denoted by Δ.

❖ Triangles can be classified on the basis of their sides and angles.

❖ Triangle in which all sides are equal is called <u>equilateral</u> triangle.

❖ Triangle in which two sides are equal is called <u>isosceles</u> triangle.

❖ Triangle in which all the three sides are different is called <u>scalene</u> triangle.

❖ <u>Right angled Triangle</u> : -

A triangle whose one angle is called. 90°

❖ <u>Acute - angled triangle</u> : -

All angles of this triangle are acute.

❖ <u>Obtuse - angled triangle</u> : -

In this triangle, at least one angle is an obtuse angle.

❖ The sum of 3 angles of a triangle is 180°.

A QUADRILATERAL

❖ A quadrilateral is a four - sided closed figure. It has four vertices, and four angles.

❖ The sum of four angles of a quadrilateral is 360°.

❖ Square, rectangle, parallelograms etc. are examples of quadrilateral.

SYMMETRY

❖ Symmetrical shapes can be folded into two matching equal halves

❖ The place from where symmetrical shapes are folded is called the line of symmetry.

❖ A symmetrical shapes can not be folded into two equal halves.

❖ A symmetrical shapes do not have a line of symmetry.

❖ The line of symmetry is also known as mirror line or line of reflection.

❖ If a figure can be folded such that one part of it exactly matches with the other then the figure has a line of symmetry.

❖ A square has four lines of symmetry, rectangle has two lines of symmetry and a triangle (whose 3 sides are equal) has 3 lines of symmetry.

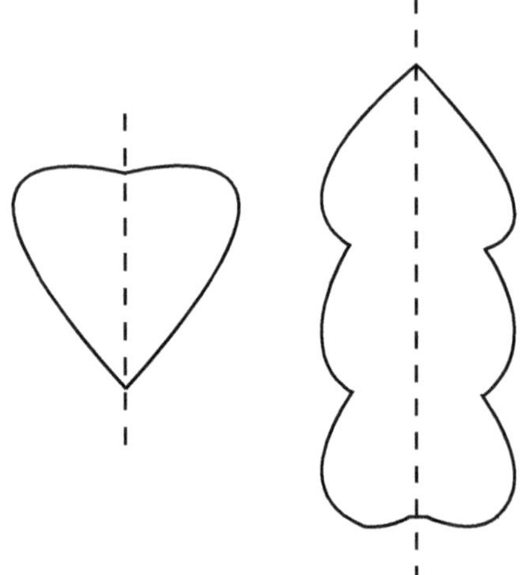

❖ Some figures have only one line of symmetry. Eg,

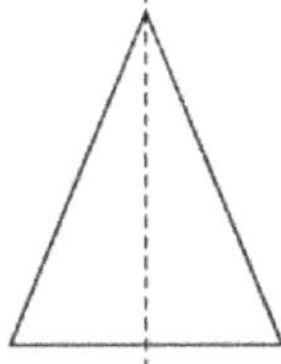 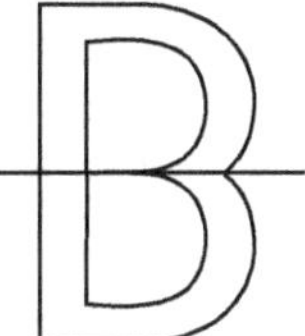

Some figures have no line of symmetry. For example:

Some figures have infinite lines of symmetry. For example: a circle has infinite lines of symmetry

TESSELLATIONS

We can fit some shapes of tiles such that there are no gaps and they do not overlap. These tilings are called tessellations.

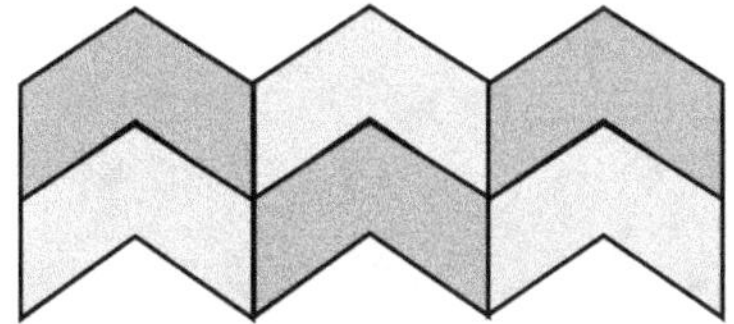

Tessellating shape

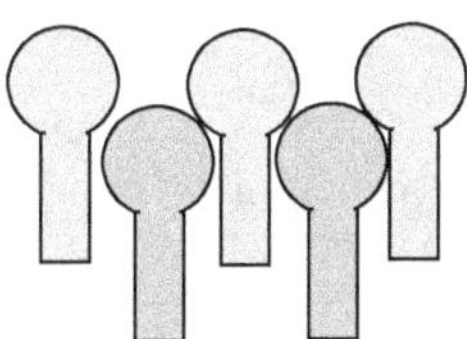

Shape that does not tessellate

3-D Shapes

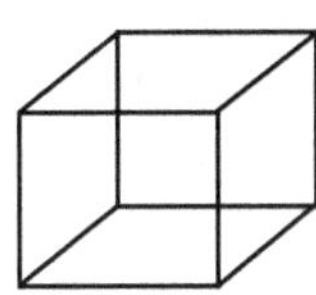

Cube

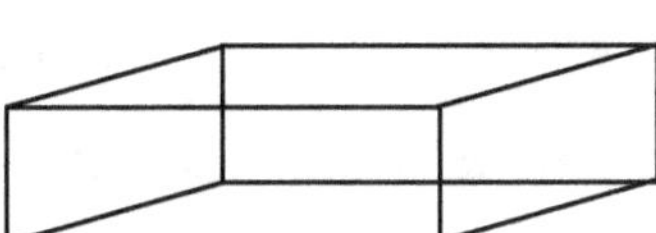

Cuboid

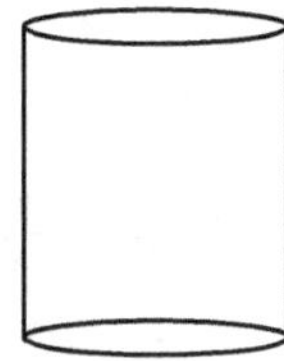

Cylinder

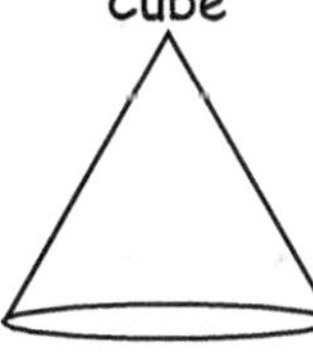

Cone

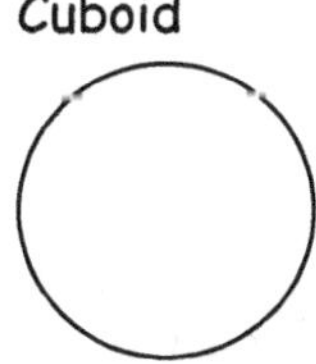

Sphere

Hemisphere

Multiple Choice Questions

LEVEL 1

Direction (Qs. 1 to 3): Arrange the shapes given in the following questions in their increasing size.

1. **Square.** [Mental Mathematics]

   A.　　B.　　C.　　D.

   (a) ABCD　　(b) ACBD　　(c) ABDC　　(d) ACDB

2. **Rectangle.** [Mental Mathematics]

   A.　　B.　　C.　　D.

   (a) DACB　　(b) DABC　　(c) DBAC　　(d) DBCA

3. **Circle**

   A.　　B.　　C.　　D.

   (a) BACD　　(b) BCAD　　(c) BCDA　　(d) BADC

4. **Which of the following is the net of a 6-faced cube ?**

   (a)　　(b)　　(c)　　(d)

5. **Chandu is making spins using cardboard. He made wrong spins and only one correct spin. Find the correct one among the following spins.**

   A.　　B.　　C.　　D.

   (a) D　　(b) C　　(c) B　　(d) A

Direction (Qs. 6 and 7): Look at the picture given below and answer the questions that follow:

6. How many faces in all does a lunch box have ?   [Mental Mathematics]

    (a) 3   (b) 4

    (c) 5   (d) 6

7. Which of the following is the face of the lunch box ?

    (a)   (b)   (c)   (d)

8. Circle : radius :: cube : ?   [Mental Mathematics]

    (a) edge   (b) diameter   (c) circumference (d) perimeter

9. 60° : acute angle : : 120° : ?   [Mental Mathematics]

    (a) right angle   (b) obtuse angle   (c) straight angle (d) reflex angle

10. An angle that is greater than 180° but less than 360° is known as a

    (a) straight angle   (b) obtuse angle   (c) acute angle   (d) reflex angle

11. 90° : right angle : : 360° :

    (a) reflex angle   (b) whole angle   (c) straight angle (d) acute angle

Direction (Q. 12): Tessellation are tiling pattern with no gaps in between the tiles.

12. Which of the following can tessellate ?

    (a)   (b)   (c)   (d)

13. Protractor : angle : : compass : ?

    (a) rectangle   (b) square   (c) side   (d) circle

14. The longest chord of a circle is _________.   [2011]

    (a) Equal to the radius   (b) Two times of the radius

    (c) Three times of the radius   (d) Four times of the radius

15. Which of the following is a drawing of the lunch box?

    (a)   (b)   (c)   (d)

16. Some shapes can be fitted together, edge to edge. This is called

    (a) paper folding   (b) tiling   (c) paper cutting (d) tangrams

17. Which shape can be used to till the pattern given below?

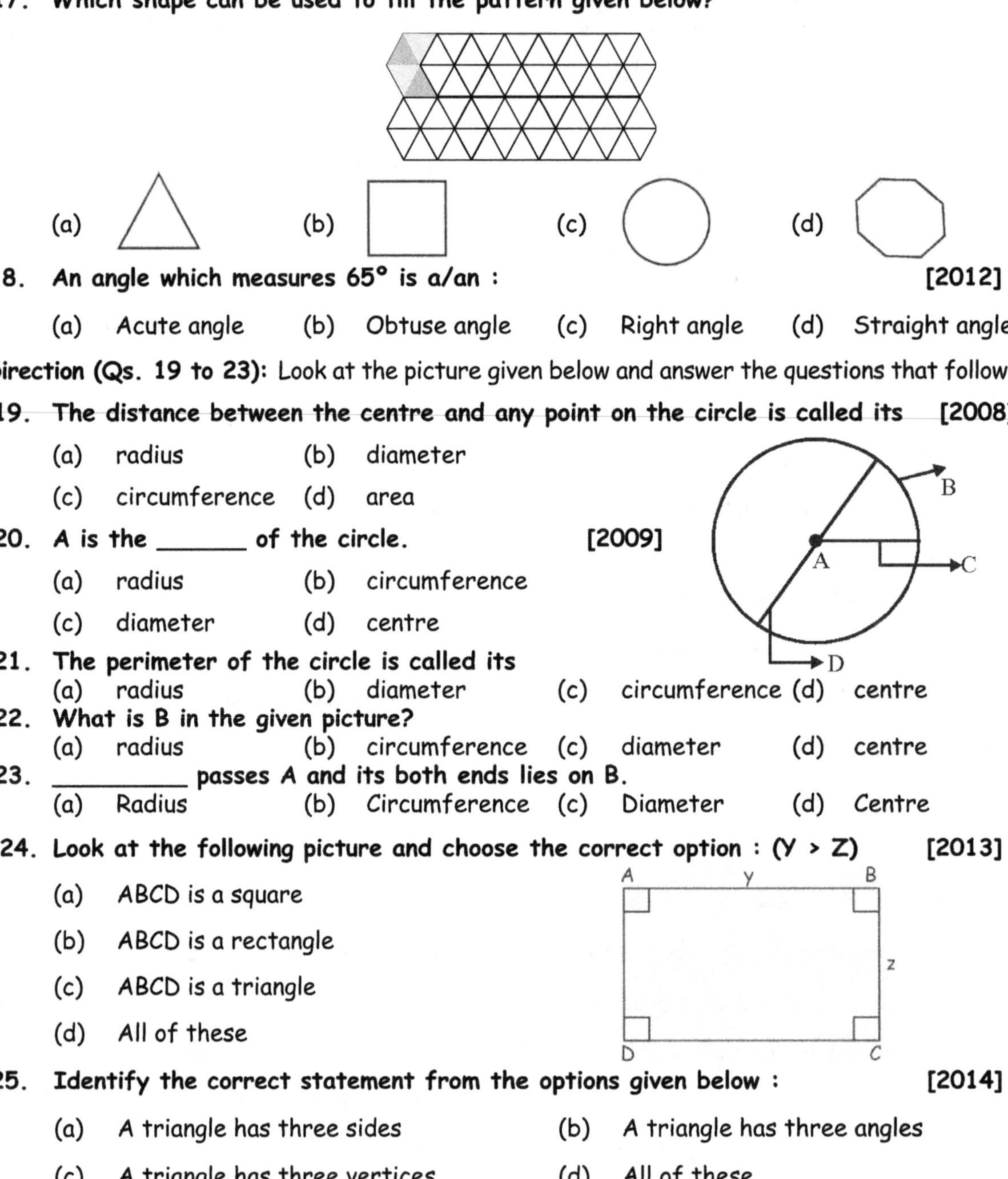

(a) △ (b) ▢ (c) ◯ (d) ⬡

18. An angle which measures 65° is a/an : [2012]

    (a) Acute angle (b) Obtuse angle (c) Right angle (d) Straight angle

Direction (Qs. 19 to 23): Look at the picture given below and answer the questions that follow:

19. The distance between the centre and any point on the circle is called its [2008]

    (a) radius (b) diameter

    (c) circumference (d) area

20. A is the _______ of the circle. [2009]

    (a) radius (b) circumference

    (c) diameter (d) centre

21. The perimeter of the circle is called its
    (a) radius (b) diameter (c) circumference (d) centre

22. What is B in the given picture?
    (a) radius (b) circumference (c) diameter (d) centre

23. _________ passes A and its both ends lies on B.
    (a) Radius (b) Circumference (c) Diameter (d) Centre

24. Look at the following picture and choose the correct option : (Y > Z) [2013]

    (a) ABCD is a square

    (b) ABCD is a rectangle

    (c) ABCD is a triangle

    (d) All of these

25. Identify the correct statement from the options given below : [2014]

    (a) A triangle has three sides (b) A triangle has three angles

    (c) A triangle has three vertices (d) All of these

26. How many line segments are there in a quadrilateral? [2015]

    (a) 2 (b) 4 (c) 6 (d) 5

27. On the basis of following features identify the correct figure. [Critical Thinking]
    A. It is a closed figure.
    B. It is not bounded by straight line segments.

    C.   It is bounded by a curved line.

    D.   Every point on this curved line is at equal distance from a fixed point inside the figure.

    (a)   Square   (b)   Circle   (c)   Polygon   (d)   Triangle

28. **On the basis of following features identify the correct name.**   **[Tricky]**

    A.   It is the gap between the two rays.

    B.   The symbol that is used to represent it is '$\angle$'.

    C.   Vertex of it always in the middle.

    D.   The unit for measuring it is degree. (°).

    (a)   Ray   (b)   Line Segment   (c)   Angle   (d)   Temperature

29. **Identify the pentagon from the following options.**   **[2015]**

    (a)   (b)   (c)   (d)

30. **If radius of the circle is first odd prime number, then find its diameter.** **[2016]**

    (a)   15 units   (b)   10 units   (c)   6 units   (d)   9 units

31. **How many letters in the given word have at least one line of symmetry?**
WATERING   **[2018]**

    (a) 4   (b) 6   (c) 5   (d) 3

32. **How many of the following figures have no line of symmetry.**   **[2018]**

    (a) 2   (b) 3   (c) 4   (d) 5

33. **Select a figure from the options which when placed in the blank space of given figure would complete the pattern.**   **[2019]**

    (a)   (b)

    (c)   (d)

34. **For a project Simmi cut a piece of paper into a shape with 4 sides, but none of them are of the same length. What is the shape of the paper?**
    [2021]

    (a) Rectangle   (b) Quadrilateral   (c) Square   (d) Pentagon

35. How many of the following figures have vertical line of symmetry?

[2022]

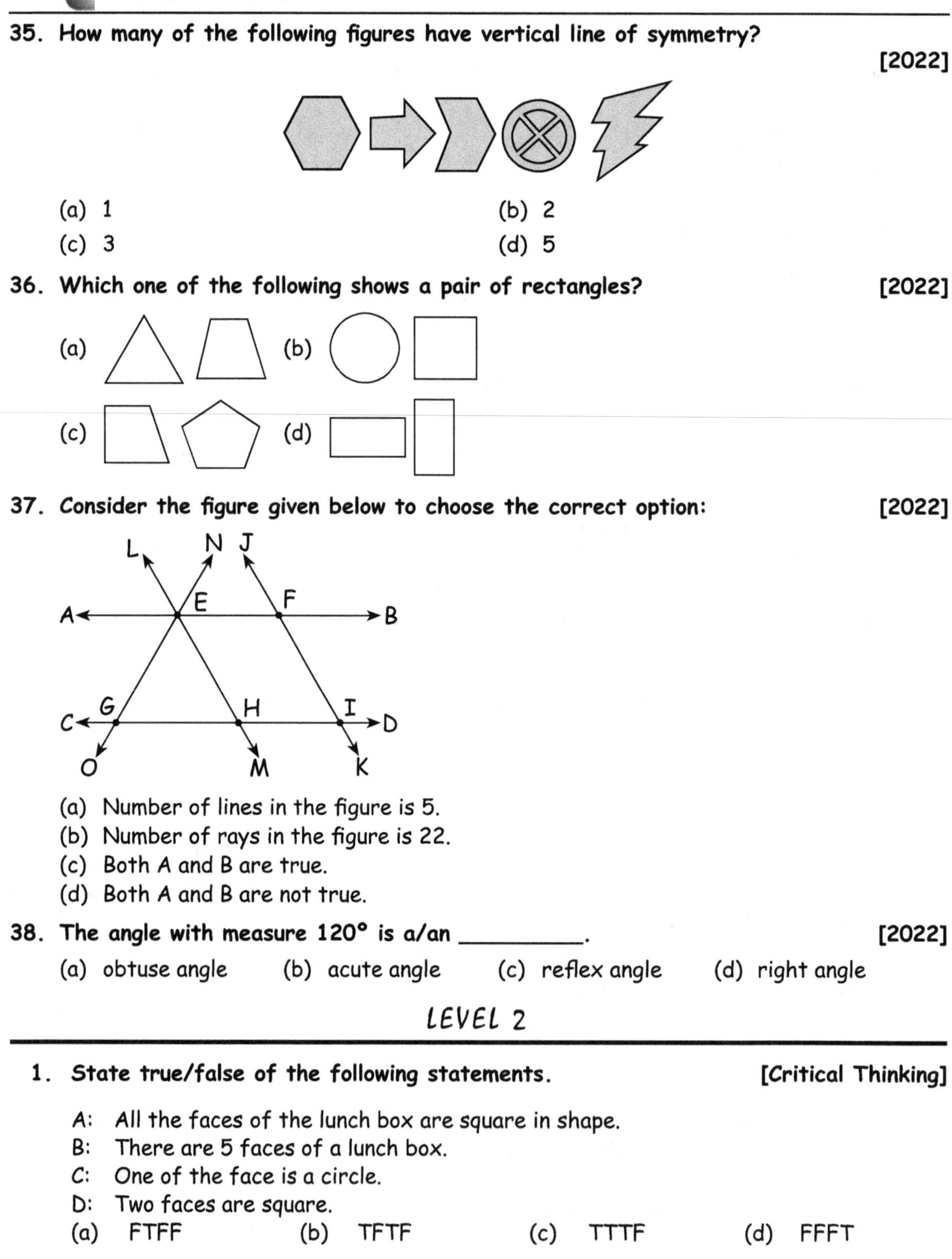

(a) 1

(b) 2

(c) 3

(d) 5

36. Which one of the following shows a pair of rectangles?   [2022]

(a)   (b)

(c)   (d)

37. Consider the figure given below to choose the correct option: [2022]

(a) Number of lines in the figure is 5.
(b) Number of rays in the figure is 22.
(c) Both A and B are true.
(d) Both A and B are not true.

38. The angle with measure 120° is a/an ___________.   [2022]

(a) obtuse angle   (b) acute angle   (c) reflex angle   (d) right angle

LEVEL 2

1. State true/false of the following statements.   [Critical Thinking]

A: All the faces of the lunch box are square in shape.
B: There are 5 faces of a lunch box.
C: One of the face is a circle.
D: Two faces are square.

(a) FTFF   (b) TFTF   (c) TTTF   (d) FFFT

2. **State true/ false for the following statements.** [Tricky]

   A: Diameter of a circle is twice its radius.

   B: Circumference of a circle is the line passing through its centre.

   C: The centre of the circle is 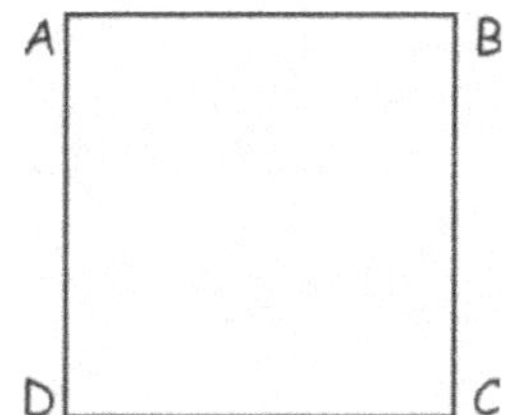

   D: Perimeter of circle is also called its circumference.

   (a) TFTT   (b) FFTT   (c) TTFF   (d) FTFF

3. **ABCD is a square given below. Which one of the following is not true about it.** [2011]

   (a) $3 \times \angle A = 270°$

   (b) $\angle A + \angle B = \angle C + \angle D$

   (c) $4AB = AB + BC + CD + DA$

   (d) $AD - DC + DA = AB + BC$

4. **Match the following solid shape with its face.** [Mental Mathematics]

List I	List II
A.	1.
B.	2.
C.	3.
D.	4.

```
        A   B   C   D                      A   B   C   D
(a)     4   3   2   1          (b)   4   2   3   1
(c)     4   3   1   2          (d)   4   2   1   3
```

5. **If**

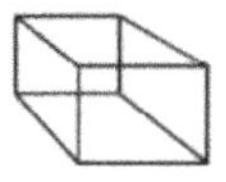 : 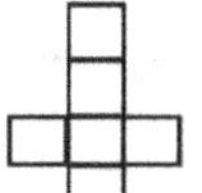 :: ? : 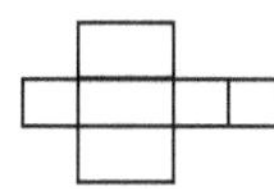

(a) 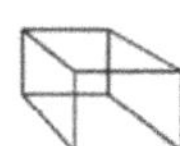   (b)    (c)    (d) 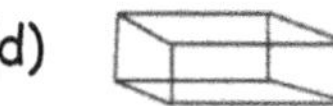

6. Find the measure of the greatest angle.   [2013]

    (a)   35°

    (b)   55°

    (c)   90°

    (d)   40°

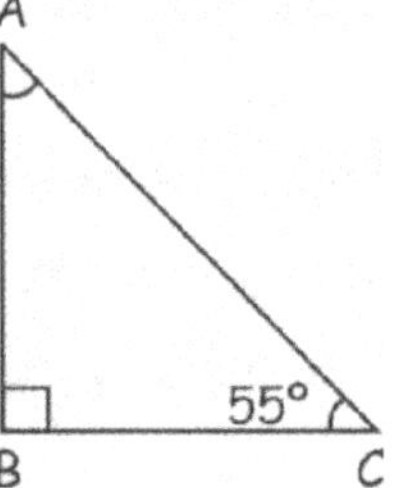

7. Complete the table given below: [Critical Thinking]

S.No.	Solid Shape		Number of faces
1.		A.	
2.		B.	
3.		C.	
4.		D.	
5.		E.	

A:	(a)	3	(b)	4	(c)	5	(d)	6
B:	(a)	3	(b)	4	(c)	5	(d)	6
C:	(a)	3	(b)	4	(c)	5	(d)	6
D:	(a)	3	(b)	4	(c)	5	(d)	6
E:	(a)	3	(b)	4	(c)	5	(d)	6

8. How many squares are there in the following picture ?   [2017, Tricky]

    (a) 23

    (b) 24

    (c) 25

    (d) 26

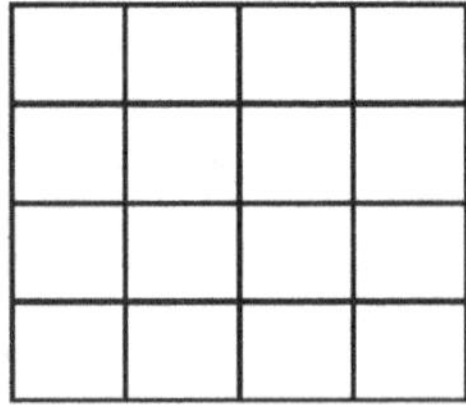

9. Symmetrical shapes are those which can be folded into two matching equal halves. The place from where they are folded is called the line of symmetry. In the following figures, the dotted line shows the line of symmetry.

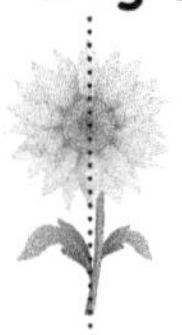 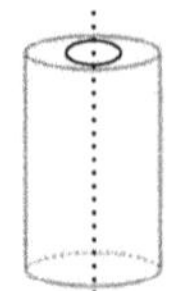  

Read the passage given above and answer the following questions based on it.

A. A rectangle has ______________ lines of symmetry. [2008]

(a) one   (b) two   (c) three   (d) four

B. A square has ______________ lines of symmetry. [2009]

(a) one   (b) two   (c) three   (d) four

C. A circle has ______________ lines of symmetry.

(a) one   (b) two   (c) three   (d) Infinite

Direction (Qs. 10 to 15): Chinky was playing with a magic box. The magic about the box was it had number on it and the numbers on the opposite faces of the box add to 7. If the box looks like the picture given below then answer the questions that follow :

10. Which number men on the opposite side of 2 ?

(a) 3   (b) 4   (c) 5   (d) 6

11. In the picture, which number will be at the bottom ?

(a) 3   (b) 4   (c) 5   (d) 6

12. Which number will chinky see if the turns left turn 2 i.e

(a) 3   (b) 4   (c) 5   (d) 6

13. What will this box look like if you opened it up ?

(a) A   (b) B   (c) C   (d) D

14. Match the following : [2012]

(i) ←——————————→

(ii) ——————————

(iii) ——————————→

(a) One end point
(b) Two end points
(c) No end points

(a) (i)-b, (ii)-a, (iii)-c
(b) (i)-c, (ii)-b, (iii)-a
(c) (i)-a, (ii)-b, (iii)-c
(d) (i)-c, (ii)-a, (iii)-b

15. Given below a step by step method to draw a circle by using compass. Choose the correct option to arrange them in a correct order. [Tricky]

A. Move the pencil arm around, keeping the metal arm fixed.
B. Keep the metal point of the compass fixed on the paper.
C. Stretch the arm of the compass that holds the pencil

(a) ABC   (b) CBA   (c) BCA   (d) ACB

Direction (Q. 16): Read the sentence and fill up the blanks with correct option.

16. A right angle measures ____(i) ____. An ____(ii)____angle is less than 90°. A ____(iii) ____ angle measures equal to two right angles. An obtuse angle_is greater than a ____(iv)____ angle and less than a straight angle. A 150° angle is an ____(v)____ angle.

    (a) (i) 90°   (ii) acute   (iii) straight   (iv) right
         (v) obtuse

    (b) (i) 180°   (ii) obtuse   (iii) acute   (iv) 90°
         (v) straight

    (c) (i) 30°   (ii) straight   (iii) acute   (iv) right
         (v) obtuse

    (d) (i) 90°   (ii) straight   (iii) acute   (iv) obtuse
         (v) right

17. Given below three triangles with their length of sides. Choose the correct name for each triangle based on their sides.   **[2010, Tricky]**

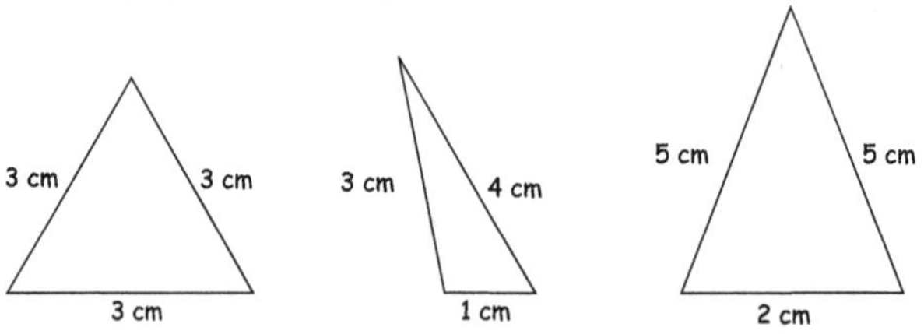

	A	B	C
(a)	Scalene triangle,	isosceles triangle,	equilateral triangle
(b)	Isosceles triangle,	scalene triangle,	equilateral triangle
(c)	Equilateral triangle,	scalene triangle,	isosceles triangle
(d)	Equilateral triangle,	isosceles triangle,	scalene triangle

18. Consider the following statements.   **[Tricky]**

    A: The sum of 3 angles of a triangle is 360°.

    B: The sum of 4 angles of a quadrilateral is 180°.

    Which of the statement(s) given above is/are correct?

    (a) A only   (b) B only

    (c) A and B both are correct   (d) Neither A nor B.

19. Which of the following squares must be shaded so that the given figure is symmetrical?   **[2013]**

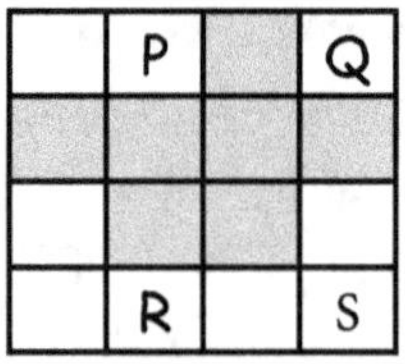

    (a) P

    (b) Q

    (c) R

    (d) S

20. How many more squares of side 1 cm must be added to the given figure to form a square of side 5 cm? **[2016]**
    (a) 9
    (b) 11
    (c) 20
    (d) 25

Direction (Qs. 21 and 22) WHICH SHAPE AM I?

21. I have no corners.   **[Tricky]**
    I have no parallel sides.
    I only have a curved edge.
    I have a centre.
    I am a ______________.
    (a) rectangle   (b) square   (c) triangle   (d) circle

22. I have 4 angles.   **[Critical Thinking]**
    The angles add upto 360°.   I have 2 sets of parallel lines.
    I am a ______________.
    (a) square   (b) triangle   (c) circle   (d) parallelogram

Direction (Qs. 23 and 32): Which of the following statements are True or False?

23. **Statement A:** A symmetrical shapes are those that cannot be folded into two equal halves.
    Statement B: Asymmetrical shapes are those that can be folded into two equal halves.
    Statement C: A triangle has three lines of symmetry.
    Statement D: A square has two lines of symmetry.
    Choose the correct option.   **[Critical Thinking]**
    (a) FTFT   (b) FFTT   (c) FTFF   (d) TFTF

24. Which of the following statements are True or False?
    Statement A: In right-angled triangle, one angle is a right angle i.e., of 90°
    Statement B: In acute-angled triangle all angles are 90°.
    Statement C: In obtuse-angled triangle, at least one angle is an obtuse angle.
    Statement D: Triangles can also be classified on the basis of angles.
    (a) TTFT   (b) TFTT   (c) FTTT   (d) TTTF

25. Identify the obtuse angle from the following options.   **[2014]**
    (a) An angle greater than 0° and smaller than 90°
    (b) An angle exactly of 90°
    (c) An angle greater than 90° and smaller than 180°
    (d) An angle exactly of 180°

26. Rahim draws a rectangle, Rohan draws a pentagon and Reshma draws a hexagon. If the pattern continues, which figure will be drawn next?   **[2016]**
    (a) Square   (b) Octagon   (c) Nonagon   (d) Heptagon

27. **Which of the following figures is not symmetric?** [2020]

(a) 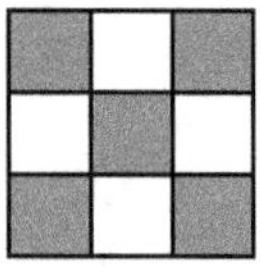   (b) 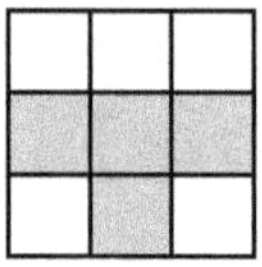   (c) 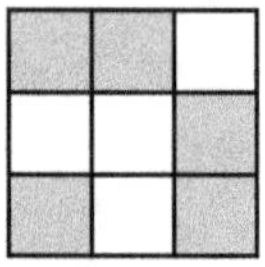   (d)

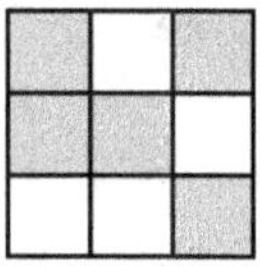

28. **The smallest number of squares that must be shaded so that the figure has a line of symmetry is __________.** [2021]

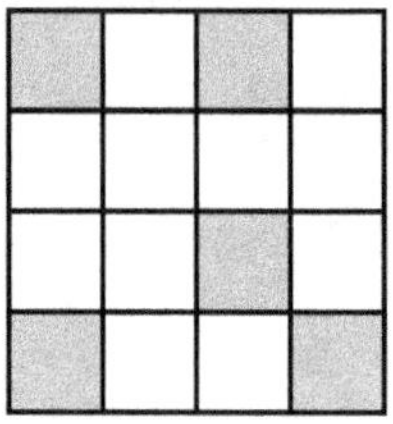

(a) 2

(b) 3

(c) 4

(d) 5

29. **Select the INCORRECT option.** [2021]

(a) A square has all four sides equal.

(b) A rectangle has two lines of symmetry.

(c) A figure which has the same start point and end point is called a closed figure.

(d) Diameter of a circle is always less than its radius.

30. **Select the INCORRECT statement.** [2022]

(a) A line can be extended on one side.   (b) A line segment has two end points.

(c) A ray has one end point.   (d) Two lines can intersect at one point only.

31. **How many triangles are there in the following figure?** [2022]

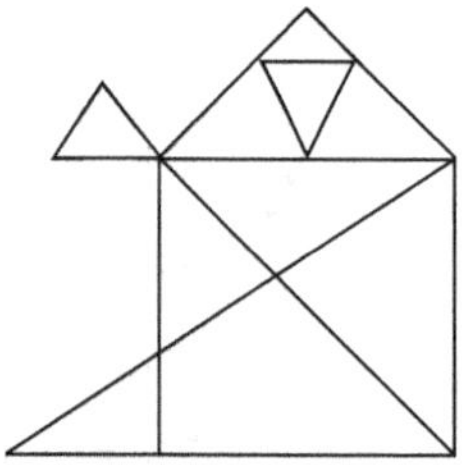

(a) Less than 9

(b) 10

(c) Between 11 to 14

(d) More than 14

32. **Minimum how many unit squares must be shaded so that the given figure has at least one line of symmetry?** [2022]

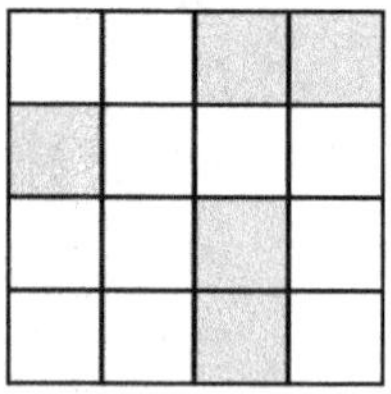

(a) 0

(b) 1

(c) 2

(d) 3

RESPONSE GRID

LEVEL 1

1. a b c d   2. a b c d   3. a b c d   4. a b c d   5. a b c d
6. a b c d   7. a b c d   8. a b c d   9. a b c d   10. a b c d

11. a b c d   12. a b c d   13. a b c d   14. a b c d   15. a b c d
16. a b c d   17. a b c d   18. a b c d   19. a b c d   20. a b c d
21. a b c d   22. a b c d   23. a b c d   24. a b c d   25. a b c d
26. a b c d   27. a b c d   28. a b c d   29. a b c d   30. a b c d
31. a b c d   32. a b c d   33. a b c d   34. a b c d   35. a b c d
36. a b c d   37. a b c d   38. a b c d

LEVEL 2

1. a b c d   2. a b c d   3. a b c d   4. a b c d   5. a b c d
6. a b c d   7. a b c d   8. a b c d   9. a b c d   10. a b c d
11. a b c d   12. a b c d   13. a b c d   14. a b c d   15. a b c d
16. a b c d   17. a b c d   18. a b c d   19. a b c d   20. a b c d
21. a b c d   22. a b c d   23. a b c d   24. a b c d   25. a b c d
26. a b c d   27. a b c d   28. a b c d   29. a b c d   30. a b c d
31. a b c d   32. a b c d

Solutions with Explanation

LEVEL 1

1. **(d)** The increasing order size of square is A C D B. Therefore, the answer is option (d) ACDB.

2. **(d)** The increasing order size of rectangle is D B C A. Therefore the answer is option (d) DBCA.

3. **(c)** The increasing order size of circle is BCDA. Therefore, the answer is option (c) BCDA.

4. **(b)** Net of a 6 – faced cube look like 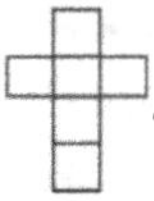 . Therefore, the answer is option (b).

5. **(a)** The correct spin is 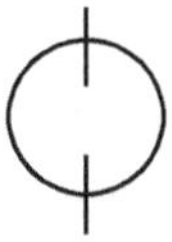 is . Therefore, the answer is option (a) D.

6. **(d)** A lunch box has 6 faces. Therefore, the answer is option (d) 6.

7. **(c)** 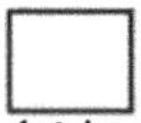 is one of the faces of lunch box. Therefore, the answer is option (c) (side face)

8. **(a)** Circle : radius :: Cube : edge

9. **(b)** An angle that is greater than 90° but is less than 180° is known as an obtuse angle.

10. **(d)** Reflex angle

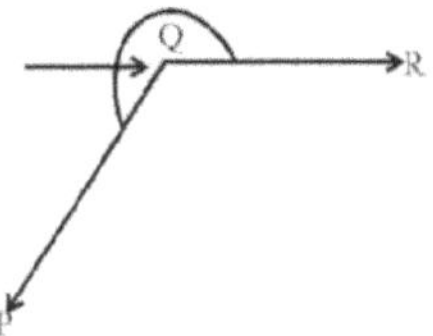

11. **(b)** 90° : right angle : : 360° : whole angle

12. **(c)**
13. **(d)** We can draw a circle with the help of a compass.
14. **(b)** Longest chord of a circle is two times of the radius.
15. **(d)** The drawing of the lunch box is 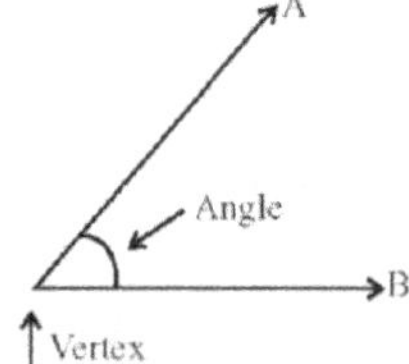 .

   Therefore, answer is option (d).
16. **(b)** Some shapes can be fitted together, edge to edge. This is called tiling.

   For eg:

17. **(a)**
18. **(a)** 65° is an acute angle.
19. **(a)**   20. **(d)**   21. **(c)**   22. **(b)**
23. **(c)**
24. **(b)** ABCD is a rectangle.   25. **(d)**
26. **(b)** A quadrilateral has 4 line segments.
27. **(b)** Circle. It is closed and bounded by curved line.

28. **(c)** Angle

29. **(b)** It is a pentagon.
30. **(c)** First prime odd number = 3. So, diameter is 2 × 3 = 6 units.
31. **(c)**   32. **(b)**   33. **(a)**
34. **(b)** Quadrilateral.
35. **(b)**   36. **(d)**   37. **(c)**   38. **(a)**

LEVEL 2

1. **(d)** Since, all the faces of the lunch box are not square in shape; So, statement A is false.
   Since, there are 6 faces of a lunch box. So, statement B is false.

   Since, no face is circle. So, statement C is false.
   Since, two faces are squares. So, statement D is true.

   Therefore, the answer is option (d) FFFT
2. **(a)** Statement A is true.

   The line passing through the centre of a circle is a diameter. So, statement B is false.
   The centre of the circle is (•). So, statement C is true
   Statement D is true.

   Therefore, the answer is option (a) TFTT.
3. **(d)** As AD – DC + DA = AB + BC is incorrect
4. **(a)**   5. **(d)**
6. **(c)** Measure of the greatest angle is 90°.
7. A :   (d) 6   B: (c) 5   C: (b) 4   D: (c) 5   E: (d) 6

8. **(d)** There are 26 square in the given picture

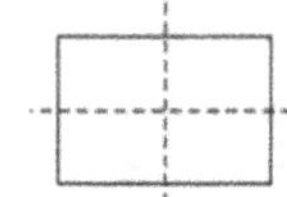

Therefore, the answer is option (d) 26.

9. **A.** **(b) two** **B.** **(d) four** 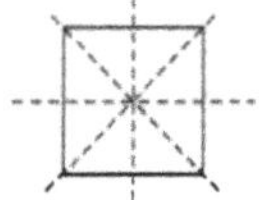 **C.** **(d) infinite** 

10. **(c)** Since the numbers on the opposite faces of the box add to 7. So, the number on the opposite side of 2 will be 7-2 = 5. Therefore, the answer is option (c) 5.

11. **(d)** Since, the top number is 1. So, the number at the bottom will be

7 − 1 = 6. Therefore, the answer is option (d) 6.

12. **(b)** If Chinky turns left turn 2 then the box will become Here ? is the

number on the opposite side of 3. So, the number will be 7 − 3 = 4. Therefore the answer is option (b) 4

13. **(c)** The box will look like, therefore, the answer is option (c) C.

14. **(b)** i → c,   ii → b,   iii → a

15. **(c)** BCA is the correct order to draw a circle by using a compass.

16. **(a)**

17. **(c)** Equilateral triangle: All sides are equal.

Scalene triangle: All three sides are different.
Isosceles triangle: Only two sides are equal.

18. **(d)** Neither statement A correct nor statement B.

The sum of 3 angles of a triangle is 180°

The sum of 4 angles of a quadrilateral is 360°.

19. **(a)** P Must be shaded

20. **(c)** 20.

21. **(d)** Circle

22. **(d)** Parallelogram

23. **(d)** 1st and 3rd statements are true and 2nd and 4th statements are false.

24. **(b)** TFTT   **25.** **(c)**

26. **(d)** Heptagon will be drawn next.

27. **(d)**   **28.** **(b)**

29. **(d)** Diameter of a circle is always two times of its radius.

30. **(a)**   **31.** **(d)**   **32.** **(c)**

NAME	FIGURE	AREA	PERIMETER CIRCUMFERENCE
TRIANGLE		$A = \dfrac{b \times h}{2}$	$P = MN + NP + PM$
PARALLELOGRAM		$A = b \times h$	$P = DE + EF + FG + GD$
RHOMBUS		$A = b \times h$	$P = b + b + b + b$ $P = 4b$
RECTANGLE		$A = L \times w$	$P = L + w + L + w$ $P = 2L + 2w$
SQUARE		$A = l^2$	$P = l + l + l + l$ $P = 4\,l$
TRAPEZIUM		$A = \dfrac{(B + b) \times h}{2}$	$P = MN + NP + PR + RM$
CIRCLE		$A = \pi r^2$	$C = 2\pi\,r = \pi d$

LEARNING OBJECTIVES

This lesson will help you to:—

- ❖ outline the boundary of a shape.
- ❖ identify shapes like square, rectangle and circle and separate it from other shapes.
- ❖ explore intensively the area and perimeter of simple shapes.
- ❖ estimate the area and perimeter of a shape.
- ❖ find the area and perimeter of a shape using grid method.

QUICK CONCEPT REVIEW

Diagrams/pictures

Perimeter

1. The distance around the edge of a shape is called boundary or perimeter of the shape. It is always measured in single unit, that is cm, m, km etc.

   The perimeter of fig. 1 is the total distance around it.

   The total distance around the fig. 1

   $= 3\,m + 2\,m + 2\,m + 3\,m + 2\,m + 5\,m = 17\,m$

   ∴ Perimeter of fig. 1 = 17 m.

   Hence, the sum of all the lengths of shape is called its perimeter.

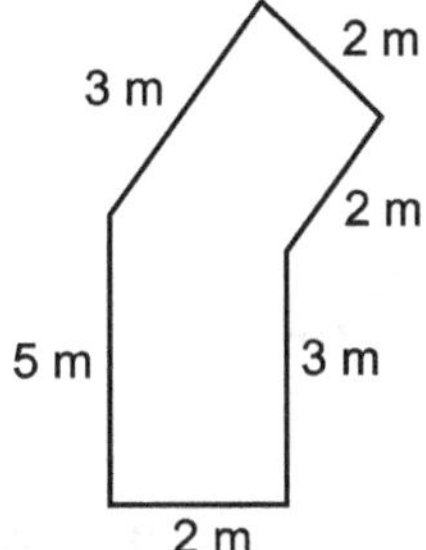

Fig. 1

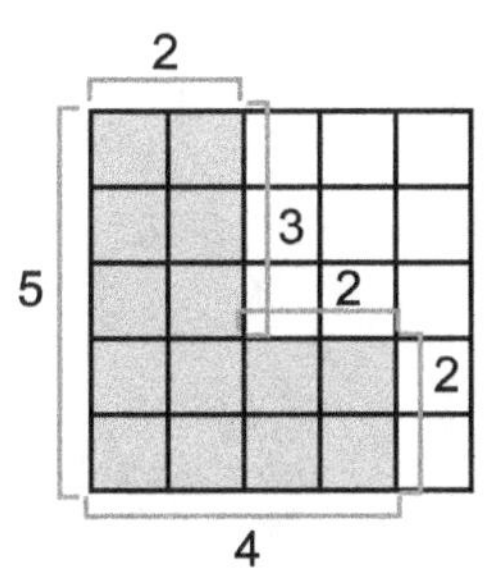

Fig. 2

Real Life Examples

- ❖ Knowledge of area and perimeter helps in installing a garden.
- ❖ The perimeter can be used to calculate the length of fence required to surround a yard or garden.
- ❖ The perimeter of a wheel (its circumference) describes how far it will roll in one revolution.
- ❖ The amount of string wound around a spool is related to the spool's perimeter.
- ❖ Area can be understood as the amount of material with a given thickness that would be necessary to fashion a model of the shape.
- ❖ Area is the amount of paint necessary to cover the surface with a single coat.

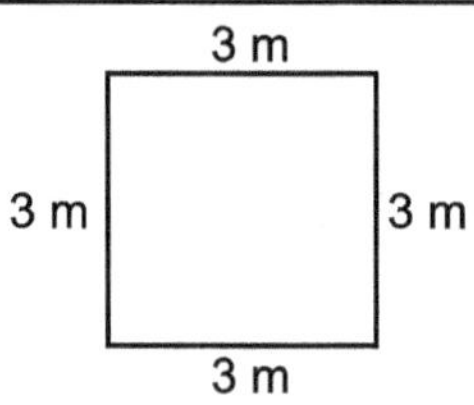

Fig. 3

Area and perimeter of a circle of radius 'r'

Area = πr^2 and perimeter

= $2\pi r$, where $\pi = \dfrac{22}{7}$ or 3.17

Perimeter of circle whose radius is 7m in fig. 5

= $2\pi r = 2 \times \dfrac{22}{7} \times 7 = 44m$

Amazing Facts

❖ A circle has the shortest perimeter of all shapes with the same area.

❖ Area and perimeter are two calculations performed on many geometrical shapes. Perimeter is a measure of distance around a shape; for example, someone might want to figure out the perimeter around their garden before buying material to make a fence so that they know how much material to buy. Area is a measure of the amount of surface something covers. For example, someone might want to know how much space their garden takes up.

❖ Area and perimeter are often grouped together because one can be used to help you figure out the other. For example, if you know the perimeter of a square, you can easily figure out the area, and vice-versa.

Here, each square is of side 1 unit.

Perimeter of shaded region

= 2 units + 5 units + 4 units + 2 units + 2 units

+ 3 units = 18 units

2. Perimeter of a square is the sum of the length of its sides.

Perimeter of square in fig. 3

= Sum of the sides of the square

= 3 m + 3 m + 3 m + 3 m or

= 4 × 3 m = 12 m.

Thus, perimeter of a square = 4 × side

3. Perimeter of a rectangle is the sum of the length of its sides.

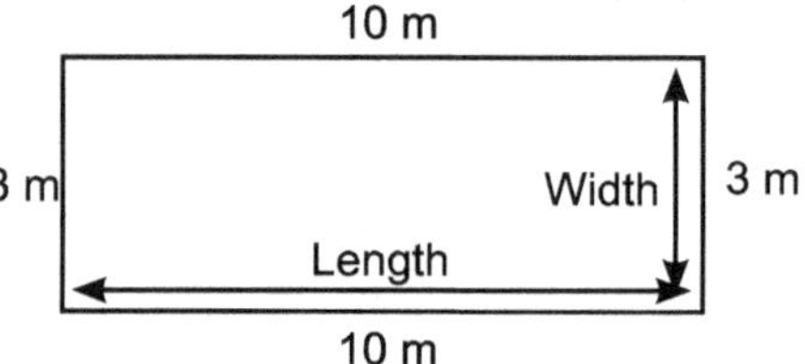

Fig. 4

Perimeter of rectangle in fig. 4

= sum of the sides of the rectangle

= 3 m + 10 m + 3 m + 10 m or

= (3 m + 3 m) + (10 m + 10 m)

= (2 × 3 m) + (2 × 10 m)

= 2 × (3 m + 10 m)

= 2 × (13 m) = 26 m

Thus, perimeter of a rectangle = 2 × (length + width)

4. Perimeter of a circle is the distance around the circle.

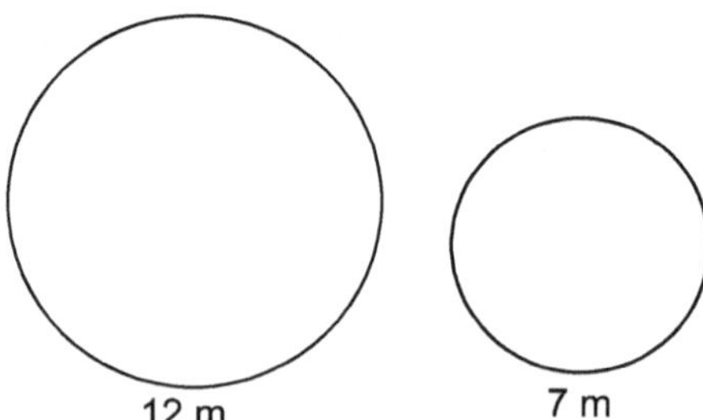

Fig. 5

Also, perimeter of a circle is known as circumference of it.

AREA

Area is the total number of square units that fill a given shape.

Area of fig. 6

= Total number of squares in the shape

= 26 square units.

When we divide a square into squares of length 1 unit, then we can see that we get same number of squares in rows and columns.

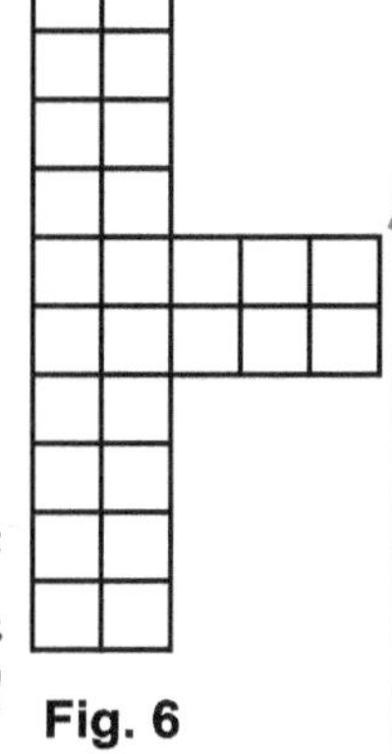

Fig. 6

In this case, we can multiply the number of squares in any one row with the number of squares in any one column to get the area of the square.

In fig. 7,

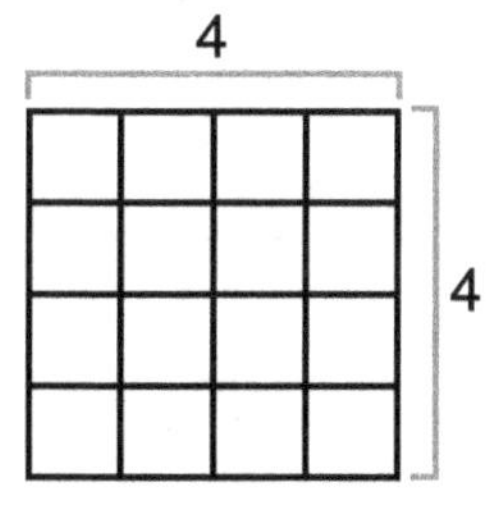

Fig. 7

Area of square = (Number of squares in row) × (Number of squares in column)

= 4 × 4 = 16 square units

Thus, area of a square = side × side.

When we divide a rectangle in squares of length 1 unit, then we can see that we get more number of squares in either rows or columns. In this case, we can multiply the number of squares in any one row with the number of squares in any one column to get the area of the rectangle.

In fig. 8, the area of rectangle

= (Number of squares in one row)

×(Number of squares in one column)

= 7 × 5 = 35 square units

Historical Preview

❖ The first recorded use of areas and perimeters in the West was in ancient Babylon, where they used it to measure the amount of land that was owned by different people for taxation purposes.

❖ The mathematics of Egyptian geometry is documented by examples of rules for determining areas and volumes of common plane and solid objects. They appear to be based on trial and error results and observations as opposed to theoretical proof.

Example: Find the perimeter and area of a rectangle whose length is 5 m and breadth is 4 m.

Solution:

Perimeter of a rectangle

= 5 + 5 + 4 + 4

= 18 m

Area of a rectangle

= length × breadth

= 5 × 4

= 20 sq. m

Shortcut to problem solving

❖ To find the perimeter of different figures, we can use certain formulae.

➢ Perimeter of a square
   = 4 × side.

➢ Perimeter of a rectangle
   = 2 (length + breadth).

➢ Perimeter of a triangle
   = a + b + c.

where a, b, c are the sides of the triangle.

❖ To find the area of different figures, we can use certain formulae.

➢ Area of a square
   = side × side.

➢ Area of a rectangle
   = length × breadth.

➢ Area of a triangle
   = $\dfrac{1}{2}$ × base × height.

Example: Find the perimeter and area of a rectangle whose area is 80 sq. m and breadth is 8 m.

Solution:

Length = $\dfrac{\text{Area}}{\text{Breadth}}$

= $\dfrac{80}{8}$

= 10 m.

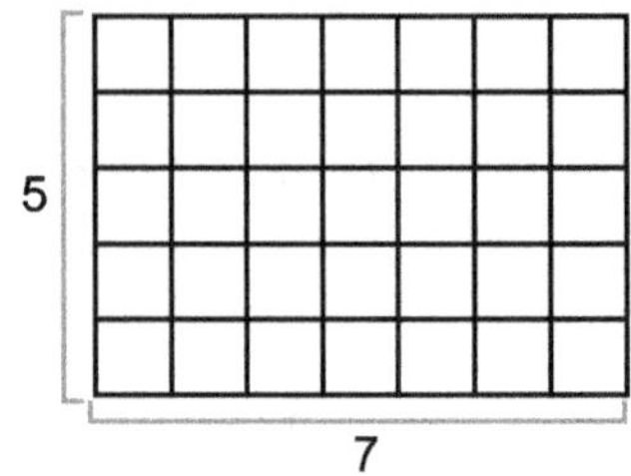

Fig. 8

Thus, we have area of rectangle = length × breadth (width)

Note: We can use the formula to measure the area of triangle = $\dfrac{1}{2}$ × base × height.

Examples

1. Suresh bought a mat as given below. He wants to know whether he can spread that mat in his living room.

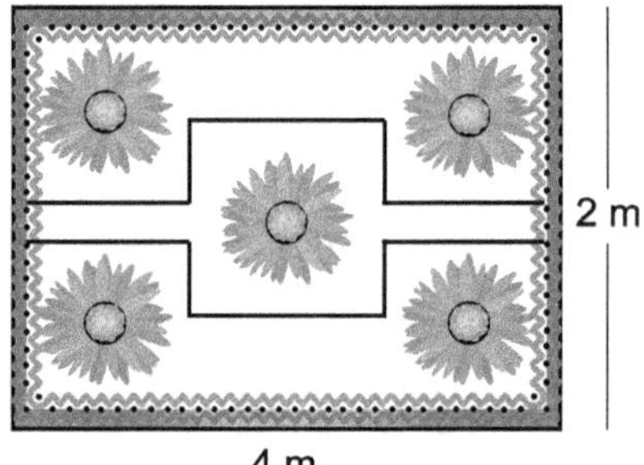

Let us find the area of the mat.

The mat is divided into squares of length 1 m. So, we get 4 squares in each row and 2 squares in each column.

∴ The area of mat = 4 × 2 = 8 square metre.

2. Sangeeta aunty bought a new saree for her nephew's wedding. She want to stitch a new matching lace around its boundary.

To find the length of the lace required to stitch around the boundary of the saree, we need to find its perimeter.

Perimeter of saree = 5 m + 2 m + 5 m + 2 m = 14 m

Thus, 14 m lace is required for the saree.

CHARTS/FLOWCHARTS

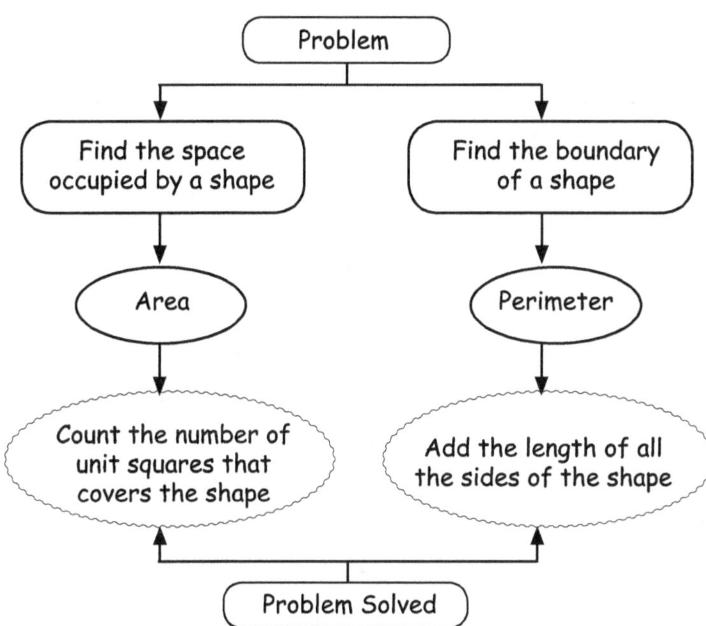

Misconcept/concept

Misconcept: When a unit square is removed from a given shape then both its area and perimeter get reduced by square unit and a unit respectively.

Concept: When a unit square is removed from a given shape then its area gets reduced by a square unit but its perimeter either remains same or gets increased by few units.

Note: Example for the concept is elaborated for you after flow chart.

For example: Consider the square given below divided into unit squares.

Perimeter = 5 + 5 + 5 + 5

= 20 units

Area = 5 × 5 = 25 square units.

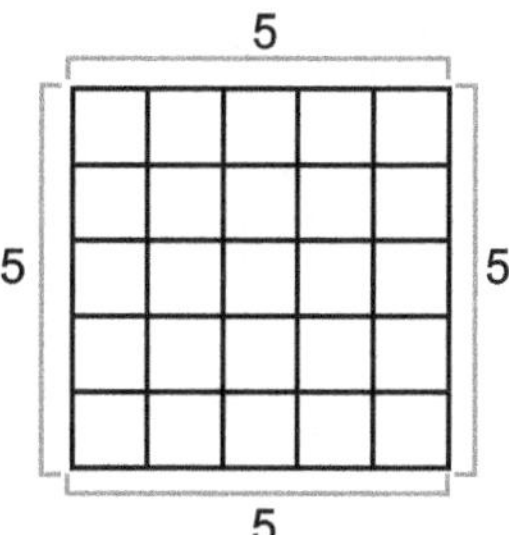

(i) Let us now remove a square unit from it and then calculate the area and perimeter of the whole square.

Perimeter = 5 + 5 + 5 + 2 + 1 + 1 + 1 + 2

= 22 units

Area = 24 square units.

(ii) Let us now remove a square unit from the corner and then calculated the area and perimeter of the whole square.

Perimeter = 4 + 1 + 1 + 4 + 5 + 5

= 20 units

Area = 24 square units.

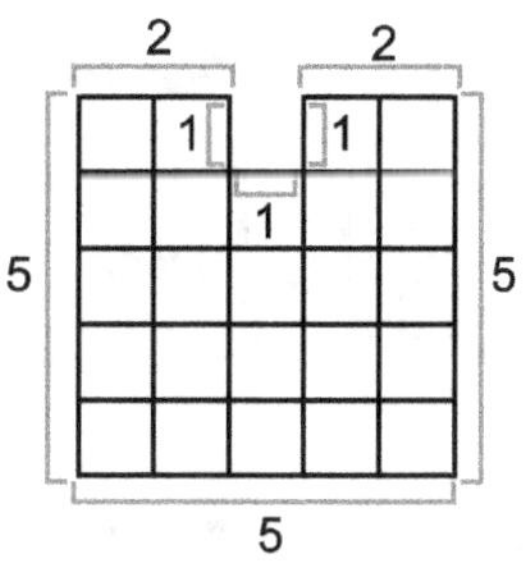

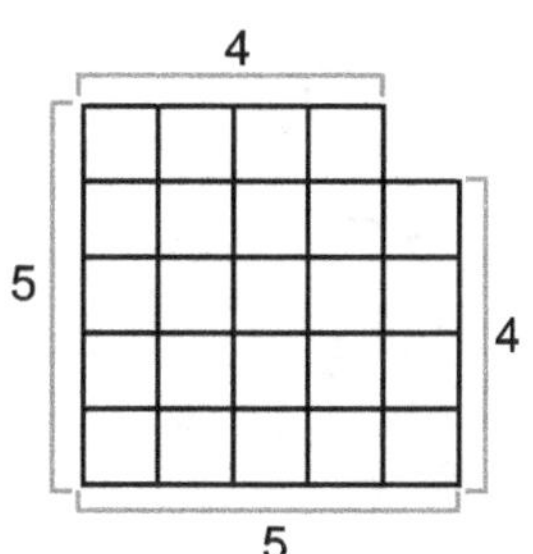

Thus, we can see that when we remove unit square from a shape then its area gets reduced by a square unit and its perimeter either remains the same or gets increased by few units.

Multiple Choice Questions

LEVEL 1

Direction (Qs. 1 to 3): Look at the picture given below and answer the questions that follow:

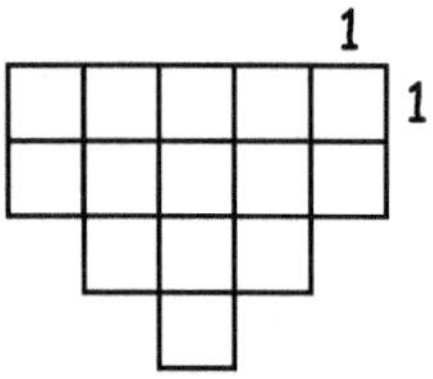

1. If Area : 14 square cm :: Perimeter : ?   **[Mental Mathematics]**

   (a) 15 cm   (b) 16 cm
   (c) 17 cm   (d) 18 cm

2. If perimeter of 1 small square is 4 m then what is the area of the whole figure?

   [Mental Mathematics]

   (a) 14 square metre   (b) 15 square meter
   (c) 16 square metre   (d) 17 square metre

3. If Area : 14 square feet :: Perimeter : ?   **[Mental Mathematics]**

   (a) 15 feet   (b) 16 feet   (c) 17 feet   (d) 18 feet

Direction (Qs. 4 to 7): Timsy is drawing some figures of given area. Find the odd one out in the following questions :   **[Mental Mathematics]**

4. Area = 6 square cm.

   (a) 3 cm / 2 cm   (b) 4 cm / 2 cm   (c) 2 cm / 3 cm   (d) 6 cm / 1 cm

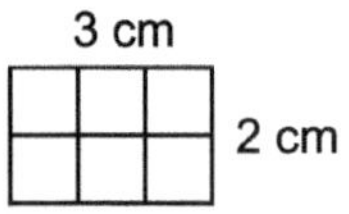

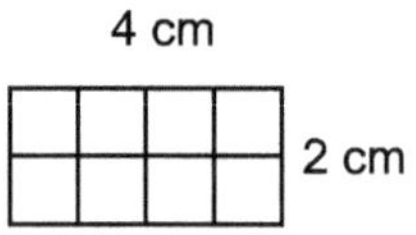

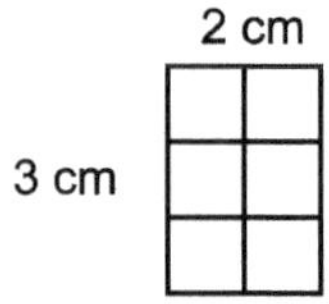

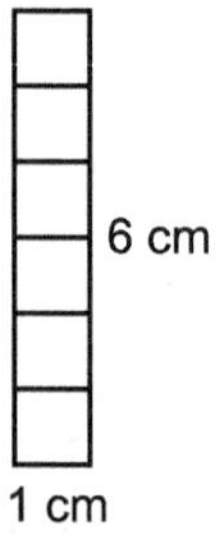

5. Area = 12 square feet.

   (a) 3 feet / 4 feet   (b) 4 feet / 3 feet   (c) 6 feet / 2 feet   (d) 4 feet / 2 feet

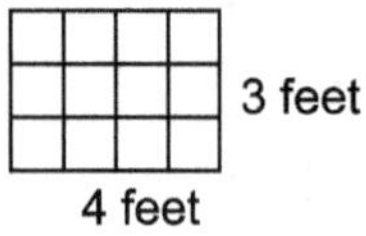

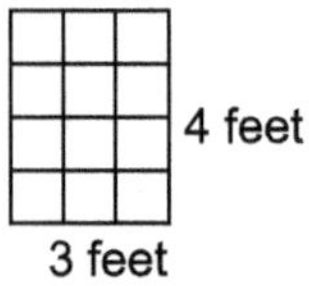

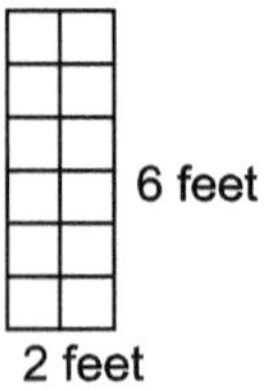

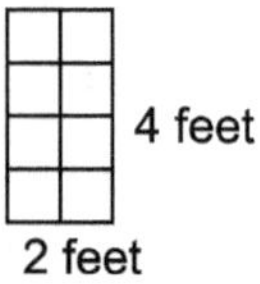

6. Area = 8 square cm

   (a) 2 cm / 2 cm   (b) 2 cm / 4 cm   (c) 4 cm / 2 cm   (d) 8 cm / 1 cm

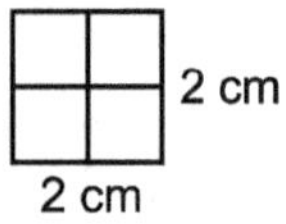

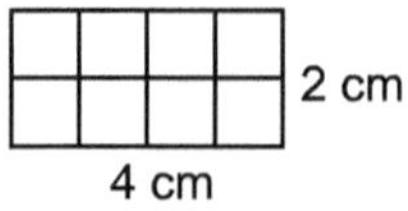

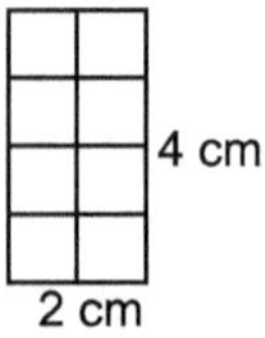

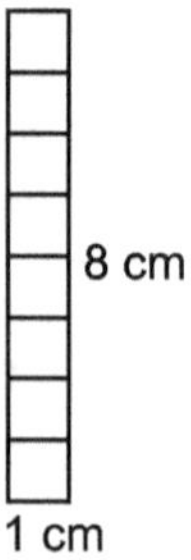

7. **Area = 16 square metre**

(a) 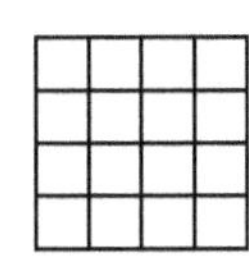

(b) 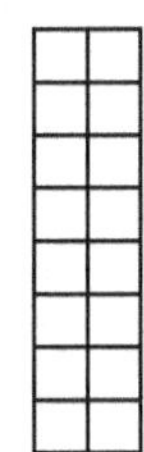

(c) 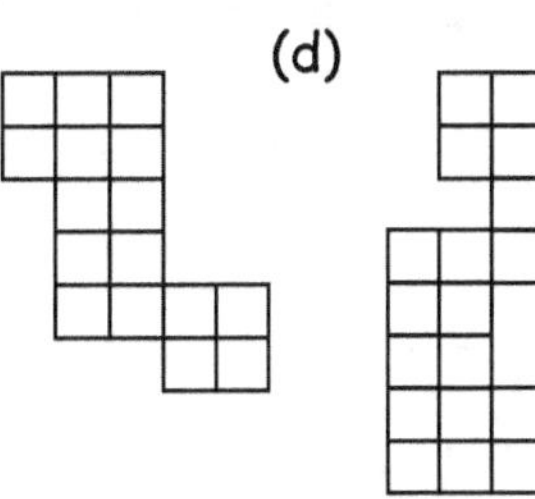

(d)

Direction (Qs. 8 to 10): Find the perimeter in units of the figures given in the following questions whose each edge of length 1 unit.   **[Mental Mathematics]**

8. 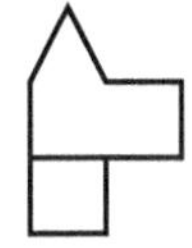

(a)   7   (b)   8   (c)   9   (d)   10

9.

(a)   7   (b)   8   (c)   9   (d)   10

10.

(a)   6   (b)   7   (c)   8   (d)   9

11. **What is the perimeter of square of side 9 cm?**

(a)   35 cm   (b)   36 cm   (c)   37 cm   (d)   38 cm

12. **What is the area of 11 unit squares?**   **[Mental Mathematics]**

(a)   110 square units   (b)   100 square units

(c)   11 square units   (d)   10 square units

13. **Which of the following statement describes the term 'perimeter' correctly?**

(a)   Perimeter can be defined as the amount of surface covered by any figure or object.

(b)   The sum of all the lengths of a figures is called its perimeter.

(c)   The multiplication of all the lengths of a figure is called its perimeter.

(d)   None of the above.

14. Which of the following shape is suitable with the area $5\frac{1}{2}$ cm². [Mental Mathematics]

(a) 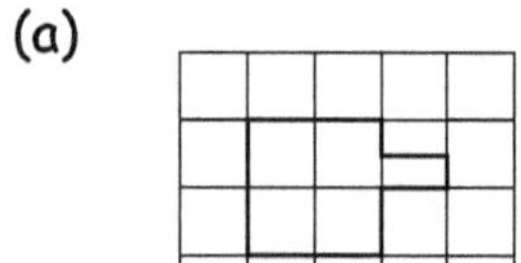 (b) 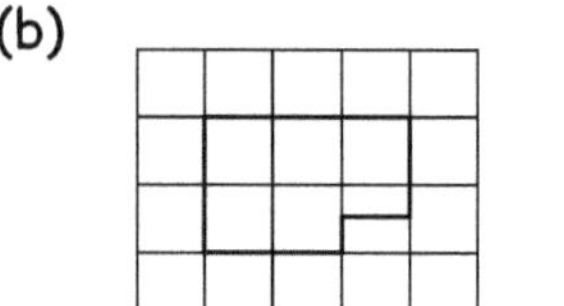 (c) 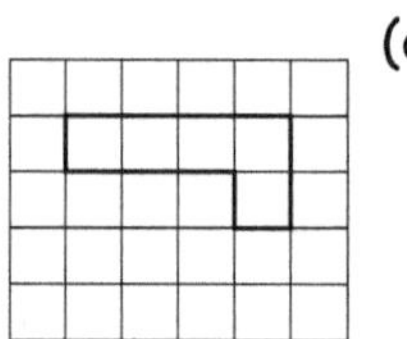 (d) 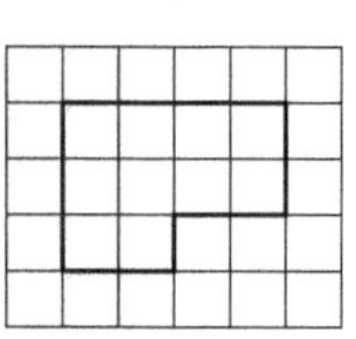

15. Weight : Kilogram : : _____________ : Metre.

   (a)   Area   (b)   Volume   (c)   Perimeter   (d)   Rupees

16. Find the perimetre of the figure given below :   [2011]

   (a) 34 cm   (b) 20 cm

   (c) 24 cm   (d) 32 cm

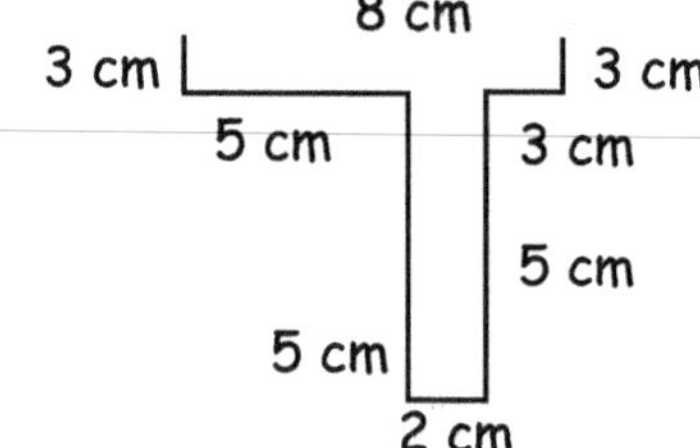

17. Arrange the following figures in increasing order according to their area.

[Critical Thinking]

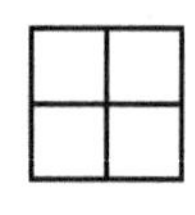   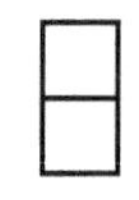   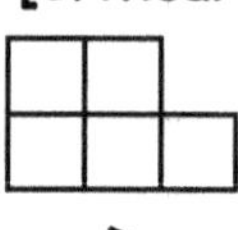

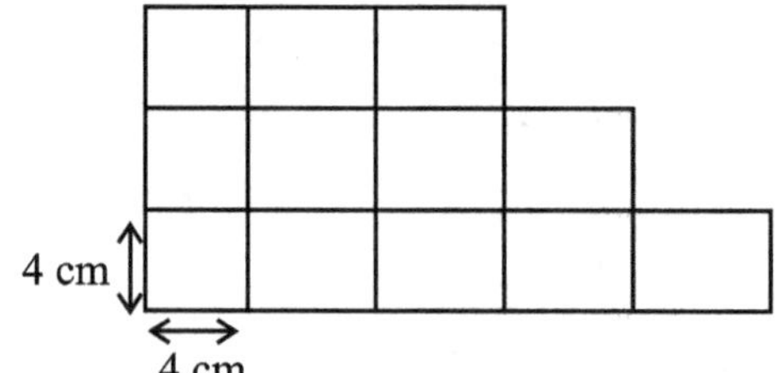

A   B   C   D

   (a)   C D A B   (b)   A C D B   (c)   C A D B   (d)   B A C D

18. If the given figure is made up of identical squared, then find its perimeter. [2016]

   (a)   68 cm

   (b)   60 cm

   (c)   64 cm

   (d)   62 cm

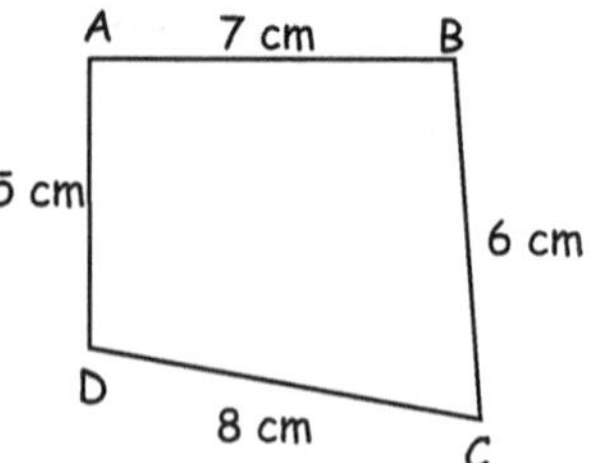

19. Find the perimeter of a square whose length of each side is 3 cm.   [2013]

   (a)   13 cm   (b)   12 cm   (c)   14 cm   (d)   18 cm

20. Find the perimeter of the following figure.   [2015]

   (a) 62 cm

   (b) 26 cm

   (c) 4 cm

   (d) 14 cm

21. Find the area of the figure given below:

(a) 16 square metre

(b) 17 square metre

(c) 18 square metre

(d) 19 square metre

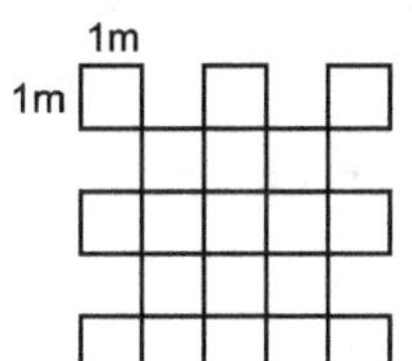

22. Find the perimeter of the given figure. [2016]

(a) 24 cm

(b) 21 cm

(c) 14 cm

(d) 17 cm

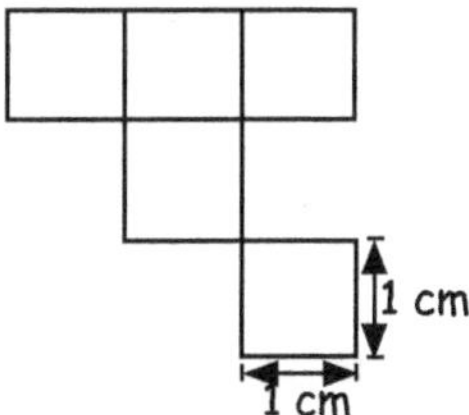

23. The given figure is obtained by removing some small squares from a big rectangle. The length of one side of a small square is 2 cm. Find the perimeter of the figure. [2013]

(a) 28 cm

(b) 42 cm

(c) 56 cm

(d) 160 cm

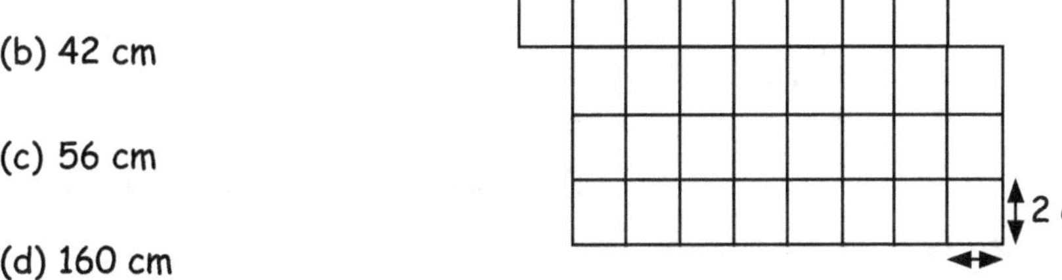

Direction (Qs. 24 to 26): Chinku is making a design using coloured papers. He cut out a square of side 10 cm as shown in fig. A. Then he cut out small squares of side 1 cm from various sections of the large square as given in fig. B. Look at the figures and answer the questions that follow: **[Critical Thinking]**

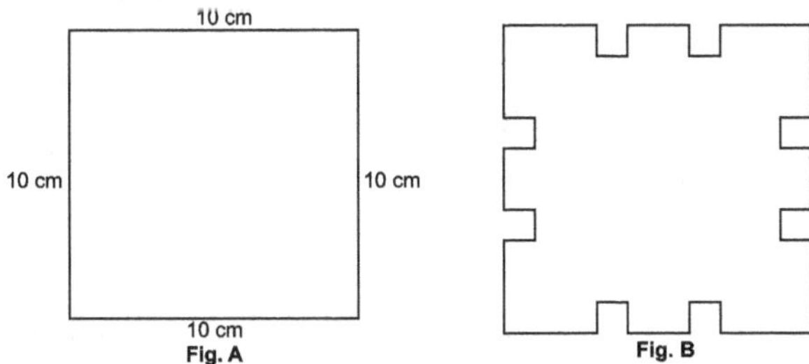

24. What is the perimeter of fig. A? [2009]

(a) 40 cm (b) 50 cm (c) 60 cm (d) 70 cm

25. What is the perimeter of fig. B? [2008]

(a) 46 cm (b) 56 cm (c) 66 cm (d) 76 cm

26. What is the difference in the perimeter of fig. A and fig. B?

    (a) 6 cm   (b) 10 cm   (c) 16 cm   (d) 26 cm

27. Find the perimeter of the given figure?   **[2016]**

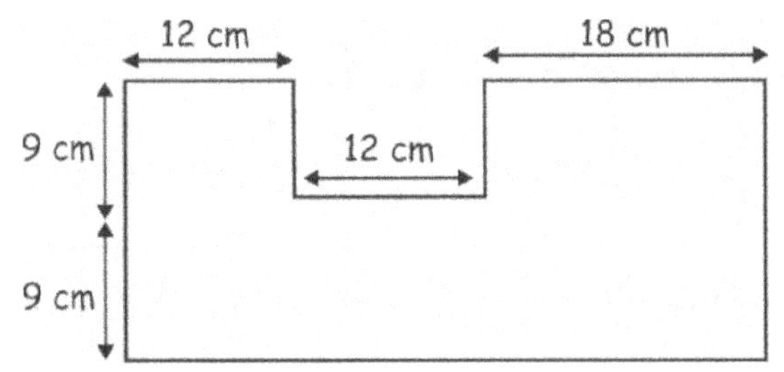

    (a) 160 cm

    (b) 142 cm

    (c) 138 cm

    (d) 130 cm

Direction (Qs. 28 to 30): Dimensions of different Parks in a locality is given in a table. Read the table given below and answer the questions that follow: **[Critical Thinking]**

Park	Length	Width
A	50 m	20 m
B	30 m	10 m
C	70 m	30 m
D	25 m	15 m
E	65 m	25 m

28. Which of the following Park has largest boundary?

    (a) Park A   (b) Park C   (c) Park E   (d) Park B

29. Which of the following Park has smallest boundary?

    (a) Park D   (b) Park A   (c) Park E   (d) Park C

30. Which of the following Park has same boundary as that of Park B?

    (a) Park A   (b) Park C   (c) Park D   (d) Park E

31. Find the perimeter of the given figure, if all the sides are of length

    3 tens – (10 ones + 4 ones) cm.   **[2013]**

    (a) 110 cm   (b) 128 cm

    (c) 138 cm   (d) 150 cm

32. Find the perimeter of the given figure (not drawn to scale).   **[2014]**

    (a) 88 cm

    (b) 93 cm

    (c) 98 cm

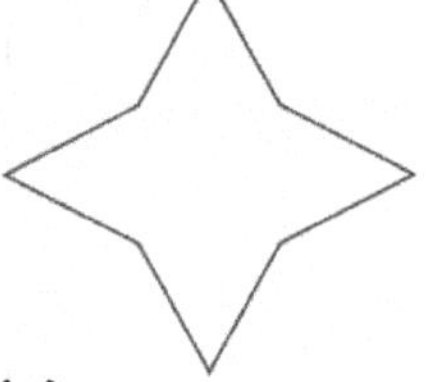

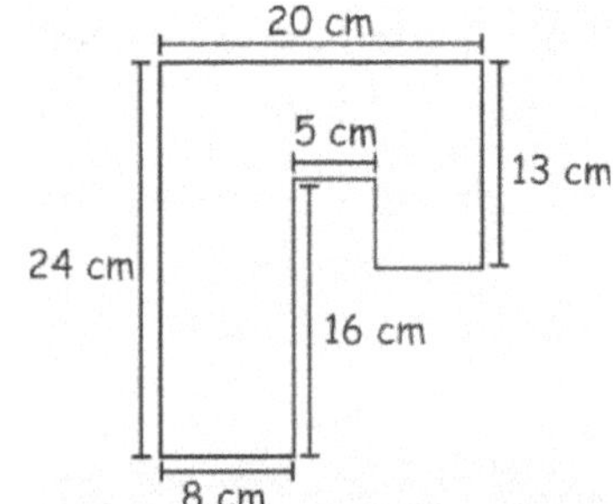

  (d)   103 cm

33. Find the perimeter of the given figure.   [2021]

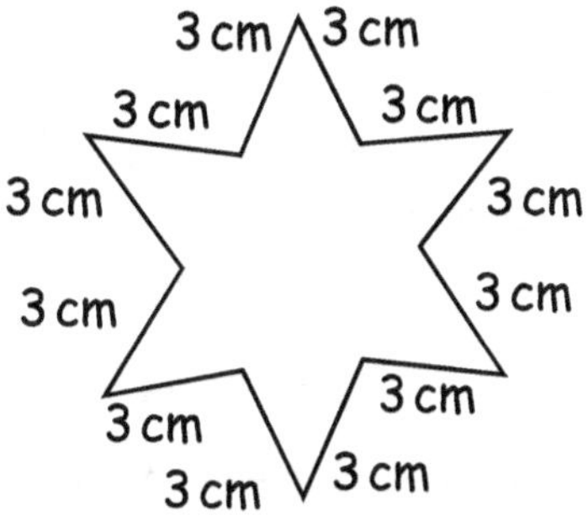

  (a) 36 cm

  (b) 30 cm

  (c) 34 cm

  (d) 42 cm

34. Find the perimeter of the figure (not drawn to scale) given below.   [2022]

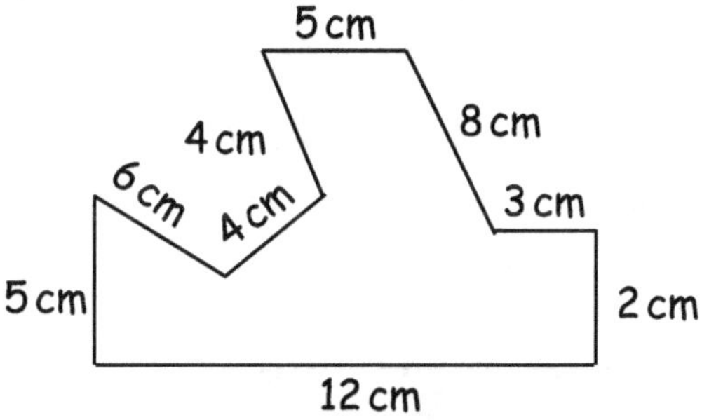

  (a) 47 cm

  (b) 43 cm

  (c) 49 cm

  (d) 51 cm

35. The perimeter of the given figure is 49 cm. Find the length of BC.   [2022]

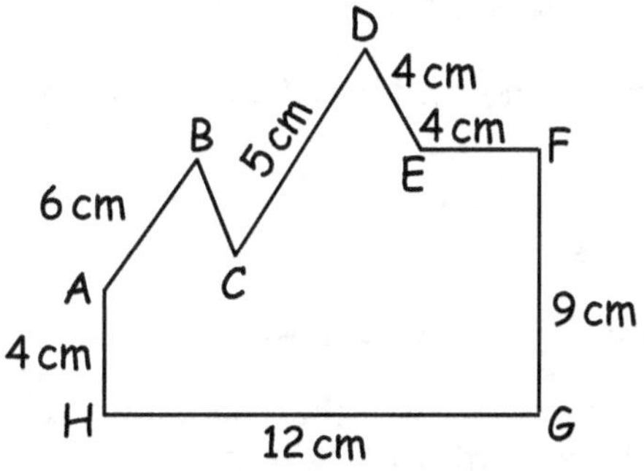

  (a) 5 cm

  (b) 4 cm

  (c) 3 cm

  (d) 6 cm

LEVEL 2

1. Parul went for shopping. She wanted to buy some bangles for her sisters. Shopkeeper showed him some bangles of different sizes. Arrange the following bangles in decreasing order according to the boundary of the bangles.

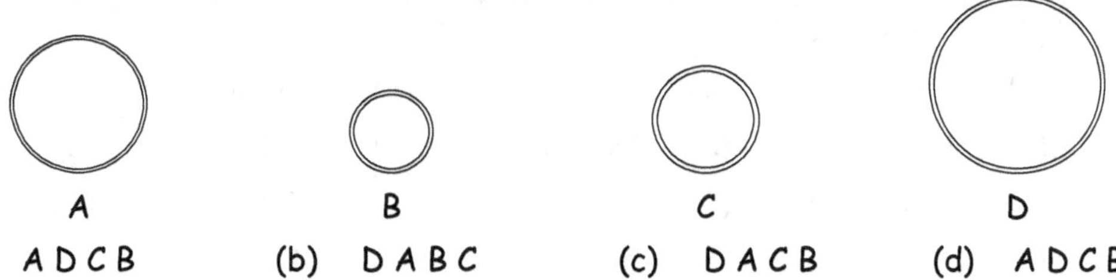

  (a)   A D C B   (b)   D A B C   (c)   D A C B   (d)   A D C B

2. Figure (i) and (ii) shows two identical rectangles X and Y which are arranged differently. What is the difference between the perimeter of both the figures. **[2015]**

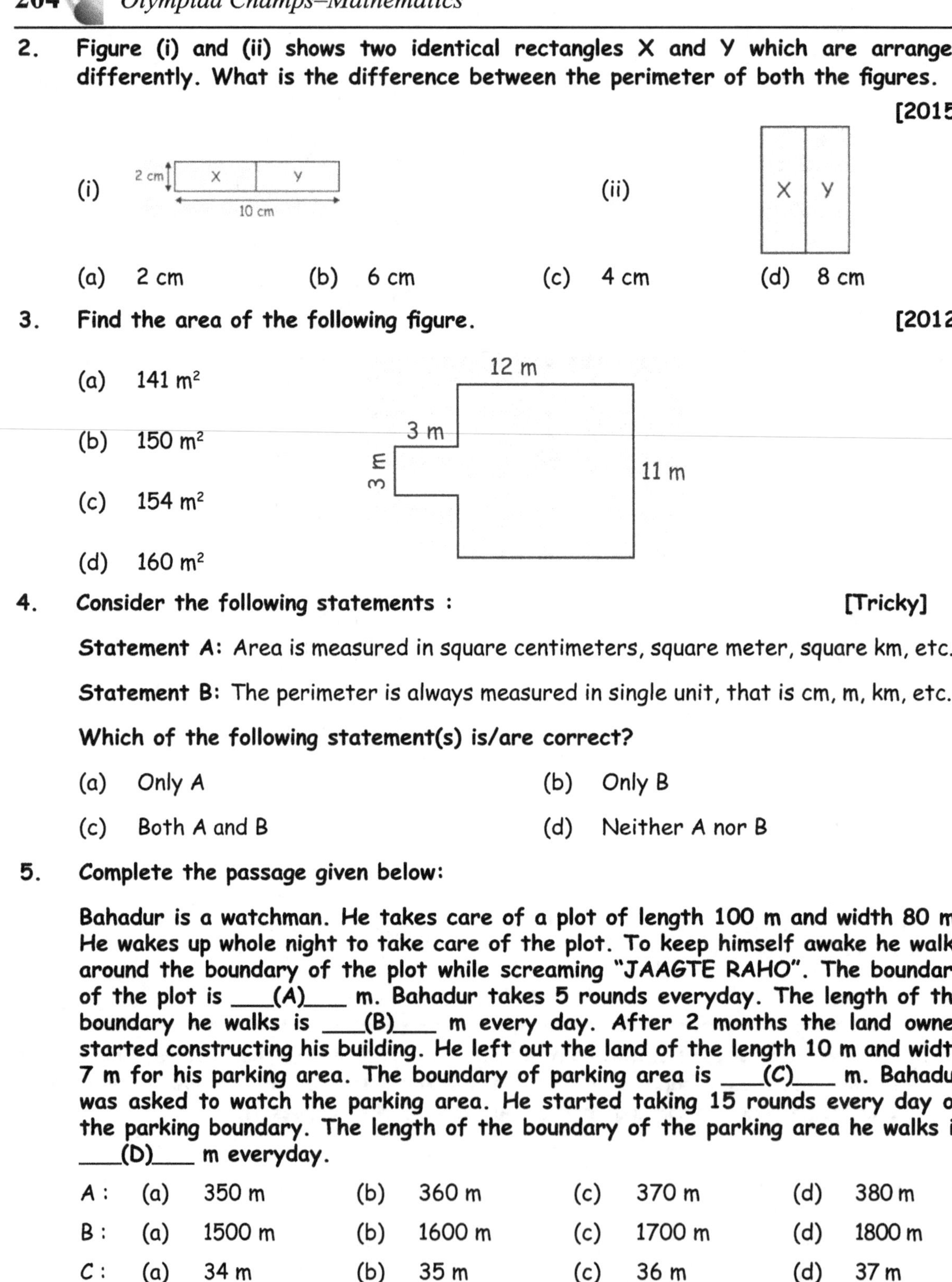

(a) 2 cm   (b) 6 cm   (c) 4 cm   (d) 8 cm

3. Find the area of the following figure. **[2012]**

(a) 141 m²

(b) 150 m²

(c) 154 m²

(d) 160 m²

4. Consider the following statements :   **[Tricky]**

   Statement A: Area is measured in square centimeters, square meter, square km, etc.

   Statement B: The perimeter is always measured in single unit, that is cm, m, km, etc.

   Which of the following statement(s) is/are correct?

   (a) Only A   (b) Only B

   (c) Both A and B   (d) Neither A nor B

5. Complete the passage given below:

   Bahadur is a watchman. He takes care of a plot of length 100 m and width 80 m. He wakes up whole night to take care of the plot. To keep himself awake he walks around the boundary of the plot while screaming "JAAGTE RAHO". The boundary of the plot is ____(A)____ m. Bahadur takes 5 rounds everyday. The length of the boundary he walks is ____(B)____ m every day. After 2 months the land owner started constructing his building. He left out the land of the length 10 m and width 7 m for his parking area. The boundary of parking area is ____(C)____ m. Bahadur was asked to watch the parking area. He started taking 15 rounds every day of the parking boundary. The length of the boundary of the parking area he walks is ____(D)____ m everyday.

A :	(a) 350 m	(b) 360 m	(c) 370 m	(d) 380 m
B :	(a) 1500 m	(b) 1600 m	(c) 1700 m	(d) 1800 m
C :	(a) 34 m	(b) 35 m	(c) 36 m	(d) 37 m
D :	(a) 500 m	(b) 510 m	(c) 520 m	(d) 530 m

6. If radius of a circle is doubled then the area of the circle will be : **[2014]**

    (a) 2 times   (b) 4 times   (c) 6 times   (d) 8 times

7. Perimeter of a square is 20 cm, find the area of the square. **[2011]**

    (a) 25 cm²   (b) 20 cm²   (c) 16 cm²   (d) 10 cm²

Direction (Qs.8 to 12): Students of class 4 went for a picnic to a garden. The garden was divided into two sections. One section was full of flowers and the other section was full of grass. Look at the picture of the garden given below and answer the questions that follow:

8. State which of the following statement is correct? **[Tricky]**

    A: Perimeter of grass garden is equal to perimeter of flower garden.

    B: Perimeter of grass garden is less than perimeter of flower garden.

    C: Perimeter of grass garden is more than perimeter of flower garden.

    D: None of the above statement is true.

    (a) A   (b) B   (c) C   (d) D

9. If the length of the grass garden is 2 times the width of the flower garden then the perimeter of grass garden is

    (a) 60 m   (b) 70 m

    (c) 80 m   (d) 90 m

10. If the perimeter of the given figure is 50 cm, then find the value of x. **[2016]**

    (a) 6 cm

    (b) 7 cm

    (c) 8 cm

    (d) 9 cm

11. What is the shape of the flower garden?

    (a) Square   (b) Rectangle

    (c) Triangle   (d) Circle

12. Separate the both gardens and find the difference between the perimeter of grass garden and flower garden?

    (a)   40 m   (b)   30 m   (c)   20 m   (d)   10 m

Direction (Qs. 13 to 16): Jhilmil Aunty is making a table cloth. She wants to put a lace border around the boundary of the cloth. She bought 20 m lace from the market. Look at the picture of the table cloth given below and answer the questions that follow:

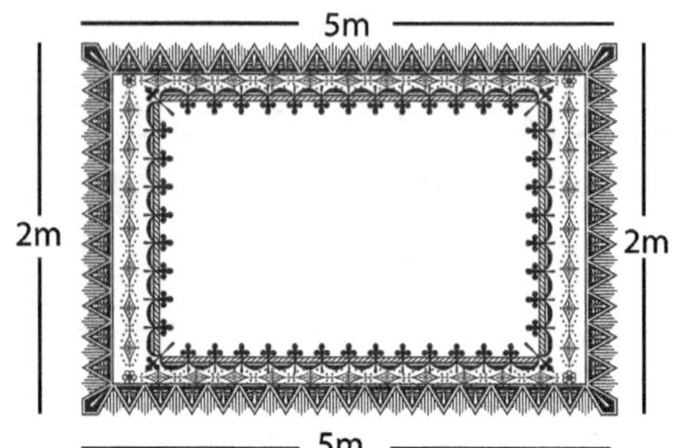

13. State true/false for the following statements: **[Tricky]**
    A: Perimeter of the table cloth is 15 m.
    B: Jhilmil aunty needs only 15 m of lace for the table cloth.
    C: Table cloth is in the shape of a rectangle.
    D: 6 m lace would be left.
    (a)   F T F T   (b)   T T F F   (c)   T F T F   (d)   F F T T

14. How much length of the lace is required by Jhilmil aunty?
    (a)   14 m   (b)   15 m   (c)   16 m   (d)   17 m

15. How much length of the lace would be left?
    (a)   5 m   (b)   6 m   (c)   7 m   (d)   8 m

16. If Jhilmil aunty gave her left over lace to Milly aunty who wants to stitch it to the border of a pillow as given below. Then how much lace would be left after completing her pillow?
    (a) 2 m
    (b) 3 m
    (c) 4 m
    (d) 5 m

Direction (Qs. 17 to 20): Look at the picture of a kitchen given below. If the kitchen is divided into unit squares, then answer the questions as given below:

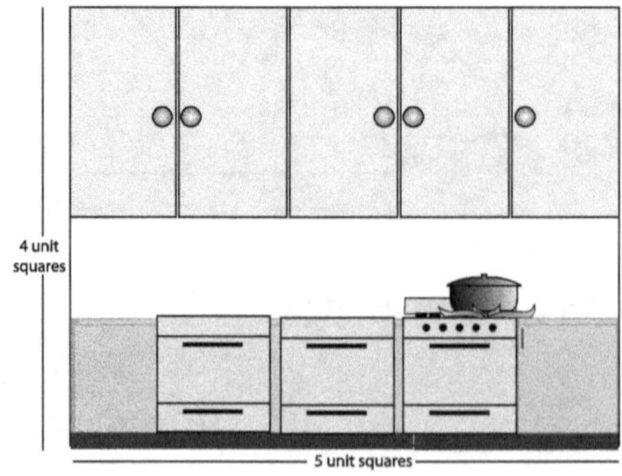

17. State which of the following statement is correct: [Critical Thinking]

    A: Perimeter of the kitchen is equal to the area of the kitchen.

    B: Perimeter of the kitchen is less than the area of the kitchen.

    C: Perimeter of the kitchen is more than the area of the kitchen.

    D: None of the above statement is true.

    (a) D   (b) C   (c) B   (d) A

18. What is the perimeter of the kitchen in units?

    (a) 18   (b) 19   (c) 20   (d) 21

19. What is the area of the kitchen in square units?

    (a) 18   (b) 19   (c) 20   (d) 21

20. Match the following figures with their perimeter.

List I	List II
A. (square, 2 cm sides)	1. 12 cm
B. (rectangle, 4 cm × 1 cm)	2. 9 cm
C. (pentagon-house: 1 cm, 1 cm, 2 cm, 2 cm, 3 cm)	3. 10 cm
D. (hexagon, 2 cm sides)	4. 8 cm

    (a) 1 2 3 4   (b) 4 3 2 1   (c) 3 2 1 4   (d) 3 1 4 2

Direction (Qs. 21 and 22): Monku is doing a Math activity at his home. He prepared a chart of a shape of a square with its boundary as 16cm as given below. Look at the figure given below and answer the questions that follow:

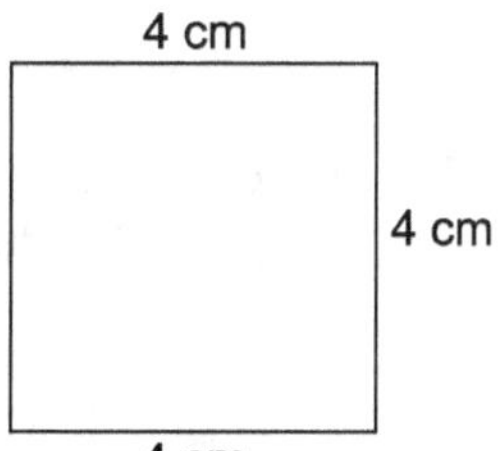

21. State true/false for the following statements.   [Tricky]

    A: If a small square of side 1 cm is cut off from the corner, then the boundary will remain the same.

B: If a small square of side 1 cm is cut off from the corner then the boundary will get increased.

C: If a small square of side 1 cm is cut off the corner then the boundary will get decreased.

D: All statements are false.

(a) F T F F　　　(b) T F F F　　　(c) F F T F　　　(d) F F F T

22. If you cut a 1 cm square to the new shape as given below then what will be the new boundary of the shape?　　　**[Tricky]**

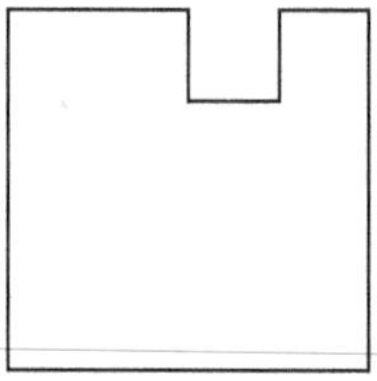

(a) 16 cm

(b) 17 cm

(c) 18 cm

(d) 19 cm

Direction (Qs. 23 to 28): Six students of Class 4 are playing a Maths puzzle game. Each of the student gives a puzzle to other five numbers. Solve all the puzzles as given below:

23. Chinky's puzzle says, "My rectangle has an area of 10 square in class and a perimeter of 14 inches." What is the figure of Chinky's rectangle?　　　**[Tricky]**

(a) 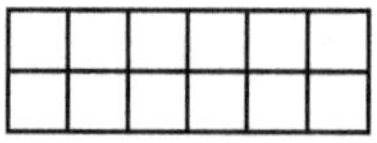　　　(b) 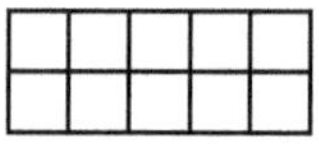　　　(c) 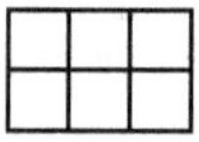　　　(d)

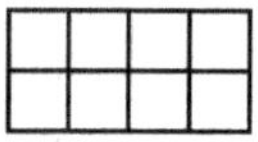

24. Monty's puzzle says, "My rectangle has an area of 6 square centimeter and a perimeter of 10 centimeter." What is the figure of Monty's rectangle?　　　**[Tricky]**

(a) 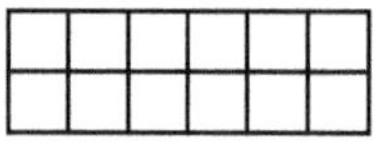　　　　　　(b)

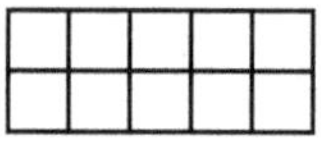

(c) 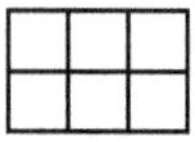　　　　　　(d)

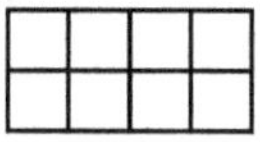

25. Pintu's puzzle says, "My rectangle has an area of 25 square metre and perimeter 20 metres." What is the figure of Pintu's rectangle?　　　**[Tricky]**

(a) 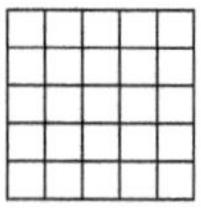　　　(b) 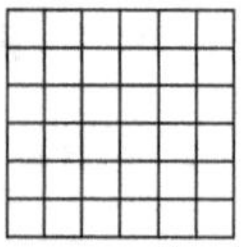　　　(c) 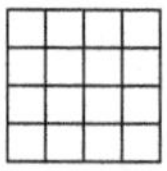　　　(d)

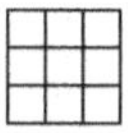

26. Bittoo's puzzle says, "My rectangle has an area of 16 square inches and perimeter of 16 inches." What is the figure of Bittoo's rectangle?　　　**[Critical Thinking]**

(a) 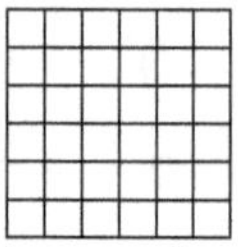　　　(b) 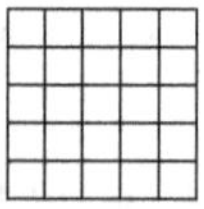　　　(c) 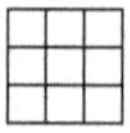　　　(d)

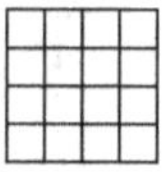

27. Tinku's puzzle says, "My rectangle has an area of 15 square feet and perimeter of 16 feet." What is the figure of Tinku's rectangle?

(a) 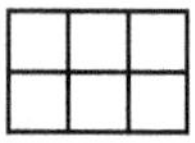　　　(b) 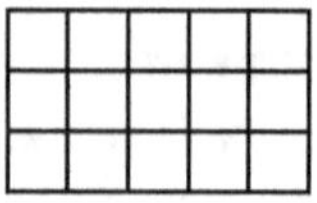　　　(c) 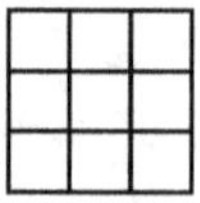　　　(d)

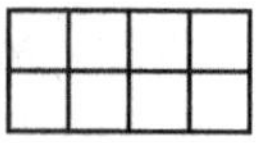

28. Bablu's p uzzle says, "My rectangle has an area of 8 square metre and perimeter of 12 metre." What is the figure of Bablu's rectangle?

(a)   (b)   (c)   (d)

Direction (Qs. 29 to 32): Anita is making bedsheets to sell it in the market. She makes bedsheets of different sizes. The table showing size and price of the bedsheet is given below. Read the table and answer the questions that follow: **[Tricky / Critical Thinking]**

S. No.	Bedsheet	Length	Width	Price
1	Small	2 m	1 m	₹ 100/-
2	Medium	3 m	2 m	₹ 200/-
3	Large	4 m	3 m	₹ 300/-
4	Extra large	5 m	4 m	₹ 400/-
5.	Deluxe	6 m	5 m	₹ 500/-

29. A customer asked for two extra large bedsheets. What is the perimeter of each bedsheet.

    (a)   17 m   (b)   18 m   (c)   36 m   (d)   34 m

30. What is the difference between the perimeter of medium bedsheets and deluxe bedsheet?

    (a)   10 m   (b)   11 m   (c)   12 m   (d)   13 m

31. A customer asked for 2 small bedsheets, 1 large bedsheet and 2 deluxe bedsheets. How much did he/she have to pay?

    (a)   ₹ 1000/-   (b)   ₹ 1500/-   (c)   ₹ 2000/-   (d)   ₹ 2500/-

32. What is the difference between the perimeter of large bedsheet and small bedsheet?

    (a)   5 m   (b)   6 m   (c)   7 m   (d)   8 m

Direction (Qs. 33 to 38): Read the passage given below and answer the questions that follow:

Ramu Kaka is a farmer. He has a land of length 100 m and width 90 m. He grows vegetables in his land and sell them in the market. But due to hot weather and no rain he suffered huge loss in his vegetable selling as he could not grow vegetables in his land so he had to sell a portion of his land of area 4000 square metre. After selling his land he again sold another portion of area 2000 square metre. Then all of a sudden the weather came in the favour of Ramu Kaka and it started raining. Ramu Kaka started making profit in his vegetable selling. He then bought a portion of land of area 3000 square metre. Then after few months he again bought another portion of land of 5000 square metre. Now he has a huge land on which he grows his vegetables. Ramu Kaka is now happy and making more and more profits every day.

33. What is the area of the land Ramu Kaka had initially?

    (a)   7000 square metre   (b)   8000 square metre

    (c)   9000 square metre   (d)   10000 square metre

34. What area of land left with him after his first sell?

(a) 4000 square metre (b) 5000 square metre

(c) 6000 square metre (d) 7000 square metre

35. What area of land left with him after his second sell?

(a) 2000 square metre (b) 3000 square metre

(c) 4000 square metre (d) 5000 square metre

36. What area of land he owned after his first purchase after making profits?

(a) 4000 square metre (b) 5000 square metre

(c) 6000 square metre (d) 7000 square metre

37. What area of land he owned now?

(a) 8000 square metre (b) 9000 square metre

(c) 10000 square metre (d) 11000 square metre

38. What is the difference between the area of land he had initially and the area of land he has now?

(a) 1000 square metre (b) 2000 square metre

(c) 3000 square metre (d) 4000 square metre

39. What is the area of a rectangle if it has 8 squares of side 1cm in each row and has 4 such rows? [2017]

(a) 30 square cm (b) 31 square cm

(c) 32 square cm (d) 33 square cm

40. On the basis of the following features identify the correct term: [2008]

A. It is always measured in square units, that is either cm^2 or m^2 or km^2 etc.

B. It can be compared by counting the number of squares of two shapes occupy.

C. It is the amount of surface, a figure covers.

(a) Perimeter (b) Volume (c) Area (d) Weight

41. Look at the picture given below. What is the area of shaded portion ? [2009]

(a) 15 cm²

(b) 72 cm²

(c) 87 cm²

(d) 57 cm²

42. State which of the following statement is incorrect?

Statement A: Boundary of Park A is more than Park B.

Statement B: Boundary of Park D is less than Park C

Statement C: Boundary of Park E is more than Park C

Statement D: Boundary of Park C is more than park A

(a) D (b) C (c) B (d) A

43. In the given figure, ABCD is a rectangle and DEFG is a square, find the perimeter of the figure. **[2018]**

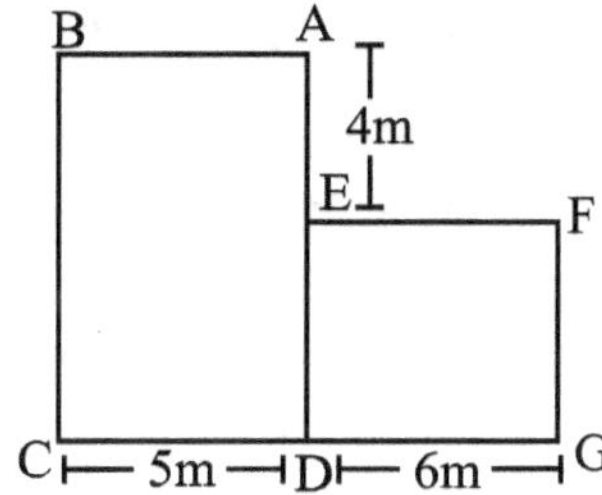

(a) 38 m

(b) 42 m

(c) 46 m

(d) 52 m

44. Find the perimeter of the shaded region. **[2018]**

(a) 150 cm

(b) 152 cm

(c) 154 cm

(d) None of these

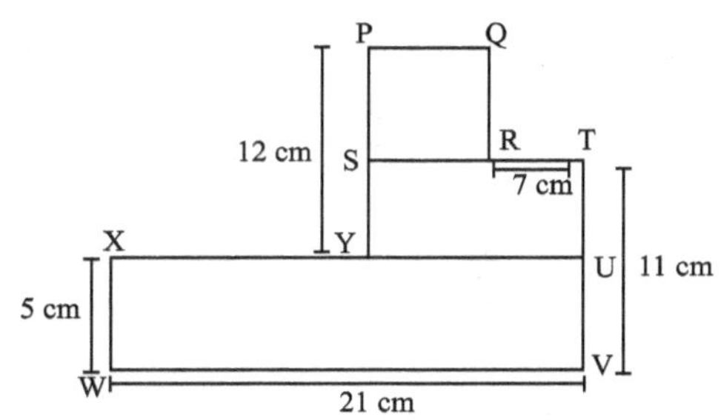

45. Given figure is made up of a square PQRS and two rectangles STUY & XUVW. Find the length of XY. **[2018]**

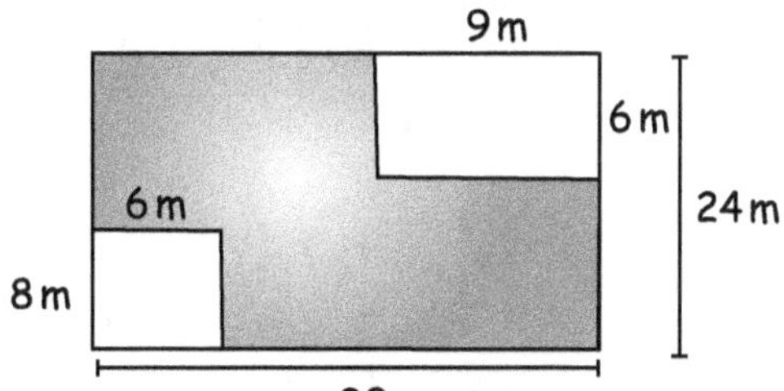

(a) 12 cm   (b) 8 cm   (c) 13 cm   (d) 6 cm

46. Find the perimeter of the given figure. **[2019]**

(a) 56 cm

(b) 50 cm

(c) 48 cm

(d) 52 cm

47. Find the perimeter of the shaded figure (not drawn to scale). **[2020]**

(a) 96 m

(b) 108 m

(c) 120 m

(d) 110 m

48. A rectangular playground is 120 m long and 80 m wide. What distance did Avantika cover in going 4 times around this field? **[2020]**

    (a) 400 m (b) 1600 m (c) 800 m (d) 3200 m

49. Which of the following has the greatest perimeter? **[2020]**

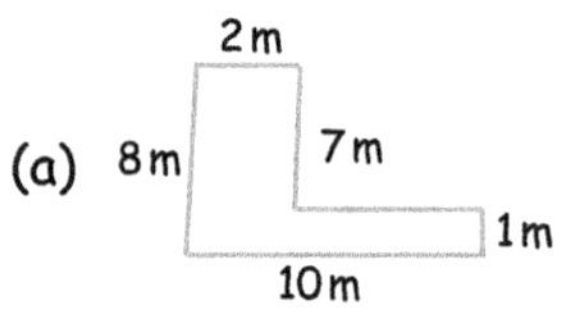

(a)

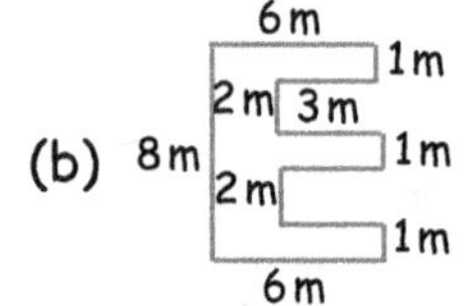

(b)

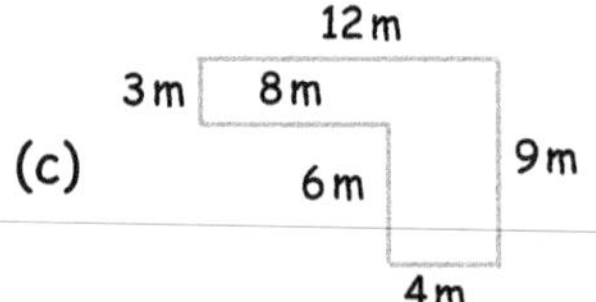

(c)

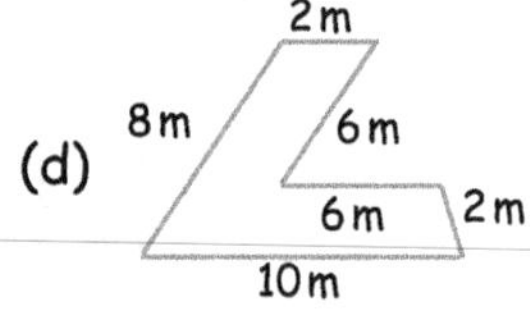

(d)

50. A rectangular playground is 150 m long and 80 m wide. What distance did Kashi cover in going 5 times around the playgronud? **[2021]**

    (a) 2 km 300 m (b) 1 km 150 m (c) 2 km 100 m (d) 3 km 300 m

51. Find the perimeter of the given figure (not drawn to scale). **[2021]**

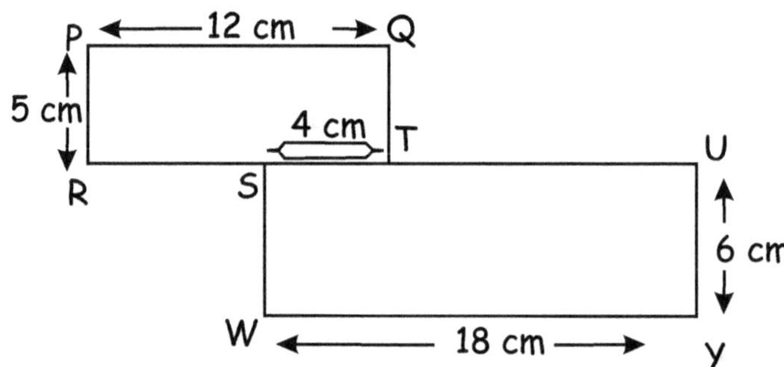

    (a) 74 cm (b) 72 cm (c) 56 cm (d) 60 cm

52. Which of the following figures has the greatest perimeter, if 1I = 1 unit? **[2022]**

(I = oneside length of a small square)

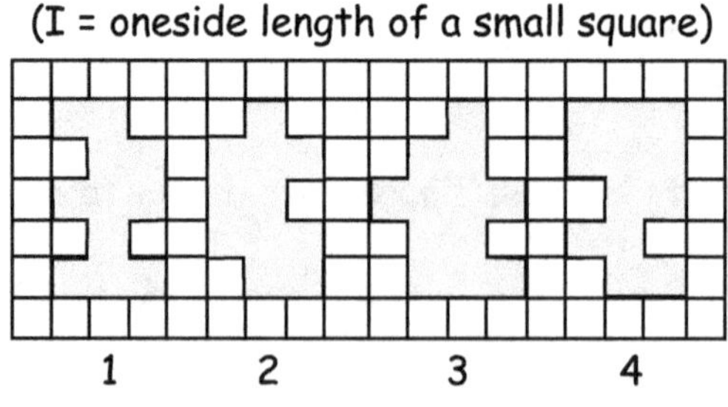

    (a) 1 (b) 2 (c) 3 (d) 4

53. There are three triangles shown below, one of which is an isosceles triangle. Find the perimeter of this isosceles triangle. **[2022]**

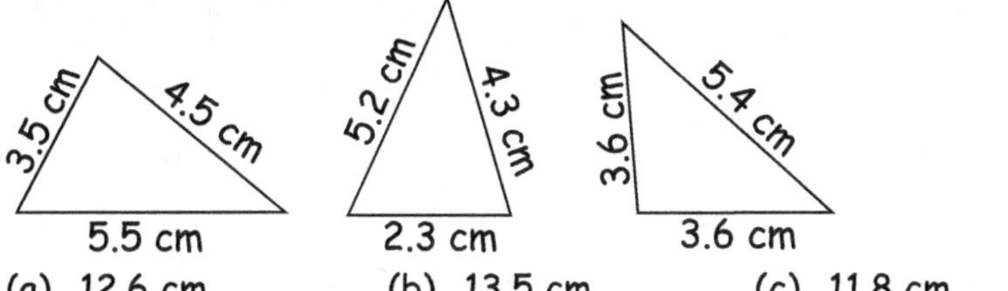

(a) 12.6 cm   (b) 13.5 cm   (c) 11.8 cm   (d) 13.8 cm

54. Find the area of the shaded portion if the area of the square ABCD is three times of the area of the triangle. **[2022]**

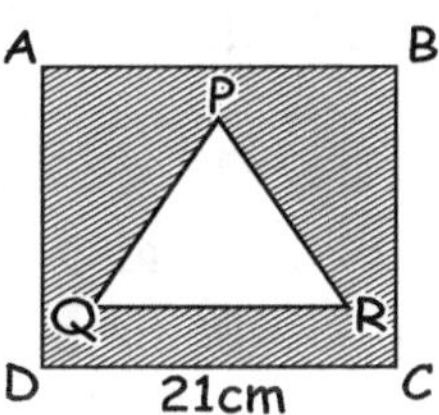

(a) 254 cm²   (b) 264 cm²   (c) 294 cm²   (d) 304 cm²

55. If each shape given below has equal line segments, then which one of the following shapes has perimeter less than 25 cm? **[2022]**

(a) 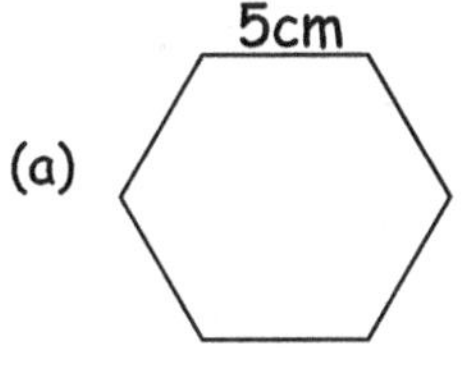

(b) 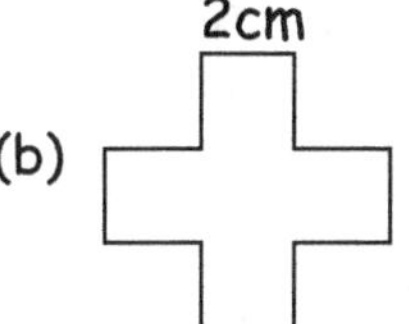

(c) 

(d) All the above

56. RISE is a rectangle in which difference between its adjacent sides is 12 cm. If area of the rectangle is 1053 cm², then its perimeter will be ____________. **[2022]**

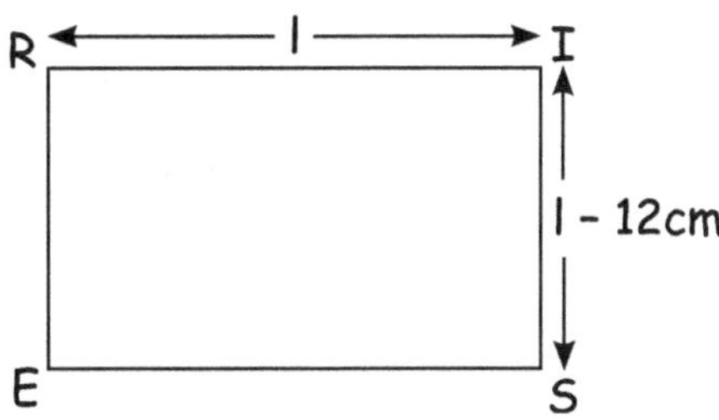

(a) 120 cm   (b) 132 cm   (c) 142 cm   (d) 150 cm

RESPONSE GRID

LEVEL 1

1. a b c d   2. a b c d   3. a b c d   4. a b c d   5. a b c d
6. a b c d   7. a b c d   8. a b c d   9. a b c d   10. a b c d
11. a b c d   12. a b c d   13. a b c d   14. a b c d   15. a b c d
16. a b c d   17. a b c d   18. a b c d   19. a b c d   20. a b c d
21. a b c d   22. a b c d   23. a b c d   24. a b c d   25. a b c d
26. a b c d   27. a b c d   28. a b c d   29. a b c d   30. a b c d
31. a b c d   32. a b c d   33. a b c d   34. a b c d   35. a b c d

LEVEL 2

1. a b c d   2. a b c d   3. a b c d   4. a b c d   5. a b c d
6. a b c d   7. a b c d   8. a b c d   9. a b c d   10. a b c d
11. a b c d   12. a b c d   13. a b c d   14. a b c d   15. a b c d
16. a b c d   17. a b c d   18. a b c d   19. a b c d   20. a b c d
21. a b c d   22. a b c d   23. a b c d   24. a b c d   25. a b c d
26. a b c d   27. a b c d   28. a b c d   29. a b c d   30. a b c d
31. a b c d   32. a b c d   33. a b c d   34. a b c d   35. a b c d
36. a b c d   37. a b c d   38. a b c d   39. a b c d   40. a b c d
41. a b c d   42. a b c d   43. a b c d   44. a b c d   45. a b c d
46. a b c d   47. a b c d   48. a b c d   49. a b c d   50. a b c d
51. a b c d   52. a b c d   53. a b c d   54. a b c d   55. a b c d
56. a b c d

Solutions with Explanation

LEVEL 1

1. **(d)** Perimeter of the figure = 18 cm.

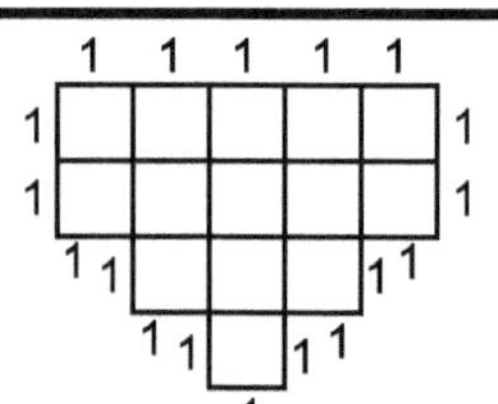

2. **(a)** Area of the figure

1	2	3	4	5
6	7	8	9	10
11	12	13		
14				

= 14 square metre

3. **(d)** Perimeter = 18 feet.

4. **(b)** The odd one is option (b)

Since, 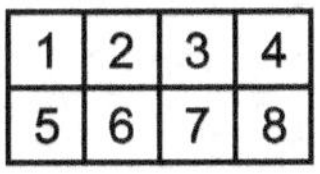

Area = 8 square cm.

5. **(d)** The odd one is option (d)

Since, 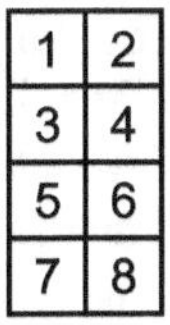

area = 8 square feet.

6. **(a)** The odd one is option (a).

Since, 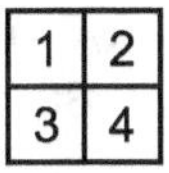

Area = 4 square cm.

7. **(d)** The odd one is option (d)

Since, 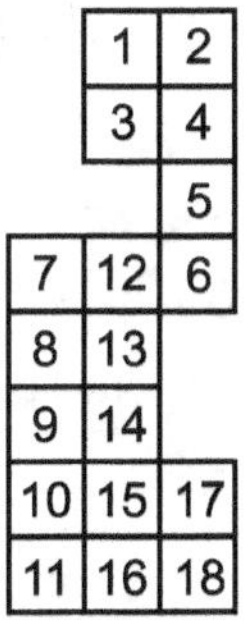

area = 18 square metres.

8. **(c)** The perimeter of the given figure = 9 units

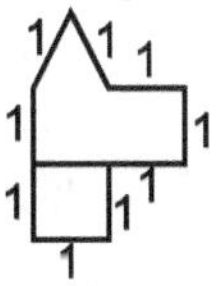

9. **(a)** The perimeter of the given figure = 7 units.

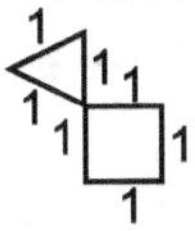

10. **(c)** The perimeter of the given figure = 8 units

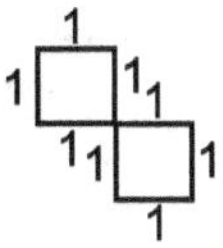

11. **(b)** Perimeter of the square of side

= 9 cm

9 cm + 9 cm + 9 cm + 9 cm = 36 cm.

12. **(c)** Area of 11 unit squares = 11 square units.

13. **(b)** Statement given in option (b) describes the term 'perimeter' correctly.

14. **(b)** Shape given in option (b) represents the area $5\frac{1}{2}$ cm^2.

15. **(c)** Kilogram is the unit to measure the weight and metre is the unit to measure the perimeter.

16. **(a)** Perimeter of the figure

= 8 + 3 + 3 + 5 + 3 + 5 + 5 + 2 = 34 cm

17. **(c)** Area of A = 4 square units

Area of B = 8 square units

Area of C = 2 square units

Area of D = 5 square units

Therefore, the answer is option (c) C A D B.

18. **(d)** Boundary of Park E = 180.

So, Park : 180

19. **(b)** Perimeter of square = 4 × 3 = 12 cm

20. **(b)** Perimeter of the figure = 7 + 5 + 8 + 6 = 26 cm

21. **(b)** 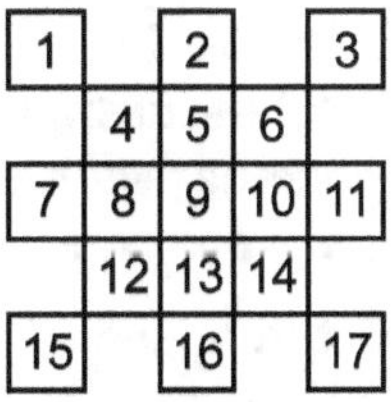

Area of the given figure = 17 square metre

Therefore, the answer is option (b) 17 square meter.

22. **(c)** Perimeter of the figure = 14 cm

23. **(c)** Perimeter of the figure = 2 × 28 = 56 cm

24. **(a)** Perimeter of fig A = 10 cm + 10 cm + 10 cm + 10 cm = 40 cm

25. **(b)** Perimeter of fig. B

= 3 + 1 + 1 + 1 + 2 + 1 + 1 + 1 + 3 + 3
+ 1 + 1 + 1 + 2 + 1 + 1 + 1 + 3 + 3 + 1
+ 1 + 1 + 2 + 1 + 1 + 1 +3 + 3 + 1 + 1 +
1 + 2 + 1 + 1 + 1 + 3 = 56 cm.

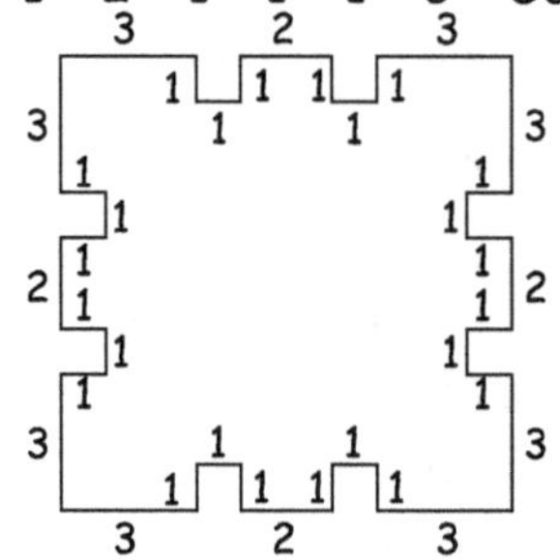

26. **(c)** Perimeter of fig. A = 40 cm.
Perimeter of fig. B = 56 cm.
Difference = 56 cm – 40 cm
= 16 cm.

27. **(c)** 138 cm

28. **(b)** Boundary of Park A
= 50 + 50 + 20 + 20 = 140 m
Boundary of Park B
= 30 + 30 + 10 + 10 = 80 m
Boundary of Park C
= 70 + 70 + 30 + 30 = 200 m

Boundary of Park D
= 25 + 25 + 15 + 15 = 80 m
Boundary of Park E
= 65 + 65 + 25 + 25 = 180 m
Park C has largest boundary.

29. **(a)** Since, Park D has smallest boundary. Therefore, the answer is option (a) Park D.

30. **(c)** Park B and Park D has same boundary as 80m. Therefore, the answer is option (c) Park D.

31. **(b)** Perimeter of the figure
= 8 × 16 = 128 cm.

32. **(a)** Perimeter of the figure = 20 + 24 + 24 + 20 = 88 cm.

33. **(a)** Perimeter = Sum of all sides = 36 cm

34. **(c)** Perimeter of the figure
= 12 + 2 + 3 + 8 + 5 + 4 + 4 + 6 + 5
= 49 cm

35. **(b)** The perimeter of the figure = 49 cm

49 cm = 6 + BC + 5 +4 + 4 + 9 + 12 + 4

49 cm = 45 cm +BC

BC = 4 cm

LEVEL 2

1. **(c)** The decreasing order of the bangles is D A C B.
Therefore, the answer is option (c).

2. **(c)** Difference between perimeters
= 28 cm – 24 cm = 4 cm.

3. **(a)** Area of the figure = 3 × 3 + 12 × 11
= 9 + 132 = 141 m².

4. **(c)** Both the statements are correct.

5. **A:** **(b)** The boundary of the plot
= 100 m + 100 m + 80 m + 80 m
= 360 m.

　B: **(d)** Length of the boundary Bahadur walks = 5 × 360 m -= 1800 m.

　C: **(a)** Boundary of parking area
= 10 m + 10 m + 7 m + 7 m = 34 m.

　D: **(b)** The length of the boundary of parking area Bahadur walks
= 15 × 34 m = 510 m.

6. **(b)** If original area = πr², then new area = π (2r)²=4πr².

7. **(a)** Side of a square = $\frac{20}{4}$ = 5 cm.

So, area of the square = 5 × 5 = 25 cm².

8. **(c)** Perimeter of grass garden = 30 m + 10 m + 30 m + 10 m = 80 m.
Perimeter of flower garden = 10 m + 10 m + 10 m + 10 m = 40 m.
So, perimeter of grass garden is more than perimeter of flower garden. Hence, statement C is correct.

9. **(a)** Length of grass garden = 2 × (10)
= 20 m.

Now, perimeter of grass garden =
2 (length + width)
= 2 (20 + 10) = 60 m.

10. (b) X = 50 cm – (12 cm + 3 cm + 4 cm + 16 cm + 4 cm + 4 cm) = 7 cm

11. (a) The shape of flower garden is a square.
Therefore, the answer is option (a) square.

12. (a) The perimeter of grass garden
= 80 m.
The perimeter of flower garden
= 40 m.
Thus, difference = 80 m – 40 m
= 40 m.

13. (d) Since, perimeter of the table cloth
= 5 m + 2 m + 5 m + 2 m = 14 m.
∴ Statement A is false.
Since, perimeter is 14 m, so Jhilmil aunty needs only 14m of cloth. So, statement B is false.
Since, the table cloth is in the shape of a rectangle so statement C is true.
Length of lace left = 20 m – 14 m = 6 m. So, statement D is true.
Therefore, the answer is option (d) F F T T.

14. (a) Jhilmil aunty require 14 m of lace.
Therefore, the answer is option (a) 14 m.

15. (b) Length of the lace left would be 6 m. Therefore, the answer is option (b) 6 m.

16. (c) Perimeter of pillow = 70 cm + 30 cm + 70 cm + 30 cm = 200 cm
= 2 m (as 1 m = 100 cm)
Milly aunty will use 2 m of lace.
Length of lace left = 6 m – 2 m = 4 m

17. (c) Perimeter of the kitchen = 4 + 5 + 4 + 5 = 18 units.

Area of the kitchen = 20 square units.
Since, perimeter of the kitchen is less than its area so statement B is correct.

18. (a) Perimeter of the kitchen is 18 units.

19. (c) Area of the kitchen is 20 square nits.

20. (b) Perimeter of A = 2 cm + 2 cm + 2 cm + 2 cm
= 8 cm ⟶ 4
Perimeter of B = 1 cm + 4 cm + 1 cm + 4 cm
= 10 cm ⟶ 3
Perimeter of C = 1 cm + 2 cm + 3 cm + 2 cm + 1 cm
= 9 cm ⟶ 2
Perimeter of D = 2 cm + 2 cm + 2 cm + 2 cm + 2 cm + 2 cm
= 12 cm ⟶ 1
Therefore, the answer is option (b) 4 3 2 1.

21. (b) Boundary of the square = 4 cm + 4 cm + 4 cm + 4 cm = 16 cm.
If a small square of side 1cm is cut off from its corner from the shape would become:

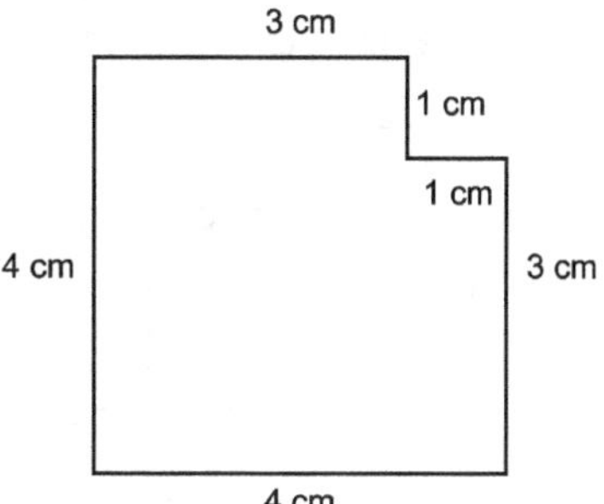

Boundary of new shape
= 4 cm + 3 cm + 1 cm + 1 cm + 3 cm + 4 cm = 16 cm
Boundary remains same.
So, statement A is true and B, C, D are false.

Therefore, the answer is option (b) T F F F.

22. **(c)** Perimeter of original square = 16 cm.

New Shape :

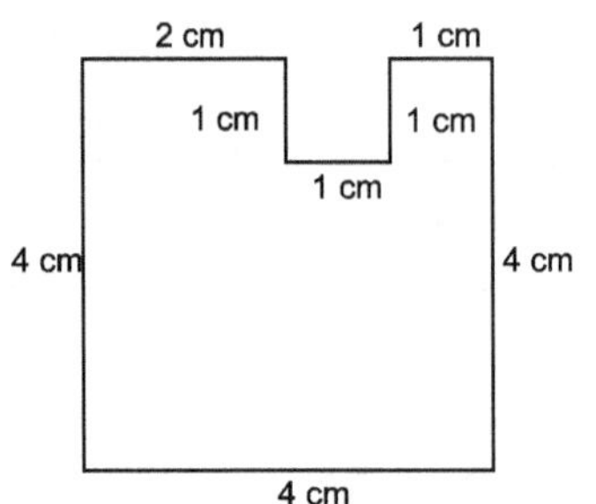

Perimeter of new shape

= 2 cm + 1 cm + 1 cm + 1 cm + 1 cm + 4 cm + 4 cm + 4 cm = 18 cm

23. **(b)** Chinky's puzzle :

Area = 10 square inches

Figure : 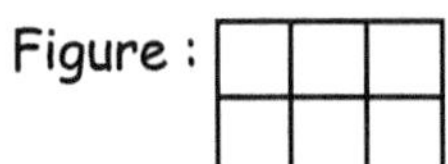

Perimeter = 14 inches

24. **(c)** Monty's puzzle :

Area = 6 square cm

Figure : 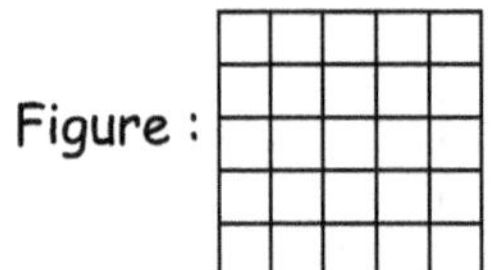

Perimeter = 10 cm

25. **(a)** Rinku's puzzle :

Area = 25 square metres

Figure :

Perimeter = 20 m

26. **(d)** Bittoo's puzzle :

Area = 16 square inches

Perimeter = 16 inches.

Figure : 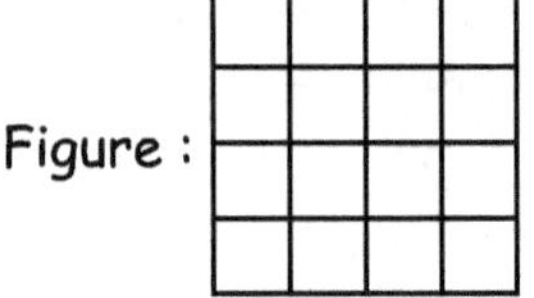

27. **(b)** Tinku's puzzle :

Area = 15 square feet

Figure : 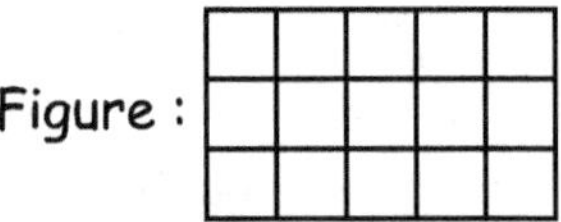

Perimeter = 16 feet

28. **(d)** Bablu's puzzle :

Area = 8 square metres

Figure : 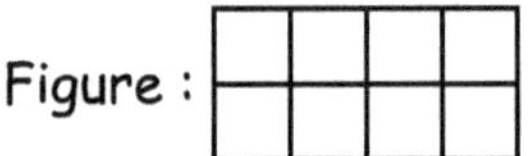

Perimeter = 12 metres.

29. **(b)** Perimeter of extra large bedsheet = 5 m + 5 m + 4 m + 4 m = 18 m.

30. **(c)** Perimeter of medium bedsheet = 3 m + 3 m + 2 m + 2 m = 10 m. Perimeter of deluxe bedsheet = 6 m + 6 m + 5 m + 5 m = 22 m. Difference = 22 m – 10 m = 12 m.

31. **(b)** Price of 2 small bedsheets = ₹ 100/- + ₹ 100/- = ₹ 200/-

Price of 1 large bedsheet = ₹ 300/-

Price of 2 deluxe bedsheet = ₹ 500/- + ₹ 500/- = ₹ 1000/-

Total amount the customer has to pay = ₹ 200/- + ₹ 300/- + ₹ 1000/- = ₹ 1500/-

32. **(d)** Perimeter of large bedsheet = 4 m + 4 m + 3 m + 3 m = 14 m. Perimeter of small bedsheet = 2 m + 2 m + 1 m + 1 m = 6 m. Difference = 14 m – 6 m = 8 m.

33. **(c)** The area of land Ramu Kaka had initially = 100 m × 90 m = 9000 square metre

34. **(b)** Area of land left after first sell
= 9000 square metre – 4000 square metre = 5000 square metre.

35. **(b)** Area of land left after second sell
= 5000 square metre – 2000 square metre = 3000 square metre.

36. **(c)** Area of land owned after first purchase
= 3000 square metre + 3000 square metre = 6000 square metre.

37. **(d)** Area of land he owned now
= 6000 square metre + 5000 square metre = 11000 square metre.

38. **(b)** Difference between the area of land he had initially and he had now
= 11000 square metre – 9000 square metre = 2000 square metre.

39. **(c)** The given rectangle is

1	2	3	4	5	6	7	8
9	10	11	12	13	14	15	16
17	18	19	20	21	22	23	24
25	26	27	28	29	30	31	32

The area of the rectangle = 32 square cm.

40. **(c)** All given features relates to the term 'Area'.

41. **(d)** Area of bigger rectangle = 9 × 8
= 72 cm²
Area of smaller rectangle = 5 × 3
= 15 cm²
∴ Area of shaded portion = 72 – 15
= 57 cm².

42. **(b)** Since, boundary of Park E is less than Park C, so statement C is incorrect.

43. **(b)** Perimeter of figure = 5 + 6 + 6 + 6 + 4 + 5 + 10 = 42 m

44. **(d)** None of these

45. **(b)** TU = 11 – 5 = 6 cm
PS = 12 – 6 = 6 cm
YU = 6 + 7 = 13 cm
XY = 21 – YU = 21 – 13 = 8 cm

46. **(c)** Total perimeter = 12 cm + 2 cm + 3 cm + 3 cm + 3 cm + 3 cm + 3 cm + 3 cm + 9 cm + 5 cm + 2 cm
= 52 cm

47. **(b)**

48. **(b)** Length of playground = 120 m
width of playground = 80 m
So Perimeter = 120 × 2 + 80 × 2
= 240 + 160
= 400 m
Total length covered by Avantika in 4 rounds = 4 × 400 = 1600m

49. **(b)**

50. **(a)** Rectangular playground's Length = 150 m

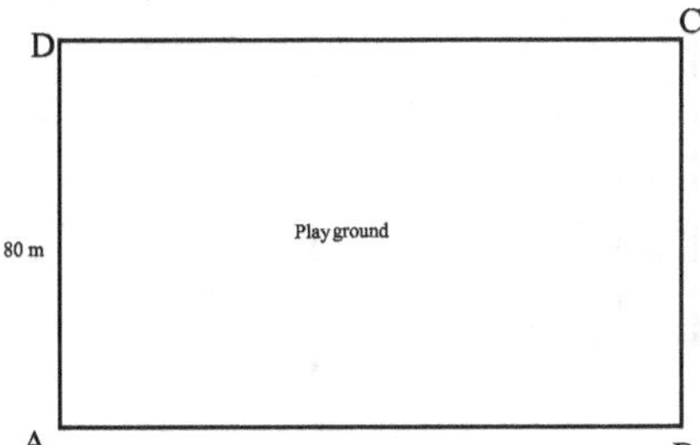

Width = 80 m
In one Round of playground kashi
Cover the length = 150 × 2 + 80 × 2
= 460 m
So, In 5 rounds kashi cover the total length = 5 × 460 m
= 2300 m
OR   2 km 300 m

51. **(a)** Perimeter of the given figure = 18 + 6 + 14 + 6 + 5 + 12 + 5 + 8
= 74 cm

52. **(a)**

53. **(a)**

54. **(c)**

55. **(b)**

56. **(b)**

Name : _________________________   Score : _________________________

Pictograph – Jam Factory

Teddy's Food Factory exports bottles of Jam. The pictograph shows the number of bottles exported each day. Use the information from the graph to answer the questions.

Jam Bottles Exported	
Day	Number of Jam Bottles
Monday	Jam Jam Jam Jam Jam Jam Ja
Tuesday	Jam Jam Jam Jam
Wednesday	Jam Jam Jam Jam Jam Jam
Thursday	Jam Jam Jam Jam Ja
Friday	Jam Jam Jam Jam Jam Jam Jam Jam

Key

Jam = 600 Jam Bottles

1) Which of the two days did they export fewer bottles of jam? _________________

2) How many key images would represent 6600 bottles of jam? _________________

3) How many more bottles of jam were exerted on Friday than Monday? _________________

4) How many bottles of jam where exported on Wednesday and Thursday altogether? _________________

5) How many bottles did Teddy's Food Factory export each week? _________________

15
Chapter

Data Handling

LEARNING OBJECTIVES

This lesson will help you to:—
- ❖ collect data from different sources.
- ❖ record data using tally marks.
- ❖ prepare tables for recording data.
- ❖ represent data in terms of pictograph choosing appropriate unit for displaying data.
- ❖ represent data in terms of bar graphs choosing appropriate unit for displaying data.
- ❖ represent data in terms of pie-chart.
- ❖ recognize patterns in the data.
- ❖ draw inferences from the data.

QUICK CONCEPT REVIEW

Data Handling

Data handling is a process of collection, organization and representation of data in various forms. Data is collected from different sources; then the collected data is organized in order to record it for further use. The recorded data is then represented using graphs and charts.

Process of Data Handing

Favourite ice-cream of students of class 4.

Step 1: Collection of data

Ask each student about their favourite ice-cream and note down in your notebook.

Amazing Facts

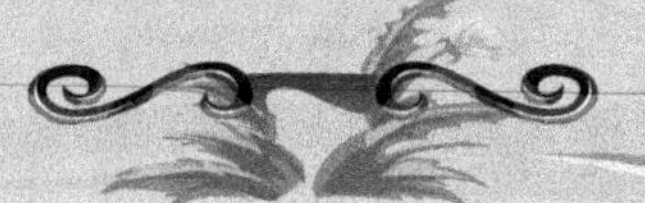

❖ Data handling is also known as statistics.

❖ The horizontal and vertical lines in the bar graph is called axis of bar graph.

Frequency of an observation is the number of times a given observation occurs in the given data. For example, if observation 'x' is occuring 10 time in a data, then frequency of x is 10. The sum of all the frequencies in a give data gives the total number of items or observations in the data.

Step 2: Organization of data

For organization of data use tally marks against each ice-cream and prepare a table.

Use of tally marks:

Write '|' for 1 student against the ice-cream.

Write '||' for 2 student against the ice-cream.

Write '|||' for 3 student against the ice-cream.

Write '||||' for 4 student against the ice-cream.

Write 'N̶J̶' for 5 student against the ice-cream.

Write 'N̶J̶|' for 6 student against the ice-cream.

Write 'N̶J̶||' for 7 student against the ice-cream.

Write 'N̶J̶|||' for 8 student against the ice-cream.

Write 'N̶J̶||||' for 9 student against the ice-cream.

Write 'N̶J̶ N̶J̶' for 10 student against the ice-cream.

For example:

Ice-cream	Tally marks	Number of students
Vanilla	||||	4
Chocolate	N̶J̶ N̶J̶ |	11
Strawberry	N̶J̶ ||	7
Mint	N̶J̶ ||||	9
Black current	N̶J̶	5

Step 3: Recording the data

For recording the data prepare a table for the ice-cream and number of students who likes that ice-cream.

For example:

Ice-cream	No. of students
Vanilla	4
Chocolate	11
Strawberry	7
Mint	9
Black current	5

Step 4 : Representation of data

Data is represented using graphs and charts. Here, we would show you representation of data through:

A. Pictograph

B. Bar graph

C. Pie-chart

A. Representation of data using pictograph (Refer Table 2)

Vanilla	V V V V
Chocolate	C C C C C C C C C C C
Strawberry	S S S S S S S
Mint	M M M M M M M M M
Black current	B B B B B

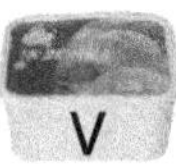 = 1 student of class 4.

Mode

Mode of a given data is the observation that comes maximum number of time in the given data. For example, mode of 1, 1, 2, 2, 2, 3, 4, 4, 5, is 2

B. Representation of data using bar graph (Refer Table 2)

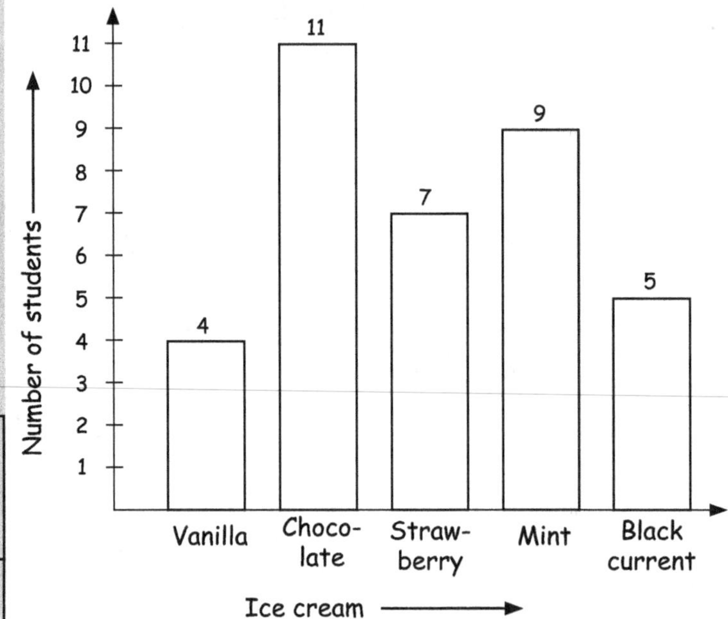

C. Representation of data using Pie-chart

Consider the following data: There are 20 students in class 4. Out of them 5 like vanilla ice-cream and rest of them does not like vanilla ice-cream.

5 out of 20 likes vanilla ice-cream.

i.e., $\dfrac{5}{20}$ students of class 4 likes vanilla ice-cream.

i.e., $\dfrac{1}{4}$ students of class 4 likes vanilla ice-cream.

∴   The pie-chart becomes

Students of class 4

Thus, using the above given four steps one can perform the task of data handling for various forms of data available in various sources.

Misconcept/Concept

Misconcept: The number of pictures in a pictograph represents the frequency and one picture means 1 object.

Concept: The number of pictures in a pictograph represents the frequency but one picture does not always represent 1 object.

For example: Number of cycles sold in 3 days.

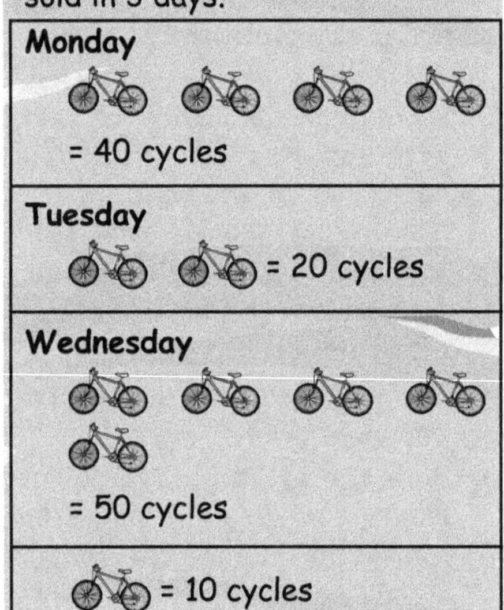

Average

Average or Mean of a given data is obtained by adding all the observations and dividing the sum obtained by the number of observations

Examples:

1. A Pictograph showing number of students going school through different modes of transport.

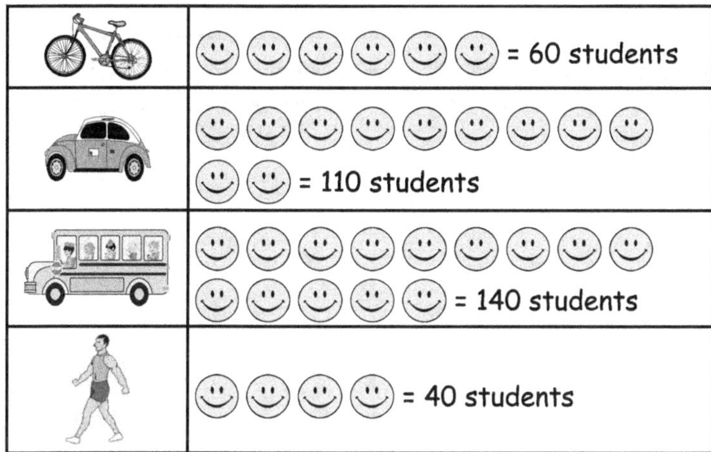

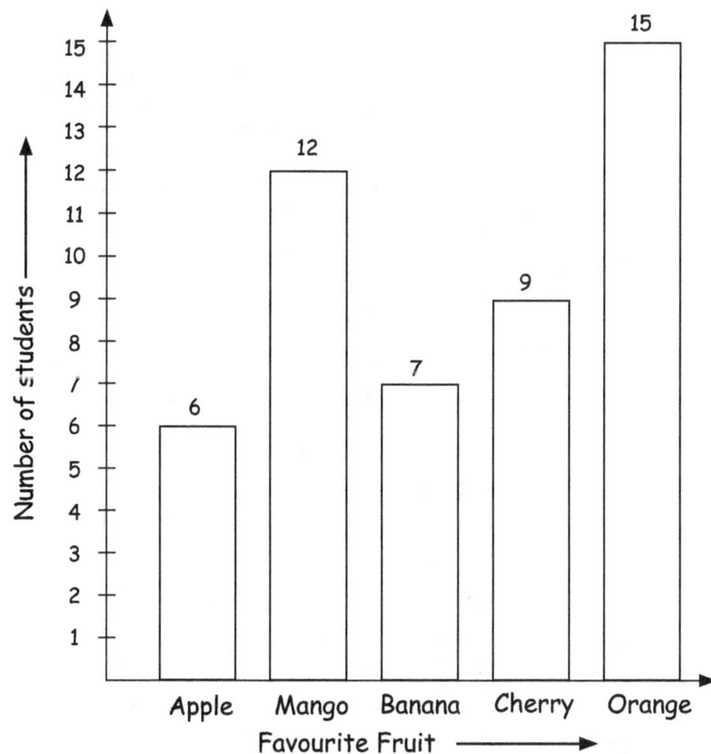

2. A bar graph showing number of students and their favourite fruit.

Shortcut to problem solving

❖ Read the data carefully as the smallest detail may change the meaning of the whole data collected. For example, if you are collecting data about number of students who likes mango or apple and a student says he/she does not like apple, then that does not mean he/she likes mango.

❖ Record the data in tabular form because tables help to understand the data.

❖ Try to understand the data provided carefully before jumping to answer the questions.

❖ Relate the data given in table with charts and graphs and draw them to have better understanding of it.

❖ Be very careful of the units used in the tables. For example, height of students in cm or feet.

❖ Take care of the scale used in charts and graphs. For example, 1 picture of cycle = 10 bicycles, etc.

Do You Know?

<u>Histogram</u>: In a histogram bars are drawn but without any gaps.

Multiple Choice Questions

LEVEL 1

Direction (Qs. 1 to 5): A boat takes visitors out into the sea to watch dolphins swimming. The bar chart shows the number of people that went out on each boat. Read the chart given below and answer the questions that follow: **[Mental Mathematics]**

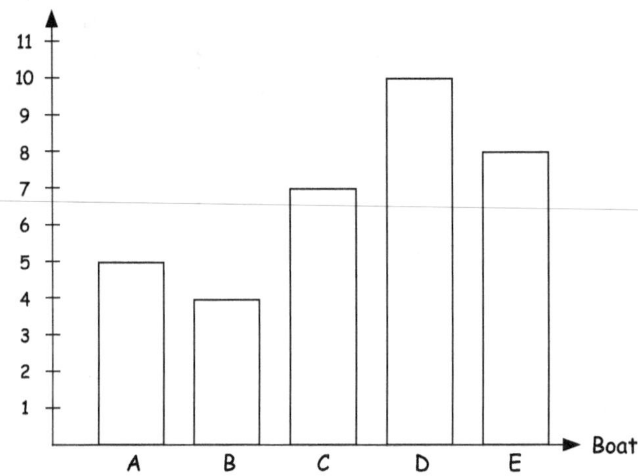

1. **If Boat A : 5 :: Boat D : ?**
    (a) 4 (b) 5
    (c) 10 (d) 8

2. **Find the odd one out.**
    (a) Boat A : 5 (b) Boat B : 4
    (c) Boat C : 8 (d) Boat E : 8

3. **How many more people went on boat D than boat A?**
    (a) 5 (b) 4
    (c) 3 (d) 2

4. **How many less people went on boat C than boat E?**
    (a) 1 (b) 2
    (c) 3 (d) 4

5. **How many people went all together?**
    (a) 31 (b) 32
    (c) 33 (d) 34

Direction (Qs. 6 to 12): The table given below shows the number of people watching at various football grounds. Round each number to the nearest thousand and put the answers in the right hand column. Then answer the questions that follow: **[Mental Mathematics]**

Team	Attendance	Rounding
Aryans	2876	
Champions	6453	
Royals	3386	
Devils	4691	
Panthers	9304	
Tigers	5771	
Shera	6852	

6. **Which team was watched by most people?**
    (a) Champions (b) Tigers
    (c) Shera (d) Panthers

7. **Which team was watched by least people?**
    (a) Champions (b) Aryans
    (c) Tigers (d) Devils

8. **Find the odd one out.**
    (a) Tigers (b) Aryans
    (c) Zebras (d) Panthers

9. How many more people watched panthers than Aryans? (use rounding)
   (a) 4000   (b) 5000
   (c) 6000   (d) 7000

10. How many less people watched Royals than Shera? (use rounding)
    (a) 4000   (b) 5000
    (c) 6000   (d) 7000

11. If Tigers : 6000 :: Champions : ?
    (a) 5000   (b) 6000
    (c) 7000   (d) 8000

12. If Devils : 5000 :: ? : 7000
    (a) Champions   (b) Tigers
    (c) Shera   (d) Royals

13. The horizontal bar graph given below shows Anshi's income from January to May.   [Mental Mathematics]

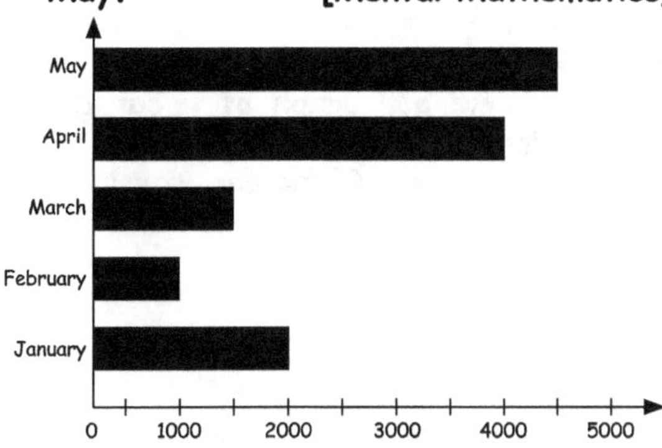

Study the graph and answer the questions that follow:

In which month did Anshi earn thrice the amount of money earned in March.
    (a) May   (b) January
    (c) February   (d) April

14. Anshi saved $\left(\dfrac{1}{5}\right)^{th}$ of the amount of money she earned in May. How much money did she spend in that month?
    (a) ₹ 900   (b) ₹ 3600
    (c) ₹ 3500   (d) ₹ 1700

Direction (Q. 15): The following bar chart shows the number of animals in a animal shelter.

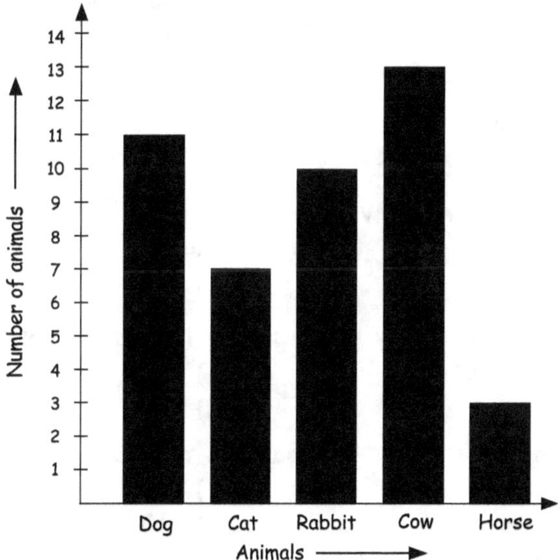

State True/False for the following statements.   [Tricky]

Statement A: The number of rabbits is less than dogs.

Statement B: The number of horse is least.

Statement C: The number of cow is less than dogs.

Statement D: The number of cats is less than rabbits.
    (a) TTFF   (b) TTFT
    (c) FFTT   (d) FTFT

Direction (Qs. 16 to 22): Tara kept a record of the birds she saw each day for a week. She presented her observation as a pictograph. Read the pictograph given below and answer the questions that follow: [Critical Thinking]

Type of bird	Numbers of Birds
Sparrow	
Seagull	

Pigeon	
Crow	
Parrot	
Bulbul	

= 5 birds

16. How many crow did she see?

(a) 20 (b) 25
(c) 30 (d) 35

17. How many more pigeon than sparrow?
(a) 40 (b) 50
(c) 30 (d) 20

18. How many less parrots than seagull?
(a) 40 (b) 30
(c) 20 (d) 10

19. Which bird was seen as many times as bulbul?
(a) sparrow (b) seagull
(c) crow (d) pigeon

20. State true/false for the following statements. [Tricky]

Statement A: Piegeon was seen more than crow.

Statement B: Bulbul was seen less than seagull.

Statement C: Sparrow was seen equal times as parrot.

Statement D: Pigeon was seen more than bulbul.

(a) F T T F (b) T F F T
(c) F T F T (d) T F T F

21. Which bird was seen maximum number of times?
(a) Bulbul (b) Seagull
(c) Crow (d) Pigeon

22. Which bird was seen minimum number of times?
(a) Parrot
(b) Crow
(c) Bulbul
(d) Sparrow

23. Look at the following picture of speed and time bar graph of a car and tell during which one of the following hours speed of the car was increased maximum.

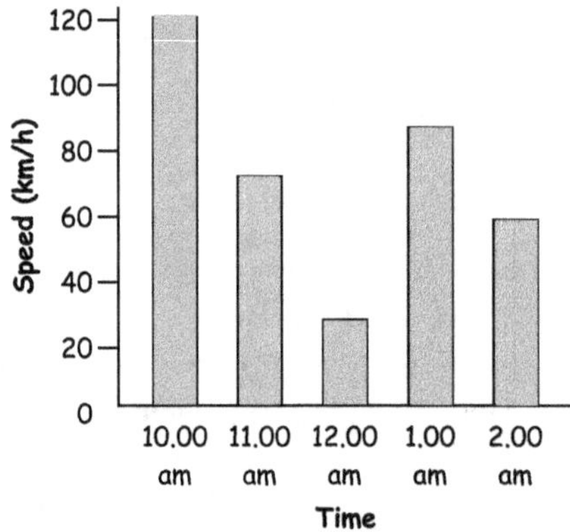

(a) 10.00 am - 11.00 am
(b) 11.00 am - 12.00 am
(c) 12.00 am - 1.00 pm
(d) 1.00 pm - 2.00 pm

Direction (Qs. 24 to 29): Lalit asked some shoppees how they had travelled to a super market. He recorded their answers on a tally chart and then draw a pictograph to show his results. Read the graph given below and answer the questions that follow:

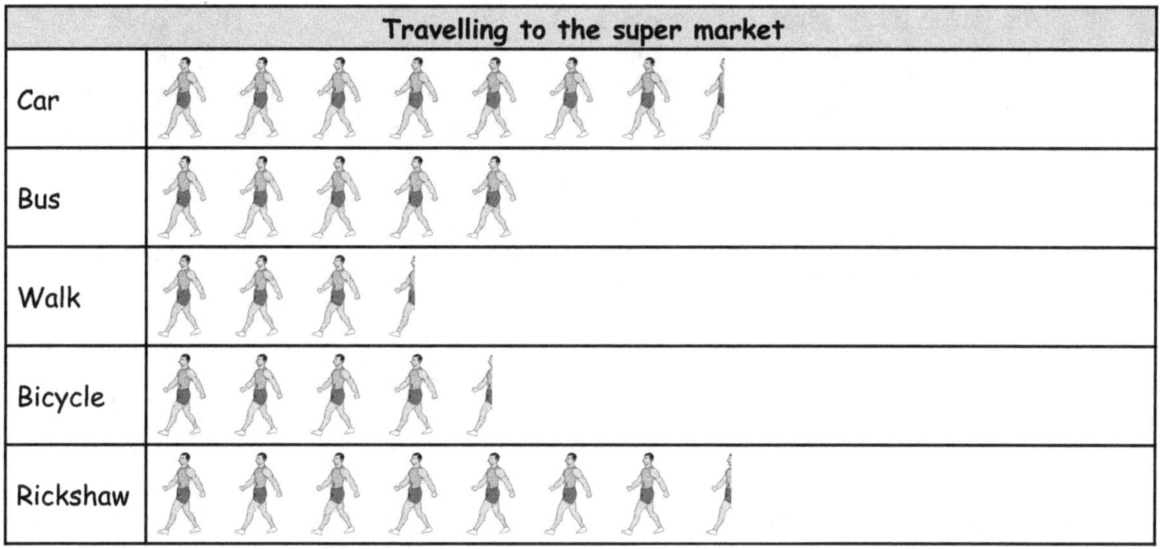

Travelling to the super market	
Car	
Bus	
Walk	
Bicycle	
Rickshaw	

 = 2 customers   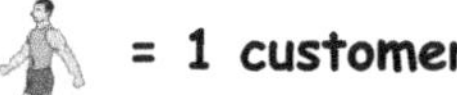 = 1 customer

24. Match the following:

	List I		List II
A.	Bus	1.	Ң‖
B.	Walk	2.	Ң Ң Ң
C.	Bicycle	3.	Ң Ң
D.	Car	4.	Ң‖‖‖

      A B C D   A B C D

(a) 3 2 4 1   (b) 3 2 1 4
(c) 3 4 1 2   (d) 3 1 4 2

25. Arrange the following vehicles used by people in increasing order: **[2012]**

A. Car   B. Walk
C. Bicycle   D. Rickshaw

(a) B D C A   (b) B C D A
(c) B C A D   (d) B D A C

26. Which vehicle is most used by people for travelling to super market?

(a) Car   (b) Rickshaw
(c) Bus   (d) Bicycle

27. Which vehicle is least used by people for travelling to super market?

(a) Bicycle   (b) Walk
(c) Rickshaw   (d) Bus

28. How many more people prefer Bicycle over walking?

(a) 1   (b) 2
(c) 3   (d) 4

29. How many less people prefer? Both are equal, so difference is zero?

(a) 1   (b) 2
(c) 3   (d) 4

30. On the basis of following features identify the correct term. **[2008]**

A. It can show more than one set of data.

B. In this we represent the data through horizontal bars or vertical columns.

C. It has a title to explain the information given in the graph.

D. It has horizontal and vertical scales.

(a) Pictograph   (b) Bar-graph
(c) Circle-graph   (d) Tally marks

31. Which of the following statements are True or False? Choose the correct statement.

A. Representing numerical data by picture symbols is called a pictograph. **[Tricky]**

B. The collection of information in the form of numerical figures, is called numerical data.

C. A circular graph which represents a given data is known as a pictograph.

D. It is possible to show two kinds of information on one bar-graph.

(a) T T T F

(b) T T F T

(c) T F T T

(d) F T T T

32. In the following bar-graph students from different classes who participated in a competition has been shown. [2017]

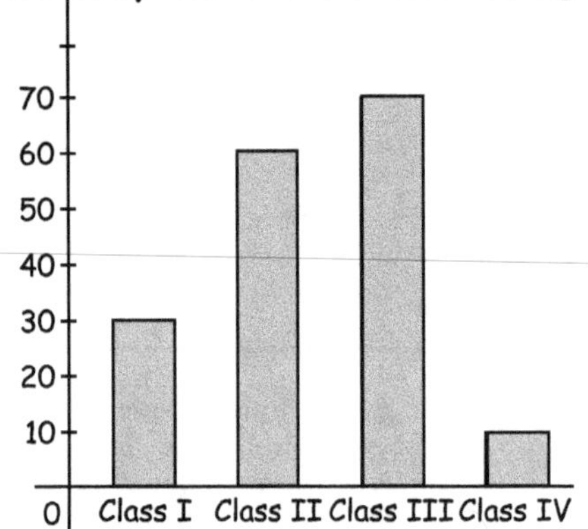

How many students participated in the competition from Class-IV?

(a) 30

(b) 60

(c) 10

(d) 70

33. The given table shows the number of chairs sold by 2 factories over a period of 4 months. [2014, Tricky]

Months	Factory P	Factory Q
September	2545	1389
October	1864	1354
November	900	1268
December	1217	2513

How many more chairs did factory Q sell than factory P in December?

(a) 1864

(b) 1183

(c) 1296

(d) 1543

34. What is the difference between the total number of members in the basket ball club in 2015 and 2016? [2016]

Members of Basketball Club		
	2015	2016
Men	3205	2804
Women	4801	6408
Boys	1600	2000
Girls	2405	1807

(a) 1587

(b) 1008

(c) 1597

(d) 2205

35. The given table shows the number of books read by students of a school :

Number of books read	0	1	2	3	4	5
Number of students	245	870	965	1120	844	762

How many students read more than two books? [2018]

(a) 3691

(b) 2571

(c) 2966

(d) 2726

36. The given table shows the petrol used by Vivek in a week. Find the total quantity of petrol used by Vivek on Monday, Wednesday Friday and Saturday. [2018]

Monday	3 L 560 ml
Tuesday	4 L 325 ml
Wednesday	3 L 780 ml
Thursday	4 L 105 ml
Friday	5 L 325 ml
Saturday	4 L 875 ml

(a) 17 L 540 ml

(b) 16 L 540 ml

(c) 16 L 225 ml

(d) 18 L 85 ml

Directions (Qs. 37–38) : Study the given table and answer the following questions.

Colours	Red	Yellow	Orange	Pink
No. of Marbles	26	34	52	47

37. What fraction of total marbles are of red colour? [2018]

(a) $\dfrac{52}{159}$

(b) $\dfrac{26}{159}$

(c) $\dfrac{47}{160}$

(d) $\dfrac{37}{160}$

38. What fraction of total marbles are not of orange colour? [2018]

(a) $\dfrac{107}{159}$

(b) $\dfrac{52}{159}$

(c) $\dfrac{107}{160}$

(d) $\dfrac{133}{160}$

LEVEL 2

Direction (Qs. 1 to 3): Mrs. Shalini's class was planning a party. They had to decide what they would have to eat. The student shose the following. Read the table given below and answer the que stions that follow:

S. No.	Student	Food choice
1	Tine	Pizza
2	Luni	Burger
3	Chinky	Pie
4	Mintu	Burger
5	Ali	Burger
6	Zafar	Pizza
7	Wahida	Burger
8	Ricky	Pizza
9	Vicky	Pie
10	Micky	Pizza
11	Billu	Burger
12	Deepu	Pizza
13	Sunita	Pizza
14	Munni	Burger
15	Abhay	Pizza

1.Complete the tally chart: **[Critical Thinking]**

Food	Tally marks
Pizza	A : _____________
Burger	B : _____________
Pie	C : _____________

A: (a) ЖIIII   (b) ЖII   (c) ЖI   (d) Ж
B: (a) ЖIIII   (b) ЖII   (c) Ж   (d) ЖI
C: (a) I   (b) II   (c) III   (d) IIII

2. **State true/false for the following statements:** [Tricky]

    A: Number of pizza is more than burger.

    B: Tally marks of pie is |||.
    C: Tally marks of burger is ᴺᴶ|||.
    D: Pie is least favourite.

    (a) F T T F   (b) T F F T   (c) F T F T   (d) T F T F

3. **Find the odd one out.**

    (a) Pie   (b) Pizza   (c) Sandwich   (d) Burger

4. **If** ▢▢▢▢▢ **represents 45 TV sets, how many TV sets does** ▢▢▢ **represents?** [2012]

    (a) 9   (b) 18   (c) 27   (d) 36

Direction (Q. 5): The bar chart given below shows the number of people who get on a bus on Monday.

Number of People
110, 100, 90, 80, 70, 60, 50, 40, 30, 20, 10
Red   Green   Blue   Yellow   Violet
Bus

5. **Read the bar chart given above and complete the passage given below:**

It was bright sunny Monday this week. Many people went out for work. many buses were running from stop to stop to pick and drop people. Buses were helping people to reach their destinations. Five buses namely red, green, blue, yellow and violet bus were running on the street. ______(A)______ people boarded blue bus. ______(B)______ bus had more people than violet bus. Yellow bus had ______(C)______ people in it but ______(D)______ bus had less people than yellow bus. ______(E)______ People boaded green bus. The maximum number of people boarded ______(F)______ bus and minimum number of people boarded ______(G)______ bus.

A : (a) 50   (b) 60   (c) 70   (d) 80

B : (a) Green   (b) Blue   (c) Red   (d) Yellow

C : (a) 50   (b) 60   (c) 70   (d) 80

D : (a) green   (b) blue   (c) red   (d) yellow

E : (a) 70   (b) 80   (c) 90   (d) 100

F : (a) yellow   (b) red   (c) blue   (d) green

G : (a) violet   (b) red   (c) yellow   (d) blue

6. **Pinku, Ravi, Brijesh and Raghu are friends. The graph shows the toy cars each of them have. What can we conclude from the given graph?** **[2015]**

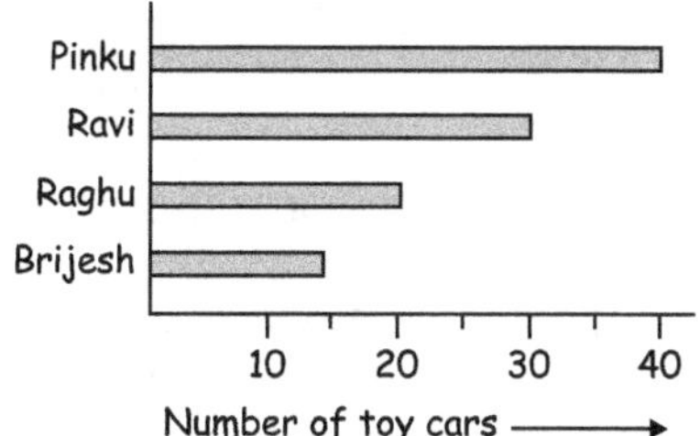

(a) Brijesh has one-third the number of toy cars Pinku has

(b) Three children have more than 20 toy cars

(c) Ravi has twice as many toy cars as Brijesh

(d) Brijesh has 1 toy car less than Raghu

7. **The pictograph shows the amount of rain received by a city over a few years.**

	Rain fall for six years
1996	🎈🎈 🎈🎈 🎈🎈
1997	🎈🎈 🎈🎈
1998	🎈🎈🎈🎈 🎈🎈🎈🎈 🎈
1999	🎈🎈 🎈🎈 🎈🎈
2000	🎈🎈 🎈🎈
2001	🎈🎈 🎈🎈 🎈🎈 🎈

In which year city received 140 cm of rain. Each 🎈 = 20 cm of rain   **[2016]**

(a) 1999   (b) 2000   (c) 2001   (d) 1997

8. **The given list shows the number of bikes of each colour in a parking lot.**

Red	🏍🏍🏍🏍🏍
Yellow	🏍🏍🏍🏍
Black	🏍🏍
Blue	🏍🏍🏍

❖ **There are 18 red bikes.**   ❖ **There are 16 yellow bikes.**

❖ **There are 6 black bikes.**   ❖ **There are 10 blue bikes.**

Which of the following statement completes the pictograph?

(a) Each ![bike] means 5 bikes.   (b) Each ![bike] means 4 bikes.

(c) Each ![bike] means 2 cars.   (d) Each ![bike] means 3 cars.

9. See the table below and answer the following question :

Items	Price
Dozen of Spoons	₹ 30
Dozen of Plates	₹ 71
Dozen of Tea cups	₹ 41
A Pot	₹ 23
A Bowl	₹ 13
A Pistle	₹ 5

Which item is the most expensive? [2013]

(a) Dozen of plates (b) Dozen of tea cups
(c) A pot (d) A pistle

10. In the given pictograph, wheat produced by different states of India during the year 2010 has been shown.

Punjab	🌾🌾🌾🌾🌾🌾🌾🌾🌾	Haryana	🌾🌾🌾🌾
Uttar Pradesh	🌾🌾🌾🌾🌾🌾	Rajasthan	🌾🌾
Madhya Pradesh	🌾🌾🌾	Other	🌾

One 🌾 represents 10 lakh tons of wheat.

Which one of the following states is the leading state in wheat production? [2014]
(a) Punjab (b) Haryana
(c) Uttar Pradesh (d) Rajasthan

Direction (Qs. 11 to 15): The Venn diagram given below shows favourite brands of leading actresses in Indian film industry. Read the diagram and answer the questions that follow:

[Critical Thinking]

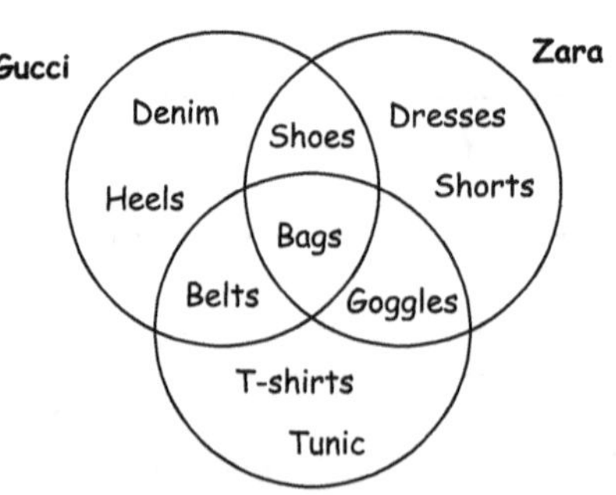

11. Which item is favourite in all 3 brands?

   (a) Denim   (b) Goggles   (c) Bags   (d) Belts

12. Which item is liked in Gucci and United Colours of Benetton only?

   (a) Bags   (b) Belts   (c) Shorts   (d) Dresses

13. Which item is liked in Gucci and Zara only?

   (a) Shoes   (b) Heels   (c) Belts   (d) Goggles

14. Which item is liked in Zara and United Colours of Benetton only?

   (a) Bags   (b) Shoes   (c) Goggles   (d) T-shirts

15. Find the odd one out.

   (a) Dress   (b) Shorts   (c) Shoes   (d) Tunic

Direction (Qs. 16 to 21): Tina made a pictograph to show how many rainy days her town had during the first half of the year.

☂ = 2 rainy days

Rainy Days	
Jan	☂ ☂ ☂ ☂
Feb	☂ ☂ ☂ ☂ ☂
March	☂ ☂ ☂
April	☂ ☂ ☂ ☂ ☂
May	☂ ☂ ☂ ☂ ☂ ☂ ☂
June	☂ ☂ ☂ ☂ ☂ ☂ ☂ ☂

16. Match the following: **[Tricky]**

	List I		List II
A.	June	1.	卌 IIII
B.	Jan	2.	卌 卌 卌 I
C.	April	3.	卌 III
D.	May	4.	卌 卌 III

     A B C D   A B C D   A B C D   A B C D

(a) 2 3 1 4   (b) 2 3 4 1   (c) 2 1 4 3   (d) 2 1 3 4

17. Which was the rainest month?

   (a) May   (b) June   (c) Feb   (d) Jan

18. Which was the dryest month?

   (a) Jan   (b) May   (c) March   (d) April

19. How many rainy days were there during the first three months?

   (a) 21   (b) 22   (c) 23   (d) 24

20. What is the difference between the number of rainy days in Jan and May?

(a) 2   (b) 3   (c) 4   (d) 5

21. How many rainy days were there altogether?

(a) 60   (b) 61   (c) 62   (d) 63

22. Which of the following statement is/are correct?   **[2011]**

     A.   When we give information (data) about a quantity through pictures, it is called a 'Bar graph'.

     B.   When we give information (data) about a quantity through horizontal or vertical bars, the graph is called a Bar graph.

(a) Only A   (b) Only B   (c) Both A and B   (d) Neither A nor B

Direction (Qs. 23 to 26): Read the passage given below and answer the questions that follow:

Children usually get ill during change of weather. They also get sick due to their bad eating habits. They don't wash their hands and does not keep themselves clean. There are many diseases which can happen due to various germs around us. Chintu got fever so her mother decided to make a tally chart of the diseases that her family members had when they were children.

Read the chart given below and answer the questions that follow:

S.No.	Disease	Tally marks
1	Flu	ⅣⅡ ⅣⅡ ⅣⅡ ‖
2	Measles	‖‖
3	Mumps	‖
4	Chicken Pox	ⅣⅡ ∣
5	Colds	ⅣⅡ ⅣⅡ ⅣⅡ ⅣⅡ ‖‖

23. How many more children had chicken pox than measles?   **[2010]**

(a) 1   (b) 2   (c) 3   (d) 4

24. Which disease happened most of the times?

(a) Flu   (b) Chicken pox   (c) Colds   (d) Measles

25. Which disease happened least number of times?

(a) Flu   (b) Measles   (c) Mumps   (d) Chicken pox

26. How many less children had mumps than measles?

(a) 1   (b) 2   (c) 3   (d) 4

Direction (Qs. 27 to 30): A Venn diagram showing even numbers and multiples of 3 is given below. Read the diagram and answer the questions that follow: **[2009]**

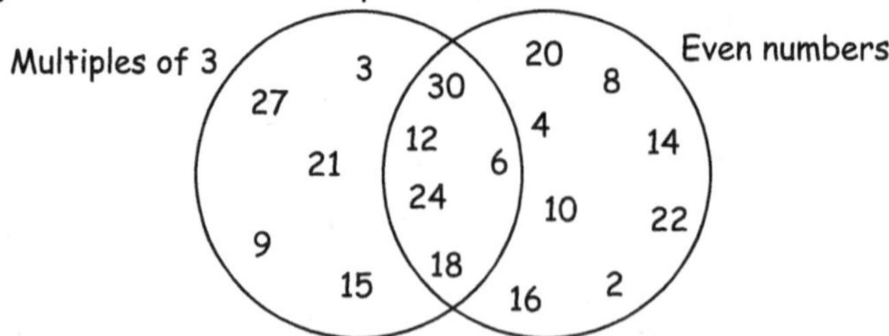

27. How many even numbers are multiples of 3?

(a) 4   (b) 5   (c) 6   (d) 7

28. How many even numbers are not multiples of 3?

(a) 5 (b) 6 (c) 7 (d) 8

29. How many numbers are multiples of 3 but are not even numbers?

(a) 5 (b) 6 (c) 7 (d) 8

30. Find the odd one from the following

(a) 6 (b) 12 (c) 15 (d) 24

Direction (Qs. 31 to 36): Hari is a barber. He used a pictograph to show how busy he had been during the first week in his new shop. Read the pictograph and answer the questions that follow :

✂ = 2 customers

Haircuts	
Monday	✂ ✂ ✂
Tuesday	✂ ✂ ✂
Wednesday	✂ ✂ ✂ ✂
Thursday	✂ ✂ ✂
Friday	✂ ✂ ✂ ✂ ✂
Saturday	✂ ✂ ✂ ✂ ✂ ✂ ✂
Sunday	✂ ✂ ✂ ✂ ✂ ✂ ✂

31. Match the following: [2011]

	List I		List II
A.	Monday	1.	卌 I
B.	Thursday	2.	卌 III
C.	Wednesday	3.	卌 卌 卌 I
D.	Sunday	4.	卌 I

```
     A  B  C  D                    A  B  C  D
(a)  4  2  1  3              (b)  4  1  2  3
(c)  4  3  2  1              (d)  4  2  3  1
```

32. Arrange the following days from busiest day to quickest day.

A. Saturday B. Friday C. Tuesday D. Wednesday

(a) A C D B (b) A C B D (c) A D B C (d) A B D C

33. Which was the busiest day?

(a) Saturday (b) Wednesday (c) Friday (d) Monday

34. Which was the quickest day?

(a) Sunday (b) Wednesday (c) Thursday (d) Friday

35. How many more customers were there on Friday than Wednesday?

(a) 1 (b) 2 (c) 3 (d) 4

36. How many less customers were on equal no. of customer so, difference = 0.

(a) 1 (b) 2 (c) 3 (d) 4

Directions (Qs. 37-38) : Study the given graph showing the number of stickers collected by five friends and answer the following questions.   [2018]

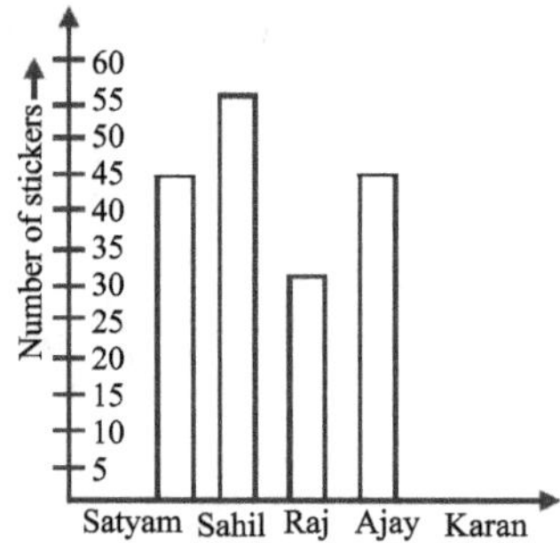

37. How many stickers Sahil must give to Ajay. So that they both have equal number of Stickers?

    (a) 10   (b) 5   (c) 8   (d) 3

38. If the total stickers collected were 225, then find the number of stickers collected by Karan?

    (a) 50   (b) 45   (c) 55   (d) 40

39. Nakul, Mehul and Naina were sitting on the see-saw at the playground. Which of the following bar graphs correctly shows the weight of the three children?   [2018]

(a)
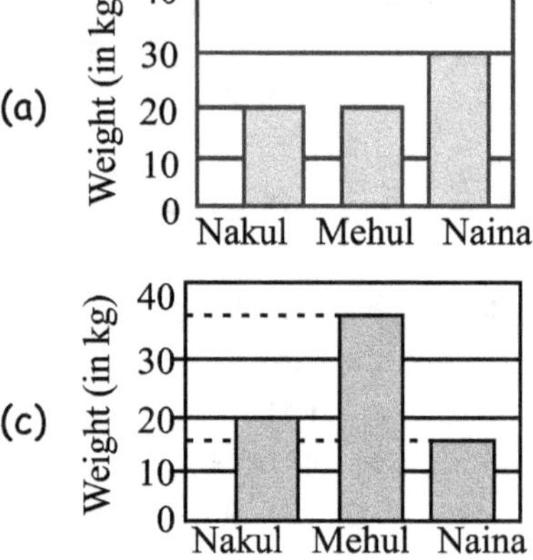

(c)

(b)

(d)
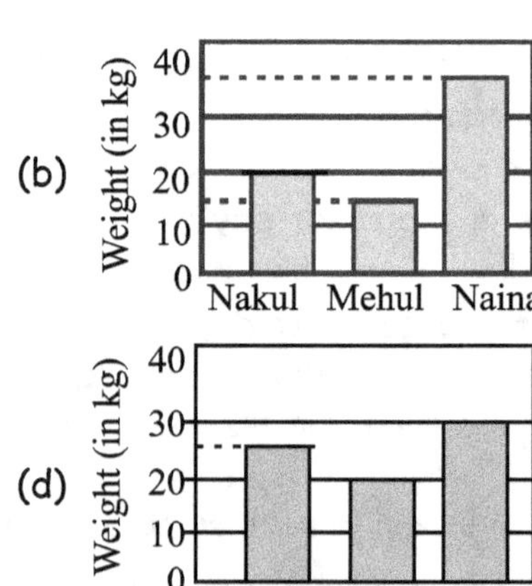

Directions (Qs. 40-41): The given bar graph shows Ravi's savings from January to May. Study the graph carefully and answer the following questions.

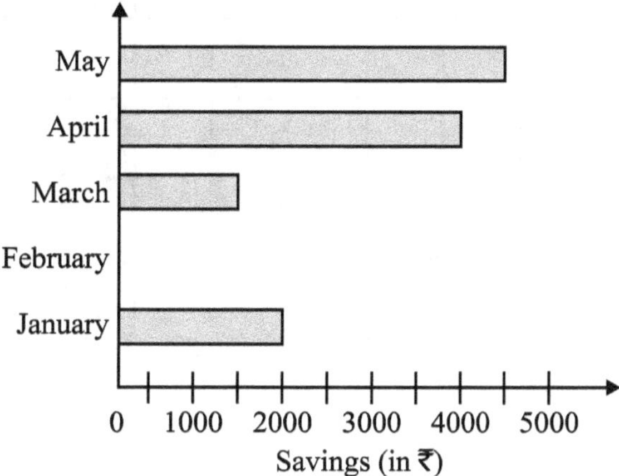

40. If Ravi saved a total of ₹15000 from January to May, then how much did he save in February? **[2019]**
    (a) ₹2500   (b) ₹2000
    (c) ₹3000   (d) ₹4500

41. If Ravi spent $\left(\dfrac{1}{5}\right)^{th}$ of the amount of money he saved in April, then how much did he earn in that month? **[2019]**
    (a) ₹3200   (b) ₹800
    (c) ₹4800   (d) ₹4000

42. The bar graph given below represents the marks scored by four friends in a test. Study it carefully and answer the following question. **[2021]**

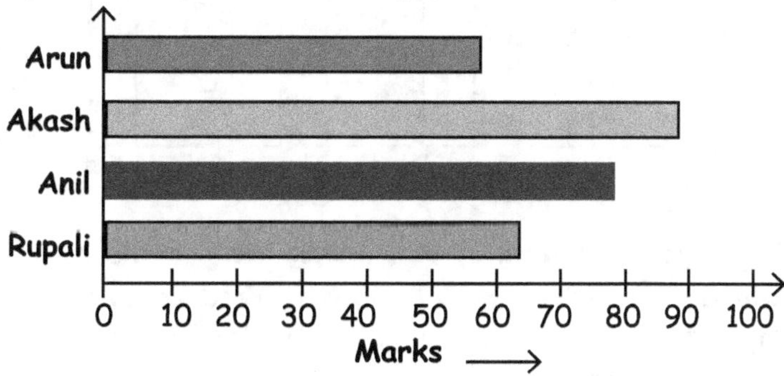

   Which two students scored a total of 125 marks? **[2021]**
    (a) Rupali and Anil   (b) Arun and Anil
    (c) Akash and Arun   (d) Rupali and Arun

43. The given bar graph represents the milk flavours liked by the students of a class. Study the graph carefully and answer the following questions.

                                               [2021]

   (A) Which milk flavour is liked by exactly 40 students?
   (B) How many students likes Rose, Badam and Pista flavours altogether?

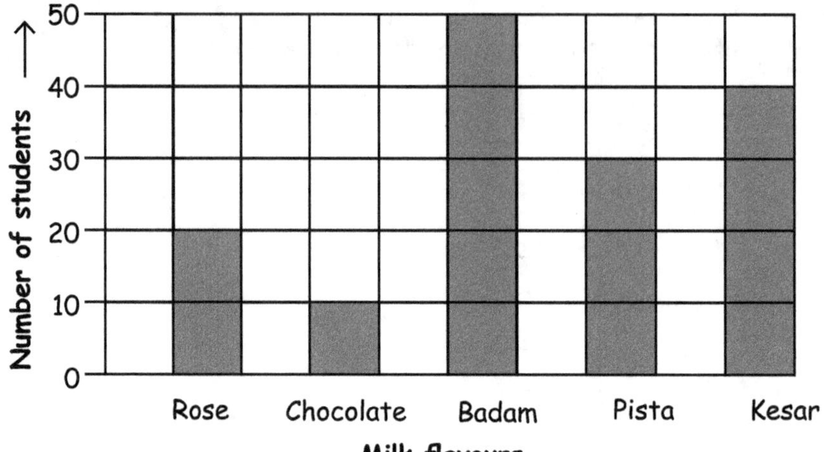

	A	B		A	B
(a)	Pista	110	(b) Badam	100	
(c)	Kesar	110	(d) Kesar	100	

44. The given bar graph shows the number of people who visited the zoo over a period of 7 days. **[2022]**

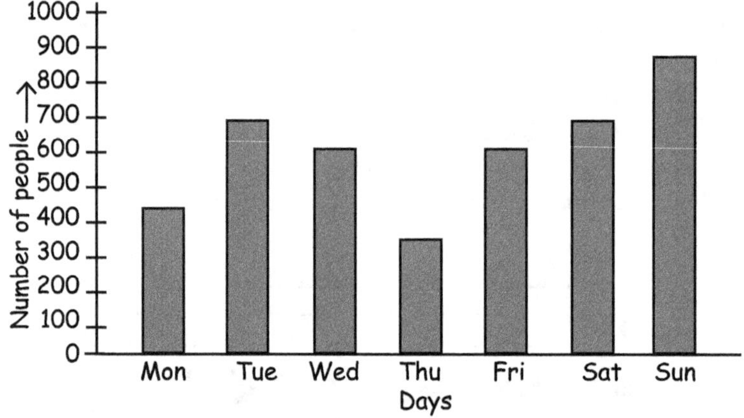

On which two days did a total of 900 people visit to the zoo?

(a) Tuesday and Wednesday (b) Wednesday and Friday

(c) Thursday and Friday (d) Monday and Thursday

45. Look at the following table: **[2022]**

Article	Price
1 Chair	₹546
1 Table	₹890
1 Fan	₹450

Ashwin bought 7 chairs, 5 tables and some fans. He paid total ₹10972. How many fans did Ashwin buy?

(a) 4 (b) 5 (c) 6 (d) 7

46. The given line graph tells us about the distance of five employees of an organization from their homes to their work places. **[2022]**

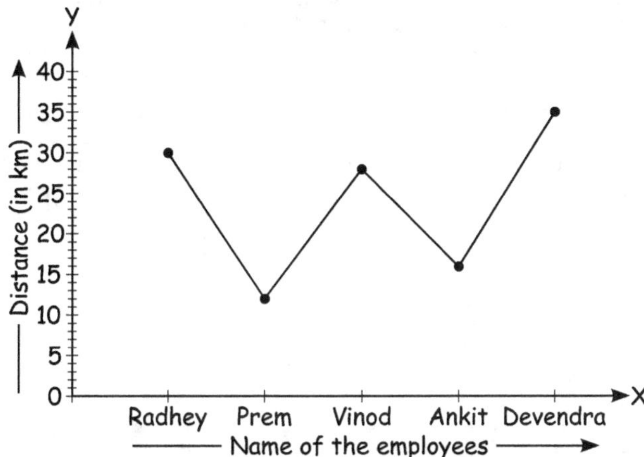

Which one of the following has his home nearest to his organization?

(a) Radhey   (b) Prem   (c) Vinod   (d) Ankit

47. Given bar graph represents the number of viewers who watched 5 different channels A, B, C, D and E. **[2022]**

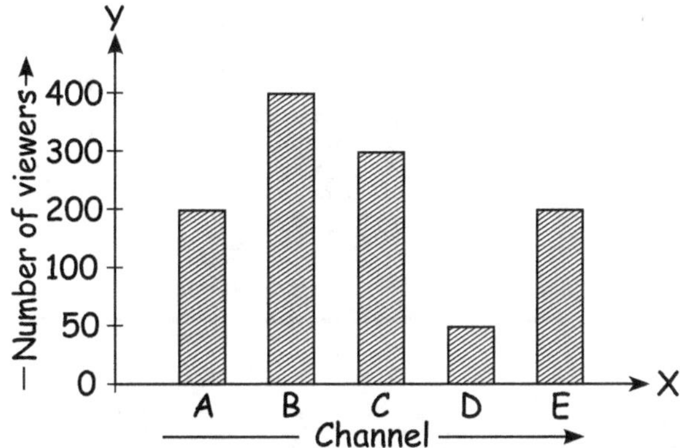

How many more viewers watched the channels B and C altogether than the channel E?

(a) 500   (b) 300   (c) 400   (d) 450

RESPONSE GRID

LEVEL 1

1. a b c d 2. a b c d 3. a b c d 4. a b c d 5. a b c d
6. a b c d 7. a b c d 8. a b c d 9. a b c d 10. a b c d
11. a b c d 12. a b c d 13. a b c d 14. a b c d 15. a b c d
16. a b c d 17. a b c d 18. a b c d 19. a b c d 20. a b c d
21. a b c d 22. a b c d 23. a b c d 24. a b c d 25. a b c d
26. a b c d 27. a b c d 28. a b c d 29. a b c d 30. a b c d
31. a b c d 32. a b c d 33. a b c d 34. a b c d 35. a b c d
36. a b c d 37. a b c d 38. a b c d

LEVEL 2

1. a b c d 2. a b c d 3. a b c d 4. a b c d 5. a b c d
6. a b c d 7. a b c d 8. a b c d 9. a b c d 10. a b c d
11. a b c d 12. a b c d 13. a b c d 14. a b c d 15. a b c d
16. a b c d 17. a b c d 18. a b c d 19. a b c d 20. a b c d
21. a b c d 22. a b c d 23. a b c d 24. a b c d 25. a b c d
26. a b c d 27. a b c d 28. a b c d 29. a b c d 30. a b c d
31. a b c d 32. a b c d 33. a b c d 34. a b c d 35. a b c d
36. a b c d 37. a b c d 38. a b c d 39. a b c d 40. a b c d
41. a b c d 42. a b c d 43. a b c d 44. a b c d 45. a b c d
46. a b c d 47. a b c d

Solutions with Explanation

LEVEL 1

1. **(c)** Number of people went to boat D = 10

2. **(c)** Since, 7 people went on boat C. So, the odd one is Boat C : 8.

3. **(a)** Number of people went on boat D = 10
   Olumber of people went on boat A = 5
   Difference = 10 – 5 = 5

4. **(a)** Number of people went on boat C = 7.
   Number of people went on boat E = 8.
   Difference = 8 – 7 = 1

5. **(d)** Total number of people = 5 + 4 + 7 + 10 + 8 = 34
   Therefore, the answer is option (d) 34.

Team	Attendance	Rounding
Aryans	2876	3000
Champions	6453	6000
Royals	3386	3000
Devils	4691	5000
Panthers	9304	9000
Tigers	5771	6000
Shera	6852	7000

6. (d) Since, Panthers were watched by most people.

7. (b) Since, Aryans were watched by least people.

8. (c) There is no Zebras team. So, the odd one is Zebras.

9. (c) Number of people watched Panthers = 9000

Number of people watched Aryans = 3000

Difference = 9000 – 3000 = 6000

10. (a) Number of people watched Royals = 3000.

Number of people watched Shera = 7000.

Difference = 7000 – 3000 = 4000.

11. (b) Since Champion's attendance after rounding = 6000.

12. (c) Since, Shera's attendance after rounding = 7000.

13. (a) Anshi Earned in March = 1500.

Thrice of 1500 = 1500 × 3 = 4500.

Hence, she earned 4500 in May.

14. (b) Amount earned in May = 4500.

Amount saved = $4500 \times \dfrac{1}{5}$ = 900.

She spend = 4500 – 900 = ₹ 3600.

15. (b) The number of dogs = 11

The number of cats = 7

The number of rabbits = 10

The number of cows = 13

The number of horse = 3

Since, the number of cows is more than dogs. Thus, statement C is incorrect.

∴ The answer is option (b) C.

16. (c) There are 6 crows in the chart So, 5 × 6 = 30 crows.

17. (d) Number of pigeon = 8 × 5 = 40

Number of sparrow = 4 × 5 = 20

Difference = 40 – 20 = 20

18. (d) Number of parrots = 3 × 5 = 15

Number of seagull = 5 × 5 = 25

Difference = 25 – 15 = 10

19. (b) Number of seagull = 5 × 5 = 25

Number of bulbul = 5 × 5 = 25

20. (b) Number of pigeon = 40

Number of crow = 30

Statement A is true.

Number of bulbul = 25

Number of seagull = 25

Statement B is false.

Number of sparrows = 20

Number of parrot = 15

Statement C is false.

Statement D is true.

Therefore, the answer is option (b) T F F T.

21. (d) Pigeon. **22. (a)** Parrot.

23. (c) 12 : 00 am– 1 : 00 pm is the time when the speed of the car was increased maximum.

24. (d) A : Bus = 10 people = ⟶ 3

B : Walk = 7 people = ⟶ 1

C : Bicycle = 9 people = ⟶ 4

D : Car = 15 people = ⟶ 2

Therefore, the answer is option (d) 3 1 4 2.

25. **(b)** A : Car = 15 people
B : Walk = 7 people
C : Bicycle = 9 people
D : rickshaw = 14 people
Therefore, the answer is option (b) B C D A.

26. **(a)** Since, car is most used by people.

27. **(b)** Since, walk is least used by people.

28. **(b)** Number of people use bicycle = 9
Number of people use walking = 7
Difference = 9 – 7 = 2

29. **(a)** Number of people use rickshaw = 14

Number of people use car = 15
Difference = 15 – 14 = 1

30. **(b)** Bar-graph.

31. **(b)**

32. **(c)** 10 students participated from class iv.

33. **(c)** 2513 – 1217 = 1296 chairs

34. **(b)** As 13019 – 12011 = 1008

35. **(d)** 1120 + 844 + 762 = 2726

36. **(a)** Monday → 3 L 560 ml
Wednesday → 3L 780 ml
Friday → 5L 325 ml
Saturday → 4 L 875 ml
Total → 17 L 540 ml

37. **(b)** $\dfrac{26}{159}$

38. **(a)** $\dfrac{107}{159}$

LEVEL 2

1. A: **(b)** 卌 ||
B: **(d)** 卌 |
C: **(b)** ||

2. **(b)** Number of pizza = 7
Number of burger = 6
Statement A is true.
Number of pie = 2
Statement B is false.
Tally marks of burger = 卌 |
Statement C is false.
Statement D is true.
Therefore, the answer is option (b) T F F T.

3. **(c)** Since, there was no child who suggested sandwich so the odd one is sandwich. Therefore, the answer is option (c) sandwich.

4. **(c)** It represents 9 + 9 + 9 = 27

5. A: **(c)** 70. B: **(a)** green.
C: **(b)** 60. D: **(c)** red.

E: **(d)** 100. F: **(d)** green.
G: **(b)** red.

6. **(c)** Ravi has twice as many toy cars as Brijesh as 30 = 2 × 15

7. **(c)** In 2001, 140 cm of rain was received.

8. **(b)** Each means 4 bikes.

9. **(a)** Dozen of plates is most expensive.

10. **(a)** Punjab is the leading state in wheat production.

11. **(c)** Bags. **12.** **(b)** Belts.

13. **(a)** Shoes. **14.** **(c)** Goggles.

15. **(d)** Since, dress, shorts and shoes comes under the brand Zara and tunic come under the brand united colours of Benetton.
Therefore, the answer is option (d) Tunic.

16. **(a)** A : June = 16 days = 卌 卌 卌 | ⟶ 2
B : Jan = 8 days = 卌 ||| ⟶ 3
C : April = 9 days = 卌 |||| ⟶ 1
D : May = 13 days = 卌 卌 ||| ⟶ 4

Therefore, the answer is option (a) 2 3 1 4.

17. **(b)** Since, June is the rainest month. Therefore, the answer is option (b) June.

18. **(c)** Since, March is the dryest month. Therefore, the answer is option (c) March.

19. **(c)** Number of rainy days during first 3 months
= 8 + 9 + 6 = 23 days
Therefore, the answer is option (c) 23.

20. **(d)** Number of rainy days in Jan = 8 days.
Number of rainy days in may = 13 days.
Difference = 13 – 8 = 5 days.
Therefore, the answer is option (d) 5.

21. **(b)** Total number of rainy days
= 8 + 9 + 6 + 9 + 13 + 16 = 61 days.
Therefore, the answer is option (b) 61.

22. **(b)** Only B is correct.

23. **(b)** Number of children who had chicken pox = 6.
Number of children who had measles = 4.
Difference = 6 – 4 = 2.
Therefore, the answer is option (b) 2.

24. **(c)** Since, cold happened most of the times.
Therefore, the answer is option (c) colds.

25. **(c)** Since, mumps happened least number of times.

26. **(b)** Number of children who had mumps = 2.
Number of children who had measles = 4.
Difference = 4 – 2 = 2
Therefore, the answer is option (b) 2.

27. **(b)** There are five numbers
6, 12, 18, 24, 30.
Therefore, the answer is option (b) 5.

28. **(d)** The even numbers which are not multiples of 3 = 20, 8, 4, 14, 10, 16, 2, 22
Therefore, the answer is option (d) 8.

29. **(a)** Multiples of 3 which are not even numbers = 27, 3, 9, 21, 15
Therefore, the answer is option (a) 5.

30. **(c)** 6, 12 and 24 are even numbers which are multiples of 3 but 15 is a multiple of 3 but not an even number. So, 15 is the odd one. Therefore, the answer is option (c) 15.
Therefore, the answer is option (c) mumps.

31. **(b)** A : Monday = 6 customers = ⑤| ⟶ 4.
B : Thursday = 5 customers = ⑤ ⟶ 1.
C : Wednesday = 8 customers = ⑤||| ⟶ 2.
D : Sunday = 16 customers = ⑤ ⑤ ⑤| ⟶ 3.
Therefore, the answer is option (b) 4 1 2 3.

32. **(d)** A : Saturday = 16 customers
B : Friday = 10 customers
C : Tuesday = 6 customers
D : Wednesday = 8 customers
Therefore, the answer is option (d) A B D C.

33. **(a)** Saturday is the busiest day.
Therefore, the answer is option (a) Saturday.

34. **(c)** Thursday is the quickest day.
Therefore, the answer is option (c) Thursday.

35. **(c)** Number of customers on Friday
= 10

Number of customers on Wednesday = 7

Difference = 10 – 7 = 3

Therefore, the answer is option (c) 3.

36. **(b)** Number of customers on Sunday = 13

Number of customers on Saturday = 15

Difference = 15 – 13 = 2

Therefore, the answer is option (b) 2.

37. **(b)** 5

38. **(a)** 50

39. **(d)**

40. **(c)** Money saved in January = ₹2000

Money saved in March = ₹1500

Money saved in April = ₹4000

Money saved in May = ₹4500

Total money saved from January to May = ₹15000

∴ Money saved in February

= ₹15000 + (₹2000 + ₹1500 + ₹4000 + ₹4500)

= ₹3000

41. **(c)** Money spent in April = $\dfrac{1}{5} \times$ ₹4000

= ₹800

∴ His income in April = ₹4000 + ₹800

= ₹4800

42. **(d)** Arun's score in Test = 60

Akash's score in Test = 90

Anil's score in Test = 80

Rupali's score in Test = 65

Sum of Arun and Rupali's marks in Test = 60 + 65 = 125

43 **(d)** (I) Kesar milk flavour is exactly liked by 40 students

(II) Total no. of students who like Badam, Rose, Pista flavour altogether

= 50 + 20 + 30

= 100

44. **(d)** Monday (500) + Thursday (400) = 900

45. **(c)**

46. **(b)**

47. **(a)**

Number Patterns

Name : __________________________   Class : ____________

Complete each sequence and describe the number patterns.

195 , 210 , 225 , 240 , ___ , ___ , ___   What pattern? ________

415 , 395 , 375 , 355 , ___ , ___ , ___   What pattern? ________

323 , 348 , 373 , 398 , ___ , ___ , ___   What pattern? ________

162 , 197 , 232 , 267 , ___ , ___ , ___   What pattern? ________

310 , 285 , 260 , 235 , ___ , ___ , ___   What pattern? ________

541 , 521 , 501 , 481 , ___ , ___ , ___   What pattern? ________

456 , 486 , 516 , 546 , ___ , ___ , ___   What pattern? ________

945 , 865 , 785 , 705 , ___ , ___ , ___   What pattern? ________

411 , 471 , 531 , 591 , ___ , ___ , ___   What pattern? ________

988 , 933 , 878 , 823 , ___ , ___ , ___   What pattern? ________

16 Chapter

Miscellaneous

❖ Beautiful patterns surround us. You can see them on trees, clouds, on bodies of water. You can even see them on plants, on animals and on our very skin. The very tips of our fingers prove just that. There is also no doubt that patterns are just as mysterious as they are beautiful. In fact, there are some patterns that are so perfect that they self-replicate.

Try It!

Example : Find the odd one out from 10, 13, 16, 26

Solution : 26 is the odd one out as $10 = 3 \times 3 + 1$

$13 = 4 \times 3 + 1$

$16 = 5 \times 3 + 1$

$26 = 5 \times 5 + 1$

LEARNING OBJECTIVES

This lesson will help you to:—

❖ apply the knowledge of series completion and odd one out.

❖ use coding decoding.

❖ understand mathematical reasoning.

❖ study mirror image and embedded figures.

❖ use different patterns, number ranking, and alphabetical test.

QUICK CONCEPT REVIEW

Odd One Out

In odd one out we need to identify the odd one among the four options. Students can improve their aptitude skill by practicing the questions and answers on odd one out.

Coding-Decoding

Coding is a method of transmitting a message between the sender and the receiver that no third person can understand it. The coding and decoding one's ability of deciphering the rule and breaking the code to decipher the message will be tested to know.

For example:

' bcd' is coded as 'def' then 'True' is coded as..........

Answer: b – d (+2)

c – e (+2)

d – f (+2)

+2 letters are considered in this code.

True – Vtwg

Answer = Vtwg.

Embedded Figures

Finding common geometric shapes in a larger design—this simple assessment helps in developing a sense of observation about many things around us. The Embedded figures test was developed for research, but it has now become a recognized tool for exploring analytical ability, social behavior, body concept, preferred defense mechanism and problem solving style as well as other areas.

Patterns

Patterns are all around us! Finding and understanding patterns gives us great power. With patterns we can learn to predict what will come next, discover new things and better understand the world around us. Many patterns we can see around us have symmetry.

Try It!

Example : If SWEETY : 6 : : RAM : x, then value of x is

(a) 3   (b) 4

(c) 5   (d) 8

Solution : SWEETY has 6 letters and RAM has 3 letters so value of x is 3.

Example : If A is father of B and C is mother of B. Also, C has a daughter D. What is relation of D with B. How can we say that B is boy/son of A & C. There is no information about this.

Solution : D is daughter of C who is mother of B So, D is sister of B.

Multiple Choice Questions

LEVEL 1

Direction (Qs. 1 to 15): Find the odd one out.

1. 51, 64, 78, 91, 104, 117.
[Mental Mathematics]
(a) 51   (b) 78
(c) 104   (d) 130

2. 147, 125, 103, 81, 58, 36, 14.
[Mental Mathematics]
(a) 147   (b) 103
(c) 58   (d) 14

3. 5, 15, 45, 137, 411, 1233.
[Mental Mathematics]
(a) 137   (b) 1233
(c) 5   (d) None of these

4. 17, 21, 26, 30, 34, 38, 42.
[Mental Mathematics]
(a) 21   (b) 26
(c) 30   (d) None of these

5. 22, 33, 47, 55, 66, 77, 88.
[Mental Mathematics]
(a) 22   (b) 47

(c) 66   (d) 88

6. Which is the odd one out?
[2008] [Mental Mathematics]
(a) 10 + 9   (b) 19 - 0
(c) 95 ÷ 5   (d) 19 × 0

7. Which is the odd one out?
[Mental Mathematics]
(a) 55 - 44   (b) 121 ÷ 11
(c) 11 + 1   (d) 11 × 1

8. 8, 27, 64, 120, 216, 343.
[Mental Mathematics]
(a) 27   (b) 120
(c) 343   (d) None of these

9. 14, 28, 40, 54, 68, 82, 96.
[Mental Mathematics]
(a) 14   (b) 40
(c) 68   (d) 96

10. Which is the odd one out?
[2008] [Mental Mathematics]

(a) 1 + 5 (b) 18 - 12
(c) 3 × 2 (d) 6 ÷ 3

11. Find the odd pair of numbers.

[Mental Mathematics]

(a) 55 - 42 (b) 69 - 56
(c) 48 - 34 (d) 95 – 82

12. Find the odd pair of numbers.

[2010] [Mental Mathematics]

(a) 18 - 45 (b) 16 - 40
(c) 14 - 28 (d) 8 – 20

13. Find the odd pair of numbers.

[Mental Mathematics]

(a) 12 - 21 (b) 71 - 88
(c) 72 - 27 (d) 36 – 63

14. Find the odd pair of numbers.

[Mental Mathematics]

(a) 13 - 31 (b) 62 - 52
(c) 45 - 54 (d) 16 – 61

15. Find the odd pair of numbers.

[2009] [Mental Mathematics]

(a) 62 - 37 (b) 74 - 40
(c) 85 - 60 (d) 103 – 78

Direction (Qs. 16 to 25) Complete the series.

16. AZ, GT, MN, ?, YB   [Tricky]
(a) KF (b) RX
(c) SH (d) TS

17. AZ, CX, FU, ?
(a) IR (b) IV
(c) JQ (d) KP

18. AZ, BY, CX, ?
(a) EF (b) GH
(c) IJ (d) DW

19. DKY, FJW, HIU, JHS, ?
(a) KGR (b) LFQ
(c) KFR (d) LGQ

20. ?, SIY, OEU, KAQ, GWM, CSI
(a) WNE (b) WNB
(c) WNE (d) WMC

21. CMW, HRB, ?, RBL, WGQ, BLV
[2010]
(a) MWG (b) LVF
(c) LWG (d) WMX

22. BXJ, ETL, HPN, KLP, ?
(a) NHR (b) MHQ
(c) MIP (d) NIR

23. QPO, SRQ, UTS, WVU, ?   [2008]
(a) XVZ (b) ZYA
(c) YXW (d) VWX

24. JE, LH, OL, SQ, ?
(a) WV (b) WX
(c) VW (d) XW

25. AD, EH, IL, ?, QT   [2009]
(a) LM (b) MN
(c) MP (d) OM

Direction (Qs. 26 and 27): Answer the following questions related to coding and decoding.

26. If PALE is coded as 2134, EARTH is coded as 41590, how can PEARL be coded in that language?   [Tricky]
(a) 25430 (b) 29530
(c) 25413 (d) 24153

27. If ROSE is coded as 6821, CHAIR is coded as 73456 and PREACH is coded as 961473, what will be the code for SEARCH?   [Tricky]
(a) 216473 (b) 246173
(c) 214673 (d) 214763

28. Which numbmer replaces the question mark?   [Tricky 2016]

(a) 10 (b) 11
(c) 13 (d) 7

29. If BAG = 10, then PAGE = ?

[2016]

(a) 27 (b) 29
(c) 34 (d) 22

30. Find the odd one out.   [2017]

(c) 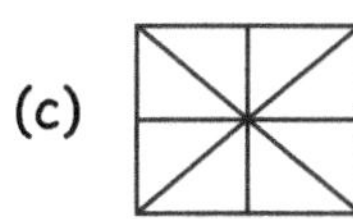   (d) 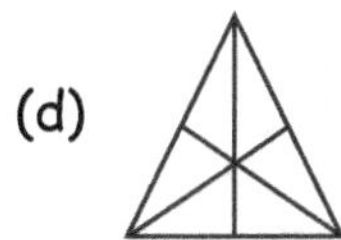

31. The given pictograph shows the different types of vehicles in a locality. There are __________ fewer scooters than cars in the locality.   **[2020]**

Vehicles	Number of vehicles
Car	⭐ ⭐ ⭐ ⭐
Bus	⭐ ⭐ ⭐
Motorcycle	⭐ ⭐ ⭐ ⭐ ⭐
Scooter	⭐ ⭐
Bicycle	⭐
	Each ⭐ represents 20 vehicles.

  (a) 0   (b) 20   (c) 40   (d) 60

32. Vishal draws some figures as given below.   **[2020]**

How many closed figures does he draw?   **[2020]**

  (a) 2   (b) 3   (c) 4   (d) 5

33. Find the successor of the number which is 365665 more than the product of 27 and 31.

  (a) 366501   (b) 366502   (c) 366503   (d) 366504   **[2022]**

LEVEL 2

Direction (Qs. 1 to 8): There is some relationship between diagrams A & B. The same relationship persists between C & D. Find the right diagrams for D from the alternatives.

1.   **[Critical Thinking]**

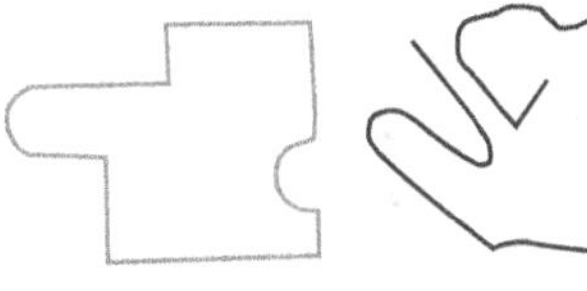

  (a) 1   (b) 2   (c) 3   (d) 4

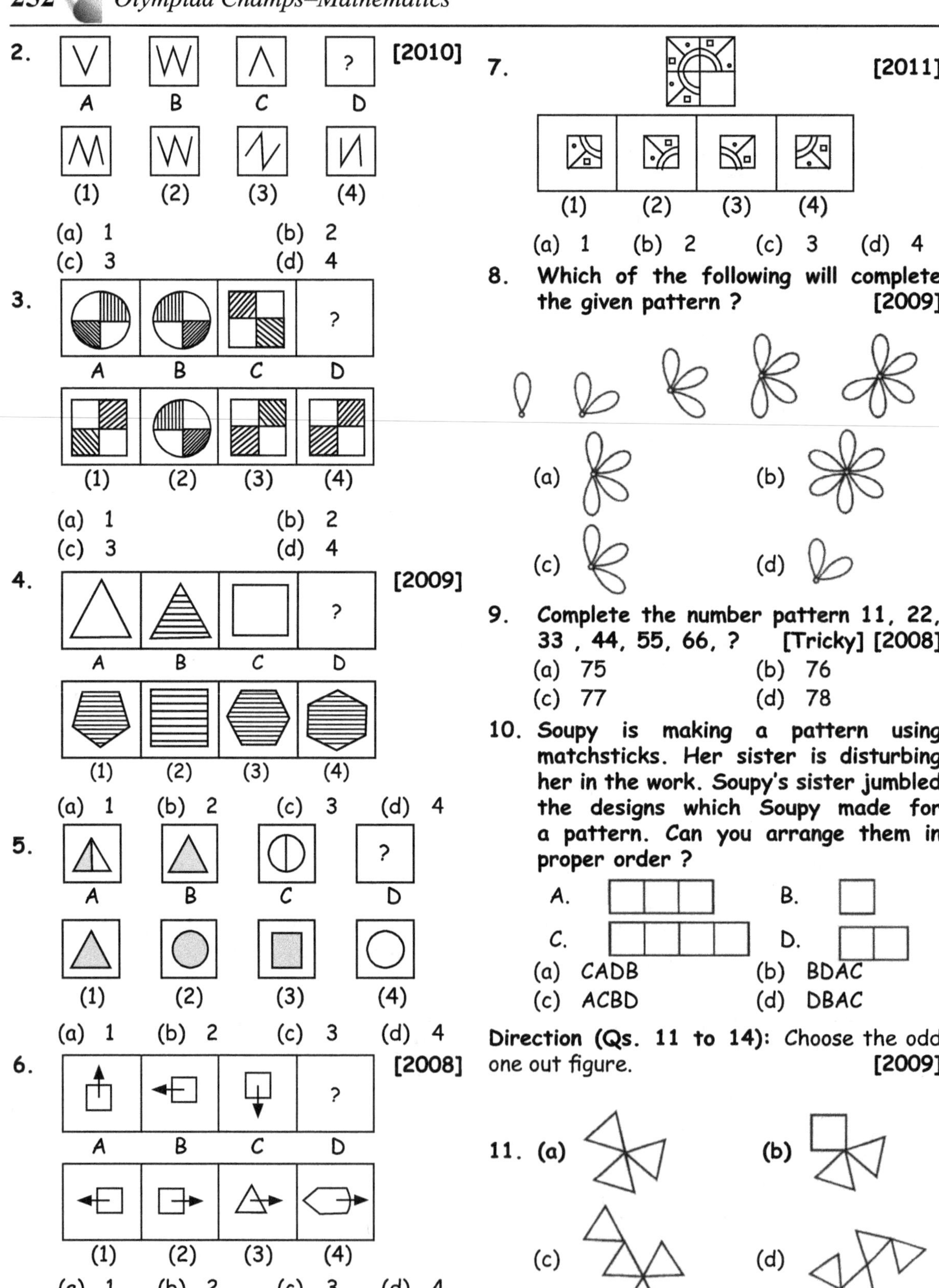

2. [2010]

(a) 1   (b) 2
(c) 3   (d) 4

3.

(a) 1   (b) 2
(c) 3   (d) 4

4. [2009]

(a) 1   (b) 2   (c) 3   (d) 4

5.

(a) 1   (b) 2   (c) 3   (d) 4

6. [2008]

(a) 1   (b) 2   (c) 3   (d) 4

7. [2011]

(a) 1   (b) 2   (c) 3   (d) 4

8. **Which of the following will complete the given pattern ?** [2009]

9. **Complete the number pattern 11, 22, 33, 44, 55, 66, ?** [Tricky] [2008]
(a) 75   (b) 76
(c) 77   (d) 78

10. **Soupy is making a pattern using matchsticks. Her sister is disturbing her in the work. Soupy's sister jumbled the designs which Soupy made for a pattern. Can you arrange them in proper order ?**

A.   B.

C.   D.

(a) CADB   (b) BDAC
(c) ACBD   (d) DBAC

Direction (Qs. 11 to 14): Choose the odd one out figure. [2009]

11. (a)   (b)

(c)   (d)

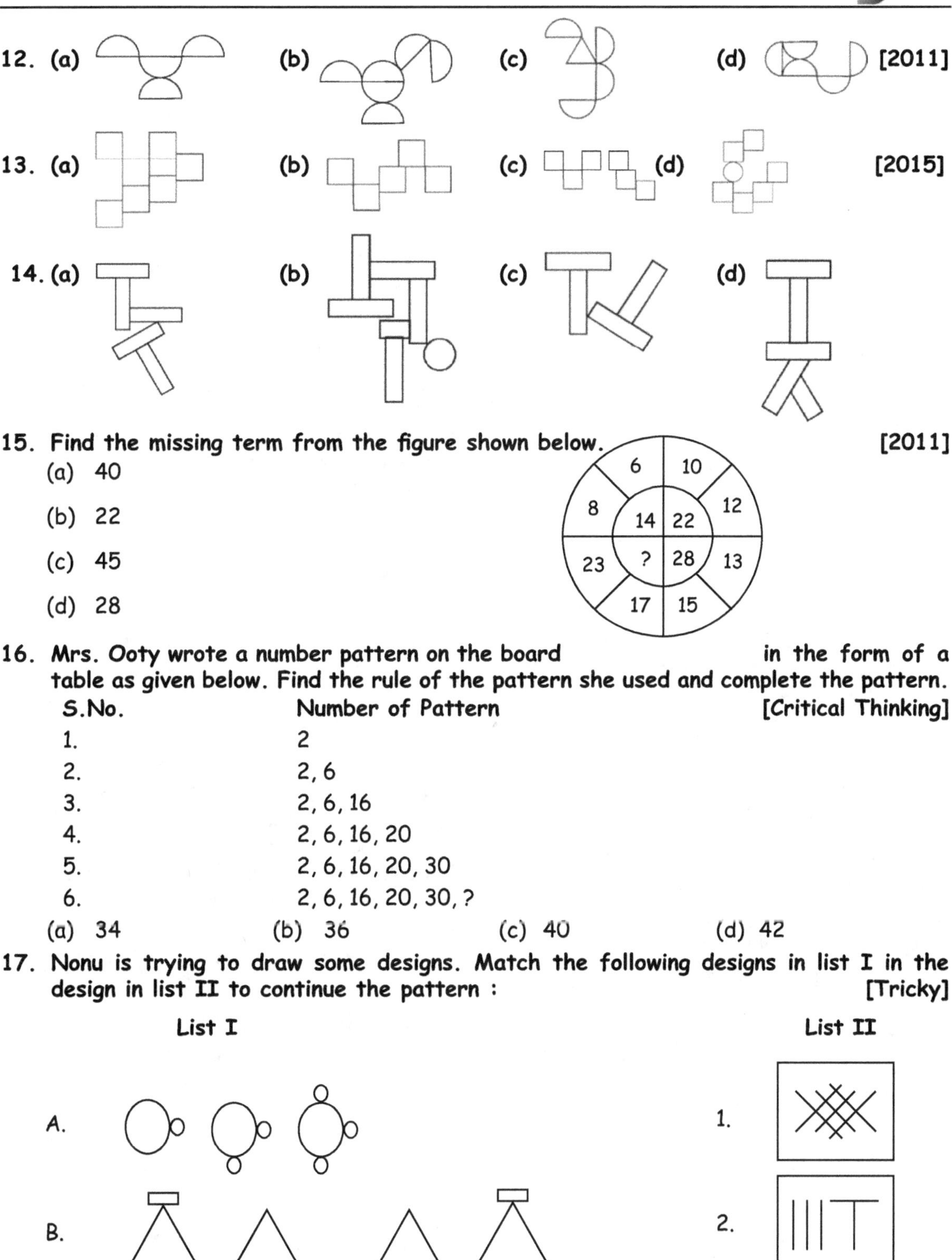

12. (a)　　(b)　　(c)　　(d) **[2011]**

13. (a)　　(b)　　(c)　　(d) **[2015]**

14. (a)　　(b)　　(c)　　(d)

15. Find the missing term from the figure shown below. **[2011]**
- (a) 40
- (b) 22
- (c) 45
- (d) 28

16. Mrs. Ooty wrote a number pattern on the board in the form of a table as given below. Find the rule of the pattern she used and complete the pattern. **[Critical Thinking]**

S.No.	Number of Pattern
1.	2
2.	2, 6
3.	2, 6, 16
4.	2, 6, 16, 20
5.	2, 6, 16, 20, 30
6.	2, 6, 16, 20, 30, ?

- (a) 34
- (b) 36
- (c) 40
- (d) 42

17. Nonu is trying to draw some designs. Match the following designs in list I in the design in list II to continue the pattern : **[Tricky]**

List I　　　　List II

A.　　　　1.

B.　　　　2.

C. ＼ ╳ ＼＼ ╳╳ ＼＼＼

D. | ┬ ||| ┬ | ┬

	A	B	C	D			A	B	C	D
(a)	4	3	1	2	(b)		2	4	3	1
(c)	3	4	1	2	(d)		3	2	1	4

Direction (Qs. 18 to 20) : Agent X is trying to crack a secret message to track criminals. Can you crack the messages in the following questions:

18. 5 G 7 U 9 N : GUN :: 2 F 1 O 4 U 6 N 8 D : ?   [Tricky]
    (a) GUN   (b) FOUND
    (c) 579   (d) 21468

19. 1 W 2 E 3 A : WEA :: ? : PON [Tricky]
    (a) 1 P 2 O 3 N   (b) 3 P 2 O 1 N
    (c) 4 P 5 O 6 N   (d) 6 P 5 O 4 N

20. 2 B 2 U 2 L 2 L 2 E 2 T : BULLET :: ? : F I R E D
    (a) 1 F 1 I R 1 E 1 D
    (b) 3 F 3 I 3 R 3 E 3 D
    (c) 4 F 4 I 4 R 4 E 4 D
    (d) 2 F 2 I 2 R 2 E 2 D

Direction (Qs. 21 and 22) : Pinny is making some patterns of numbers on the board. Can you figure out which patterns are true and false in the following questions:

21. A. 1, 2, 3, 3, 2, 1, 1, 2, 3, ...
                              [Critical Thinking]
    B. 2, 2, 4, 4, 6, 6, 6, 8, 8, ...
    C. 1, 1, 0, 2, 2, 0, 3, 3, 3, ...
    D. 2, 4, 6, 8, 10, ...
    (a) T T F F
    (b) T F T F
    (c) T F F T
    (d) F F T T

22. A. 2, 7, 12, 17, 22, ...
    B. 10, 20, 30, 40, 50, ...

C. 11, 22, 33, 55, 66, ...
D. 3, 6, 9, 13, 15, ...
(a) T T F F   (b) T T T F
(c) F F T T   (d) F T T F

Direction (Qs. 23 to 25) : Billu is trying to solve a puzzle with patterns. He can only use numbers from 10 to 9 to complete a pattern. Help Billu complete the patterns given in the following questions:

23. 1, 1, 2, 1, 1, 3, 1, 1, ...   [2008]
    (a) 3   (b) 1
    (c) 2   (d) 4

24. 7, 8, 9, 9, 8, 7, ...   [2012]
    (a) 8   (b) 9
    (c) 7   (d) 6

25. 5, 3, 1, 0, 5, 3, 1, 0, ...   [2013]
    (a) 0   (b) 1
    (c) 5   (d) 3

Direction (Qs. 26 and 27) : Bageera wrote few number patterns in his maths book. His maths teacher found some patterns incorrect. Can you figure out wihch pattern is incorrect in the following questions:

26. A. 99, 96, 93, 90, ...   [2015]
    B. 101, 110, 011, 101, 011, 110, ...
    C. 80, 60, 40, 20, ...
    D. 100, 150, 200, 250, 300, ...
    (a) C   (b) D
    (c) A   (d) B

27. A. 31, 51, 71, 91, 111, ... [2016]
    B. 4, 9, 14, 19, 24, 29 , ...
    C. 2, 4, 3, 9, 4, 15 , ...
    D. 1, 10, 100, 1000, 10000, 100000 , ...
    (a) C   (b) A
    (c) B   (d) D

28. **Choose odd one from the following :** [2012]
    (a) Ray   (b) Radius   (c) Diameter   (d) Chord

29. **Complete the series. 1, 4, 9, 16, _______, 36.** [2014, Tricky]
    (a) 22   (b) 23   (c) 24   (d) 25

30. **Find the odd one out.** [2016]
    (a) $\dfrac{14}{N}$ (b) $\dfrac{18}{R}$ (c) $\dfrac{27}{U}$ (d) $\dfrac{8}{H}$

31. **Find the number using the given clues.** [2018]
- **The number is the predecessor of a two digit even number.**
- **The number is a multiple of 3.**
- **Sum of digits of the number is an even number.**

    (a) 87   (b) 99   (c) 93   (d) 66

RESPONSE GRID

LEVEL 1

1. a b c d   2. a b c d   3. a b c d   4. a b c d   5. a b c d
6. a b c d   7. a b c d   8. a b c d   9. a b c d   10. a b c d
11. a b c d   12. a b c d   13. a b c d   14. a b c d   15. a b c d
16. a b c d   17. a b c d   18. a b c d   19. a b c d   20. a b c d
21. a b c d   22. a b c d   23. a b c d   24. a b c d   25. a b c d
26. a b c d   27. a b c d   28. a b c d   29. a b c d   30. a b c d
31. a b c d   32. a b c d   33. a b c d

LEVEL 2

1. a b c d   2. a b c d   3. a b c d   4. a b c d   5. a b c d
6. a b c d   7. a b c d   8. a b c d   9. a b c d   10. a b c d
11. a b c d   12. a b c d   13. a b c d   14. a b c d   15. a b c d
16. a b c d   17. a b c d   18. a b c d   19. a b c d   20. a b c d
21. a b c d   22. a b c d   23. a b c d   24. a b c d   25. a b c d
26. a b c d   27. a b c d   28. a b c d   29. a b c d   30. a b c d
31. a b c d

Solutions with Explanation

LEVEL 1

1. **(b)** Add 13 to each number.
2. **(c)** We have to subtract 22 from each number.
3. **(a)** We have to multiply 3 to each number.
4. **(b)** We have to add 4 to each number. If we add 4 to 21 it is 25 not 26.
5. **(b)** Except option (b) all are multiples of 11.
6. **(d)** 7. **(c)**
8. **(b)** All the others are cube e.g.- 2's cube is 8, 3's cube is 27 and so on.
9. **(b)** 10. **(d)**
11. **(c)** Subtract the numbers;

    55 – 42 = 13

    69 – 56 = 13

    48 – 34 = 14

    95 – 82 = 13

    Here, 48 – 34 = 14 which is not similar to the other.

    Therefore, 48 – 34 is the odd pair of numbers.
12. **(c)** Multiply 2.5 to the first number to get the second number.

    18 × 2.5 = 45

    16 × 2.5 = 40

    14 × 2.5 = 35

    8 × 2.5 = 20

    Hence, 14 × 2.5 ≠ 28

    Therefore, 14 - 28 is the odd pair of numbers.
13. **(b)** 14. **(b)**   15. **(b)**
16. **(c)** First letter moves 6 steps forward. Second letter moves 6 steps backward.
17. **(c)** The first letter moves 2, 3, 4 ... steps forward. The second letter moves 2, 3, 4 ... steps backward.
18. **(d)** The first letter moves one step forward. The second letter moves one step backward.
19. **(d)** The first letters are alternate. The second letter of moves one step backward to obtain the second letter of the successive term. The third letter moves two steps backward to obtain the third letter of the subsequent term.
20. **(d)** The letters move four steps backward to obtain the letters of the next term.
21. **(a)** The letters move five steps forward.
22. **(a)** The first, second and third letters move three steps forward, four steps backward and two steps forward respectively.
23. **(c)** Each term consists of three consecutive letters in reverse order. The first letter and the last letter of the next term are the same.
24. **(d)** The first letter moves 2, 3, 4 ... steps forward. The second letter moves 3, 4, 5 ... steps forward.
25. **(c)** The letters move four steps forward.
26. **(d)** The letters are coded accordingly P as 2, E as 4, A as 1, R as 5 and L as 3. So PEARL is coded as 24153.
27. **(c)** The letters are coded accordingly S as 2, E as 1, A as 4, R as 6, C as 7 and H as 3. i.e., 214673.
28. **(b)** As 10 + 6 + 2 = 18 and $\dfrac{18}{2} = 9$

    Also 12 + 3 + 5 = 20 and $\dfrac{20}{2} = 10$

    So, 9 + 8 + 5 = 22 and $\dfrac{22}{2} = 11$
29. **(b)** P = 16, A = 1, G = 7, E = 5

    So, PAGE = 16 + 1 + 7 + 5 = 29

30. **(d)** As it has 6 parts and other figures have been divided into 8 parts.

31. **(c)** Number of cars = 4 × 20 = 80
Number of Scooters = 2 × 20 = 40
Scooters Difference = 80 – 40 = 40

32. **(b)** **33.** **(c)**

LEVEL 2

1. **(d)** **2.** **(a)** **3.** **(a)** **4.** **(b)**
5. **(d)** **6.** **(b)** **7.** **(d)**
8. **(b)** Since, the rule of the pattern is to add one petal.

Therefore the answer is option

(b).

9. **(c)** The rule is table of 11
11 × 1 = 11, 11 × 2 = 22, 11 × 3 = 33,
11 × 4 = 44, 11 × 5 = 55, 11 × 6 = 66,
11 × 7 = 77

10. **(b)** The proper order of designs will be

B. 

D. 

A.

C.

Therefore, the answer is option (b) BDAC.

11. **(b)** **12.** **(c)** **13.** **(d)** **14.** **(b)**
15. **(a)** As 6 + 8 = 14,

10 + 12 = 22, 15 + 13 = 28
and 23 + 17 = 40

16. **(a)** Here, the rule is add 4 then add 10

i.e. 2 + 4 = 6, 6 + 10 = 16
16 + 4 = 20, 20 + 10
= 30, 30 + 4 = <u>34</u>
The next number will be 34.

17. **(a)**
18. **(b)** S G 7 U 9 N : G U N
∴ 2 F 1 O 4 U 6 N 8 D : F O U N D

Therefore, answer is option (b) FOUND.

19. **(c)** 1 W 2 E 3 A : W E A
∴ 4 P 5 O 6 N : P O N

20. **(d)** 2 B 2 U 2 L 2 L 2 E 2 T : B U L L E T
∴ 2 F 2 I 2 R 2 E 2 D : F I R E D

21. **(c)** A. 1, 2, 3, 3, 2, 1, 1, 2, 3
Here, the sequence 1, 2, 3 is being repeated first in the same order then in the opposite order of numbers. This pattern is true.

B. 2, 2, 4, 4, 6, 6, 6, 8, 8
In this pattern even numbers are occurring two times but 6 is occuring three times. Thus, this pattern is false.

C. 1, 1, 0, 2, 2, 0, 3, 3, 3
In this pattern, the rule is number will occur two times followed by 0. But here 3 is occurring 3 times. Thus, this pattern is false.

D. 2, 4, 6, 8, 110
In this pattern, the rule is even numbers. Thus, the pattern is true.

Therefore, the answer is option (c) T F F T.

22. **(a)** A. 2, 7, 12, 17, 22, ...
Here, the rule is add 5.
2 + 5 = 7 + 5 = 12 + 5 = 17 and so on. Thus, the pattern is true.

B. 10, 20, 30, 40, 50, ...
Here, the rule is table of 10.
10 × 1 = 10, 10 × 2 = 20, 10 × 3 = 30 and so on.

C. 11, 22, 33, 55, 66, ...
Here, the rule is table of 11.

11 × 1 = 11, 11 × 2 = 22, 11 × 3 = 33, 11 × 4 = 44, is missing, then 11 × 5 = 55 and so on. Thus, the pattern is false.

D.   3, 6, 9, 13, 15, ...

3 + 3 = 6 + 3 = 9 = 9 + 3 = 12. But we have 13. Thus, the pattern is false.

Therefore, the answer is option (a) T T F F.

23. (d)   1, 1, 2, 1, 1, 3, 1, 1, ...

Here the rule is two times 1 followed by number from 2 then 3, then 4 and so on.

∴   The next number is 4.

24. (c)   7, 8, 9, 9, 8, 7, ...

Here, the rule is to write the three consecutive numbers in opposite order.

∴   The next number is 7.

25. (c)   5, 3, 1, 0, 5, 3, 1, 0, ...

Here, the rule is to repeat the set of four numbers 5, 3, 1, 0.

∴   The next number is 5.

26. (d)   A.   99, 96, 93, 90, ...

Here, the rule is subtract 3.

∴   99 – 3 = 96 – 3 = 93, 93 – 3, 90

Thus, the pattern is correct.

B.   101, 110, 011, 101, 011, 110, ...

Here, the rule is to change the position of 0. 1st in centre, then at right, then at left.

Likewise, the next three numbers should be 101, 110, 011 but we have 101, 011, 110.

Thus, the pattern is incorrect.

C.   80, 60, 40, 20, ...

Here the rule is subtract 20.

80 – 20 = 60 – 20 = 40 – 20 = 20

Thus, the pattern is correct.

D.   100, 150, 200, 250, 300, ...

Here, the rule is add 50.

100 + 50 = 150 + 50

= 200 + 50 = 250 + 50 = 300.

Thus, the pattern is correct.

Therefore, the answer is option (d) B.

27. (a)

A.   31, 51, 71, 91, 111, ...

Here, the rule is add 20.

31 + 20 = 51 + 20 = 71 + 20 = 91 + 20 = 111

Thus, the pattern is correct.

B.   4, 9, 14, 19, 24, 29, ...

Here, the rule is add 5.

4 + 5 = 9 + 5 = 14 + 5 = 19 + 5 = 24 and so on.

Thus, the pattern is correct.

C.   2, 4, 3, 9, 4, 15, ...

Here the rule is number then (number × number) and numbers moves from 2, 3, 4, 5, ... So the pattern should be

2, 2 × 2 = 4, 3, 3 × 3

= 9, 4, 4× 4 = 16

Thus, the pattern is incorrect.

D.   1, 10, 100, 1000, 10000, 100000, ...

Here the rule is add a zero or '0'.

Thus, the pattern is correct.

Therefore, the answer is option (a) C.

28. (a)   Ray is the odd one out as rest of the terms are related to a circle.

29. (d) $1 = 1^2, 4 = 2^2, 9 = 3^2, 16 = 4^2, 25 = 5^2, 36 = 6^2$

30. (c)   U has 21 and not 27 code

31. (c)